A humanistic psychology of education
Making the school everybody's house

Richard A. Schmuck and Patricia A. Schmuck

 NATIONAL PRESS BOOKS

Library of Congress Catalog Card Number: 73-93345
International Standard Book Numbers: 0-87484-303-0 (paper)
0-87484-304-9 (cloth)

Manufactured in the United States of America
National Press Books
285 Hamilton Avenue, Palo Alto, California 94301

Editor: London Green
Designer: Nancy Sears
Production: Michelle Hogan

To Julie, who said,
"school is everybody's house,"
and to
Allen, Jordan, Pam, and Rhonda

Contents

Preface

To proclaim that American society is constantly changing is hardly profound: change has become an undeniable fact of our daily lives. But the changes sought in America in the 1970s are unique. They no longer involve merely technological growth, as they have in the past. Today the emphasis is on altering interpersonal relationships, and the educational process is integrally involved in the changing scene. The contemporary focus for change is people-centered and the schools are viewed as an important setting for such change.

In America there has been a growing outcry that many of our traditional schools are emotionally destructive. The surge of alternative schools attests to the sincerity and determination of the critics. Further, alternative schools have attracted not only alienated underachievers and drop-outs but also bright, creative, and "successful" students, as well as a large number of well qualified teachers seeking lively alternatives to the traditional methods of public schools.

The school criticisms themselves are neither partisan nor privileged. They come from citizens in many segments of society, and both from "educational romantics" providing personal testimony on school conditions, such as Herbert Kohl (1969) and James Herndon (1965, 1971) and also from the authors of more detailed and documented analyses, such as Silberman's *Crisis in the Classroom*. These books are being read by many: most are available in general bookstores, some have been offered as popular book club selections, and a few have climbed the best-seller lists. Perhaps most tellingly, such books have made parents and students increasingly aware of their relative powerlessness in choosing from among the educational options available. In some communities, for example, parents and students are now demanding parity with professionals in deciding how schools should be run.

The issues in question among these new groups have to do primarily with *relationships* among school participants. Increasingly few criticisms seem to be aimed at curricula, facilities or instructional strategies, while criticisms about joylessness, fear, mutual lack of respect among teachers and students, the absence of spontaneity, growing alienation, and personal disinterest have become dominant. The crisis of our schools lies in interpersonal conditions; the changes demanded are in the area of human relationships.

Unfortunately, the words "humanistic" and "humanized" are virtually shibboleths today; there are humanistic psychologists, humanistic sociologists, humanistic educators, humanistic chemists, humanistic engineers, and even humanistic real estate brokers and used car salesmen. Despite this, we do use the words "humanistic" and "humanized" throughout this book because we think they still communicate specific and important meanings and indicate most clearly the values we want to bring to schools. We use the words "humanistic" and "humanized" to refer to measurable social phenomena. Humanized schools, as we see them, are those where the environment sets the stage for successful personal encounter; where ideas, facts, and feelings are openly expressed; where conflict is brought out into the open, discussed, and worked on; where emotions share equal prominence with the intellect; and where learning activities integrate the personal interests of students and the learning goals of the school. Schools with humanistic climates have new educational options and ways of relating, and different kinds of discussion from those in schools that are not humanistic. Humanistic schools are places where, for example, teachers and students can be more open and truthful with one another, and where they can interact as individuals in addition to carrying out their tasks of teaching and learning.

In this book, we grapple with ways of humanizing schools by using theory and research available from the social sciences—social psychology in particular. All of the social sciences have contributed to our understanding of the dynamics of school organizations. However, the concentration of social psychology has been upon the relationships *between* people—our primary target for humanizing schools. Social psychological research has demonstrated how the presence of others can affect an individual's performance and how his* self-concept is formed and reformed through association with others. This research

---

*Throughout we have sought to use the plural personal pronouns "they," "them," or "their" when we refer to persons regardless of their sex. At times, however, such usage creates awkward reading so we have interchangeably used "he" or "she" or "him" or "her" when the singular pronoun was appropriate.

has helped us in looking at groups in a variety of dimensions and has shown the interrelationships of these dimensions and their effect upon both the group and the individuals. It is primarily from this base of knowledge that we make our suggestions for changing the schools.

This book can be used effectively in many educational settings: preservice, inservice and graduate. It is meant to be practical: to shed light on what humanized schooling means, what humanized schools look and feel like, and, most important, how such schools can be created. Although it undoubtedly will be used primarily in professional courses in such areas as educational psychology, educational sociology, the foundations of education, curriculum and instruction, and educational administration, we intend it to be read also by individual educators, parents, students, and citizens interested in our schools.

We wish to acknowledge the stimulation and assistance of many people during our writing of this book. Special thanks are due to the students in Richard Schmuck's advanced educational psychology course (given during the spring of 1972 at the University of Oregon) who read and generously shared their reactions to early drafts of the first four chapters. Many of their suggestions were heeded. Others who made significant contributions were our colleagues Dick Arends, Jane Phelps, Phil Runkel, David Sonnenfeld, and Spence Wyant; their extensive, diverse, and careful criticisms were very helpful to us. Finally, we wish to thank Rosemary Briggs, Lois Newton, and Louise Olds, who assisted with the typing of many sections, and to give a special thanks to Jan Starling Sides, who worked under tight deadlines to complete the most substantial part of the typing.

Humanized schools will not materialize simply because teachers and students have developed some understanding and knowledge of the ways in which learning groups and school organizations can operate. A humanized school can be created only by the conscious practical effort of everyone involved, including educators, students, and parents. We attempt to offer here specific ideas and concrete plans of action to create a more humanized climate for learning. The value of a humanized school lies in the scope of learning available (cognitive and emotional), the respect shown for individuals (staff *and* students) and the opportunity to mold an organization which reflects the needs and goals of its members.

R.A.S.

P.A.S.

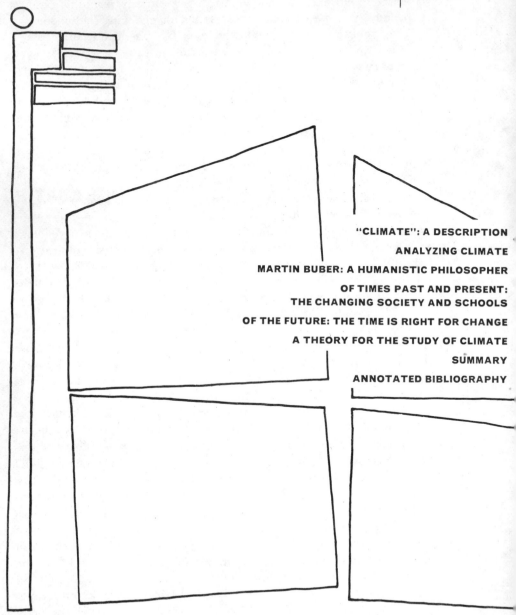

chapter

Humanized climates for learning

To the casual observer, schools are schools. Distinctions between different schools are not considered and often not even noticed. But to the people who work and play within schools—the students, teachers, administrators, and concerned parents—schools are different from one another. A school has its own vibrations and soul; different schools express tones of feeling that are both important and distinguishable from one another.

These vibrations emanate from the interpersonal relationships in the school; they compose the school's "human culture." We call these vibrations or feelings the "climate" of a school. Evidence of the "climate" can be seen in how learning activities are carried out, how play occurs, and how school participants typically interact with one another. To us, the term "climate" is useful in dealing with the culture of a school and with groups within a school such as classrooms, committees, and councils.

In this chapter, we will first elaborate on the general connotations of the term "climate" and offer an analysis of the measurable aspects of a school which determine the nature of its climate. Second, we will elaborate on what we mean by "a humanized climate for learning." We will focus on four categories of group processes and show that members of humanized schools have shared influence, that affection and confrontation are openly expressed, that such schools and their members are attractive to one another, and that people communicate with one another there freely, regardless of their status positions.

1

Third, we will indicate briefly how the values, norms, and aspirations of American culture have in the past affected our schooling methods and then show why we believe the time is right for the further humanization of schools. Fourth, we will propose a general plan of action for school personnel interested in changing their climate in planned and deliberate ways. Vital to this effort are the questioning of prevailing norms, the exploration and formulation of new goals, the clarification of new values and—as a central philosophy—the idea that individuals are more important than bureaucratic efficiency and expediency. Later chapters offer a systematic, concrete set of procedures for school participants to use in creating humanized climates for learning.

"CLIMATE": A DESCRIPTION

The cultural climate of which we have been speaking is indicated not simply by the school curriculum or organizational arrangement, but by the quality of emotional and intellectual interplay between persons and groups. A skilled observer can gather from ordinary behavior many informal cues for a primitive assessment of the climate (or *several* climates) of a school. For example, climates can be informally assessed by observing physical movements and bodily gestures. How do students move toward the principal and teachers? Do they stand close or far away? Are they physically at ease or tight and tense? How often is affection indicated by smiles, winks, or pats on the back? Do the students move quietly and unobtrusively with measured steps through the hallways or do they walk freely and easily in ways that indicate the building is truly their own? Are students reticent to approach clusters of teachers? Are teachers similarly slow to approach clusters of students? How do the students relate to one another? Are they quiet, distant, and formal, or do they talk easily and laugh spontaneously? Do hall monitors attempt to control students' behavior or do the students generally monitor their own traffic between classes? How often does hostility erupt into fighting between students? How is fighting handled by other students when it does occur? Are the classrooms neatly organized and run primarily by the teacher? Is the seating arranged for ease of interaction or for the convenience of custodial services? Are students intent on what they are doing? Are they working together within classes?

Although the physical plant as such is not a direct indicator of climate, some physical arrangements can provide clues. The most obvious example is classroom seating. Do students sit in rows facing the teacher, as in a lecture hall, or are the seats arranged in seminar style or in small groups? Do the seating arrangements shift from time to time, or do they remain the same regardless of the learning activity?

To an extent, hall decorations can indicate cultural climate. Is there a reproduction of *Whistler's Mother* or Stuart's *George Washington* hanging in the hallway, with perhaps a display of twenty-five neat pink, white, and red Valentines on a nearby bulletin board, or is there a variety of individualized projects visible to all? In some schools the hallways take many minutes to walk through because much of the open space is filled with interesting eyecatching presentations. At the same time, such attractive features can sometimes be misleading where climatic cues are concerned. The brightest, most architecturally open, and most modern facility may at first hide behavior aimed at conformity, order, and formal regimentation; likewise, dingy old buildings splashed with army surplus green paint cannot by themselves subdue intimacy or suppress interpersonal spontaneity, creativity, and the joy of discovering things with others.

In informal analysis, many critics have described current schools abstractly as sterile, demeaning, tense, and rigid. Silberman's acclaimed book, *Crisis in the Classroom* (1970) is an excellent illustration. Obviously he is a sensitive and experienced observer of the climate cues of schools here and abroad and his book provides item after item of concrete evidence to support his thesis that schools are sorely in need of improvement. He writes:

> It is not possible to spend any prolonged period of time visiting public school classrooms without being appalled by the mutilation visible everywhere—mutilation of spontaneity, of joy in learning, of pleasure in creating, of sense of self. (P. 10.)

We believe, that such statements are useful in that they point out the necessity for change. However, they do *not* point out a new direction nor lead to a *plan* for change. That is why we believe a more systematic and deliberate effort must be made to collect objective data carefully about the climate of schools—those sobering and often confusing facts that can humble our most ardent speculations. We believe that successful planned change can come only when one knows as precisely as possible what the reality is and then systematically attempts to intervene in specific and deliberate ways.

ANALYZING CLIMATE

One scheme we propose for carefully analyzing the climate of a school or school group is to observe the interactions between the various participants—between staff members, between staff members and students, and within the student culture. We analyze these interactions in terms of four categories of group processes: influence, attraction, norms and communication.

(1) *Influence.* How dominative or collaborative the relationships are is an important indicator of influence relationships in a school or classroom. Are teachers satisfied with their degree of influence in decision-making in the school? Do students believe that they have a chance to influence what and how they will study? Humanized climates are characterized by collaborative decision-making. Persons are held in high regard; they are seen as being important enough to participate in decisions affecting their work or play.

(2) *Attraction.* How close or distant participants feel toward one another is an important indicator of the level of attraction members have toward the group to which they belong. What are the friendship patterns in a classroom or a school? Are there only a few greatly liked teachers or students, with many others who feel alienated and isolated? Or do most people have at least one friend with whom they can share their joys and struggles? In a humanized school there is a high level of attraction to both the school and individuals in it. There is a place for each person, and friendship patterns are dispersed among many rather than concentrated on a few.

(3) *Norms.* The shared expectations regarding behavior constitute the norms of a school. Norms are powerful governors of an individual's behavior, especially toward other people. The actual formality or openness between people is an important indicator of the operating norms in a school. A humanized school stresses honesty and authenticity—in both affection and confrontation—between people. Lively public discussions bring "behind the scenes" or "under the table" phenomena into the open so that they can be dealt with and changed if need be.

(4) *Communication.* The patterns of communication are other important indicators of influence, attraction, and norms. Communication which is closed and primarily vertical—that is, traveling from principal to teachers to students—is often indicative of closed formal

relationships in which individuals are influential only insofar as they hold bureaucratic power. Communication in a humanized school is fluid, direct, and broad in its emotional range. The open exchange of feelings, whether pleasant or unpleasant, is a hallmark of the humanized school.

Climate involves all of these elements: influence, attraction, norms, and communication. It includes, among other things, the activities of participants working on goals for learning: for example, the ways in which people exchange curriculum materials. Climate is *not* a bulletin board filled with valentines, but valentines can offer clues to the interpersonal processes that took place while they were being constructed. It is unlikely that twenty-five students, given a variety of materials and a sense of the value of individual expression, would prepare a set of twenty five similar valentines. The students probably were directed very closely, were given little encouragement to express their own feelings about the sentiments of Valentine's Day, and were not encouraged to look critically at the misleading and superficial sentiments that can be induced by such a holiday. It is likely that this group of students, like many others, missed an opportunity to relate a celebration of love to the personal relationships in their own classroom.

Until now, educators typically have not dealt with the learning climate analytically and objectively, nor have social scientists collaborated with them to change that climate. On the contrary, learning climates, good or bad, have emerged generally without much conscious effort or overall planning. Students and teachers typically participate in classroom culture without understanding either their roles or the nature of the climate in which they operate. If American schools are to become truly humanized, we must try to fathom the complexities of group life and develop plans to improve learning climates.

MARTIN BUBER: A HUMANISTIC PHILOSOPHER

Central to our thinking about humanized schools is the work of the existentialist philosopher Martin Buber (1958). Buber teaches that people learn "how to be human" through interpersonal "meetings": brief encounters in which people communicate honestly and openly, sharing themselves with each other.* His simple yet precise analyses of the kinds of relationships which exist between people, and the terminology he develops to explain those relationships, help to clarify our thinking about humanized schools.

1. I-Thou; I-It

Buber indicates different kinds of transactions between people by the primary terms "I-Thou" and "I-It." The "I" never stands alone; I is always *in relation*. Most transactions are of the I-It variety, and do not involve true meeting. Role relationships are I-It; one person relates to another in terms of a category or function—storekeeper and shopper, conductor and passenger. In I-Thou transactions, on the contrary, each person is recognized, appreciated, respected, and valued as a *total* being. In simple language, I-Thou transactions occur when "whole persons" encounter one another on an equal basis, each with full respect for the array of qualities to be found in the other.

Schools, like other institutions, tend to foster I-It transactions. Teachers—especially in high school—are concerned primarily with the cognitive development of students within the narrow confines of specialized subjects. They think mainly of the students' level of competence or motivation *in relation to subject matter*. Even when secondary teachers strive to think of their students in broader ways, they seldom think of them as total and complex persons. One student is viewed as "a hard worker," another as "a troublemaker," and another as "conscientious." Even in elementary schools, where teachers can adopt a broader, more personal view, they tend to categorize students within a subject-matter perspective, judging students by their accomplishment in mathematics, reading, social studies, art, and physical education. Many secondary and elementary teachers nowadays claim to have growing interest in the emotional development of their students, but their rhetoric about educational goals is often unaccompanied by actual changes in interpersonal behavior. In many schools, teachers, students, and administrators have not yet begun, even

---

*For Buber, a religious philosopher, such encounters are also evidence that we are at one with God or the Universe. Since our own expertise and commitment lie primarily in humanistic social psychology, our analyses of education have a definite social scientific bias. We hope that the reader also will consider the philosophical, political, and theological implications of these ideas.

momentarily, to interact as whole persons with a full complement of human feelings, knowledge, behavioral skills, and creativity.

According to Buber, it is impossible to plan deliberately for an I-Thou transaction. The acts of planning in themselves lead to categorizing and objectifying aspects of the other. Since I-Thou transactions arise as unexpected gifts, the best we can do is to orient ourselves to be receptive to their occurrence. Unfortunately, the organizational patterns of schools keep students, teachers, and administrators isolated from one another both physically (in separate classrooms and isolated offices) and psychologically (through hierarchical decision-making procedures). Thus schools tend to rule out the possibility of the spontaneous I-Thou transactions by physically separating the participants and keeping them in role categories.

I-Thou transactions are most likely to take place in what sociologists refer to as "primary relationships": those involving spouses, parent and child, siblings, close friends, and lovers. Primary relationships are defined as rich in affect, closeness, empathy, concern, and conflict. They often have *no purpose other than* to afford emotional support, comfort, encouragement, and confrontation. In primary relationships, emotion takes on equal status with thoughts and behavioral skills. Secondary relationships, in contrast, involve interactions between role-takers during which only a small, and usually cognitive, part of each person enters the interaction. These relationships tend to be devoid of deep feelings, psychologically more distant and formal, imbalanced with regard to power, and focused specifically on a particular task or function. Relationships in schools, as in most other formal organizations, are more secondary than primary; however, primary relationships *do* occur in all formal organizations, especially within informal friendship clusters.

2. Personal relationships in schools

It is emotionally difficult for a person to interact continuously as a "thou" or for schools to offer only affect and closeness; schools will, we believe, continue to be mostly characterized by secondary relationships. It is the school's responsibility and obligation to provide opportunities for cognitive and skill development. However, too many American schools have neglected or ignored the importance of personal relationships in learning; too many schools are characterized *only* by superficial and distant relationships, covert hostility and cynicism, and little mutual concern or respect among their members. When a school pays too little attention to its members as individuals, the objectives of cognitive and skill development are hindered. Students and teachers cannot learn and work within a hostile and alienating environment. A humanized school transforms these debilitating and hindering interpersonal forces so that they can facilitate and complement formal educational objectives. A humanized school uses all of its resources; the stage is set for learning about feelings as well as information; conflict, considered grist for learning, is brought out into the open, shared, and worked on; I-Thou transactions occur with increased frequency; and individuals consider the needs and objectives of others.

OF TIMES PAST AND PRESENT: THE CHANGING SOCIETY AND SCHOOLS

Most basic textbooks on the history or sociology of education tell us that schools are mirror images of the cultures in which they operate. We agree; at no time in our history have schools *led* the way or *mapped* the direction for planned change. Schools have reflected rather than initiated the norms and values of the culture. In view of this, we hope that we are entering a new era: one in which the educative process can provide energy in leading toward a solution to some of the human problems in our society. We believe the many nonpublic alternative or free schools burgeoning across the country are one positive sign that education can perhaps make a difference in the way people lead their lives. The values and aspirations of many people—young, middle-aged, and even old; rich and poor; political and apolitical; highly and meagerly educated—are no longer consonant with the values and goals which have in the past been characteristic of our society. These people are looking for new directions. In like fashion, the free school movement repudiates much of what our public schools have stood for in the past. We would now like to explore briefly those changes which indicate that our society may be moving in new and better directions. At the same time we want to show how the schools may be instrumental in furthering such changes.

The growth of a society is, from one point of view, a struggle between the rights and well-being of the individual and the rights and security of the collective people. At different times in America's history that struggle has been resolved in different ways. We believe that the ever-tenuous balance between the individual and the collective group is now being confronted in ways different from those of the past.

1. The age of the entrepreneur

When we were a new nation, the motifs of autonomy, individualism, hard work, and self-control represented a stance adaptive to the agrarian, pioneer society of the nineteenth century. This orientation persisted through the early development of urbanization and industrialization. The best government was that which governed least. Reisman (1950) described the typical character type of this period as "inner-directed." He painted the portrait of a steadfast and dogmatic people for whom the judgments of others were not very important. They knew what was true and virtuous and were prepared to act accordingly. An extreme example of the rigidity of the inner-directed character occurred during the fateful trip of the Donner party over the Sierra Nevada mountains. In the face of death, members maintained family autonomy and competition even though with more community collaboration and sharing many of the party would probably have survived.

Similar psychological motifs persisted even through the early stages of industrialization during the latter half of the nineteenth century. Entrepreneurs were pioneer heroes allowed, and even encouraged, to use the physical environment and people *for the sake of* production. The belief persisted that good would prevail so long as strong individuals were left to their own ingenuity and allowed to build their own businesses and fortunes. Such values permeated the society. For instance, Miller and Swanson (1958) showed that the child-rearing patterns of entrepreneurial families taught the virtues of independence, self-control, and facing adversity bravely. As an example, entrepreneurial parents eschewed pacifiers as crutches for emotional security, kept their infants on tight feeding schedules, and advocated very early toilet training.

America's classrooms mirrored the norms of this era. The processes of rote learning and long hours of tedious study emphasized the virtues of hard work and self-control. Frustrating repetition and competitive drills offered the young a glimpse of the hardships and struggles they would face as adults. Books such as the *McGuffy Reader* and *Pilgrim's Progress* also taught about hard work and self-control, while providing dramatic evidence of the benefits of taking initiative and being competitively independent. Supervisors instructed teachers that learning occurred primarily through repetition and that the homily "Spare the rod and spoil the child" should be heeded. The perspective of both teachers and students was that knowledge is immutable and consequently can and must be discovered and "stamped in." The path to independence and competitive individualism was thought to be more easily traveled with a storehouse of internalized knowledge.

2. The rise of bureaucracy

As industrialization and urbanization matured in the early twentieth century, organizations and communities grew rapidly. People from rural areas migrated to the cities, and more and more of them took jobs in large bureaucracies. The themes of this era were modified to represent new responses to the environment; the concepts of accommodation, smooth working relations, loyalty, and responsibility began to define a new culture. Reisman (1950) described the character type of this period as "other-directed." Other-directed persons are those having symbolic antenna with which to sense the reactions of others. This portrait is in contrast to that of the independent inner-directed characters, with their symbolic gyroscope housed within. The other-directed persons expected that organizations would provide for them so long as they remained responsible and loyal to the organization.

Miller and Swanson (1958) showed that parents of the "other-directed" orientation reared their children differently than did the entrepreneurs. They stressed cooperation, conformity and adjustment to the changing demands of organizational life. Bureaucratic parents believed in letting their infants suck on pacifiers, fed their babies on demand, and advocated delaying toilet training until it might be accomplished without tension. The basic theme of this bureaucratic period was that one could trust the organizational world, especially if one learned to adjust to it, and that help in getting work done was available from others.

Schools gradually took on a changing role also. Like large industrial bureaucracies, they broadened their programs to provide for more of the educational and social needs of their students. The valued attribute of self-control was replaced by that of being well-rounded. Curricula were broadened to include art, music, mental hygiene, and physical education; and the school provided remedial programs, guidance programs, vocational education, and other extra services such as recreational programs and hot lunches. Teachers became concerned about how well the students got along together and tended to reduce their concern about heightening competition between students. The supervision of teachers emphasized building rapport and helping teachers to improve their human relations. "Life adjustment" became a popular phrase to describe the basic aim of the educational process.

During the 1920s and 30s a movement known as "progressive education" even attempted to focus attention upon an aspect of whole-person relationships. Progressive educators argued that students could *not* become wise and effective citizens if offered only fragmented and unconnected subjects for study. Rather, students should be helped in their learning by a problem-solving orientation in which knowledge and skills were sought to reach and understand alternatives for action. The progressive educators believed that by using problem-solving techniques to study academic subjects, their students would be better able to apply knowledge in their daily lives and to learn additional concepts when confronted with problems outside of school.

This effort became known in some circles as the "child-centered movement." It flourished mostly within university schools and private, elite schools in urban areas but did not make strong inroads into the public schools. The major influence in public schools seemed to be in the emergence of "core curricula," in which subjects such as mathematics and science or English and social studies were combined. However, in most schools a fragmented and departmentalized emphasis continued. While the child-centered movement was persuasive in confronting and disturbing some traditional views of compartmentalized knowledge and practice, it continued to emphasize cognitive development, and in fact put very little emphasis on humanizing learning climates.

Schools also took on the important function of fulfilling certain newly perceived needs of the nation-state. The schools became the bulwark of the democratic state; it was through the process of schooling that the ultimate goal of an educated citizenry could be achieved. Classes directed toward political socialization, such as those in civics and American government, became mandatory for high school graduation in many states. Schools also responded to more specific national needs by providing training to fill the new roles and jobs created by society. Federal grants served as an impetus for many school districts to update curriculum or to introduce new programs for students and teachers. As the society became more technically oriented, more complex, advanced training was required for many jobs. (While the federal government has granted support to special vocational and technical education since 1917, it has been only within the last few decades that the *basics* of education, such as mathematics, languages, and physical sciences have been given very high priority. These general areas have been earmarked as important for our future in the international sphere.)

In some ways the schools of this era were more concerned with *students* than the schools of earlier times. There was an attempt to account for individual differences, students were viewed as more than just storage places for knowledge, and the psychological needs of students were taken into consideration during educational planning. But the organizational complexity of the schools became so overwhelming that efficiency nevertheless took precedence over the needs or wishes of students and teachers. Students were treated as numbers rather than individuals: as IBM cards rather than persons. School participants were expected to fill slots and to adjust to a large number of rules. I-It transactions characterized their relationships, and, as a consequence, many students and teachers felt isolated, alienated, and lonely even in the midst of a host of people. Reisman summarized this condition in the title of his book, *The Lonely Crowd.*

3. The present

Most American schools can still be accurately described by the preceding paragraph. During the past decade the federal government attempted to improve our bureaucratized and rigid schools by financially supporting educational innovation. The impetus for this change in policy apparently continues to come from international pressures on the American nation-state. The title of one of the largest education bills symbolized this: "The National Defense and Education Act." This legislation and other similar bills supported work in the development of curricula and learning materials and in teacher training.

Although many people still believe that our schools can be improved through expenditures for hardware, buildings, supplies, curriculum, and training, we believe that improvement must come primarily in humanizing the learning climate. Moreover, we believe that schools cannot become humanized without the support and collaborative involvement of students, teachers, administrators, and parents.

Herndon (1971) summarizes well the need for collaboration of all concerned participants in this moving account of his struggles with the complex bureaucracy of a school system:

> ... We [the teachers] feel we have nothing to do with it, beyond the process of maintaining what is presented to us. Presented to us by whom? The principal? But the principal tells us at faculty meetings that this is the situation, he didn't invent it, we all must only live with it. The superintendent? He gave us an inspiring speech on opening day but beyond that he makes it clear that our problems are not his invention. We are all in the same boat, he wants to tell us. The board of education? The state board? The superintendent of public instruction? No, man, they didn't do it. Who decided that Egypt is just right for seventh graders? Who decided that DNA must be something which all kids answer questions about? Who decided that California Indians must enter the world of fourth grade kids, and that South America must be "learned" by sixth graders? (P. 90.)

Herndon's frustration is that the organization of the school seems to have no point that might serve as leverage for change. The organization, not any of the people in it, is supreme and all participants learn to submit to its structure and procedures. But how, we might ask, did the schools get that way? Herndon answers:

> Nobody, it seems, made any of these decisions. . . . The people responsible for the decisions about how schools ought to go are dead. Very few people are able to ask questions of dead men. So we treat those decisions precisely as if dead men made them, as if none of them are up to us live people to make, and therefore we determine that we are not responsible for any of them. It ain't our fault! It ain't our fault! (P. 90.)

Herndon goes on to say that he does accept some responsibility for his own actions within the schools and that he does believe that dehumanized conditions in schools result in part from the behavior of individuals. It is this view of personal responsibility and impact that we believe characterizes the contemporary era. *The adaptive behaviors of the bureaucrat and the skills of the inner-directed man are not sufficient to lead American culture into a new, more humanized era.*

Not even the active and ambitious left-wing students of the sixties who brought to national awareness the deficiencies of dehumanized bureaucracies seem to be exactly in step with the emerging period. Two liberal friends of ours, after an unsuccessful attempt to build a professional and personal community of twenty people, spent a year recouping their own energies by traveling throughout the United States. One of their impressions was that everything was quiet on college campuses and that political organizations were dormant. The streets and campus buildings had been cleared of pickets and the protesters had retreated to the intimacy of their living rooms, with friends, to find meaning and significance within personal relationships.

What Reich (1971) calls Consciousness III (and what Herndon is asking for) is a new blend of respect for interdependence and an emphasis on personal responsibility. In certain respects the new view is a blend of the entrepreneurial and the bureaucratic outlooks, intended to form a culture in which group life and individual pursuits are equally valued. Hopefully it will add up to even more than this combination; perhaps it will lead to a culture in which emotional life is blended with cognitive life, in which the present existential moment is revered, and in which I-Thou transactions and meaningful relationships are as highly cherished as "achievement" and "success."

We see enough indications of change in this direction within our schools to be optimistic. Apart from the free schools there are community schools, multi-unit schools, open campuses, and "schools without walls" being discussed and tried *within* the public schools. Students everywhere are speaking up more, asking for alternatives, confronting educators, or dropping out. The British primary school, after centuries of bureaucracy and formalism, has gradually adopted informal and fluid classrooms, at least for younger children. The American intellectual community has been nourished with the writings of a new brand of "educational romantics" such as Dennison (1969), Kozol (1967), Kohl (1969), and Marin (1969). More and more students, parents, teachers, and administrators seem to be working toward more open, informal, and personal learning situations.

OF THE FUTURE: THE TIME IS RIGHT FOR CHANGE

The counterculture and the free school movement are significant elements in the changing era. One prominent theme of countercultural attempts at change is respect for the learning process. Never before in America has a radical social movement been so focused on the im portance of education and yet been so alienated from and disrespectful of schooling. The virulent anger against public education is due primarily to the view that schools are personally and psychologically damaging. The free school movement, above all else, has tried to create schools in which *persons* have the highest value in the educative process.

We believe that the counterculture and its free schools are a response to our society which should not be ignored. We are not entirely clear about all of the reasons which have moved such a large number of people to respond in alternative ways, but we wish to discuss some of the reasons in which we believe or about which we have gathered evidence in talking to others. For example, after the loud and hopeful sixties, we are now experiencing disillusionment with the political process; there have been Vietnam and the seemingly unending conflict in the Middle East; there are continual national and international crises and an endemic racism that has no apparent solution; there is poverty still amidst our affluence long after it has been called to public attention; and there is a waste of natural resources which is reaching dramatic levels. Many people are frustrated by their evident powerlessness in solving these problems. Perhaps as a result of this frustration, more people are directing their energies to matters closer to home.

The focus on interpersonal relationships, new mystical and religious experiences, and the quality of daily life are occupying the attention of many people formerly occupied with larger social concerns. The one institution which is "close to home" yet representative of society at large is the public school. Amidst the seemingly insoluble problems of poverty, racism, war, and disillusionment with the political process, many people are angry with the schools, which still stress credentials, achievement, and success. The schools ignore the larger concerns of the society and they also ignore the "close to home" concerns of intimacy and the quality of daily life.

One of the striking aspects of the counterculture movement of the seventies is its concern for education. This movement is composed not only of societal dropouts but also of many people within the very fabric of society who are making earnest efforts through alternative schools to help young people and themselves achieve a sense of self and arrive at an intimate understanding of others. Not only young people and "long-haired freaks" but also straight middle-aged people are giving up color television sets, academic appointments, and secure jobs in industry to explore different ways of living and learning. Alternative life styles are being explored in different ways by many people in various walks of life.

The free schools that we have read about or directly observed have rejected much of the regularized and efficient pattern characteristic of public schools. There is usually a disregard for time schedules and long-term commitment. There is an emphasis on people doing what excites and interests them either individually or in small groups. There is regard for knowledge and skills, but it is believed that these can be obtained from other students as well as from a credentialed teacher. There is an atmosphere of informality—sometimes even bordering on chaos—and there is at least an attempt at collaborative decision-making by everyone in the school. Teachers are generally viewed as regular members of the group with no more rights or privileges than the students.

Already many helpful and provocative publications about alternative schools have appeared. Descriptions of different schools, dialogues about new pedagogies, and philosophical essays can be found in magazines such as *Outside the Net*, *This Magazine Is About Schools*, and *Big Rock Candy Mountain* (defunct as of 1972). Information about free schools can be secured from the *New Schools Exchange Newsletter*, about how to locate a school to one's liking (whether one is a student or a staff member) from a clearinghouse called the Teacher Drop-Out Center, and even about how to set up a school from *Rasberry Exercises*.* Many of these enterprises depend entirely on the efforts of only a few people, and consequently they face continued economic pressure. Before publication of this book many of them may be defunct. We hope that others will take their place.

One sign of the success of the free school movement is the recent book by Kozol (1972), an open criticism of those free schools that have failed to provide students (especially lower-class and black students) with basic survival skills such as reading and writing. In 1973 the alternative school movement is strong and healthy enough for

---

*The addresses are: *Outside the Net*, P.O. Box 184, Lansing, Michigan 48901; *This Magazine Is About Schools*, 56 Esplanade St. E., Suite 301, Toronto 215, Canada; and *Big Rock Candy Mountain*, Portola Institute, Menlo Park, California; *New Schools Exchange*, 301 E. Canon Perdido, Santa Barbara, California 93103; "The Teacher Drop-Out Center," Box 521, Amherst, Massachusetts 01002; and *Rasberry Exercises*, Freestone Publishing Company, 440 Bohemian Highway, Freestone (Sebastapol), California 95472.

members from within to criticize the methods and objectives of the school publicly. Even some young students can see the strengths and weaknesses of these schools. A sixteen-year-old friend of ours, for example, spent a delightful and refreshing year at the New School in Spokane, Washington, which has survived for four years. However, he found that there were too few resources there for his interest in mathematics and chemistry, so he returned to a public school to avail himself of the laboratory equipment and science teachers. His decision involved even wider options. As he said, "I want to wear my hair shoulder-length but I want to play football. I want to rap about cabbages and kings but I want some skills in case I seek a job."

We share many of the same concerns and dislikes for the old order with those young people who label themselves as part of the counterculture, but we are likewise concerned about some aspects of the counterculture and the alternative free schools that we fear are damaging and unfortunate. First, we agree with Kozol that basic cognitive skills are often neglected. Second, there are many alternative schools which we think are as damagingly anti-human as the public schools, although their rhetoric is different. Fortunately such schools, unlike our public schools, do not seem to survive very long in the private sector. Third, we are concerned that the emphasis on the individual often leads to emotional catharsis and behavioral abandon for their own sake, with too little value placed on learning interpersonal skills and making long-term agreements to build and improve relationships. The injunction, "Do your own thing," can be and often is used as a "cop-out" to avoid responsibility to others and to avoid conflict and working through issues by merely leaving the scene. Fourth, while there is a healthy skepticism of the old, the established, and the traditional, there is a growing movement toward the occult, the mystical, and the magical. It is most disturbing to us that science and especially the use of systematic procedures for problem-solving and planned improvement are being attacked as the enemy of the humanized life.

We share with many young and old the disrespect and concern for much of the old order. Yet we do not agree with those who attack science as basically anti-human or who reject any plan simply if it is systematic and deliberate. This book we hope is a constructive response to others who, like us, believe that education should be joyful, exciting, and personal but who are not ready to give up all the resources available in public schools such as materials, libraries, people who have skills and knowledge, and such nuts and bolts of education as buildings, furniture, and laboratory equipment. We are not ready to retreat from these resources or previously accumulated knowledge in order to "remake the wheel," but we are ready to meet the challenge that the alternative schools have placed upon us to pay attention to people in the schools. We think the time is right to try to do that.

A THEORY FOR THE STUDY OF CLIMATE

Knowledge of scientific findings and of the systematic procedures of the scientific method are useful and necessary tools for improving the climate of schools in planned ways. In this section we wish to lay the foundation for our strategy for humanizing the climates of schools. We will apply the basic concepts of a systems theory to schools, show one example of how systems theory has been used to view the living processes of classrooms, and finally present the basic principles of systems theory that we will use throughout the book.

1. Systems theory

Scientific activity proceeds both inductively and deductively. We have used both strategies to build our theories about schools—theories that guide our plans for intervention and improvement. In our search for deductive strategies, we have found aspects of "living systems theory" to be especially useful.* Its flexibility and generalizability have allowed for analyses of widely different levels of biological life, ranging from the unicellular amoeba to the dynamics of an organization as complex as the Library of Congress. We have used systems theory to conceptualize some of the processes and interactions of individuals, classroom groups, school organizations, entire school districts, and even their community environments. The challenge that systems theory attempts to meet is to define a wide range of living structures while still remaining precise enough to guide objective measurement. Although we will not elaborate in general on this theory,

---

*For information on living systems theory, see Miller (1955 and 1965). For applications of modern systems theory to interpersonal clusters, groups, and organizations, see Buckley (1967) and also Terreberry (1968).

we do wish to present some aspects of it that are useful for conceptualizing about learning groups.

According to systems theory, a learning group is an open system contained within a school but constantly influencing and being influenced by its members and its surrounding organizational context. It is primarily oriented to the attainment of specific goals: for example, the intellectual and emotional development of students. Any goal that it does attain, especially in the form of modified thoughts, feelings, and behaviors of its members, constitutes an output which, in turn, becomes an input for another interdependent system: for example, students' families or the other groups in the school.

In a similar vein, each group within the school district, whether it is a classroom, an administrative council, a curriculum committee, or an extracurricular student club, constitutes an interdependent subsystem. Even the district itself, as a social system, has a relationship interdependent with its internal subsystems as well as its community and regional environments. *A major objective of schools is to develop educated citizens.* The resources to achieve this mission come from other systems: teachers from colleges or other schools, an ever-changing array of students from families, and curriculum materials from publishing houses. From a deliberate combination of these resources, learning experiences are produced which develop students who, in turn, enter other classrooms, changed families, colleges, the armed services, jobs, and so forth.

The term "system" refers to any organized part of an educational institution that is working to achieve certain goals and that has a great amount of internal interaction and interdependence. Examples of systems at different levels include tutoring pairs, project groups, committees, classrooms, school staffs, and entire districts.

"System" is used to refer to the particular focus of analysis regardless of its size; the word "subsystem" refers to small systems within a larger system. Focus on a classroom as a system might lead, for example, to an analysis of such subsystems as friendship cliques or influence hierarchies among students. Likewise, the investigation of a school staff could lead to a focus on its subsystems: staff friendships and influence relationships.

The importance of the social system to the learning climate cannot be overstressed. The individual is regarded as the focus of the learning process, but it must be remembered that individual behavior and psychological experiences arise out of a cultural context and are based on interpersonal relations and influenced strongly by group norms. For too long, educational thought has been dominated by a narrowly psychological focus. To be useful to practitioners in our schools, research and analysis must include the work of social psychologists, sociologists, and anthropologists. It is to be hoped that social psychologists in particular will help to change the emphasis so that learning groups and cultures are viewed as systems. Groups and organizations, regardless of size, are, after all, more than collections of individuals. They achieve a stable existence and identifiable style even though individuals continuously come and go.

2. The class as a social system

In a theoretical essay on the dynamics of instructional groups, Getzels and Thelen (1960) used concepts from systems theory to describe the most basic features of learning groups. They wrote that the two interacting levels of human activity—the social and the individual dynamics—become integrated and result in the specific group behavior or climate. At the social level, students, teachers, and administrators behave somewhat predictably because of shared norms regarding the way in which each of them *should* behave in their respective roles. From this social perspective, behavior arises out of shared expectations rather than from each person's unique attributes; it involves primarily I-It transactions. Such expectations for a teacher usually include, for example, the idea that he or she will provide most of the leadership in the classroom and will be responsible for attendance-taking and the collection of milk money, even though these functions may be assigned to a student. The teacher will be ultimately responsible for the evaluation of student work and will act as liaison between students and the administration. Likewise, students are expected to perform work in terms of projects or assignments that will help them learn. They are expected to follow the directions of teachers and administrators and to show some evidence of learning and skill development.

The individual level of analysis introduces, of course, unique personal dynamics into the system. Each person, regardless of his role in the school, behaves as the result of a unique and inimitable configuration of cognitions, motives, and attitudes. While performing his or her prescribed role functions, one teacher, for example, will behave quite differently from another teacher who is also behaving in response to the expectations of others. People do what they think is expected of them, but they do it in unique ways.

The social and the individual dimensions interact to create the conditions for the particular group climate that emerges. This primitive framework represents a systems perspective for the social psychological analysis of school behavior. Herbert Walberg has used this framework to guide his program of research on classroom learning; we will refer to his work often throughout this book. Similar concepts have been effectively used by Katz and Kahn (1966) to delineate a social psychology of organizations which we have found useful in our analysis of the organizational climates of schools in Chapter 6. In general we have used this social and psychological framework to derive our principles for an analysis of learning climates and our suggestions for how to improve them.

3. Principles for humanizing learning climates

Five principles can be derived from systems theory. As such, they set the stage for our analysis of learning climates and suggestions for how to improve them.

(1) *Learning groups, constituted of students, teacher(s), and curriculum materials, are organized into subsystems through the communi cation of information, affect, and expectations.* A learning group, as a system, can be as small as a tutorial pair or as large as a school district. Larger systems, such as schools, become humanized to the extent that their subsystems, such as instructional or work groups, encourage I-Thou transactions and personal relationships. A system is analyzed through its subsystems. For example, to study the climate of a classroom one would look at subsystems such as helping pairs, reading groups, project groups, and friendship clusters. To study the climate of a school one would look at departmental groups, curriculum committees, and work forces, along with instructional groups. Changes in a system level come about through changes in the subsystems. *In a humanized school, subsystems are rich in affect and encourage I-Thou transactions and personal relationships.*

(2) *Learning groups aim at achieving particular goals, which are usually stated in terms of individual change or group products.* Subsystems within groups are the divisions for work that, ostensibly at least, are formed to achieve specific goals. An example of a functional subsystem within a district is a committee convened by the superin-

tendent to forecast the future so that the district can accommodate itself to changing times. One subsystem within a school might be a group of teachers and students trying to solve problems that prevent the school from reaching its goals. In the classroom, one subsystem might be a student steering committee formed to help teachers diagnose problems and arrange for new actions.

These subsystems can help to humanize the learning climate, especially if they take into account the emotional needs of members while they attempt to achieve their goals. At present most building staffs and classrooms that we have studied do not set aside time for discussing how well their interpersonal procedures are going. Furthermore, many types of school activities, such as supervisory functions carried out solely by either administrators, curriculum committees made up solely of administrators or teachers, or student governments constituted *only* of students, were devised long ago and are now inappropriate in style for the emerging culture of the 1970s. *Subsystems of a humanized school work toward shared goals. The members consider the feelings and personal goals of one another.*

(3) *Learning groups are interdependent with other systems and continually are influenced by them.* Because the outside environment is in flux continually, a learning group's adaptability and openness to deepening humanization are marks of its effectiveness. To put it another way, no ultimate or utopic learning climate is possible. Change is inevitable and must be faced.

Interdependencies present major sources of conflict between the district and its community, between subsystems within a district, and even between different parts of the same classroom group. For example, conflict arises between the district and community when increased tax levies or bond issues are requested; it occurs between subsystems within the district when a curriculum development committee attempts to keep teachers up to date; and it arises between groups in the same classroom when students disagree on the efficacy and relevance of the teacher's goals and instructional techniques. Interdependence with other systems, the requirement for continuous modification, and inherent conflicts of interest are present regardless of whether the learning group is in a public or an alternative school. *A group with a humanized climate for learning will never be free of conflict, but the members can monitor and try to reduce stress while realizing that conflict is inevitable.*

(4) *A variety of resources, competencies, knowledges, and skills, exists in most schools and groups.* In most schools, teachers and students have special interests and competencies that do not get used. It is not unusual, for example, for a school to have an expert ham radio operator whose resources are not used when a class is studying communication, mass media, or electricity. As another example, a new and effective instructional practice may have been developed by a teacher who, for various reasons, never shares it with colleagues. At another level, students commonly have many different feelings about their teachers, but they are seldom asked to communicate these feelings directly.

The variety of resources among students is much greater than is typically recognized in schools. Too often the knowledge, attitudes, and skills of students are viewed as irrelevant to or even destructive of the school's goals. This is a major error, especially in the 1970s, when cultural changes are occurring so rapidly that people educated in previous generations are out of touch with many aspects of contemporary life. Because of these rapid changes, schools need more ways of formalizing students' teaching of one another. For example, information and discussion about topics such as drugs, sex, dress, and music can be initiated and led by students. Moreover, mini-courses can be developed by curriculum committees made up of students and teachers. In one alternative school, teachers and students listed their resources early in the year and then shared these with one another. Every teacher and student was encouraged to teach at least one mini-course. The result was a series of short classes ranging from "Back Rubbing with Ease," to an American history seminar taught by a student "history buff." *A key to humanizing the learning climate lies in greater use of members' resources.*

(5) *The tenacity of a group's culture or a school's climate lies in the power of norms, how well they are adhered to, and how resistant they are to change.* Norms are shared expectations, usually implicit, that help to guide the psychological processes and behaviors of group members. Note that our definition of norms emphasizes *sharing*: norms occur in groups and are not merely intrapsychic processes. The psychological counterpart of a norm is an *attitude*; a predisposition to think, feel, and act in certain specific ways. Norms are individual attitudes *that are shared with others.* When a norm is present most persons know that their attitude is also held by others and that the others expect them to have the same attitude and behave accordingly.

Norms are therefore strong stabilizers of behavior even though often they are informal and unspoken and group members monitor them unknowingly. School life is predictable and orderly when students, teachers, and administrators behave out of a common normative framework. When teachers behave as other teachers and students expect them to behave, and when students behave according to the expectations of students and teachers, then the classroom learning climate is stable, steady, understandable, and reasonable to all participants. Members quickly discover when they have behaved contrary to expectations. When norms are broken, sanctions usually are administered to help the deviant back within the normative framework. When traditional norms are broken by many, life can become disorderly and even chaotic.

Learning climates as well as entire cultures can be described by the norms that influence the way in which people relate to one another. To us the most pertinent norms in schools revolve around closeness and distance, formality and informality, and closedness and openness. We think that educators and students need to plan rationally, deliberately, and collaboratively the sorts of norms they want to guide their interpersonal relationships. They need to ferret out the unspoken and informal expectations so that they can come to know the power of norms and to decide whether certain norms are worth keeping. *The basis for developing more whole-person relationships and I-Thou transactions in schools lies in the understanding and shaping of new norms having to do with interpersonal relationships.* In the remainder of this book, we plan to explore ways in which the norms of schools can be changed to move toward more humanized learning climates.

SUMMARY OF CHAPTER 1

The essential environment of a school is the climate of feelings and thoughts that are carried through its interpersonal interactions. Humanized school climates are characterized more fully than others by what sociologists refer to as whole-person relationships and what the philosopher Martin Buber called I-Thou transactions. These are personal, affective, and authentic encounters between persons. From our observations, we believe that the salient features of humanized learning climates involve the way in which interpersonal influence and attraction are distributed among staff and students; the extent to which communications among them are authentic and direct; and the degree to which school norms support interpersonal openness and directness.

A brief overview of American cultural history in relation to education leads us to be optimistic that our society is moving toward a more people-oriented period: an era in which feelings can be cherished just as much as information and in which people may be regarded as even more important than "success" and "achievement." We have prepared this book with the faith that schools can play their part in ushering in this new day.

This book aims to show how our schools can go about humanizing their own processes and procedures. We take the view that schools are very complex social systems and that *systemic* changes—not merely changes in individual attitudes—are required to realize humanization. From this "systems" point of view, the most powerful tool for developing humanized learning climates lies in reforming the norms that influence the interpersonal relationships among all school participants.

ANNOTATED BIBLIOGRAPHY FOR CHAPTER 1

Dennison, George. 1969. *The Lives of Children*. New York: Random House.

Dennison's book is one of several recent personal accounts of the damaging effects of some public schools and of efforts to set up a neighborhood alternative school. Dennison examines and documents the pitfalls of public schooling while introducing his own insights about people and education. Although the insights are important and helpful, he offers no guidelines or suggestions—except by way of relating his own experiences—for improvement of the public schools.

Herndon, James. 1965. *The Way It Spozed To Be*. New York: Bantam Books. 1971. *How To Survive in Your Native Land*. New York: Bantam Books.

The first book is a hair-raising account of Herndon's teaching experiences in an urban ghetto school. The second book is equally hair-raising but in a different way. Herndon tells of his experiences in a middle-class suburban school, demonstrating again how deper-

sonalized, bureaucratic organizations work against school participants and particularly against students learning humanistic values.
The second book is far superior to the first, both in the matter of
Herndon's skill in presenting his case and in his answers to basic
questions about who he is as a teacher and what he hopes to
accomplish.

Illich, Ivan. 1970. *Deschooling Society.* New York: Harper and Row.

Illich believes that the institution of the school has taken precedence
over the process of education. Schools have become the recruiting
and training grounds for a dehumanized and production-oriented
bureaucratic society. While his proposal to do away with school is
considered radical and unrealistic by many critics, he still provides
positive directions for where education could go. He proposes skill
centers for learning and the use of modern technology to bring
together those who have skills or knowledge with those who wish
to learn. He thinks schools should not be mandatory and proposes
that many people who have not obtained credentials are capable
of teaching.

Kohl, Herbert R. 1969. *The Open Classroom: A Practical Guide to a
New Way of Teaching.* New York: A New York Review Book.

This is a personal and readable volume suggesting ways teachers
can transform traditional and closed classrooms into open and informal centers for learning. Kohl's own experiences and frustrations
are very understandable, making the transition seem all the more
possible. Although this small book does not present very specific or
concrete details, it presents basic questions and assumptions that
should be answered by every teacher and offers some useful guidelines for how to move toward a more open classroom.

Nyberg, David. 1971. *Tough and Tender Learning.* Palo Alto, Ca.:
National Press Books.

This witty and refreshing but serious book about humanizing
schools is primarily focused upon relationships between people.
Nyberg sometimes appears flippant and even impudent, but he
tackles problems seriously and thoroughly, with continual references to philosophy, psychology, and literature. This book is written

for the serious student of education. While he offers much food for thought, Nyberg does not give many concrete suggestions about what to do tomorrow.

Rogers, Carl. 1969. *Freedom To Learn*. Columbus, O. Charles E. Merrill.

This is a collection of Rogers's thoughts about humanistic education, partly gathered from previous speeches and papers and partly from his recent experiences with interventions. Rogers, one of the most important humanistic psychologists of this era, discusses various levels of education—from elementary school to graduate education—noting problems and offering some general solutions.

Silberman, Charles F. 1970. *Crisis in the Classroom: The Remaking of American Education*. New York: Random House.

Silberman's three-year, Carnegie-sponsored study illustrates and demonstrates in detail the crisis facing American schools. He does not, however, do as sufficient a job of demonstrating how to "remake" education. Although this book lacks constructive guidelines for action, it is a carefully documented and readable account of the dehumanized, depersonalized, and ineffectual education typifying many public schools.

Thelen, Herbert A. 1960. *Education and the Human Quest*. New York: Harper and Brothers.

Although more than a decade old, this book still stands out as one of the best and most up-to-date critical analyses of the schools. Thelen presents a social psychological perspective on the way school groups operate and presents specific proposals for a complete overhauling of the schools. It is as applicable today—unfortunately—as it was in 1960.

chapter 2

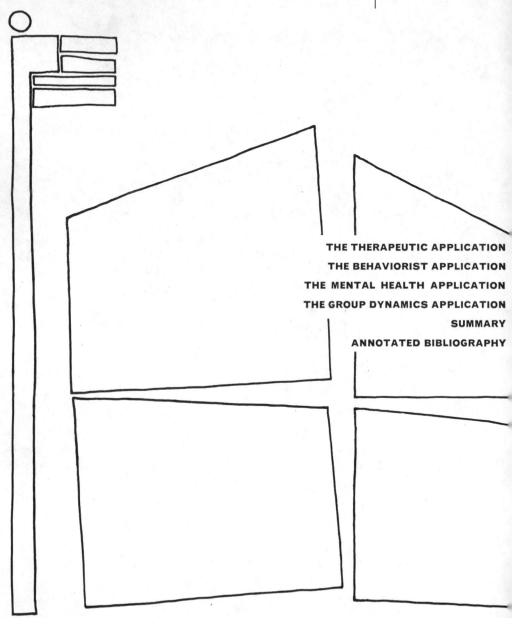

Psychological applications to changing learning climates

Psychological theory and findings have been applied to the schools in a major way only for the past twenty-five years. Although Thorndike coined the appellative, "educational psychologist," in 1903, there were only a few isolated attempts to apply the findings of psychology to the schools, until the 1950s, when behavioral research and its application in school settings began to accumulate.

The detachment of all the behavioral sciences and psychology in particular from public education can be partially explained by the traditional norms of American society regarding schooling. During the first few decades of the twentieth century, attitudes about schools emanated from an entrepreneurial value system—the schools existed to train only those who had adequate intelligence and sufficient interest. Acquisition of an education was primarily left to the individual; the schools were not seen as responsible for students who could not or would not capitalize on their benefits.

The subsequent period of bureaucratic emphasis, however, ushered in the concept that schools should be held accountable for the failure of many of the young to become educated. Americans began to expect favorable results on a large scale from the schools; but often their aspirations went unfulfilled. Schools did not act as a productive force in relation to the society's ills. In fact, they were held responsible, whether justifiably or not, for such social problems as the growing number of inmates in mental hospitals and prisons, the large number of citizens incapable of holding jobs because they lacked functional skills, and the growing number of citizens on the welfare rolls.

When commentators investigated the schools they found valid bases for criticism. They discovered students who did not learn or could not learn or were bored and unstimulated; they found students with physical impairments going unnoticed; and they found many students who were causing continual disturbances for teachers, administrators, and other students. The methods of teacher training reflected times gone past, curriculum materials were antiquated, and teaching procedures were archaic; even compulsory Latin persisted in some schools as America entered the space age.

The 1950s and early 1960s saw a growing number of influential dissidents criticizing and attacking the schools publicly. Conant's careful analyses were published in 1959 and 1964, while Mayer's popular account of the inferior conditions in American schools was published in 1961. During the 1950s large amounts of public money became available for educators and behavioral scientists to try to improve the schools. Increased expenditures for education were accompanied by the rise in stature and power of the United States Office of Education. While this governmental division had been in formal existence since 1867, its move to the newly organized Department of Health, Education, and Welfare in 1953 heralded an unprecedented allowance of federal funds for educators and behavioral scientists to promote and encourage educational research, to apply psychology to the improvement of educational processes, and to experiment with various innovations in the schools. Behavioral scientists by the hundreds were quickly drawn into attempting to solve the complex problems of public education. At the present time, however, there is a serious reduction in funding for the formerly prestigious Office of Education. This seems due in part, at least, to changes in political priorities, but also to the OE's poor record in achieving substantial changes in public education over the past twenty years.

We believe the chief reason for the failure or short-lived and partial success of the experimental programs attempted by behavioral scientists is that the innovative procedures have not directly intervened into the school's interpersonal culture. Traditional patterns and norms for interacting have been transferred to new buildings with new curriculum materials, new teaching methods, and new hardware; the quality of interpersonal relationships has remained largely unchanged. We believe that the quality of relationships among all the school par-

Psychological applications
to changing
learning climates

ticipants as they engage in the curriculum is the most critical factor in making schools more humanized institutions.

This chapter is given over to describing four types of school interventions which have their origins in different schools of psychological thought. We will show why we think each of these applications of psychological theory has fallen short in altering the interpersonal relationships between school participants and has not created basic change. The four applications are the *therapeutic*, the *behaviorist*, the *mental health*, and the *group dynamics* applications.

The therapeutic application is grounded in psychoanalytic theory and overlaps many concepts of clinical psychology; it stresses the individual's intrapsychic mechanisms (primarily those of students) but has provided few systematic concepts or tools to shed light on the influence of the environment. The behaviorist application, on the other hand, purposely ignores intrapsychic processes and deals systematically with the environmental contingencies that influence an individual's behavior. We contend that these two applications are too narrowly focused to be of much value in humanizing the multifaceted cultures of schools, which involve not only intrapsychic mechanisms and environmental contingencies, but, most importantly, the continuous interaction between the two.

The other two psychological applications, mental health and group dynamics, have considered interaction between the individual and his environment as well as the interpersonal dynamics that are inevitable within any human group. However, they, too, have fallen short in providing systematic and planned attempts to humanize the climates of our schools because they have focused on too narrow a range of school participants or have not accounted for both the cognitive and affective psychodynamics of the participants.

Our discussion of each of these applications will not provide a comprehensive description or evaluation of the particular school of thought it represents; rather we will try to indicate both the direct and indirect implications each application holds for dealing with the climates of schools and how each, by itself, fails to provide a viable method for humanizing the learning climates of schools and the groups within them.*

---

*For more comprehensive treatment of each of these schools of thought, we refer the reader to the annotated bibliography at the end of this chapter.

THE THERAPEUTIC APPLICATION

The therapeutic application stems from Freud's efforts to understand and treat people whom he defined as neurotic. Although his pioneer work in the development of psychoanalytic theory has contributed greatly to the understanding of human development and behavior, his major contribution has been in strategies for treating disturbed or abnormal persons. Similarly, the use of this application in public schools is primarily directed toward students who have emotional difficulties or who are participating in neurotic relationships which influence their academic work.

Although this application does not directly concern the climate of schools or learning groups *as a whole*, we believe it does have implications for the kinds of relationships that are established between *individuals* in the schools. In this section we will briefly describe the ideal treatment model of the therapeutic application and show how it has been used in the schools, and provide some empirical research on the efficacy of its application. The bulk of our discussion will focus on three major implications of this application for creating climates in which whole-person relationships are paramount: first, the use of diagnostic labels or categories which encourage "I-It" relationships; next, the social and political implications of placing students with psychological problems in separate, homogeneous classes; and finally, the effect of the one-sided emphasis on the intrapsychic mechanisms, resulting in an almost total neglect of environmental forces.

1. The therapeutic application in the schools

The treatment model of the therapeutic application calls for removing the client from his natural setting and bringing him to a specially trained therapist for intensive counseling. Ideally, an effective therapist can make an accurate diagnosis, prescribe the correct treatment, and skillfully carry out the treatment program until a client is cured. Cure comes about when the client understands the basic motives and reasons for his or her behavior. One assumption of psychoanalytic theory is that a person is motivated to behave by subconscious or unconscious drives; sick persons have drives that are so debilitating they cannot function effectively. The treatment is aimed at helping the client to understand the nature of his debilitating drives and to ferret out their causes. Understandably, treatment lasts over a prolonged period of time.

This therapeutic procedure, in its ideal form, is limited by one obvious shortcoming in the schools—there have never been enough therapists, enough time, or enough money to provide optimal treatment for students in need of help. Nevertheless, some educators have tried fervently to approximate such an ideal program. As the bureaucracy of schools has grown, so have their specialized services; all fifty states now have some legislation that calls for special educational programs. Mackie (1965a and 1965b) computed that 12 percent of the American student population were in special classes in 1948; in 1963 27 percent of the school children were receiving some kind of specialized instruction. She predicted that by 1970 at least 35 percent would be enrolled in special classes. It should be noted in the context of our discussion that her figures include many categories of special problem children—the physically handicapped, mentally retarded, emotionally disturbed, the gifted, and those with learning disabilities.

Since the 1950s, schools have assumed the dual responsibility of (1) serving as the society's monitoring device for determining which students have psychological problems and (2) helping such problem students. Ivan Illich reported in 1970, for example, that President Nixon had agreed with a recent proposal submitted to the Department of Health, Education, and Welfare which advocated that all children between the ages of six and eight should be tested professionally to determine their "destructive" tendencies and that obligatory treatment should be provided for them.

Most large school districts now have routine procedures for diagnosing and placing students with emotional or learning problems. Often students are first referred by their classroom teacher; each student is given the appropriate tests by the school psychologist or diagnostician, who attempts to discover the underlying causes of the student's problem; and then usually a group of people (the diagnostician, teacher, and counselor, for example) decides on the best course of action from among the alternative therapeutic procedures available. The student may be referred to a special class, placed in a treatment center, or asked to remain in the regular classroom with the additional prescription to attend one-to-one therapy or group counseling sessions once or twice a week. Schools have made great strides in finding the students who need help and in trying to provide specialized services for them.

2. The efficacy of the therapeutic application

There have been several attempts to evaluate the efficacy of the therapeutic application. In evaluation of the effectiveness of traditional therapy, Eysenck (1952), for example, reviewed twenty-four studies involving 8,000 patients who had received some type of therapy. Although the results of these therapies seemed encouraging, when Eysenck compared the results of them with two other baseline samples he found no difference between the recovery rates of those who had intensive therapy and those who had received little or no therapy. He compared the recovery rates of patients who had received intensive therapy to the recovery rates of 500 patients classified as neurotic who had been treated by their own family physicians as well as a sample of neurotic patients who were discharged from New York hospitals during a seventeen-year span after receiving little or no therapy. Although Eysenck's methods and results have been questioned and criticized by psychiatrists and psychological researchers, there does seem to be general consensus that research on intensive psychological therapy has *not* indicated that it warrants being considered successful. Berelson and Steiner (1964), summarizing the results of research on the effect of psychotherapy, conclude:

> Strictly speaking, it cannot even be considered established that psychotherapy, on the average, improves a patient's chances of recovery beyond what they would be without any formal therapy whatsoever. (P. 287.)

Evaluation of the outcomes of the therapeutic application to schools show much the same results. Meyers (1971) reviewed ten research studies on counseling within the public schools and found very few conclusively favorable results. The ten studies employed several different outcome measures, such as gradepoint average, self-esteem, attitudinal measures, sociometric ratings, and standard personality or achievements tests. Meyers also pointed out that almost all of the students had been pressured or persuaded to participate in treatment.

Other studies besides those reviewed by Meyers also offer discouraging evidence. Rothney (1963) conducted an intensive ten-year follow-up of students who had received some therapeutic help from a counselor in high school. He used such criteria for success as completion of post-high-school training or formal education, promotion in jobs, and general satisfaction with life. While the results were in the positive direction (those students who had received counseling were somewhat better off), the differences between the treatment and control groups were small and insignificant. In another comprehensive evaluation, Runkel (1962) conducted a carefully controlled study of the relationships between guidance programs in Illinois high schools and criteria centering on the students' knowledgeable decision-making about occupational choices. He found that the guidance programs played a less significant role in influencing the students' occupational decision-making than the teaching staff. And finally, in a more recent paper, Reynolds (1969) reviewed a number of studies of children with such behavioral disorders as emotional disturbance, social maladjustment, and delinquency, and reported no conclusive evidence that deviant behavior improved when the children were placed in special classes.

One might wonder why special programs persist in the face of so much evidence that they have few long-term favorable effects. For one reason, the evidence is conflicting: a few studies do show that students with psychological problems do better in special classes, or at least that they are more comfortable in special classes than in regular classrooms. Second, special classrooms do get potential or actual troublemakers out of the regular classroom. Third, the view of institutions as being more culpable than individuals, typified in bureaucratic value systems, allows individuals to abdicate their personal responsibility toward others—the bureaucracy (in this case, the schools) will provide! Fourth, the aura of mystery and competence that surrounds the expert serves to bind and limit teachers; they become unsure and unwilling to confront students who have psychological problems. Instead, they prefer to send such students to specialized personnel who have received training to cope with emotional problems. In this way teachers do not behave toward problem students as whole persons but more as objects who fit a particular diagnostic category.

3. Diagnostic labels and whole-person relationships

The primary purpose of psychological diagnosis is to increase understanding and information about another person. A diagnostic inventory is merely a methodological tool for deciding rationally on the best course of action. If that course of action does not bear fruit, then the therapist re-evaluates the original diagnosis and tries a new path. However, psychological or academic tests in school often eventuate in a *fait accompli*. Students who are diagnosed in their early years as "emotionally disturbed" or as having "limited abilities," a "learning problem," or an "adjustment problem" very often continue to fit that diagnosis for many years. Such events can mean at least two things: either the diagnostic category is correct (and in this case we may well ask why the student has not been helped) or else students tend to continue to behave in the ways expected of them *because* of the diagnosis.

A diagnostic label supported by an objective test is not merely a scientific procedure carried out by psychologists; it can come to have meaning and power itself over the lives of students insofar as their teachers' perceptions and interpretations of their classroom behavior are inevitably influenced by the labels. Several studies corroborate our view. In one study (Farina and Ring, 1970), the experimenters gave subjects background information on their co-workers; on some of the information protocols, the co-worker was identified as mentally ill, while on others this designation was deleted. Persons subsequently behaved differently toward co-workers who had been categorized as mentally ill than they did toward those who were not. The prevailing response was of sympathy or unwillingness to criticize or confront the "mentally ill" co-worker.

The well-named but controversial study, *Pygmalion in the Classroom* (Rosenthal and Jacobson, 1968), which we criticize in detail in Chapter 3, tried to show this phenomenon in reverse. Teachers were given false data indicating that certain students were "academic spurters." The authors interpreted the resulting data to mean that those students who were randomly designated to flourish intellectually actually made significant increases on subsequent intelligence test scores, reading test scores, and teachers' ratings of their personal and social adjustment. In light of several studies indicating that people will distort even stable and constant stimuli in order to maintain some congruence between their belief system and the physical world (Asch, 1956, and Ames, 1955), it is not so difficult to see why people selectively perceive and distort judgments about others whose behavior is varied, changing, and complex.

A primary objective of most diagnostic tests is to discover what is *wrong* with a student, while very few of them are designed to discover a student's strengths. A request to test a student usually means that some adult believes something is wrong with the student; the purpose of the test is to identify the nature of the difficulty, whether it is emotional or intellectual. Thus, as he interprets the results, the diagnostician understandably has a predisposition to think that something is wrong with the student. A diagnostician's competence, moreover, may be questioned if his findings indicate little or nothing wrong with the majority of students referred for testing. Very often a student's future in school is dependent upon the intuitions of teachers, which, in turn, are confirmed in some way by an objective diagnostic procedure. Students can carry the label of such results with them for a long time, either through the informal interactions of teachers or through their cumulative records, often important to future teachers and employers.

Like all of us, teachers react in preferential ways (depending on their expectations) toward students. Most advocates of the therapeutic application emphasize the importance of the specially trained expert to deal with student problems. An implicit "hands off" message is communicated to teachers: no matter how good a teacher's intentions may be, he may do significant damage to a student's psyche by intervening ineffectively. We know of one student in an elementary school who took advantage of his "emotional problems" for an entire academic year. He was on a formal waiting list for psychological treatment, and no adult staff member would assume the responsibility of confronting him: that would be the job, after all, of the therapeutic expert. As a result he was allowed to run errands for the principal's office, to read stories to the younger children, to have two lunch hours, and to do virtually anything without being held accountable for his behavior!

Labels such as "disturbed," "retarded," or "dyslexic" can also serve as a means to justify a teacher's inability to work effectively with a student. We have often seen teachers verbally write off students who have had problems beyond their control; such behavior on the part of teachers is often a convenient ploy to avoid looking at his own interaction patterns and behavioral failures with a student. Giving a semantic label to the student's problem relieves the teacher of facing his own responsibilities regarding the deviant behavior. In one teacher-training event that was designed to increase understanding of mental health principles in the classroom, most of the teachers did change their attitudes toward some problem students as a result of increased understanding (Schmuck, 1968). Whereas before the training the teachers had labeled some of their extremely active students "disturbed," in the light of some new knowledge they began to view these behaviors more as normal and increased their level of tolerance for the outgoing and active students in their classrooms. But even though some teachers do not categorize their students inappropriately, the detrimental effects of labeling students continue to be widespread.

The labeling of someone as pathological "objectifies" the other person: the labeler does not have to meet the other as a whole person. Interpersonal distance increases when one person excuses another, justifies another, or dismisses another as a peculiar type of person. When the other is labeled as pathological, the labeler usually emphasizes the other's problem as arising from within himself; the labeler moves away from looking at his or her own relationship with the other. Looking at students through a diagnostic category system likewise tends to reduce the students to impersonal objects—to "its,"—and keeps the teacher from looking carefully at the part he or she has played in influencing the students' behavior.

One of the major activities of the therapeutic application is to ferret out exceptions to the normal population and provide help for them. Too often educators assume that anyone who does not follow the pattern of most students is abnormal and needs help; the clinical label gives an air of legitimacy to this conviction. The labeling of some students as abnormal and most of the others as normal is, however, self-defeating for schools. For one thing, schools will never catch up with the need for specialized treatment of students. The reason is almost embarrassingly simple. *All students need specialized treatment.*

School personnel with the intention of being bureaucratically efficient and exhibiting their know-how try to fit each student into a specific category. If the student does not fit that category, another is tried, and if there are no appropriate categories, concerned and well-meaning teachers work diligently to create a new one. The educators find money, they find room in an already crowded building, and they provide a program to fit the needs of this new category of students.

4. Deviant behavior in a humanized school

The staff of a humanized school would view all students, and teachers for that matter, as basically different—each with his own particular "bag" of problems, skills, and strengths. The staff would make use of some diagnostic instruments or methodological tools to provide information about student strengths or weaknesses in academic areas, about their interpersonal relations, and about their interests, goals, or attitudes. The staff would teach students and parents about the objectives of each test and would make test-records accessible to both groups. The tests would be used as only one step in providing the kinds of programs and guidance that students want in their educational careers.

A humanized school would of course, have its share of students with problems—there would be norm violators, students who have problems in learning certain things, students who exhibit different types of behavior, and those who seem to make life miserable for everyone around them. A staff that aspires to build a humanized school will have to cope with such problem persons, not by dismissing them because they are "sick" or "limited" but by accepting their peculiar behaviors as legitimate individual differences. The problems that students have will not, of course, go away if they are ignored or even if they are treated as legitimate differences. It is true that many nonpublic, alternative schools that we have visited have quite a few students who would be labeled "deviant" by public school standards, and that many of these students are nevertheless flourishing in the new schools, which have much broader ranges of tolerance for different behaviors. At the same time, of course, some of the students and faculty even in these schools are clearly making both other people and themselves miserable, and obviously need more help than they are getting.

No simple recipe exists for dealing with students or faculty who present a continual irritation to other school participants. The hallmark of the humanized school is not that such behaviors will be ignored or that others will accept attacks from someone who is "sick"; rather it is that procedures will be followed that recognize the integrity of all persons and that norms in which individuals are held accountable for themselves will be promoted. One example that occurred in a free school illustrates our point. Two seven-year-old boys were making life miserable for everyone in the school by destroying people's projects, swearing at everyone, interrupting classes, and being vicious to the dogs and cats. The older students furiously approached the teacher of the younger group but the teacher refused to take responsibility for the boys' behavior. In this school there was a well-supported norm that everyone should teach someone else—many students, for instance, conducted classes for other students. There was also a norm in support of "individual freedom" and each person's accountability for his own behavior. Individuals confronted the boys by expressing their anger over what they had done or by attempting to engage them in more positive actions. A few of the older students could deal effectively with the boys, but the general problem persisted.

Two of the older students were guests at our home and discussed the problem that was so upsetting to them. They had feelings of anger and resentment toward those "little brats." They used the usual mechanisms of blaming the parents and the teacher, and even suggested that the boys were really neurotic and should be placed in a special institution. Perhaps the deviant boys were beyond the capabilities of the people in the school, but, as we suggested to our guests, very few of the available resources had really been used. For instance, the school held weekly community meetings designed to air problems and grievances, but no one had brought up the disturbing influence of the two boys even though almost everyone was affected. The few students who could manage the deviant boys had not been consulted by anybody else to find out how they handled them. The rhetoric of the school gave credence to the view that all persons were important and that all persons had something to offer others in daily interactions, but the school's participants had not joined collaborative forces to develop a milieu where all persons took responsibility for helping the boys or attempting to alter the behaviors which were so upsetting to everyone. Our two houseguests went back to their school armed with some new ideas for confronting the problem at a community meeting. The last we heard was that one of the students was in a treatment center while the other was adapting well to the free school.

5. Social and political implications

Theodore Sarbin (1970), discussing the question of whether some people should be labeled mentally ill, pointed out that solely on the basis of a clinical diagnosis our society has deprived certain persons of their liberties, their civil rights, and their capacity for self-determinism. He suggested that such labels are modern-day versions of archaic views of sin, witchcraft, and evil, and he further stated that the "myth" of mental illness has stood as an obstacle to providing policies and practices for meeting many of the social problems of our times. While it is still a moot issue as to how much liberty and self-determination students should have, the problem created by a lack of freedom can be severe for those students who do not succeed in the schools and consequently are placed in a treatment center or a special classroom. Referral of students who are deviant or who do not fit the expected pattern to special schools or classes may no longer serve even as a legal solution. An illustration of a community's response to special opportunity classes is documented in a brief prepared by the Community Council at Park School in Toronto (Martell, 1971). This brief contends that the school district, consciously or unconsciously, has discriminated against students from families with low incomes by placing those students on the bottom rung of the educational ladder, i.e., special classes or opportunity classes. The argument rests on presentation of the results of the Every Student Survey, which categorizes students in special classes according to their social class. They show:

> If for example you're classified as a "sheet metal worker" the Every Student Survey tells you that your child has 18.5 times the chance of ending up in one of these bottom streams as the child of an 'accountant, engineer or lawyer'. The figure jumps to 40 times the chance if you are retired or on workman's compensation and to 43.5 for unemployed and 67 times the chance for welfare or mother's allowance. (P. 11.)

The crux of this brief lies in questioning *why* there is such a direct connection between parental occupation and a student's placement in a special education class. The official explanation given by the school district is that these children have been tested and diagnosed as having "very limited ability" and that the special classes have been designed to provide an opportunity for them because they cannot succeed in regular classrooms. The community council points out that such classes, in fact, do not provide opportunities, but further add to a child's perpetuation in the lower socio-economic class. The special classes serve, in other words, as a final dead end.

> The end result of all this of course, is that nothing really changes for our children. To the hard 'facts' of being at the bottom of the socio-economic ladder are added the public diagnosis that you are dumb as well as the translation of that diagnosis into placement in the bottom stream classes. (P. 27.)

This brief illustrates how strongly a diagnostic category can affect the entire life of a student. The student is placed in a category and a class based on one personal aspect: in this case his learning ability *as predicted by the district's testing program*. The Park School Council does not disregard or ignore the reasons for the diagnosis of their children as having "very limited ability"; they understand that their children do have learning problems *that center primarily on reading.* The alternatives they propose are not radical; they ask for a reading program based on continual diagnosis of skill level and a chance to move up the ladder of success rather than be rooted to one spot. They ask for greater variety and availability of materials, and for more use of community resources and trained teachers. In essence the Council has asked for adequate educational facilities and programs for their children, without the stigma of the "opportunity classes" that are based on the premise that the child has failed. Hopefully, such an educational program will change the long-term effects of the students' failure syndrome.

In contrast to the use of opportunity classes that are in fact "the bottom rung of the educational ladder" is Marcus Foster's description (1971) of his experiences in an inner city school where most of the children were also on the bottom rung. His messages to these students were "you are important" and "you can learn"; the medium through which he chose to communicate the message was the simple skill of handwriting. After his students had surpassed city norms in handwriting achievement, his staff began on arithmetic, then spelling, and then grammar. After the students and the staff were stimulated by their joint achievements, they began on the more basic issues of reading, concept development, and engaging the parents and the community in the educational process. School was not a dead end but something alive for many students and teachers and even some parents. Indeed, as Foster's experiences showed, academic achievement is only one small aspect of a student's life. A humanized school will allow many parts of the self to emerge and will mirror that variety in the context of its programs as well as in its means of evaluating how well the students are doing. A major focus of the humanized school will be on enhancing self-esteem of all the participants.

6. The role of the environment

A major limitation of the therapeutic application is the assumption that the pathology resides within the individual. Thus, treatment is aimed at providing the client with the necessary psychological resources to cope with his environment, as that environment now exists. Forces of the environment are not taken into consideration, except as the demands to which a person is expected to adjust. As a consequence, there are many therapeutic designs for socializing persons gradually back into their environment, such as halfway houses and special programs in regular classrooms.

A social psychological orientation offers quite a different point of view. It suggests that not only is this "adjustment strategy" a naive and incomplete consideration of the nature of psychological problems, but also that environments themselves should be changed. Indeed, the therapeutic application may encourage the preservation of environments by providing no diagnostic label (and therefore no focus) for pathological *environments*. Unfortunately, many pathological environments do exist in our schools and the unwillingness of some students to adapt to these circumstances may well be the mark of a *sound* psychological condition on their part.

We think that it is unnecessary to present an extended discussion of the pathological environments of our schools. One macabre example of the Indian identity problem in the American school system provided by Silberman (1971) points it out only too clearly.

> The students in a sixth-grade English class in a school on a Chippewa Indian reservation are all busily at work writing a composition for Thanksgiving. The subject of the composition is written on the blackboard for the students (and the visitor) to see. The subject: "Why We Are Happy the Pilgrims Came." (P. 173.)

The psychiatrists Grier and Cobbs (1968) tell of the feelings of futility and frustration in conducting psychotherapy with blacks. They point out that in most cases the clients are not deranged but in fact have found very successful coping mechanisms (which would be labeled pathological in many clinical texts) in dealing with a very sick society. Another vivid example is provided by Bruno Bettelheim's treatise (1958) on schizophrenic reactions of prisoners in concentration camps in World War II. He maintains that the schizophrenic syndrome was functionally adaptable in that setting; the loss of one's hold on reality can be a life-saving mechanism when the reality itself is insane.

Clearly, the psychological brutality of many school environments can lead students to adopt psychologically unhealthy responses in order to cope with the external reality. In many instances, students who refuse to submit or cooperate with the regimen of a school have been put into diagnostic categories emphasizing their maladjustments, while the learning environments offered by the school have remained unscathed and unchanged. The next psychological application we discuss, the behaviorist application, deals almost exclusively with contingencies of the environment and their importance for improving schools.

THE BEHAVIORIST APPLICATION

Behaviorist psychology rejects most of the assumptions and procedures of psychoanalytic thought. For behaviorists the study of people should be an objective scientific endeavor; the phenomena to be studied must be observable and measurable. Hence the focus of behaviorist study is on observable behaviors themselves, not upon the underlying psychological dynamics of the personality. Emotions, motivational drives, and other intrapsychic mechanisms, emphasized so much by traditional therapists, are categorized by behaviorists as phenomena that cannot be observed or measured and thus are not considered the "stuff" of science.

The first attempts to apply behaviorist psychology were with patients in mental hospitals. Most behaviorists, however, were not concerned as much about the diagnostic labels of patients as they were about modifying specific problem behaviors. To the behaviorist a person is categorized as sick when he or she behaves in sick ways. The treatment for sickness is to change the behavior; a cured patient is one who no longer behaves in sick ways. Behaviorists have attended to such grossly maladaptive behaviors as vomiting, refusal to eat, head-banging, aggressive behaviors directed toward oneself or another, impotence, and withdrawal and phobic reactions of several different kinds. Psychological literature is replete with successful case histories of behavioral changes that came about through the application of *reinforcement strategies*—the primary techniques of the behaviorist.

A central premise of behaviorist thought is that behavior is learned through reinforcing contingencies in the environment. A child behaves in one way rather than another because of the witting or unwitting reinforcement of certain behaviors. In contrast, Freudians have argued that behavior is symptomatic of underlying psychological dynamics and that where one merely changes behavior (the symptoms of the sickness) the sickness is forced to take on new behavioral manifestations. The behaviorists have argued strongly against this psychoanalytic position, pointing out that in case after case of successful behavioral change, patients have offered little evidence of symptom substitution.

1. The behaviorist application in the schools

In the schools the earliest behaviorist work was carried out by Thorndike at the beginning of this century. He was quoted often (and inaccurately) to justify such popular educational practices as rote and drill and the view that "practice makes perfect". Like the other schools of psychology, however, behaviorism has not had a wide impact upon the public schools until the last two decades. The movement now led by B. F. Skinner has grown to tremendous proportions: to educators, "programmed instruction," "precision teaching," "contingency management," and "behavior modification" have become familiar phrases.

The primary view of people implicit in the behaviorist philosophy shows them as regulated by reinforcements; one can predict their responses (at least in theory) by knowing their reinforcement history and knowing what reinforcers are operating upon them at any moment in time. According to the behaviorist view, students respond to stimuli in the environment and learn behavioral patterns as a consequence of the reinforcing contingencies operating upon them. The technology of behaviorism that Skinner advocates for the schools is to decide on goals, to find the reinforcers to produce those responses, to implement a program of reinforcers that will produce the desired behaviors, and finally to measure very carefully the effects of the reinforcers and to change them accordingly.

It is on the first step of deciding upon goals where we often are in disagreement with the applications of behavioristic principles and see their shortcomings in humanizing the climate of our schools. As Neil Postman (1970) writes in his discussion of reading as a basic skill, one's strategy for instruction ultimately is a political statement:

> ... all educational practices are profoundly political in the sense that they are designed to produce one sort of human being rather than another—which is to say, an educational system always proceeds from some model of what a human being *ought* to be like. (P. 244.)

Our major disagreement with the applications of reinforcement theory to our schools is aimed not so much at the behavioral technology as with the model it implies for what a human being *ought* to be like. For instance, in an unpublished paper of reactions to the British Infant Schools (the new open and informal schools for primary-grade students), Skinner gives a partial description of what he thinks a human being ought to be, and hence what an educational institution should be.

We have been too ready to assume that the student is a free agent, that he wants to learn, that he knows best what he should learn, and that his attitudes and tastes should determine what he learns, and that he should discover things for himself rather than learn what others have already discovered. These principles are all wrong, and they are responsible for much of our current trouble. Education is primarily concerned with the transmission of culture—with teaching new members what others have already learned—and it is dangerous to ignore this function. . . . The teacher must regain control, but he must do so in ways which are not only more efficient but free of the undesirable by-products of older practices.

We quarrel with many of Skinner's points as stated here. First, we disagree that education should be viewed as the transmission of culture, or even that it can be. World cultures are changing too fast, moving in new and uncharted directions; transmission of the old ways is not the way to solve the international problems of today. Second, we disagree that teachers should regain control of students, even if they could. Young people are growing toward independence and new life styles that are in some ways a rejection of past hypocrisies and discontents in the lives of their parents. There is a plethora of issues, such as civil disobedience, the ecological crisis, and the irresponsibility of large corporations, that young people are confronting in different ways from those of any previous generation. And we think this is proper even though some of the consequences, such as the use of drugs or the impermanence of interpersonal relationships, may be detrimental to the solution of human problems. Third, we disagree with Skinner's argument that educational institutions are based on wrong assumptions about student psychology. The ideas that students are "free agents," that their attitudes and tastes should determine the form their instruction takes, and that they should discover for themselves are not "all wrong." On the contrary, we firmly believe that these are some of the principles upon which educational institutions should be built.

In essence, our primary disagreement with Skinner and many other behaviorists is not with the validity of the principles of a reinforcement psychology, but rather with their goals for public education and their view of what a human being should become. Behaviorism presents a technology that is not invalid, inappropriate, or incorrect; however, we vehemently disagree with the ends to which the technology can be used. Feelings, attitudes, motivations, and aspirations are not often considered legitimate in the rhetoric or the experiments of behaviorists.

In its lack of emphasis on the reciprocity of interpersonal relationships and in its view of man as being buffeted about by external rewards, the behaviorist's application is in stark contrast to what we think of as humanized schools. Indeed, the application of behaviorist principles can even promote distance between persons, can produce a highly authoritarian or hierarchical decision-making structure, and may even lead easily to legitimizing I-It relationships.

We do not mean to say that persons who use behaviorist principles in our schools are themselves cold, mechanistic, or unaffectionate people. Our argument is with what a behaviorist application can reap rather than with the persons who are using behaviorist techniques. While we do believe reinforcement techniques are narrow and limited, we have respect for the technological advances brought about by Skinner and other behaviorists such as Gerald Patterson at the University of Oregon. Our son attended nursery school at Educational Environments, a school based on a behaviorist orientation. We chose that school for him *not* because it was experimenting with programmed instruction or because of the school's history of success with enhancing the academic achievement of children, but because of our impression that the climate of warmth, acceptance, and excitement about learning in the preschool at Educational Environments far surpassed what we saw in any other nursery school in Eugene.

Now we wish to turn to two major behaviorist interventions in the schools: first, *programmed instruction* and the implicit assumptions it makes about learning and the nature of truth; and second, *behavior modification* as it has been applied typically in the schools. We do not intend to present a comprehensive discussion of how behaviorism relates to these two applications, but we will discuss what implications these educational strategies have for our view of the kinds of learning climates that foster whole-person relationships and I-Thou transactions.

2. Programmed instruction

The idea of programmed instruction is not new. Thorndike wrote as early as 1912:

> If by a miracle of ingenuity a book could be so arranged that only to him who had done what was directed on page 1 would page 2 become visible, and so on, much that now requires instruction could be managed in print. (Stolurow, 1969, p. 1018.)

Thorndike's "miracle of ingenuity" has come into fruition in the form of programmed instruction. While various kinds of programmed instruction are available today, we refer here to those instructional procedures that include four essential conditions: that curricula are sequentially presented, that individual students progress at their own rate, that students are required to make behavioral responses, and that immediate feedback is given with regard to the correctness of the responses.

Programs can be constructed very simply; for instance a program in handwriting may be merely a booklet of sequential instructions requiring students to proceed in small steps at their own pace by making specific notations that are corrected immediately by a teacher. A much more complex type is a computerized mathematics program requiring first a diagnostic test to pinpoint a student's conceptual or skill difficulties, resulting in a computer print-out that suggests the lessons to be followed to alleviate specific skill problems. In this computerized program the student uses only those parts of the program he needs and often his responses are corrected immediately by the computer.

New types of programs are being produced continually and technologically they are increasingly advanced. While the more complex ones are costly, they can be efficient and expedient in teaching skills and concepts and in evaluating a student's level of mastery. Furthermore, programming can be far superior to teachers' traditional methods of presentation. For instance, rote drill for a group of students is usually quite ineffective because each student is at a somewhat different level of mastery; as a result, many students probably are not listening while others are under fire. Drill can be more effective when the student works alone at his own pace.

In a review of the research on programmed instruction in the *Encyclopedia of Educational Research* (1969), Stolurow makes the following strong statement:

Research on Programmed Instruction (PI) leaves no doubt that students learn. They learn from adjunctive, linear, mathetic, branched, intrinsic and idiomorphic programming. They learn when materials are in book and machine form. Many different kinds of learners have not only learned, but also liked programs. With PI, students have learned the gamut of school subjects from algebra to zoology plus a variety of college, military and business courses and skills. ... The decision to use PI in and for education are [*sic*] not

48 Psychological applications
to changing
learning climates

simple and easy, but any doubts about its permanence or effectiveness would have to stem from prejudice or ignorance. (P. 1020.)

We do not have serious doubts about the effectiveness of programmed instruction. We do have reservations, however, about its use that we believe stem from neither prejudice nor ignorance. These reservations center on three areas: first, the narrow operational definition of learning used in programmed instruction; second, the incidental learning that might take place while using this medium of instruction; and third, the nature of truth that is implied by programmed instruction.

a. The nature of learning

The process of learning, according to most behaviorists, is itself not directly observable. A measurable change in behavior can be taken as *evidence* of learning, however. According to Skinner (1968), the mission of the schools is to shape those behaviors that give evidence of learning:

> It is true that the techniques which are emerging from the experimental study of learning are not designed to 'develop the mind' or to further some vague 'understanding' . . . they are designed, on the contrary to establish the very behaviors which are taken to be evidence of learning. (P. 26.)

Evidence of learning consists of prescribed responses to stimuli presented in a program, on a standardized test, or by a teacher's question. In a good program, the objectives are behaviorally defined, the information is presented in a logical and sequential manner, and there are methods for evaluating behaviors to be used as evidence of reaching the program's objectives. Such systematic procedures and means of evaluation are far superior to many methods of teacher-directed instruction and subjective evaluation.

However, we think that such programs do not offer a broad enough view of the process of learning or instruction. Much programmed instruction focuses primarily upon cognitive goals and tends to avoid and even reject the affective dimensions of learning. Affective processes (student attitudes, acceptance or rejection of ideas or people, student motivations, and interests that students bring to school) are always present whether or not they are stated as elements of a given instructional objective. Students also learn about themselves, about others, and about academic subject matter through their relationships with teachers and peers in the school. It is true, of course, that a hypothetical program can teach cognitive information about interpersonal relationships, about values, or about attitudes, but even then cannot account for much of the affective learning that occurs daily.

Krathwohl, Bloom, and Masia (1964) have published a useful volume about the affective facets that should be accounted for in instruction. Affective objectives can be incorporated into the curriculum and more sophisticated methods of evaluating evidence of learning can be used than judging specific responses to specific stimuli. The interpersonal life of one's own school, classrooms and surrounding community, if dealt with openly and formally, can provide many opportunities to apply knowledge, synthesize ideas, learn how to make judgments about ethical matters, and learn about aesthetics or other modes of thought.

Coleman (1972) argues in support of this point of view by suggesting that students today do not need more information or cognitive knowledge. He maintains that contemporary students are information-rich and action-poor. Methods of instruction, and in particular programmed instruction, that emphasize cognitive gains merely supply additional information to students who already have information in abundance. Coleman thinks that schools should not emphasize the accumulation of additional information, but rather should teach students, *through experience*, how to apply the knowledge they already have. Schooling could, for example, provide experiences for acting in ways that make a social difference by having students try to improve the community. Such learning experiences would of course be harder to evaluate than responses to stimuli, but people like Bloom, Hastings, Madaus (1971) have made great strides in broadening the definition of evaluation and in recommending other procedures to supply teachers with evidence of learning.

b. The medium may be the message

Marshall McLuhan (1967) has forcefully argued that the medium through which one learns is an important determinant of *what* one learns. The medium of programmed instruction presses the student to act as passive recipient; knowledge is presented as if to be "stamped in." Bruner (1961), in attempting to guard against the development of learner passivity, has advocated—along with McLuhan—that the medium of instruction should represent the process of the field of study, e.g., one learns about history by behaving as a historian or about sociology by acting as a sociologist. Programmed instruction could follow the sequence and the logic of the content area presented and in this way proffer critical information, but it represents a poor simulation of the actual discipline. One very important difference in programmed learning, as contrasted with the "discovery style" of learning advocated by Bruner and others, is that the program incorporates all of the answers. The student does not actively generate his own hypotheses nor his own sources of data, nor does he participate in testing whether his hypotheses are confirmed. The typical program does not duplicate the living activity of discovery. Programmed materials are essentially a safe way of learning; they include very little student risk, but they also generate very little of the joy of discovery.

Students using programmed instruction (as well as most traditional types of instruction) do not have a voice in determining their own learning goals, in deciding on the process for achieving those goals, or in determining how they will be evaluated. Skinner argues that students should not be "free agents" and that their tastes and interests should not determine instruction; programmed materials also support that position. In programmed instruction, the major allowance for differences between individuals is the rate at which they will proceed and the nature of difficulties any particular student may have at any step along the way. More advanced programs account for these variances; alternative branches of information and back-tracking are available for students if they have not yet mastered the material which has been presented. But the student's varying interests, motivations, and aspirations are not taken into consideration, and we believe they should be. In programming all students proceed in the same manner (except for branches) to reach the same objectives, and all receive similar treatment while doing so. Such a lock-step procedure does not take into consideration the unique and important aspects of the individual which must be paramount in the humanized school. Research by Myers (1972) corroborates this point by showing a significant decrease in self-esteem for students who have worked with programmed instructional formats for three years. The loss of self-esteem was less for the younger students who had been in IPI programs for one or two years. Could it be that the mechanical style of programmed instruction takes away a sense of individual uniqueness?

Students are not elements of an amorphous and undifferentiated mass, to be treated one like the other. They make, for instance, different responses to the very same stimuli. One study by Thompson and Hunnicutt (1944) reported that students respond differentially even to the reinforcement of teacher praise, and another study by French (1958) reported that the student's motivation makes a difference to the conditions under which he will perform best. In the Thompson-Hunnicutt study, those students who were classified as introverts behaved differently in response to praise given them by a teacher than did those students classified as extroverts. In the French study, students with high achievement motivation worked best in settings that were highly task-oriented and less personalized, as compared to those students who had high affiliation motivation. The latter preferred highly personalized work situations. Most behaviorists do not argue, of course, that the same reinforcers will work for all people, but they do argue that given a person's history of reinforcements we can predict that person's behavior in a given situation. Whether we wish to call a student's readiness his reinforcement history or his motivational state may be merely a semantic exercise. Our point is that there is something unique to each person that is not taken into consideration in the medium of programmed instruction and in most lock-step instructional procedures used in schools.

One common criticism of programmed instruction is that it may limit a student's developing repertoire of learning styles.. (See Olton and Crutchfield, 1969.) Creativity is one psychological process that has been pointed to repeatedly as obviated by programmed instruction. Creativity involves organizing disassociated elements in a new way; students who are never given the task of organizing or synthesizing their knowledge in the course of instruction will probably not know how to proceed when given the challenge. Again, programmed instruction may be able to deal with the cognitive features of creative problem-solving, but it cannot provide living situations for application. Indeed, acting creatively in relation to new understandings calls for a different view of the world of truth from that held by the behaviorists. Thorndike, and later Skinner, advocated, implicitly at least, that truth must be "stamped in" to the learner. We prefer a more dynamic view of human nature and the universe: one that asserts that the interaction between people and their environments continu ally changes both and that truth is fluid, existential, and what exists here and now.

c. The nature of truth

Programmed instruction necessarily limits and restricts the view of the world that is presented to the student. Views of the world are changing so rapidly that any particular information presented to students is bound to be out of date to some extent. It is possible for example, that even a simple machine, such as a pulley, could be used in ways not previously considered and that we risk restricting rather than expanding a student's view of the world when we claim definitively what a pulley is and what exactly it does. This criticism of programmed instruction is often presented by those who prefer a discovery or inquiry approach to instruction—one that prescribes particular methods while leaving the "dimensions of truth" up to each student to decide.

The following is an illustration of the ill effects that can arise when boundaries are imposed on students who do not yet have a well-defined view of the world.

Billy was playing with the record player motor. He had managed to get the motor to turn a Tinkertoy wheel using an elastic band belt drive. I came over and observed for a few minutes, and then we started talking about transferring the movement from a horizontal to a vertical plane. I had done it before and could see the whole experiment stretching out before me. So I gave Billy another wheel complete with spokes and showed him gears until I had almost done the experiment for him. Billy's reaction was to get up and leave! Then I realized what I had done. Is this what flexibility means, is this structuring the environment? Is this providing good motivation? No, it is essentially saying my ideas are better than yours. I left the experiment then and came back later to find Billy having solved the problem using two elastic bands—a very elegant and workable solution. I hadn't even thought of it. (Wocha, 1971, P. 33.)

Evidently Einstein was not a very good mathematician in his early years. Perhaps if he had been trained with a logical and sequential program that defined the nature of the mathematical world and reality he would not have had such a hard time of it in his youth. But then . . . .

In fairness, we do admit that there are fewer potential Einsteins than there are children who are put at a disadvantage throughout their whole lives because of not having learned the rudimentary skills necessary to function effectively in our society. A logical sequential program of "stamping in" can provide such students with the skills necessary for the freedom to be able to delve into new learning activities and thus can make an important contribution to their education.

3. Programmed instruction in a humanized school

Considering all the limitations already discussed, we still recommend some programmed materials for instruction. There are many situations and conditions that warrant the use of a logical and sequential program. There are, for instance, critical instances when students are interested in a topic and they wish to learn more about it. Their questions are personally important, their involvement is high, and they wish to seek out answers. Well-programmed materials that are accessible to students at such critical points can be very valuable. The student can become absorbed in the information and get what he or she needs and wants. Certainly the technology of an automated retrieval system is far more in keeping with the 1970s than having a student refer to an encyclopedia, which is most likely outdated or inaccessible.

Another example of the effective use of programmed instruction is in teaching basic language and computational skills to young children. But we think it is important for programmed instruction always to be optional, since there are students who seem to learn to read by merely looking at a lot of books and having someone nearby to answer their questions. Students who give evidence of learning through procedures other than programmed instruction should be permitted to use whatever procedure achieves the general goals of mastery. There may be times when one specific problem can be met—such as increasing comprehension skills or learning how to use punctuation—with the use of programmed materials. Programmed materials can be a source of rich information for cognitive mastery, and they can be used to provide additional choice in learning for students as well as teachers. Their basic riches should be exploited for the purposes of students' mastery but the technical advances themselves should never take precedence over the importance of the student as a human being.

4. Behavior modification*

Throughout our discussion of programmed instruction we have pointed out that in this system educators decide on specific objectives, on the logic and sequence of steps to reach the objectives, and on the method to be used for evaluating performance. Similarly, the use of reinforcement procedures in behavior modification almost always means that decisions like these are made by educators. We wish to focus the reader on the question of "who decides." We prefer that the students themselves have greater opportunity to make such decisions than is the case in typical behavior modification strategy.

Most often the adult professionals in power in a school or district make decisions about goals, instructional strategies, and evaluation practices, and typically they take such decision-making for granted. Usually students do not choose whether or not they will go to school. Furthermore, they do not choose whether they will be given instruction in the areas of reading, arithmetic, and other "basic subjects," nor are they asked for an opinion of the norms and sanctions of the society in general and the school in particular. Adults—both parents and teachers—usually make unilateral decisions about the school-related behavior of their children and what they should learn.

Behavior modification is a technique for altering a person's behavior in the direction of a desired end by using reinforcement contingencies in the environment. Many case studies on the application of behavior modification in the classroom describe its use to change such gross maladaptive behaviors as school phobias, physical aggression, withdrawal, and dependency. In most published case histories, teachers or counselors have brought about changes in specific behavior through the planned application of reinforcement. In most of these cases we do not argue against the fact that something should have been done: for example, a child with a school phobia so severe that she vomits or cries hysterically when her mother leaves is clearly in need of help. We ourselves successfully used the principles of behavior modification in toilet-training our son when he was three years old. Diapers were

---

*Although we use the term "behavior modification" in a general sense to refer to the deliberate use of reinforcement strategies to modify student behavior, some psychologists reserve it specifically for changing maladaptive behavior and use "contingency management" to refer to the planned change of normal behavior patterns.

a chore which *we* no longer wanted to continue. Persuasion on grounds of reason or inconvenience did not reap as much success as four days of carefully planned and consistent positive reinforcement (a small present wrapped in colorful paper) for the desired behavior of going to the toilet at the appropriate time. Although there were many moments when we had serious questions as to who was reinforcing whose behavior, we nevertheless achieved the behavioral pattern we wanted.

The application of behavior modification is a systematic and deliberate activity requiring a decision as to what behavior to change, the collection of baseline data, determination of the reward system, alteration of the environmental contingencies, collection of data, removal of the rewards to see if behavior returns to baseline, and continuation of the program until the desired behavioral patterns are reached. Typically these techniques have been used to change the behavior of one child, but currently a growing number of case histories focus on changing the behavior of *entire groups* while taking into account the social reinforcers that operate within a given group. For a compilation of several studies we refer the reader to Fargo, Behrns, and Nolen (1970).

"Token culture" classrooms (a form of behavior modification) offer experiments in changing deviant social behavior for groups of students. The tokens may be as simple as the now famous M&M candy that is given to a student for desired behavior, such as attending to a book for three minutes (thereby shaping his or her behavior toward longer periods of attention), or they may be as highly complex as using scrip to cash in for various rewards over a longer period of time. One illustrative study dealt with nine children in a special school for learning disabilities (Geiger, 1970). The teachers and consultant used a token culture and social reinforcement to modify the disruptive behavior of children in the classroom. They focused on the behaviors of hitting and pushing, making hissing noises, name-calling, and calling out before being recognized by the teacher. The program included presenting M&M candies to a student every ten minutes if he did not engage in any of the above behaviors. Moreover, the teacher tried to ignore the undesirable behaviors when they did occur. The time periods to receive the rewards gradually increased to twenty-five minutes and then to half a day. The procedure worked effectively and the undesirable behaviors of the children in the classroom were indeed modified.

Patterson (1971), in a review of studies of behavior modification, reported that token culture techniques have been overwhelmingly successful in altering deviant behavior; however, he also wrote that token culture attempts aimed at improving academic performance have not fared as well. It seems to us that behavior modification procedures work better at eliminating certain irritating behaviors than at adding new behavioral responses to a student's repertoire of behaviors. As with programmed instruction, we do not question the important role played by social reinforcement in influencing behavior. There is no doubt, furthermore, that the technology of behavior modification can be applied in many ways. We object primarily to the manner in which many applications are carried out. The "helper" or the person in authority, more often than not, makes all the decisions; he or she decides on the behavior to change, collects the data, arranges the environmental contingencies, and determines whether the program has been successful. There is no sharing of goal-setting, instructional procedures, and evaluation methods with the students.

5. Behavior modification and the humanized school

Adult control of decision-making about instruction does *not* teach students how to be independent, how to act with resourcefulness, or how to apply knowledge to their own problems. Behavior modification techniques as they are commonly used in many schools tend not to consider the students' personal goals, particular problems, or idiosyncratic methods of solving those problems. Moreover, such techniques can put the students at a disadvantage with their peers or other teachers by categorizing them as a deviant. We do think, however, that these techniques can be applied in ways that do not depersonalize an individual or single him out as an unknowing (and often undesirous) target for help.

A program of behavior modification could be planned so that the teacher and the students would decide on the goals and procedures together. For instance, if the students in a classroom continually talk out of turn, and if the talking has a disruptive influence—and, most importantly, if it "drives the teacher up a wall"—it is far better, we think, for the teacher to state his or her objections plainly and clearly rather than to attempt to modify the talking out of turn without consulting the students. When the teacher states his objections to speaking out of turn, of course, there is a chance that the students will see nothing wrong or disruptive in that sort of behavior and will suggest that the teacher change his expectations and be more tolerant of their speaking out. Perhaps the students could use reinforcement techniques to increase the teacher's tolerance level. (We do not suggest this facetiously.) If, however, the students do agree that speaking out of turn is disruptive and bothersome and that they are concerned about the feelings of the teacher, then they may decide that talking out of turn is a problem they should tackle jointly with the teacher. They can mutually agree on goals, decide collaboratively on reinforcers, and together use the technology of behavior modification to reach their goals. In this way a collective decision that takes into account the feelings and perceptions of both the teacher and the students has been made and each party is granted recognition as an important participant in the enterprise. We believe such an instructional program would indeed be more effective in the long run, both in changing the talking-out behavior and in establishing a model for solving other classroom problems.

6. Performance contracting

Collaborative and mutual decision-making about goals, methods, and rewards are used in the technique of contingency- or performance-contracting. This variation of behavior modification has been widely used with mental patients or persons suffering from such behavioral problems as obesity and smoking. In the schools, performance-contracting has been used primarily to improve academic achievement. Students make a contract to complete a particular academic task and upon its completion receive a reward. Unfortunately, contingency-contracting often is misused in many schools. Too frequently, teachers or administrators write the contract, leaving the student no options but to agree. As such, the process is not very different from that of teachers giving assignments which the students must complete. The major difference is that teachers traditionally have not given rewards (unless a letter grade for a completed assignment is considered a reward in itself) for tasks completed. If contingency-contracting is to be humanistic and effective, it must involve a contract between *two* consenting persons. After all, one-party contracting is a contradiction in both legal and humanistic terms.

7. Summary remarks

Educational technology is better because of the contributions of the behaviorists. Like any technology, it can be used or misused. We think that there is nothing inherently mechanistic, manipulative, or anti-human about the methodology itself. The principles of reinforcement can be used toward any ends. However, debate continually rages between the "inquirers" or "discoverers" and the behaviorists. While we are not in the behaviorist camp, we do not decry the methods of programmed instruction or behavior modification: they can be useful tools to educators and to students. Hilgard writes pointedly of the effect of these continuing arguments:

> If no one framework can deal with all the facets of behavior, if one framework is more clearly applicable to the description of physiological or psychological variables and another yields greater insight into an assessment of teaching techniques and materials, why force all data into one mold? Why jam a hippopotamus into a girdle? Yet this is precisely what happens when behavior modification advocates claim they have never seen an ego, or the dynamically oriented claim that M&Ms have never solved a problem.... The practitioner who uses only one point of view can only shortchange the child. (Fargo, Behrns, and Nolen, 1970, Pp. 4-5.)

THE MENTAL HEALTH APPLICATION

The mental health application, unlike those of the therapist and behaviorist, does not directly emanate from a particular school of psychology. Furthermore, its advocates and practitioners come from a diverse set of academic backgrounds such as social psychiatry, clinical psychology, social work, education, public health, and community service. The mental health application is an eclectic orientation and incorporates a flexible set of techniques rather than a fixed body of behavioral knowledge with prescribed methods. The key concept that unites the backgrounds and procedures of persons using the mental health application has been *prevention*, and their primary process of intervention has been *consultation* with teachers. The application has *not* emphasized intervening directly with students. Consultation has been aimed at increasing the teachers' understanding of the psychological makeup of students and showing how the environment or social milieu can enhance or hinder a student's psychological development.

The prevention of psychological problems of students has been attempted through consultation with those people who are constantly in direct contact with the students.

As in the therapeutic application, the person's emotions and intrapsychic mechanisms are emphasized. The emphasis on prevention rather than cure, however, has moved the mental health application away from an emphasis on sickness, and toward delineation and clarification of the characteristics of the mentally healthy person. Indeed, the question, "What is optimal mental health?" has engendered many definitions of the characteristics of the mentally healthy person. One frequently quoted and comprehensive list was provided by Marie Jahoda (1958), who classified six general areas of mental health, with an extensive listing of more precise subcategories under each one. The six areas are: (1) positive attitudes toward self, (2) optimal growth, development and self-actualization, (3) psychic integration, (4) personal autonomy, (5) realistic perceptions of the environment and (6) adequate environmental mastery. This list guides the work of many practitioners using the mental health application.

Concomitant with the emphasis on individual mental health there is also emphasis on the environment and its role in enabling individuals to achieve and maintain the favorable characteristics of an integrated and fully functioning self. A person's mental health is thought to grow out of the accumulated bits and pieces of daily experience; the person learns to feel competent by being competent, to feel successful by being successful, to feel accepted by being accepted, and to love by being loved. One's behavior presents evidence of one's feelings about self and one's attitudes toward others. Unlike the behaviorists, however, the mental health orientation considers behavior to be inextricably intertwined with affective and motivational processes. Behaviors which alienate others or which follow patterns of defeat and failure are related to feelings about self and others which have developed over a series of daily—and perhaps mostly minor—occurrences. The emphasis on the social milieu also indicates that by altering environmental contingencies (especially social relationships) one can also change feelings and behaviors. Unlike behaviorism, however, the mental health application has no standard or precise technology to alter the environment. This is because the mental health application specifies that a person's unique personality characteristics must be matched with particular contingencies in the environment for favorable changes to occur. In fact, the openness of the mental health

Psychological applications
to changing
learning climates

application to situational variables and its flexibility in adapting various techniques is one of its major strengths, as pointed out by Morse in an introduction to Newman's book about mental health consultation (Newman, 1967):

> If there is one basic asset in this type of consultation, it is flexibility. When one leaves the defining perimeters of the professional office, new things begin happening. . . . If one tries to help, no matter what, there is nothing constant but the helping methodology. What one does depends upon how one can help. The flexibility in technique runs all the way from testing and research to advice and oblique conversation. All the old "thou shalts" give way to this flexibility. The consultant role may mean serving as an expert in one situation and passive non-direction in another. (P. ix.)

1. The mental health application in schools

The various programs and intervention strategies of the mental health application, like those of the other applications, have been in operation in schools for only the last two decades. In 1946, Congress enacted the National Mental Health Act, under which the National Institute of Mental Health was created. Most of the services and programs of this act centered on community agencies or treatment centers and clinics. In 1955, however, the Joint Commission on Mental Illness and Health began to point the way for the public schools to take a major step in the prevention of mental illness. However, prevention has remained more a dream than a reality. Programs for the backlog of students *already* in serious trouble have often taken priority over programs optimistically designed to help those students having either potential problems, minor problems, or developmental crises not considered abnormal. Many mental health consultants have spent much of their time in helping *teachers* come to grips with students who have caused problems to themselves and others. But even when the consultant has dealt directly with very sick children, his or her approach has been more equalitarian as compared to the elitist orientation inherent in the therapeutic application or the behaviorist's emphasis on professional control of the environmental contingencies of a school.

We view the mental health application as a step toward the creation of more humanized schools. First, the practice of describing various attributes of the healthy person, in contrast to an emphasis on the diagnosis of sickness, represents an attempt to approximate the complexity and totality of a human being; it stresses the integration of all the parts of a person and does not encourage a simplistic categorization of people based on a few attributes.

Second, interest in the tones of feeling in the interpersonal environment has led the advocates of the mental health application to characterize the dimensions of a healthy learning climate and to train teachers in procedures for creating such climates in their classrooms. This focus on the social environment is illustrated in the treatment procedure of "milieu therapy" for seriously disturbed youngsters. Milieu therapy consists of planned psychological help from all the key persons in an individual's life. The proponents of milieu therapy argue that a few hours of intensive therapy, by itself, does not change a person's basic attitudes and behaviors. Changes in the disposition of an individual are brought about only through examining the accumulated bits and pieces of everyday life. Milieu therapy marshals all the key individuals in a person's environment for engagement in a treatment program for the person. Fritz Redl's (1959a and 1959b) therapy with hyperaggressive boys, for example, included not only counseling but active work with the ward staff, teachers, and all other related personnel, who were trained in procedures such as role-playing and life-space interviewing, so that the neurotic boys were worked with consistently in all of their daily routines, from eating breakfast to doing school work to going to bed at night. Similar strategies can be activated in the classroom when the teacher and the entire peer group work together to change their own social environment.

2. Teacher-training as an intervention strategy

The training of teachers has been the primary type of consultation used by those making the mental health application. This emphasis on training teachers is guided by the obvious fact that there will never be enough well-trained teachers in mental health, along with the theory that teachers, in their daily encounters with students, can have most significant impact on students and should therefore help to organize learning situations so that classroom instruction will add up to a constructive rather than a destructive experience. We believe the interest in training teachers arose as more and more behavioral scientists became aware of the destructive potential of schooling and as they came to see the naive and often unintended rejection of students by well-meaning but poorly or incompletely trained teachers. Too many teachers have viewed their primary purpose as the teaching of subject matter and have not seen the psychological well-being of students as their province or function. Many teachers have not recognized the close relationships between a student's feelings about himself and other people and his performance of academic tasks. In fact, too many teachers have believed that students' emotions should be *subdued* on the basis that strong feelings interfere with academic learning. The mental health application has sought to change the level of teachers' insight into the psychodynamics of students and has introduced some instructional procedures to foster student growth toward favorable mental health.

The role of consultant-trainer of teachers has become a major element in mental health interventions. This consultant role is defined less as an expert diagnostician and prescriber (such as in the therapeutic and behaviorist applications) than as a collaborator and fellow problem solver. In mental health consultation, programs and practices are mutually decided upon by the teachers and the consultants. Iscoe *et al.* (1967) illustrated one particular aspect of this consultant-trainer role in a description of a mental health program for schools. They trained graduate students to become child-behavior consultants. The students' previous training had been in the clinical procedures of diagnosis and prescription. As child behavior consultants, their role was to *help teachers* solve the problems of students within their classrooms, rather than to give therapy or consultation directly to the children. Iscoe *et al.* described some difficulties encountered by the graduate students, who were asked to perform in ways quite different from those for which their formal training as diagnosticians had prepared them. The graduate students felt frustrated and concerned over never working directly with the children. They also had to develop trust and rapport with the teachers while helping the teachers to decide on the best course of action for the students. Whereas the elitist expert essentially can ignore the teachers' perceptions and prescribe treatment for students in a controlled therapy situation, Iscoe's mental health consultants had to live through the classroom problem with the teacher and help her to take appropriate action. The consultants did not have the security or safety of the isolated office, were compelled to work with adult professionals rather than troubled students, and were challenged to seek practices and programs to help problem children within the normal confines of the classroom.

Because the mental health application has seemed to many to be more useful and beneficial in the long run, many applied behavioral scientists, formally trained in clinical psychology, psychiatry, social psychology, and psychiatric social work, have adopted the role of consultant-trainer for teachers despite its difficulties. Ruth Newman's book, *Psychological Consultation in the Schools* (1967) vividly describes some procedures of the consultant-trainer. Present as constant themes in the book are the importance of being a sympathetic listener and supportive prober and working within a *problem-solving* orientation. We believe, with Newman, that the concentration upon helping teachers to help themselves and their students is an important step toward humanizing the schools. The mental health application has removed the aura and mystique of the elitist expert, replacing an unbalanced helping relationship with the equalitarian, consultative relationship.

The attempts of mental health consultants to help teachers become more understanding and sympathetic toward students' needs and feelings have provided many behavioral scientists with a new sympathy and concern for the plight of the teacher. Behavioral scientists as consultants have been confronted with the complex realities of the classroom and school; as a consequence they have been less prone to dismiss teacher problems as being due to a lack of psychological sophistication or proper technique. Most mental health application programs have included a focus on the interpersonal relationship between the consultant and the teacher. Consequently, many of these programs have included confrontations as well as mutual support between consultant and teacher, which in turn has led to a greater focus on adult psychology. The mental health application has accepted teachers as having a full complement of feelings and motives. As a result, the relationship with consultants has often provided teachers with the human support and sympathy necessary to help them improve in teaching: the sort of soft shoulder so often lacking in a principal or a teacher's colleagues.

An experience of one of the authors illustrates very clearly the effect of the relationship between the consultant and the teacher. Dr. William Morse of the University of Michigan was serving as a mental health consultant to the school in which Patricia Schmuck was teaching. His help was invaluable at a critical time for her. At one point during the school year she was feeling very depressed. She felt both incompetent and inadequate, and everything that happened in the classroom seemed to corroborate her feelings about herself as a teacher. Most of the problems centered on one student who had irritated the entire class, and in her mind, the classroom problems of distrust and competition had become insoluble. Other teachers in the school merely gave such advice as "Tighten up the controls," or extended sympathy of the "I'm sure glad I don't have him in my class" kind. However, during a conference with her, Bill Morse was sympathetic but also very confrontative. He urged her to clarify the classroom problem, to define clear goals, to identify her own feelings, and to look at her behaviors in relation to the students. He became angry at her "pouring salt into her wounds" and said, in effect, "There is nothing wrong with you. There is plenty wrong with that kid and plenty wrong between the two of you. See what's wrong with him. Look at *him* and not only yourself. When you have seen him as a total person, with all his problems and his strengths, then, and only then, can you begin to deal with him somehow." She did begin to clarify goals and objectives. The major goal was to eliminate the grossly disruptive behaviors such as standing on top of the desk and yelling or running out of the room. With special attention and some stated agreements (for example, "If you don't leave the room once this morning you can be excused ten minutes early"), they came to understandings that made life tolerable, and sometimes even pleasant, for each other. The next year the student was admitted to a treatment center.

As in this case, student behaviors can often have the effect of lowering a teacher's self-esteem and feelings of professional competence. A teacher must look past himself, however, to encounter the other meaningfully. We believe that any attempts to humanize schools that do not take into account the feelings of both students *and* teachers is doomed to failure. An indispensable feature of the humanized school is that it grants a kind of sacredness and uniqueness to all persons, including the teachers and the administrators. Attempts to bypass the professionals or to ignore them as persons will only lead further in the direction of impersonal and anti-human schools.

3. Case study of a mental health intervention

We now describe one of the studies of Richard Schmuck (1968) to illustrate a mental health intervention in school. Although the results did not run entirely as expected, the study's systematic design and mental health goals make it appropriate to discuss here. After a presentation of the study in some detail, we will explain why we think the intervention failed and elaborate on the limitations of the mental health application for humanizing the schools.

In 1961 a pilot program for seriously maladjusted children was established in some elementary schools in Philadelphia through the joint efforts of the Mental Health Association of Southeast Pennsylvania and the Philadelphia School District. The results of the pilot study suggested that many problem children could be helped within the regular school classroom. These results, plus the increasing number of students in need of special services (12,000 students in grades 1 through 6, as compiled by a 1961 survey) led the department of student psychological services in the district to adopt a new approach in handling the problem students. A Special Advisory Committee on the Experimental School Project was developed to train classroom teachers to deal directly with the problem students in the classroom. Dr. Anne M. Edelman, a counseling psychologist and associate professor of educational psychology at Temple University, was appointed the director and Richard Schmuck was appointed research specialist to evaluate the project.

Goals of the project were fourfold: (1) to assist teachers in understanding and coping with behaviors of emotionally or socially handicapped students, (2) to further the teachers' general understanding of the psychology of human behavior, (3) to develop the teachers' understanding of the connection between a student's mental health and the student's performance of academic tasks, and (4) to help the teachers to develop new methods for teaching students from urban ghetto backgrounds.

The participating schools and teachers were selected on the basis of specific criteria. Each school had (1) a counselor, (2) a large number of emotionally disturbed children as indicated by the 1961 survey, and (3) a principal who was supportive of the program. Fifty-nine teachers from six elementary schools volunteered to participate in the study. Three schools were in middle or upper middle socio-economic areas of the city and three schools were from lower socio-economic areas. Further, two schools that received no consultation whatsoever were used for purposes of comparison.

Six consultants were chosen to work with the teachers; all were professionals in the fields of child psychiatry, psychology, social work, child development, or education. The consultants met with Dr. Eli

Bower and Dr. Ruth Newman, both of whom had extensive backgrounds and national recognition in mental health in the schools, and Mr. Morris Berkowitz and Dr. Phyllis Schaeffer of the Philadelphia Public Schools, to develop their intervention strategies. This was clearly a highly experienced, competent group of persons.

Each consultant met with a group of teachers in each school for fifteen sessions. The consultants also visited classrooms and had individual meetings with teachers upon request. While each consultant had somewhat different ideas and his or her own style in working with teachers, all the sessions were oriented toward problem-solving discussions about the teachers' relationships with students, other teachers, and parents. Each consultant kept a log in which he or she described the major themes and issues of his group of teachers.

The evaluation of the project included four pre-test and post-test questionnaires for teachers and students. The questionnaires written for teachers were aimed at obtaining data on how the teachers viewed themselves as teachers, how they viewed their students according to categories relevant for the classroom, how they thought about classroom mental health factors, and how they related the mental health factors to academic performance. Finally there was a questionnaire designed to measure how the teachers thought they would handle typical student problems in the classroom. The results of these questionnaires for teachers generally indicated positive and significant changes in the teachers' self-esteem, in their understanding of mental health principles and the ways in which these are related to academic learning, and in the ways in which the teachers thought they would handle problem situations in the classroom.

The questionnaires for students centered on the students' perceptions of informal group processes in the classroom, self-esteem, sociometric measures of classroom friendships and helping relationships, and the students' attitudes toward school and academic work. Analyses indicated *no* improvement in any of these student measures as a result of the consultation. Apparently, the group processes in the classrooms were unaffected by the mental health consultation with teachers.

The findings of this study were similar to the results of a more comprehensive three-year mental health program for Michigan schoolteachers (Cutler and McNeil, 1966). Cutler and McNeil found, just as Schmuck did, that consultations helped the teachers' feelings about themselves, increased the teachers' understandings of mental health principles, and helped the teachers associate dimensions of mental health with dimensions of subject-matter learning. On student measures, although there were directional changes of showing students having more favorable views of themselves, school, and academic work, none of these changes was statistically significant.

4. Weaknesses of the mental health application

We believe the mental health application can be superior to the therapeutic and behavioristic applications for reaching the goal of humanizing schools. The mental health application accentuates the complex totality of persons and the inextricable connections between one's emotions and academic performance. It encourages teachers themselves to confront and appreciate the unique qualities of individual students rather than to refer the students to a specialized person to deal with only one aspect of the student's life. It takes into account the fact that teachers also need guidance and help. Further, the mental health application focuses on creating classroom climates that foster favorable mental health among the students and teachers.

The results of the two careful studies we have summarized indicate serious weaknesses in the mental health application, however. The dynamics of the classroom peer group seem *not* to be affected significantly by the teacher's growth and understanding of mental health principles. We think this is true for two reasons. First, while the mental health application appreciates the influence of the social environment upon the individual, it does not focus enough on the dynamics of the classroom group as an entity. Mental health analyses give attention more to individuals or to two persons in interaction; they are focused primarily on the teacher's interactions with one student at a time. The classroom obviously is more than a collection of individuals; it is a complex web of interactions governed by formal and informal norms that are played out in how work gets done, how decisions are made, and how students respond to teacher direction or help. When a teacher gives direction, it is true that responses to it are mediated by the teacher's relationship to each individual, but also any student's response is influenced by the prevailing feelings and attitudes that exist within the group as a whole. Most of these peer group processes are subtle and informal. These affective undercurrents are part of any group that works together, and knowledge or increased insight about *individual* personalities will not change the basic dynamics of the group. The teacher's behavior, as well as that of students, is affected by these informal norms; to cope with group dynamics in an intellectual exercise is quite different from coping with the intentions, feelings, and attitudes inherent in living classroom interactions. Cognitive training and increased insight do not necessarily or easily lead to behavioral changes, especially in teaching.

The second reason for the failure of mental health interventions, we believe, lies in the dynamics of the teacher's adult peer group. A teacher's work in the classroom is influenced by his colleagues' values and opinions about the definition of good teaching. In Chapter 4 we describe the primary influences on teachers' attitudes and values regarding teaching and we present research evidence to show that the norms of the faculty and other teachers constitute one of the strongest influences on a teacher's behavior. Communication in the teachers' lounge has more influence on teachers' attitudes and behaviors than many training programs for teachers. Most of this group influence grows out of a neophyte teacher's informal interactions with colleagues.

The importance of the teacher peer group is illustrated by one finding in Richard Schmuck's evaluation of the mental health project in Philadelphia. An analysis of the logs kept by consultants showed that there was a negative association between the success of teachers (those teachers who made the most gains in the four questionnaires) and the number of times the teacher asked for individual help from the consultant. Personal conferences with the consultant were available to all teachers upon request. The frequency of such sessions ranged from one school which had only seven individual conferences to another school in which thirty-six individual conferences took place. Those schools that showed *most* significant changes in teachers had *fewer* individual consultations than schools where no changes occurred. Conversely, the schools that had the most individual consultations showed the least change in teacher understandings. We hypothesize that those faculties that changed the most had developed peer group norms in support of colleagues helping each other, so consequently they did not have to seek many individual sessions with the consultant. We further hypothesize that those teachers who had to depend on the one-to-one counsel of the consultant received very little support from their colleagues in sharing and discussing their results with each other.

In summary, the mental health application can be powerful for humanizing schools because it takes into consideration both personality dynamics and social processes as important components of change. However, its focus on the individual and on dyadic interpersonal relationships between teacher and student restricts its scope of analysis by neglecting the dynamics of the group life that are a major part of any school. Consulting with teachers is a necessary step, we believe, but the mental health application relies too heavily on cognitive experience and intellectual understanding; it de-emphasizes the very important affective dimensions of the classroom group as well as the teachers' peer group, both of which can have profound effects on how students and teachers behave in the classroom.

The fourth and last application, that of group dynamics, shares many of the same assumptions of the mental health application, but broadens the scope of analysis to include group life and directly deals with the ways attitudes and feelings are expressed through the formal and informal interactions that constitute part of the life in any classroom group.

THE GROUP DYNAMICS APPLICATION

Advocates of the group dynamics application take for granted that both psychodynamics and reinforcements from the social environment simultaneously influence behavior. A key psychological attribute, *the self-concept*, is viewed as being formed and modified by interactions with other persons, by one's perceptions of his relationships with others, and by past interpersonal experiences and feelings. The self-concept is *not* viewed as developing from an unfolding of instinctual drives or merely through operant conditioning. Group practitioners do not typically work with persons who have severe emotional or behavioral disorders; like the mental health consultants, they emphasize the normal and healthy rather than the abnormal or deviant. Consequently, group training programs tend to aim toward maximizing individual potential and self-awareness rather than toward rendering treatment. Since individual behavior takes place within a social context, large-scale behavioral change involves essentially changing the interactional experiences that take place in social settings.

Group dynamics trainers, like mental health consultants, strive to act as equals and facilitators in collaboration with clients. The major differences between these two applications is that while mental health practitioners emphasize the individual's feelings and relationships with one or two others, the group practitioners stress interpersonal interaction within a group along with the emotions and cognitive insight and understanding of the participants. Even though many mental health training programs use a group as the context for the training, they do not typically deal with the processes of the group as such. The group dynamics application takes a broader view of the complex interpersonal relationships that exist within a group and directs participants' attention to the existential, here-and-now interpersonal processes.

Only during the last two decades has the group dynamics application grown in popularity, diversity, and magnitude. Interest has burgeoned to such an extent that we expect most people who read this book will have either participated in some kind of group training experience or read about it. We believe too, that the burgeoning involvement in group training is another indication of the movement toward a new American consciousness (Reich, 1971). Participation in groups offers the opportunity for closeness that is not widely available in depersonalized neighborhoods and bureaucratic organizations. Group experiences also represent one answer to the search for a workable balance between the individual's desire for independence and his wish to be part of a supportive community.

1. The group dynamics application in the schools

The group dynamics application has come into prominence in the schools during the past two decades. A comparison of two articles written on the dynamics of classroom groups highlights the changes that have occurred over that period of time. The first article, written in 1950 by Trow et al., had relatively little research evidence to support its theoretical premises, whereas the second, published in 1966 by Glidewell et al., showed the dramatic progress of empirical research and the application of group theory to the school setting.

The group dynamics application has gained momentum, we think, because personal alienation and a lack of community feeling persist in many schools despite significant innovations in physical facilities, programming, curriculum materials, and instructional methods. We believe, in fact, that one-to-one therapy, programmed instruction, and teachers' uses of behavior modification methods may be exacerbating the interpersonal tension and increasing the sense of alienation and the feeling of unconcern found within classrooms. The use of the mental health application has changed teachers' information and insight about psychology, but surveys indicate that it has not altered the interpersonal relationships that normally exist today in classrooms and school buildings. Use of the group dynamics application as an intervention strategy is designed to bring people together, confront them with their differences, clarify individual goals, establish joint goals, and find procedures through which the participants can learn to work both interdependently and effectively. Group training places emphasis on the sharing of current personal feelings as a means to establish desirable patterns of relationships for the present and the future.

Systematic focus on the ways interpersonal relations are experienced is the major contribution which the group dynamics application can make toward creating environments facilitating I-Thou transactions. Although Buber warns against analyzing or objectifying true meetings between people, we do not believe that most of the methods offered by group practitioners necessarily undermine I-Thou transactions. The purpose of the training group as a vehicle for change is to help knock down barriers and facades between people and to encourage I-Thou transactions. The training group is not meant, however, to be the primary setting for meaningful exchange between persons. There are some who rightly argue that the artificiality and contrived nature of a training group lessens the authenticity of the encounters between the people in it. The group as a training ground should be conceived only as an *approximation* of reality. Those who must return frequently to group training to find the communication and meaning that they are missing in their daily personal lives have not achieved in the real world the goals of their previous group experiences.

Group training for school personnel also is meant to help them understand and appreciate in particular the complexity and importance of human relationships. Those teachers or principals who learn what the group dynamics application has to offer, and who attempt to apply it in their classrooms or schools, should be able to have closer and more productive encounters with their students and each other. Moreover, the capacity to analyze and understand the dynamics of human interaction is important for all persons in the school, including teachers, principals, students, counselors, secretaries, custodians and cooks. Of course, to persist in objectifying and intellectually analyzing every personal encounter is to miss the moments of Buber's "meetings" as those occur. We expect that the most satisfying memories of school have to do with such personal encounters, whether they are with coaches, secretaries, teachers, or other students.

2. Types of groups

With the rise of group training has come a diversification of objectives and methods. The T-group (training group) is generally considered to be the father of group dynamics application. It was born in 1947 through the efforts of the founding fathers of the National Training Laboratories,* (Kenneth Benne, Ronald Lippitt and Leland Bradford), following the principles set down initially by Kurt Lewin. While today the T-group takes many forms and styles, in its first decade it followed a fairly clear and consistent model:

> The group leader was a process observer and reporter, a relatively inactive trainer who attempted to keep attention on process rather than content and to keep interaction in the "here and now," continually dealing with perceptions and feelings that members generated about each other within the group setting. Since then the model has become considerably broadened to encompass a wide variety of "intervention styles," theories of leadership and behavior change. . . . (Gibb, 1971, P. 852.)

The group movement has developed an almost unending list of training events and varieties. (The above quotation is from a comprehensive review prepared by Gibb. For fun, the reader may enjoy skimming the intentionally comic list written by Criswell and Peterson in 1972.) To specify just a few of these types, there are encounter groups such as those espoused by Rogers (1970), Gestalt groups which follow the theories of Perls (1969), bio-energetic groups after Lowen (1967), and transactional analysis groups following Berne (1964), subsequently popularized by Harris (1969). A host of different programs on various aspects of creative personal growth is sponsored by the Esalen Institute,† and there are many specialized groups, such as Synanon for drug problems, Alcoholics Anonymous, and Weight Watchers, which use group methods to solve specific behavioral problems. Additional groups in many communities are continuously being formed to focus on specific life concerns such as divorce, sexual problems, child-rearing, and marriage. Most of these group experiences have been popularly categorized under the generic label of sensitivity training. However, distinct theoretical and proce-

---

*National Training Laboratories, Institute for Applied Behavioral Science, P.O. Box 9155, Rosslyn Station, Arlington, Virginia 22207.

†Esalen Institute, 1776 Union St., San Francisco, Ca. 94123.

dural differences exist among many of these group experiences. Appreciating and understanding these differences is very important, especially when applying training interventions to the humanization of schools.

We find it useful to distinguish among three general types of group training experiences. First are those groups concerned with individual dynamics that aim to help individuals with personal problems, such as drugs, impotence, or divorce. In the schools students with scholastic or behavioral problems may engage in such group therapy under the guidance of a psychologist or a counselor. During such training attention is *not* directed to the processes of the group as such or upon changing the nature of the social processes in the classroom or school. We categorize this sort of group as therapeutic. It is actually closely related to the mental health application and we do not plan to discuss it here. The two types of group training we do plan to discuss are categorized as *personal growth* and *group process* training.

3. Personal growth and group process training

These two types of training groups share as their ultimate purpose the desire to change individual attitudes, behaviors, and the social setting of the participants. Their main differences center on the relative emphasis each places upon personal growth and changing group processes. To illustrate the principles in practice we present two case studies. The first study was carried out by Rogers (1969), who used the encounter group (personal growth) in attempting to humanize the Immaculate Heart School District in Los Angeles. The second study emphasized the group process orientation and resulted from Richard Schmuck's program for Michigan teachers. The two interventions share many similarities.

In both, a "safe climate" for the training group is developed so that members can openly express their personal perceptions and feelings about themselves and others; both attempt to build mutual trust to facilitate interpersonal confrontation as well as support; both place value upon the capabilities and attitudes that the participants bring to the group; and in both, while the facilitator is highly experienced his role as expert is de-emphasized and usually he participates actively in a personal and human way. The features that distinguish personal growth groups from the more group-process-oriented training events have to do with their objectives and some of their methods.

a. The objectives of personal growth and group process training

Rogers defines the encounter group as "an avenue to personal fulfill-ment and growth." (1970, p. 162.) He defines group process training as aiming to "improve the learnings and abilities of the participants in such areas as leadership and interpersonal communication." (1969, P. 305.)

Rogers's version of the encounter group has a therapeutic bias even though it was *not* developed from a psychoanalytic perspective or from concepts of mental illness. Rogers proposes that the problems of contemporary man do not reside so much in his psyche as in his relationships with other human beings.* Rogers advocates that through the experience of the group, persons can learn to work out some of their basic concerns such as: Am I loved? Am I loving? Am I lovable? Can I care? Can I understand another? and Can I accept another? The relational problems of human existence are those upon which the encounter group focuses, and it is in the safe climate of the group that people can explore and discover answers for themselves.

Those who hold more of a group process orientation would not disagree with Rogers's basic premises. The group process practitioners place a different emphasis, however, on the group experience and attempt to achieve different objectives. The focus of the group process experience arises from group dynamics research which has demon-strated the ways in which formal and informal group processes con-tinually affect individual behavior. Group-oriented training mainly explores the processes of group communication, influence, norms, and attraction, in contrast to *personal* emotional dynamics. These group processes are brought into the open so they can be analyzed, under-stood, and perhaps changed. Although the group process orientation encourages contact and communication with others, it makes the basic assumption that contemporary people cannot communicate meaning-fully unless they have *learned* to do so. On the contrary, many people have learned to *hide* their emotions and therefore must be *trained* to

---

*This point of view is shared by many behavorial scientists. For instance, Rollo May's (1969) account of the malaise of contemporary man emphasizes his in-ability to have the will to love; Eric Fromm's (1962) writings stress man's striving for individual freedom within the context of loving another; and the social psy-chologist Sarbin (1970) argues that the use of pathological labels has actually blocked basic encounters between people and has impeded the development of workable solutions to important social issues.

communicate openly and directly with one another. In group process training, such communication skills as paraphrasing and checking one's impressions of another are practiced so that individuals can maximize their abilities to enter into meaningful dialogue. In line with this, the group process orientation also is distinctly task-focused: groups of people work on a task together so they can maximize their productivity both as individuals and as a group.

b. Methods of personal growth and group process training

The two types of groups use different methods to achieve their purposes. Regarding personal growth training, Rogers states:

> There is no organized encounter group. There is simply freedom of expression—of feelings and thoughts—on any personally relevant issue. (1970, P. 161.)

He also maintains that as a facilitator,

> I try to avoid using any procedure that is *planned*, I have a real 'thing' about artificiality. (1970, P. 56.)

We do not mean to imply that Rogers does not use tools such as role-playing, psychodrama, or group exercises. He does stress, however, that such techniques can be contrived gimmicks; they must occur spontaneously in order to "express what one is actually feeling at the time." (1970, P. 57.)

Group process training methods are typically quite different from this. The content concerns the group itself. Personal issues unrelated to the group are discouraged and even viewed as inappropriate for discussion. Topics such as one's marriage or one's concerns about sexuality or child-rearing are not discussed unless they bear directly on how the participant is relating with others in the group. While spontaneity is encouraged, there also is usually a planned agenda that includes lectures, visual presentations, and simulations of group processes such as decision-making or other exercises to serve as vehicles for learning. Generally the agenda remains flexible and changes as the group moves through different stages and issues. Frequently the members themselves are involved in setting or changing the training design.

Another difference in method lies in the functions performed by the leader. While both training groups stress the leader's role as a *facilitator* (who reacts as an individual and avoids the role of the expert who objectively interprets and gives answers about behavior), there are distinct differences in the types of interventions that the trainer makes in each group. For instance, regarding the personal growth groups, Rogers writes:

> I make comments on the group process very sparingly. They are apt to make the group self-conscious; they slow it down, giving the members the sense that they are under scrutiny. Such comments also imply that I am not seeing them as persons but as a sort of a lump or conglomeration, and that is not the way I want to be with them. (1970, P. 57.)

In contrast, the trainer with a group process emphasis attempts early to establish norms supporting continued attention to group procedures such as problem-solving and decision-making. One way he develops this orientation is to initiate comments about the group processes and to encourage members to do the same. For instance, when an intense exchange occurs between two members, it is typical for someone to comment on the processes of that exchange. Was help asked for? How? How was help given? In group process training, norms are formed that encourage interrupting any "moment" and then looking at it in an analytical way. Moments are sacred but they are also investigated and discussed.

4. Two case studies of the group dynamics application in the schools

We will now describe how personal growth and group process training have been used as interventions in schools. Basically these types of training share the goals of changing members' attitudes and behaviors and helping persons carry over their learning from the group to their work setting.

a. Personal growth training

Rogers's project was carried out in the Immaculate Heart School District in Los Angeles (consisting of a small Catholic college, several high schools, and many elementary schools). Although there was some training of high school and elementary school participants, no evaluations of these groups were available, so we will discuss only the training of college personnel. Immaculate Heart College is an interesting institution in itself; it is no ordinary small Catholic girls' college. For two years preceding the intervention, the sisters of the Immaculate Heart College Community had been planning a series of reforms related to the role of education in religious life. The work of Sister Corita, concerned with both political commentary and new directions in graphic arts, is only one example of the kind of climate that prevailed at the college. The Sisters had already participated in many controversies with more conservative elements of the Catholic Church hierarchy.

Rogers and his staff at the Center for the Study of the Person were called upon to work with the college in its movement toward a more humanized community. Their plans for the project began in 1967 and were outlined in a Rogers article published in 1969. The intervention strategy consisted primarily of a series of encounter groups to sensitize the individual participants and eventually to change the culture of the college itself by increasing the participation of learners and the communication between all facets of the college.

Since Rogers's staff was interested in obtaining an objective evaluation of their intervention, they hired the services of two behavioral scientists, Dr. Mort Shaevitz and Dr. Don Barr, who subsequently prepared an interim evaluation (1968). The report indicated that each encounter group met for two weekends. Although the report did not include a description of the encounter groups, we assume that they closely followed the Rogerian orientation that we have already described. The groups probably were very loosely structured, emphasized exploring the concerns of individuals, and probably did not carry out any contrived exercises or simulations about one's role in the college.

The evaluative data consisted of interviews with participants and of observations of changes in college policies or procedures. The interview questions were analyzed from two points of view: how worthwhile participants felt the workshop was for them personally, and how worthwhile they felt it was in helping them to carry out their roles at the college. While no numerical or statistical tabulations were reported, Shaevitz and Barr did show that participants of a wide variety of ages, years of experience, and roles in the university felt that the encounter groups were both professionally and personally beneficial. However, two groups gave especially negative reports: the administrators, who felt that the encounter groups were neither personally nor professionally worthwhile, and many students, who indicated that although the encounter groups were meaningful, they seemed unrelated to their roles as students.

Shaevitz and Barr also described some actual changes in behavior as evidence that the encounter groups were effective in bringing about some changes in the organization of the college. They cited examples of teachers who changed teaching styles and administrative leaders who allowed for wider participation in decision-making within their departments. We must point out, however, that these changes took place in a college that *already* was very amenable to change. Also the contemporary mood on most college campuses supported the idea of an increased range of influence in decision-making. Although the report gave some support to the position that the encounter groups changed some individuals, we do not believe the data are convincing evidence that the college was changed very much as an organization or that classrooms became more humanized as a result of the encounter group experiences.

It is difficult, of course, to assess the full impact of the encounter groups on the Immaculate Heart College because the evaluative data are incomplete. Apparently, however, the personal growth training led to some controversy among Immaculate Heart staff members; as a result, the services of other consultants were subsequently used. This second group of consultants was lead by Jack Fordyce, whose philosophy and training strategy are different from those of Rogers. Fordyce emphasized more of a group process orientation as a means to building teams of personnel in the college to work together effectively. An exciting and unique graphic presentation of the various changes that occurred in Immaculate Heart College after Fordyce entered is available in a publication edited by Pendel and Hennessey (1971), titled *On the Move*.

b. Group process training

The second study, representing more of a group process training program than the Immaculate Heart project, was conducted by Richard Schmuck. Although Schmuck's project shared some of the goals and procedures of the Rogers's project, the intervention was aimed more clearly at educating individuals to make changes in the schools to which they belonged. The focus was largely on the teachers' back-home classrooms, not on the entire school culture. Comparisons between the two projects illustrate quite different training techniques. Although

Schmuck and his staff also used the vehicle of the intimate and personal T-group, their emphasis was more on the participants as teachers than on their personal problems and concerns as individuals. They also used a much wider array of training events, including planned role-playing and systematic problem-solving.

The design of the study called for two experimental groups and one control group. The focal experimental group consisted of forty teachers, all of whom participated in a daily, full-day four-week summer workshop and a number of bi-monthly follow-up meetings, lasting until the following December. The second experimental group met weekly for four months in the fall. The control group received no training.

The summer workshop spent its first week in sensitivity training (with focus on personally relevant issues *as well as* the dynamics of group formation and development), supplemented by theory presentations, discussions of application to the classroom, and group dynamics skill exercises. The second week of the workshop emphasized cognitive understanding of the classroom as a human relations setting. Since the teachers had already spent a week together working intensively, these discussions about theory often became very involving and emotional. During the third week, the teachers visited classrooms and attempted to apply their cognitive learning to analyze what was happening in those classrooms. During the fourth week, the teachers used role-playing to simulate classroom situations and thereby developed specific and concrete plans for what they each would try in their own classrooms in the fall. After school began they met bi-monthly with the training staff to discuss the strengths and weaknesses of their efforts to apply what had been learned during the summer.

The second group met weekly for four months while school was in session; they did not have the sensitivity training or an extended period together in a workshop situation. They received cognitive training about classroom group processes and discussed ideas they planned to try in their classroom. The training was very much like that provided by mental health consultants.

Evaluation of the two different training groups centered on changes in student perceptions of the classroom group processes and of their attitudes toward peers, school, self, and teacher. Other evaluative data came from logs kept by both groups of teachers and from observations made on their classrooms by outsiders. The data showed many significant differences in the classrooms of the two groups of teachers subsequent to training. The student questionnaires, for example, indicated that the workshop group tried more instructional innovations and that the student peer group processes in their classes were changed more in the predicted direction. Workshop teachers had peer groups, for example, that were more diffuse in their friendship patterns; i.e., nearly every student felt that someone in the classroom was his friend. In contrast, the other experimental group of teachers and the control group had peer groups in which friendships were more hierarchical; i.e., only a few students were liked and many other students felt they had no friends in class. Students of the workshop teachers, compared with students of the other groups, also felt that they had greater power to influence their peers and teacher and to determine classroom activities. The intervention was considered successful, since teachers who experienced intensive training in group process skills did change their teaching behavior. Unfortunately, however, budget was not available to make follow-up evaluations to test whether the changes in teaching behavior endured beyond several months after the training interventions.

c. A comparison of personal growth and group process orientations

We have described two case studies illustrative of two types of group training for educators. It is, however, virtually impossible to compare directly these two studies or to determine which orientation is more effective. First, the two were aimed at changing different variables; Schmuck's intervention focused on improving classroom group processes and Rogers's intervention focused on humanizing the culture of the college. Second, the different evaluative schemes used do not lend themselves easily to comparison. Third, the primary training event in Rogers's study lasted for two weekends, whereas Schmuck's primary training event involved four weeks and bi-monthly meetings for four months.

An outstanding study by Friedlander (1968) may help in comparing the effectiveness of these two types of group training. He studied a research and development laboratory of the Armed Services, but we believe it has application for the two types of school interventions described above. Friedlander studied three types of group interventions. Group A was most similar to an encounter group in that it experienced an unstructured three-day workshop devoted to the expression of feelings between members. Group B was highly cognitive and work-related, similar to Schmuck's second experimental group that met weekly for four months. Group C was most similar to the T-group used with the teachers in Schmuck's summer workshop; it involved personal dimensions but also was significantly related to work issues. Also, like Schmuck's, Group.C met with the consultant prior to the first training session in order to diagnose its problems and to plan the agenda for the training. After the laboratory session, members of Group C met again to evaluate the methods they were using to achieve their objectives.

Friedlander used measures of group effectiveness and personal involvement to assess the effects of his three training strategies. The members of Group A became highly involved and the group developed high morale. However, Group A experienced no basic changes in its effectiveness as a work force. Group B, the cognitively trained work-related group, had the smallest number of personal or group changes. The members of Group C, which involved an integration of personal and work-related issues and extensive pre- and post-laboratory work, scored highest on group effectiveness in their work.

5. Strengths and weaknesses of the group dynamics application

The conclusions of the studies carried out by Rogers, Schmuck, and Friedlander, along with evidence from other research (see Gibb, 1971), indicate that group training, whether it is person- or group-centered, can have a profound effect in changing an individual's perception of himself and his behavior in relation to other people. The group provides a unique medium for dealing with personal concerns; it offers a setting for learning about others in depth and allows first-hand experience regarding the kinds of relationships that are possible. A group training experience can serve as a useful model of what can be achieved in relationships with others even within a highly bureaucratic setting. We therefore advocate the use of group training for faculty teams in the schools as well as for learning groups. One application of this method with learning groups, for example, has been described by George Brown (1971), who offers suggestions to enable teachers to increase the personal awareness and psychological growth of students. In general, we feel that the use of the group dynamics application can be invaluable in helping people to relieve their isolation and to pursue meaningful contact and dialogue with others.

At the same time, however, we do not share Rogers's degree of conviction that:

> The learnings in the group experience tend to carry over, temporarily or permanently, into the relationship with peers, students, subordinates, and even to superiors, following the group experience. (1969, P. 307.)

Individual insight and self-awareness resulting from a group experience do not necessarily lead to changes in behavior in other situations. Campbell and Dunnette (1968), in a comprehensive review of research on the transfer effect of group training, point out the many problems confronting any researcher trying to discover how the learning gained in a laboratory situation transfers to real-life work settings. They tentatively conclude:

> Examination of the research literature leads to the conclusion that while T-group training seems to produce observable changes in behavior, the utility of these changes for performance of individuals in their organizational roles remains to be demonstrated. (P. 73.)

Their review primarily covers T-group experiences and does not offer evidence about the transferability of groups that are oriented toward personal growth. Except for recent research by Yalom, Lieberman, and Miles (1973), very little systematic research exists on personal growth groups, and in fact leaders of such groups seem to have some bias against doing types of research other than anecdotal case studies. From the findings of Campbell and Dunnette and Friedlander, and from our own experience, we conclude that educators can benefit from group training both personally and professionally *only* if certain conditions are met during the training.

First, as indicated by Friedlander's results, we think it is imperative that the training includes a personal growth component *and* that it relates directly to professional role behavior. Behavioral change is complex and involves personal insight and awareness as well as a repertoire of behavioral skills. While for implementing a teaching strategy there may be no standard recipe that accounts for all the various and subtle processes of learning groups, group training *can* offer the opportunity to try out new behavior, to discover how one's professional behavior affects others, and to learn about the methodological tools and behavioral skills that must accompany an effort to change one's style of leadership.

Second, people who aim through training to change not only their own behavior patterns but the pattern of the system to which they belong must be realistic in evaluating their sphere of influence. Thus, we would expect teachers to make some impact on their classrooms, but probably not on the culture of the entire school (unless the majority of their colleagues also decided to make changes in their behaviors). Likewise, we would expect a principal to have some impact on the procedures of the faculty but probably not on larger subsystems of the community.

Third, in order for any major change effort to endure, there must be a continuation of support and dialogue among the people concerned. Teachers, principals, superintendents, and students are not merely autonomous individuals: they are linked by formal and informal relationships, and their "product" is the result of a group effort. The most dedicated and skilled teacher cannot survive in a school where nearly every behavior is in opposition to the norms and procedures of the staff. In fact, as previously indicated, we know of *no* follow-up studies which show that teachers' behavioral changes endured for a very long period of time after the close of the training intervention. To us this indicates not that interventions are by nature ineffective, but that unless a specially trained teacher has support from colleagues, he will either leave the school or revert to the school's prevailing norms, regarding teaching.

We have spent the first decade of our professional lives working with aspects of the group dynamics application—Richard in action research with the schools and Patricia in teaching and curriculum development. The group dynamics application has been our major interest and its importance has been summarized in our text, *Group Processes in the Classroom* (1971). Throughout this period we have wondered what difference better classroom climates alone make in humanizing educational institutions as a whole. Our conclusion has been that *they make considerable difference—but not enough.* Focus on the classroom alone does not change the surrounding subsystems that continually influence what can happen within a classroom. We know of *many* excellent teachers who create exciting and challenging classroom environments where persons are paramount and I-Thou encounters are cherished and where there is support and confrontation between the members of the classroom. However, the efforts of a few teachers are miniscule and the rewards of a year of teaching are quickly diminished when the students return to depersonalized and anti-human classrooms the following year.

Many initially successful teachers cannot—and do not—continue to teach in this atmosphere. They burn out and resort to more traditional ways of relating to students, or they leave teaching entirely. Humanized learning groups must operate within a larger school culture that encourages and sustains a milieu that is in itself person-oriented. Too often teachers who value students as whole persons are impeded by the prevailing norms and structures of their colleagues or the principal. *The group dynamics application, stressing only the individual or the processes of one subsystem, thus falls short of bringing about changes in the culture of the school.*

None of the four psychological applications which we have discussed has dealt with the *systemic* and *cultural* features of the school as a whole in a planned and deliberate way. While the group dynamics application is broader than the other three and directly attempts to create environments that encourage free cognitive exchange and emotional expression, even this application is not broad-based enough to deal with the relationships among participants in different subsystems of the school culture. *Teachers, principals, superintendents, supervisors, counselors, students, and parents must all be involved in the process of reforming and humanizing education.* To humanize the educational process, all such people and the subsystems in which they work should be fully involved in determining where they want to go and how they will get there. Only in this way will a school truly become everybody's house.

SUMMARY OF CHAPTER 2

From among the various behavioral sciences, educators have drawn most often upon the concepts and procedures of psychology. For the first half of the twentieth century, however, even psychology like the other behavioral sciences for that matter—was little used to guide the improvement of educational programs. In contrast, during the past twenty-five years, four different schools of psychological thought have been applied in attempts to improve learning climates. We refer to these as the *therapeutic*, the *behaviorist*, the *mental health*, and the *group dynamics* applications.

Although each of these psychological applications has made useful contributions to the solution of particular educational problems, all have been limited in relation to the kind of systemic change that would truly humanize the culture of the school. The therapeutic and behavior applications have been especially ineffective. The former has helped educators to note the importance of emotional dynamics of individuals, but by the same token it has drawn attention away from the power of environmental forces. The latter has provided educators with a useful technology for teaching certain kinds of skills, but its elitist educational goals and reinforcement strategies have worked to undermine the development of whole-person relationships and I-Thou transactions between teachers and students.

The mental health and group dynamics applications seem to us to hold the most potential for humanizing learning climates, but they have been unsuccessful in changing school cultures despite their beneficial influence on certain teachers. The mental health application has prodded educators to take into consideration both personality dynamics and social processes as important components of the educational process, but its focus on the individual and on dyadic interpersonal relationships between teachers and students has restricted its impact on the dynamics of group life. The group dynamics application perhaps has come closest to offering methods for humanizing the school, but its focus on the small group has limited its impact on the structural and normative aspects of the larger school organization, which itself tends eventually to conventionalize even the most strongly humanized classroom processes.

ANNOTATED BIBLIOGRAPHY FOR CHAPTER 2

The therapeutic application

Bettelheim, Bruno. 1949. *Love Is Not Enough*. New York: The Free Press.

Bettelheim follows psychoanalytic concepts and procedures in the educational treatment of emotionally disturbed children; he encourages little formal structure and high acceptance and encouragement for the open expression of emotions. Change is brought about through the therapists and teachers interpreting and working on the emotional expressions of children. Bettelheim is easy to read; his style is informal and articulate. This book is a classic in illustrating the positive aspect of the therapeutic application for the schools.

Pearson, Gerald. 1954. *Psychoanalysis and the Education of the Child.* New York: Norton Book Co.

Pearson discusses how psychoanalytic concepts and methods can be applied to public schools. He discusses sex education, the structure of schools, and generally how to treat children who have psychological problems. He recommends greater use of psychoanalytically trained professionals in the schools to work with children who have emotional problems.

The behaviorist application

Fargo, George, Charlene Behrns, and Patricia Nolen. 1970. *Behavior Modification in the Classroom.* Belmont, Ca.: Wadsworth Publishing Co., Inc.

This book contains a variety of articles dealing with the ethics, theory, and application of behaviorist principles in schools. It is a useful volume showing the types of research that have been carried out in classrooms with students of different ages and sociological characteristics. It also has a chapter on the role of the counselor and other special service personnel and discusses how they can employ the methods of behavior therapy.

Meacham, Merle, and Allen E. Wiesen. 1970. *Changing Classroom Behavior: A Manual for Precision Teaching.* Scranton, Pa. International Textbook Co.

This book is a straightforward and internally consistent presentation of precision teaching—the system and logic of behavioristic psychology—and how it is carried out in the classroom. The book also discusses ethical questions and how precision teaching can be applied in classes for normal, retarded, socially deprived, and disturbed youngsters.

Skinner, B. F. 1971. *Beyond Freedom and Dignity.* New York: Alfred A. Knopf.

This controversial book is required reading for any serious student of human behavior. Skinner maintains that freedom and dignity are illusory concepts that have only served to block man's attempts to create an equitable society; instead he proposes large-scale application of a science of human behavior (Skinner's own brand of behaviorism) to solve the problems of contemporary society. It is a valuable book full of challenging premises, assumptions, and questions which he tries to answer.

The mental health application

Newman, Ruth. 1967. *Psychological Consultation in the Schools.* New York: Basic Books, Inc.

Five case studies showing applications of mental health concepts in public and private schools are presented. Each study describes in detail the design, procedures, daily problems, and general results of a different consultation effort.

Redl, Fritz, and William Wattenberg. 1951. *Mental Hygiene in Teaching.* New York: Harcourt, Brace, and World.

Redl and Wattenberg make generous use of psychoanalytic concepts, yet they translate the traditional therapeutic strategy into one which emphasizes more the environmental milieu and they present a variety of educational methods to work with disturbed children. Many of the suggestions and tools in this book are not only for use with emotionally disturbed children but can be adopted for use by teachers and children everywhere.

Seidman, Jerome M. 1963. *Educating for Mental Health: A Book of Readings.* New York: Thomas Y. Crowell Co.

This is a well organized book of fifty-six articles previously published in social science or education journals. Seidman has selected articles that are authoritative, practical, and clearly written; many are classics of educational psychology. He includes two major sections on students, entitled "Understanding Children and Adoles cents" and "Helping Children and Adolescents." A third section presents articles on the topic of "Improving Parent and Teacher Effectiveness." This compendium offers some of the very best work done on the mental health application in schools.

The group dynamics application

Bradford, Leland, Jack Gibb, and Kenneth Benne. 1964. *T-Group Theory and Laboratory Method*. New York: John Wiley and Sons, Inc.

Eighteen different articles are presented by the editors as well as other contributors active in the T-Group movement. The book contains the theory, process, application, evidences of success, and pitfalls of the T-Group. One very useful chapter by Matt Miles looks specifically at comparisons between the T-Group and the classroom.

Luft, Joseph. 1970. *Group Processes: An Introduction to Group Dynamics*. Palo Alto, Ca.: National Press Books.

This small volume is in its second edition and is a thorough, explicit, and adequate description of the field of group dynamics and how it applies to many settings, including the classroom.

Rogers, Carl. 1970. *Carl Rogers on Encounter Groups*. New York: Harper and Row.

This is Rogers's explanation and description of an encounter group, how it proceeds, and how he functions as a facilitator, with some evidences of success from personal accounts and some predictions for the future. It is a readable and important book about the personal growth side of the group dynamics application.

Schmuck, Richard, and Patricia Schmuck. 1971. *Group Processes in the Classroom*. Dubuque, Iowa: Wm. C. Brown.

The theory and research of group dynamics are explained and illustrated through examples in the schools. It is a book about learning groups: how to understand and change them through the use of the principles of group dynamics. It is intended for practitioners in the field and has many specific, concrete examples and suggestions for use in humanizing learning groups.

Solomon, Lawrence, and Betty Berzon. 1972. *New Perspectives on Encounter Groups*. San Francisco: Jossey-Bass, Inc.

This book presents twenty-four chapters by many different authors covering an array of issues about encounter groups and other types of group experiences. It contains theoretical articles as well as data-based research reports. An article about Rogers's personal growth intervention at Immaculate Heart College is included.

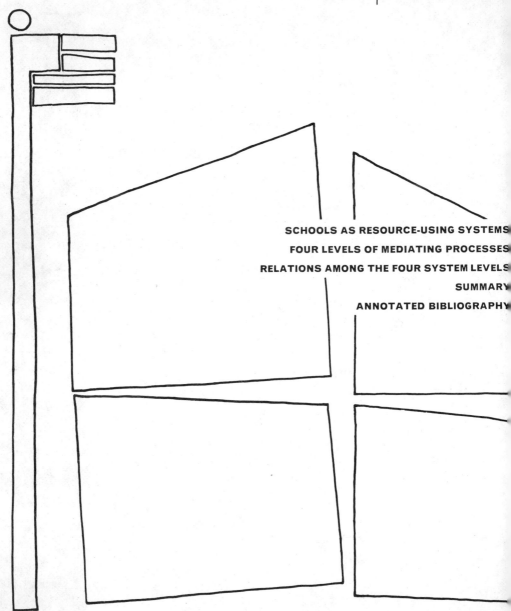

chapter 3

A human systems application: systems theory applied to schools

This is a textbook on the application of behavioral sciences to education, albeit *not* a typical one. Texts in educational psychology, for example, have traditionally covered topics such as child development, cognitive learning, student motivation, and individual differences. We have already touched on these topics in Chapter 2 and will deal only indirectly with them throughout the rest of this book. Texts used in educational foundations perennially have gone into topics such as cultural changes in the society, the nature of the school curriculum, formal characteristics of the school organization, and teachers as professionals. We already have discussed the first of these in Chapter 1 and will touch on each of the other three topics in subsequent chapters.

Perhaps this text comes closest in organization and treatment to texts in the sociology of education, which typically include discussions of the student peer group, the school as a bureaucratic organization, and the relationships between the school and community. However, this book is different from most such texts in its emphasis on planned change of schools. Topics covered in most texts for professional education, even when they have a definite behavioral science bias, seldom deal directly with the planned humanizing of classroom and school climates. Even those books in the social psychology of education that we annotate at the end of this chapter give short shrift to systemic change in schools. This chapter introduces a theory to correct this lack; this book introduces the elements of an operational strategy for humanizing schools.

We think that efforts to humanize schools typically have fallen short for at least three interrelated reasons. First, as we have noted previously, whole-person relationships do not develop among school participants as a result of particular strategies of psychological intervention or by virtue of specific educational practices or programs. Instead, we think attention must be given to modifying a school's entire culture by altering such basic elements of interpersonal relationships as influence, attraction, communication patterns, and norms.

Second, by focusing largely upon the introduction of new resources from the outside, schools do not encourage more I-Thou transactions. Academically better prepared students and professional staff or new curricular programs and physical arrangements will not, in themselves, humanize the culture of the school. The daily human interactions, regardless of the particular persons or curriculum materials involved, must be focused upon for improvement.

Third, a school's humanization will *not* take place as the result of partial changes or specific innovations in only one of its subsystems. Whole-person relationships and I-Thou transactions are likely to flourish only when comprehensive changes in influence, attraction, communication, and norms occur simultaneously at four system levels of the school.

We will describe and analyze the four system levels using the concepts of social psychology and systems theory. The four system levels are: (1) the individual—students, teachers, and administrators; (2) the learning group—classrooms and committees; (3) the school organization—the social procedures of the levels working together; and (4) the external environment—school board, budget, and parents. It is our belief that further understanding of the levels of the educational system—particularly the second and third levels—will enable us to plot a practical strategy for humanizing schools.

SCHOOLS AS RESOURCE-USING SYSTEMS

Social psychologists such as Katz and Kahn (1966), who write about systems theory, describe groups and organizations as open, living systems; they are open to environmental resources and they are living in the sense that they use them to develop products that are put back into the environment. Both learning groups and school organizations are examples of such open, living systems. Learning groups are embedded within, and constantly influencing and being influenced by, the culture of the school as a whole. In turn, schools are open systems contained within the larger context of a district and a community. Although, unfortunately, the importance of human interaction often is over-looked by educators, it is *people* who represent the primary resources entering, being processed by, and leaving the school. And, from our point of view, a school's organizational efficiency should be evaluated in terms of how well it produces people who can engage skillfully with others and who can enter into the I-Thou relationships previously described. Furthermore, we think that a school's efficiency in such human terms will be determined largely by the quality of the inter-personal relationships that occur inside the school and within its learning groups. It is, in other words, the quality of the group pro-cesses mediating the incoming "people-resources" and the outgoing "people-products" that will determine the school's potentiality for humanizing American culture.

In the past, however, analyses of school effectiveness usually have *not* been approached from a humanistic perspective. Typically, for instance, the school's products have been evaluated in terms of intel-lectual achievement. When cognitive goals and achievement are espoused, the level of academic competence of incoming students can be very important. For example, in summarizing the Coleman report, Dentler (1966) writes:

> What the child brings with him to school as strengths or weaknesses determined by his social class is the prime correlate of school achievement. It is influenced—offset or reinforced—most substan-tially not by facilities, curriculum, or teachers but by what other pupils bring with them as class-shaped interests and abilities. In practical terms, as the proportion of white pupils increases in a school, achievement among Negroes and Puerto Ricans increases because of the association between white ethnicity and socioeco-nomic advantage. (P. 29.)

Resources often complained about in relation to school achieve-ment are poorly trained teachers, inadequate curriculum materials and teaching aids, and even the classroom facility itself. (See, for example, Sexton, 1961.) Neophyte teachers, for example, are often thought to be less capable than more experienced teachers, and since schools in lower-class neighborhoods generally have more new teach-ers than schools in middle-class areas, this is often advanced as a reason why lower-class students learn and achieve less than others.

Although this causal chain seems doubtful in light of Coleman's (1966) results (which showed that teachers, by themselves, have little effect on academic achievement of students), the explanation is still often proposed that classroom teaching in general attracts the less capable college students, who then receive an inadequate pre-service education from poorly prepared college instructors who know little about the realities of the classroom. Such poorly prepared teachers, it is said, do not facilitate student achievement.

Other critics have argued that even the most able students and the most competent teachers cannot produce high academic achievement when curriculum materials are not high in quality, abundant, individualized, well programmed, and accompanied by audio-visual resources. Some critics even have focused upon the physical classroom and building facilities as representing barriers to school achievement.

A great deal of money granted to school districts, research and development centers, and regional laboratories by government and private foundations typically is earmarked for improving the quality of resources in hopes of improving cognitive achievement of students. Grants, for instance, are being offered to increase the cognitive skills of entering culturally disadvantaged children, to upgrade both pre-service and inservice teacher training, to build larger- and better-equipped libraries, and to encourage more individualized instruction and the use of more programmed materials and audio-visual learning aids. All of these educational activities and aims can be especially important for increasing achievement levels of students, but alone they fall short because they do not account for the interpersonal processes which inevitably occur in learning. To facilitate academic achievement, more attention should be given to the quality of group processes in the school.

Figure 3-1 illustrates the school as a resource-using system. During the entrepreneurial and bureaucratic historical periods in America, a school's efficiency was defined by the degree to which its resources were optimally integrated and processed to produce students of high academic achievement or vocational skill. That is to say most schools were judged in terms such as the number of students going on to college or obtaining good jobs. We believe that in the mid-1970s much more emphasis should be placed on the quality of the relationships developed as a result of daily experience in the school. The focus on humanizing our schools should be on changing the quality of the mediating group and organizational interactions of the schools.

FIGURE 3-1

SCHOOL AS A RESOURCE-USING SYSTEM

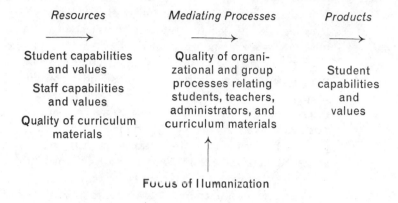

Resources	Mediating Processes	Products
——→	——→	——→
Student capabilities and values	Quality of organizational and group processes relating students, teachers, administrators, and curriculum materials	Student capabilities and values
Staff capabilities and values		
Quality of curriculum materials		

Focus of Humanization

FOUR LEVELS OF MEDIATING PROCESSES

Since the daily episodes occurring in schools and learning groups are very complex, we need to select a limited set of categories for analysis if we are to build social settings which encourage interpersonal relationships and I-Thou transactions. To focus on the school's *mediating processes* we have defined four levels for analysis: the person, the learning group, the school organization, and the school's environment. Each of the four is interrelated with the others and forms part of the whole human system that constitutes the school in living process. We will first discuss each separately and then show how all of them interact with one another.

1. The person

Although the avowed purpose of American schools has always been the education of individuals, our schools have tended *not* to strive deliberately toward the goal of developing psychologically robust and vital persons. American schools have tended to emphasize cognitive knowledge and vocational skills; affective development has generally not been viewed by educators as an appropriate province for schooling, and where the concept has been supported, attention has been given to emotional dynamics in the belief that such a program is supportive of *cognitive* goals. As we indicated in Chapter 2, with the rise in popularity of psychology, educators have begun to adopt the point of view that thoughts and feelings cannot be easily separated. Nonetheless, this view of the integration of cognition and affect during learning has not led to very many real changes in teaching. Indeed, in following a therapeutic prescription, teachers have tended to *remove* from their classes students that they think have "emotional problems," placing them in separate classrooms under the guidance of specially prepared teachers. The giving of attention to students' feelings and the role they play in classroom interactions continues to be viewed pessimistically even among many advocates of mental health and group process applications. Many educators still take the position that a student's feelings have little connection to work and consequently are not to be discussed in the normal classroom.

This orientation cannot continue to prevail among educators if schools are to become more fully humanized. One of the most profound facts of human existence is that everyone faces conflict, anxiety, and turmoil, and that these emotional experiences are normal and even natural. They occur in intensified ways especially during the childhood and adolescent years, when directions are unclear and identities are not yet crystalized. One major challenge for schools, then, is how to confront developmental conflict constructively and creatively as a part of the educational program. Both Erik Erikson (1950) and Abraham Maslow (1967) point to emotional dilemmas that exist throughout life. Erikson has discussed such developmental issues as establishing *trust* with others, achieving personal *autonomy*, and being *productive*: issues that confront all people throughout their lives. We think that schools should deliberately plan to treat these human issues as part of the very fabric of the educational process.

One of Maslow's (1967) delightful descriptions of self-actualizing people presents a challenge for schools to achieve:

> They listen to their own voices; they take responsibility; they are honest; and they work hard. They find out who they are and what they are, not only in terms of their mission in life, but also in terms of the way their feet hurt when they wear such and such pair of shoes and whether they do or do not like eggplant or stay up all night if they drink too much beer. All that is what the real self means. They find their own biological natures, their congenital natures, which are irreversible or difficult to change. (P. 30.)

If schools are to help facilitate personal growth of the sorts described by Erikson and Maslow, we think that they must actively strive to build more whole-person relationships: those relationships which are concerned with the unique combination of all parts of a person rather than one or two qualities, such as baseball skill or reading proficiency. Although schooling has traditionally been future-oriented (to prepare responsible, thoughtful, and skillful adults), we think that facilitating the growth of whole persons requires the development of more personal and emotionally expressive relationships in school. By focusing not only on the future but more on the here-and-now existential episodes of school life, schools can make a difference in the extent to which individuals mature into humanized, mentally healthy persons.

2. The learning group

Most school activities are carried out within small groups. The traditional class of from twenty-five to thirty students is perhaps the most typical learning milieu; however, many other types exist, ranging from tutoring pairs to large cross-grade groupings. All learning groups, regardless of size, have both social and individual features. As we noted in Chapter 1, the social and individual dimensions interact to create conditions for the particular classroom climate that emerges. We must attend to both dimensions as we strive to build more whole-person relationships in schools.

The social aspects of learning groups have to do with the ways in which various members work toward implementing the official or specified goals of the group. One social feature, for example, is the manner in which any student is expected to perform the role of learner by the teachers, the school district in general, and the adult community at large. Other social features center on the resolution of such key issues as: how academic objectives are set, how decisions about curriculum are made, and how the rules for behavior are made and enforced. Every formal learning group faces such questions and must resolve them either publicly or implicitly. The traditional answers to these social questions have developed more often from needs peculiar to the past or for the sake of bureaucratic efficiency than from the intention of facilitating full relationships between people.

The individual aspects of a learning group comprise the manner in which each member relates to other members as persons. Especi-

A human
systems 99
application

ally in learning groups that meet over prolonged periods, emotional undertones arise in most of the interpersonal relationships. High levels of feeling exist from day to day; teachers and students have feelings of closeness or distance for others which are mostly communicated by nonverbal gestures.

Both Bion (1948) and Thelen (1954) have described the inevitable emotions which arise between people, especially in relationships in settings where youngsters are present. They maintain that the first relationships a person experiences are in the family, and that those relationships are saturated with emotionality and feelings. From a person's family experiences, he or she learns basic ways of relating to other people. The transfer from family to learning groups is direct for young people because they are simultaneously living in both.

Several nonschool studies shed light on the relation of the social and individual aspects of groups. In their study of the German army during World War II for instance, Shils and Janowitz (1948) showed that the organizational breakdown of the German army arose largely from the dissolution of friendship among soldiers in small fighting units rather than from significant flaws in the formal organization of the military. The supportive relationships of closeness among the soldiers were necessary for the realization of the formal goals of winning the war.

In a similar study, Goodacre (1953) showed that the informal relationships among American soldiers also had significant influence on success in reaching the larger goal of winning the war. Men in the squads which performed better reported many interpersonal ties in their groups, "buddying around" after duty hours, having fewer group disagreements, and thinking highly of their own squad, as compared with men in poorly performing squads.

Walberg (1968b) has shown that significant relationships exist between social and individual features of classroom groups. For example, he showed that classrooms in which formal authority, goal-setting, and communication were tightly controlled by the teacher exhibited a great deal of interpersonal conflict and tension among the students. In such highly formalized classes, the teacher dominated and the students maintained their places in the "pecking order." Students were discouraged from airing their grievances, did not partake in decision-making, and talked very little with the teacher. Tension was channeled off through interpersonal catharsis within the peer group. In contrast, Walberg found interpersonal tensions mitigated in classes in which a great deal of both favorable and unfavorable dialogue occurred between teacher and students and where more decision-making was shared between them. In these groups, whole-person relationships were more characteristic and affective ties within the peer group were stronger.

Although educators generally have not considered student friendships relevant to individual students' cognitive and affective development, our research evidence (Schmuck, 1963, and Schmuck, 1966) and experience indicate that they are related. In fact, the friendships classmates have for one another, along with their willingness to help and support one another, represent important ingredients for the enhancement of individual academic achievement. Moreover, learning groups in which friendship and influence are dispersed among many peers have more supportive work norms and are more cohesive than groups in which the friendship and influence processes are hierarchical. Strong relationships with others are not only valuable in themselves; they also can enhance cognitive development in the classroom.

3. The school organization

Although learning groups usually are relatively autonomous from one another, the characteristics of the school organization can influence the climate of a learning group. The school organization comprises the cultural context for its learning groups. It is constituted by the processes through which all important subsystems work together, including community and other outside forces, social and individual dimensions of staff and faculty-student relationships, and the curriculum and other academic materials. Learning groups are unlikely to become humanized unless humanized relationships and I-Thou transactions characterize the total organization of the school.

Teachers have tended to underestimate the power of the school organization for helping or inhibiting the humanization of their own learning climates. We believe that six features of school organizations are necessary ingredients for creating and maintaining humanized climates in learning groups: (1) a high degree of trust, openness, and supportiveness among staff members, (2) skillfull communication and constructive openness among the staff and with students, (3) equalization of influence among staff members, (4) staff norms that view students as curious, active, and wishing to be productive and challenged, (5) a principal who is viewed by both teachers and students as supportive, collaborative, and helpful, and finally (6) students having the opportunity to view congenial and supportive relationships among staff members.

We think that most efforts to make learning climates more humanistic collapse or are absorbed into the school's traditional processes without effect because too little attention is given to the organization in which the reforms are attempted. Since schools are human organizations, any major innovation in curriculum or teaching procedures implies a change in the school's culture. The relationships between teachers and administrators, for example, are bound to change, especially when the teacher tries a new way of allowing freedom for more students. Often attempts at changing relationships within a classroom influence not only the students and teachers involved but also the relationships between the principal and other teachers, among teachers themselves, and among the counselors, nurse, social worker, nonprofessional staff, and other students. As a result, authority relationships, role definitions, communication networks, status groupings and even friendships are forced to change. During this arduous change process, the innovation itself often fails or is restricted to conform to the old, more impersonal way of doing things.

A number of relationships between a school organization and attempted innovations have recently been demonstrated in the Cooperative Project for Educational Development (1970). No relationship was found between innovativeness and per-pupil expenditures. Indeed, the research tended to confirm our position that school culture is the major factor related to success in innovation. The project showed that both school-district and building-level innovativeness were functions of organizational variables such as the degree of leadership-sharing and personal support provided by the principal, the staff's perception of a normative system favoring creativity and a high degree of trust among colleagues, and the degree of initiation of innovative proposals by teachers.

4. The school's environment

Whether schools become more humanized depends in large part on how well they cope with their external environment and especially with the variety of demands posed by different parts of their community. The informal community groups, along with the many formal organizations that surround and influence schools, are increasingly complex, diverse, and in flux. Transactions between organizations within the community, the community's informal clusters, and the school often create pressures that exceed the school's ability to predict and plan adequately for the future. Compared to other organizations, such as industrial firms, hospitals, and government bureaus, schools have less autonomy and control over outside demands. For example, school personnel do not influence the general shape of the community's job market and cannot even accurately prepare students to fit into jobs because the needs and demands of the job market are continuously in flux. Many school districts do not have control over their own budgets much less control over changes in community feelings and attitudes toward the schools. School personnel cannot predict accurately how the society may change, nor can they plan for specific needs of the future with precision. This condition of the "ambiguous future" is one more reason why we believe that the school should aim primarily at humanizing its interpersonal relations in the present. After all, the need for emphatic and supportive interpersonal relationships exists daily and will continue to exist as long as human systems persist.

Change in American schools comes about more often than not by crisis-oriented legislation; pressures from state and federal agencies, teachers' associations, and textbook publishers; and rulings by central office administrators, rather than from the planned attempts of educational professionals or participants in local schools. As Bassett (1970) has pointed out, innovation in American schools tends to come from *outside*. By contrast, he describes the situation in Britain, where changes, especially those involved in humanizing primary classrooms, have come from the professionals themselves working together within specific schools.

In America there have been several occasions on which large-scale pressures (none of which have been to humanize the schools) have been exerted on schools from the outside. One such pressure resulted from the so-called Sputnik scare of the late 1950s, which made greatly increased funds available for a renewed emphasis on science and foreign languages. Another example was the flurry of interest in New Math during the early 60s; in that case the push came initially from selected university academics and later from the publishers of popular magazines such as *Life* and *Look*. Subsequently, many parents understandably became interested in making sure that their youngsters received the best possible instruction in mathematics. New math programs were adopted throughout the nation without sufficient empirical evidence of their effectiveness. Moreover, they did *not*, in fact, diffuse rapidly, because the interests, curiosities, and competencies of teachers were not congruent with them.

The Kent school district in Kent, Washington, with which we are thoroughly acquainted, is an excellent example of the vulnerability of a school to its surrounding environment and of its inability to predict accurately the changes in that environment. The population and affluence of the Kent community grew rapidly during the 1960s because of the success and growth of the Boeing aerospace complex. In order to keep abreast of these changes, the Kent school board hired a management consulting firm to make ten-year projections about population growth, enrollment figures, financial needs, and additional possibilities for financing. Kent administrators also asked the consultants to advise them on how to change the organization of the district and schools to cope successfully with the future.

Abrupt changes occurred during the late sixties and early seventies when the economic environment changed drastically. Boeing was beset by hard times, many of their large contracts were terminated and inflation grew rapidly. Moreover, the district financial officer, with the help of a state auditor, discovered a major deficit in the district budget. Within three years the consulting firm's planned projections proved totally invalid; their recommendations for changes in the central office were useless and many interesting innovations had to be terminated.

Fortunately, one innovation that did survive (and is still flourishing) was a cadre of communication consultants within the district charged with helping subsystems to function more competently and humanistically. This group consists of assistant superintendents, principals, counselors, and teachers who function part-time as "group process consultants" to various subsystems within the district. This sort of innovation, which we will discuss in Chapters 6 and 7, carries the potential for helping a school to deal effectively with its external environment while still emphasizing humanized interpersonal relationships within.

A human systems application

RELATIONS AMONG THE FOUR SYSTEM LEVELS

To achieve deeper understanding of barriers that arise in attempting to humanize schools, we now consider some of the relationships that exist among these four levels of mediating processes. First, we will discuss the person's impact on the group in which he is most centrally involved. Although we are primarily concerned with the student's impact (or lack of it) on the learning group, we will also discuss the teacher's influence within learning groups and the principal's impact on the school organization. We will go on to delineate some of the ways in which learning groups influence students and teachers. Then we will discuss how the organizational processes of a school influence both its learning groups and individual members. Finally, we will show how the environment can influence the school organization, the learning groups, and the persons within them.

1. The impact of the individual on the group

Individuals are not merely cogs in an ongoing system. In this section we will show how students and (primarily) teachers influence their learning groups and how principals make a significant impact on the school organization.

a. Student influence on learning groups

The power of students to shape their school climates has always been limited in American schools. In the past, however, this state of affairs has not typically aroused much frustration and anger among students or public. Students for the most part accepted their subservient roles at school, at least until the late 1950s. Then, with the increased affluence of the sixties and seventies and the accompanying rise in expectations for personal autonomy and well-being and the burgeoning concern for racial and social justice, the powerless position of students became very obvious to them.

A popular phrase of the late fifties to describe wide-spread alienation in America was that of the *organization man*. It referred to a member of a bureaucracy whose uniqueness and individuality had been lost within the machinery of impersonal rules and procedures. Reisman's phrase for the same phenomenon was "other-directed"; Coleman viewed high school students, in the same vein, as being interested primarily in superficialities and appearance, popularity, and comfortable interpersonal relations.

These lonely, depthless feelings of the fifties were transformed into virulent anger during the sixties. The descriptive language changed to phrases such as "*student as nigger*," by which students were depicted as totally powerless, and yet acting in collusion with teachers to *maintain* their low status. Teachers similarly were viewed as unconsciously collaborating pawns working within a large educational bureaucracy and without distinctiveness or power. They were exhorted by some critics of education to "drop out" or to subvert the establishment behind the closed doors of their classrooms. But the bigness of schools made isolated attempts at radical change minuscule in effect.

As we proceed through the seventies, some students and educators are showing a fresh confidence in school as an institution by making public attempts to improve learning climates. Along with the large number of alternative free schools, there are many instances within the public schools of attempts at humanizing relationships. Traditional school organizations and impersonal large classes are being transformed into smaller schools within schools and project groups within classes are being developed. Students are better able to influence their peers and teachers when working in small groups of five to twelve. Teachers are able to influence students more by working with them on an individual basis and by forming guidance and tutoring relationships in small groups.

Although students still do not wield the sort of power in learning groups that teachers do, some of them can have significant impact through their peer group influence. Such influence is especially prominent in elementary schools, where classes remain intact for large portions of the school day, but peer group relationships can be very influential during the high school years as well.

Research has confirmed common assumptions about who the popular students are. Popular students are typically outgoing and socially effective, physically attractive, and well coordinated. In most social settings, students are in some respect rejected if they are limited in attractiveness or physical ability, if they have difficulties in relating socially, if they have intellectual limitations, or if they are neurotically passive or aggressive. There are some socio-economic class differences in regard to which attributes are considered most valuable; for instance, lower-class boys tend to value physical prowess more than their middle-class counterparts. In schools characterized by middle-class values, lower-class students are rejected by their peers often because of their overt aggression or passive dependency.

Some ideas developed by Atkinson and Feather (1966) are helpful in conceptualizing the psychodynamics of a student attempting to influence his peer group. They argue that behavior is influenced by the three psychological processes of motive force (M), expectance (E), and incentive value (I): tendency to act $= (M) \times (E) \times (I)$. Students with a strong need for power (M), for example, will attempt to influence their peers provided they expect to succeed in the attempt (E), and they believe they will receive some reward for being influential (I). Atkinson and Feather view the motive force as a relatively stable aspect of the personality, instilled during the early years. The expectation for success derives both from past successes in similar circumstances and the student's perceptions of the current ones. The incentive value is the expected pay-off for attempting influence. Each of these variables must be present and positive for the student to attempt influence. Thus, even when a student has a high need for power, he will *not* attempt to influence his peers unless he has some expectation of being influential and thinks that he will be rewarded for it. Students with a high motive force accompanied by low expectations and incentive generally feel frustrated and depressed by their relations with peers.

Characteristics of the group itself can also be important in determining how strongly individual students will influence it. Groups in which many of the members attempt influence have leaders who facilitate the emergence of high expectations and incentives for mutual influence. In the classroom group the teacher's behavior can be very important in raising expectations and incentives for interpersonal risk-taking and initiating influence attempts. The teacher who listens respectfully to student discourse and who talks to students openly about his own feelings tends to encourage students to venture forth with influence attempts. In contrast, teachers who monopolize air-time and who direct their students a great deal tend to reduce student influence attempts—at least public ones—and also to reduce effective influence between peers. Student influence attempts are likely to be most effective in classes where teacher and students support and encourage one another to act openly and truthfully.

Following a different sort of theory, Walberg carried out some illuminating research on the effects of students on their classroom climates. In a study on physics classes, for example, Walberg and Anderson (1968) found that students who measured high in *scientific creativity* (interest in inquiry, in experimentation, and in working with laboratory material) formed quite a different classroom climate from students who measured high on *scientific achievement* (regard for physics as important, especially in application). Groups high in creativity had tense climates characterized by competition, friction, and a sense of individual isolation, whereas climates of achievement-oriented groups were comfortable, democratic and equalitarian, goal-directed, and characterized by little friction among the members.

In another study, Walberg (1969) found significant differences between what he termed highly cognitive climates (emphasizing achievement and understanding) and noncognitive climates (emphasizing interest and activity) in science classes. Students in the cognitive climates had high I.Q.'s and high grades and viewed their classes as difficult. Those in the noncognitive climates were highly involved in extracurricular science projects, liked school, and saw their classes as interpersonally comfortable.

Although Walberg's research does not show unequivocally that individual students had impact on their group learning climates, it does appear that students with similar psychological characteristics formed a particular kind of miniculture in the school. We can only speculate about the social processes by which this occurred. It is evident that the predominant attitudes of the students interacted with those of the teacher and with the content of the physics curriculum. Since Walberg attempted to keep teacher characteristics and the curriculum constant between groups, differences in climate seem to have been due mostly to peer group interactions and to the norms that developed between each group of students and their teacher. Particular norms emerged because the students in each class commenced interaction with one another in unique and idiosyncratic ways; for example, the students in the cognitive climates entered into intellectual combat, while the "noncognitive" students were more problem-focused. In addition, instruction in each class was geared to allow the individual characteristics of students to emerge; it encouraged students to work in small groups and do independent study.

It would be encouraging, indeed, for the humanization of American schools if we could declare from Walberg's results that the personal predilections of students have a significant impact upon learning climates. Students who feel that they can influence other students, their teacher, and the activities in their classrooms feel good about themselves, feel good about school, and achieve at levels consonant with their intellectual abilities (Schmuck, 1966). Unfortunately, student influence depends a great deal on the teacher's behavior and the structure of the curriculum. In too many classrooms students influence learning activities only *in spite of* the teacher's actions and the curriculum structure. Students who feel powerless and unable to make a personal mark upon their classes tend to be unhappy with school and usually do not perform up to their intellectual capabilities as indicated by I.Q. scores.   Need for power

b. Teacher influence on learning groups

Teachers have the major responsibility for providing the curriculum and for guiding the growth and development of students. Since no other position for formal authority exists in the classroom, teachers have the highest formal potential for interpersonal influence. As a result educational research is replete with articles about teachers, their attitudes, personality characteristics, behaviors, and the effects of these on student achievement, attitudes, and personality development. An underlying assumption in much of this research, however, has been that the classroom is constituted of two-person units, with the teacher largely involved in determining his interaction with each student. In contrast, we believe that the classroom group undergoes much more complex interpersonal processes, with teachers acting as members and mediators rather than as mere controllers of interaction in two-person units. We believe that teachers should attempt to facilitate rather than control transactions between themselves and all participants in the learning group. (For details on our position see Schmuck and Schmuck, 1971.)

Regardless of how the learning group is conceptualized, however, most teachers do in fact influence the norms, communication patterns, interpersonal attractions, and influence relationships in the classroom. Students continually respond to teacher gestures and behaviors and in turn initiate behaviors to which the teacher must react. Teachers' influences are also continually mediated by students' responses, individually and collectively, formally and informally. For example, a specific direction from the teacher may create a flurry of communication between students; they may agree to follow the direction or as a group refuse to follow it. We wish to focus now on how teachers' personalities, attitudes, and behaviors contribute to the classroom climate.

We have found that teachers whose classrooms have favorable climates—those with widespread friendships, evidence of respect and caring, strong feelings of power and involvement, and norms that support individuals working at different rates on different learning tasks, and those in which students can influence both each other and the teacher about classroom procedures—differ cognitively, attitudinally, and behaviorally from teachers with less favorable climates. We do not believe that favorable classroom climates emerge randomly; our own teaching experiences and research have proven to us that developing favorable learning climates requires a certain cognitive orientation as well as deliberate effort and special interpersonal strategies. Teachers with favorable learning climates tend to see many more of the complexities of the interpersonal world and to understand how they might affect student behavior and academic learning. For another, the teachers with favorable climates tend to adopt a democratic and equalitarian relationship with their students. They ask for suggestions, listen carefully to ideas, and react generally with respect and evidence of caring. We have also found that teachers with favorable learning climates talk often with a wide variety of students, encourage students to talk and to influence one another, use a great deal of praise, and are honest about their personal values and preferences. When called upon to control student behavior, they tend to make goal-directed comments such as "Class, it's too noisy. I am having trouble hearing you and understanding what you want to say." In contrast, teachers of classes with less favorable social climates typically talk with only a few students (implying favoritism), rebuke students publicly, and are not as generous with their praise.

Classrooms that have more negative learning climates are typified by threatening and anxiety-producing interpersonal relations, by a small powerful clique isolated from most classmates, and by a feeling of powerlessness and neglect among most students. We refer to classes with a small powerful clique as "centrally structured"; in contrast are diffusely structured classes in which nearly every student is included within a friendship cluster. Such sociometric patterns constitute core aspects of classroom climates.

Some research by Walberg (1968a) casts light on how certain types of teachers influence the development of peer group structures. Using teacher scores on a variety of personality measures, he found

A human systems application

that the classes of teachers who were unclear about how affiliative or aggressive to act were low in esprit de corps and were centrally structured. Many teachers reduce this appearance of ambivalence by becoming more distant from their students. A teacher can maintain distance, for example, by reminding students of the hierarchical power relationship through dominating verbal statements. The interpersonal relationships in such classes are thus monopolized by the teacher, and in response the students tend to form alliances with students who are coping best with the teacher.

Another personality style strongly influencing the learning climate is that of the self-centered teacher: a style similar to that of the laissez-faire leader described in the classic study by Lewin, Lippitt, and White (1939). Self-centered teachers run very loosely organized classes; students are poorly supervised and much behavior of both teacher and students is characterized by passivity and withdrawal. The self-centered teacher does not use the power of the position to initiate close interpersonal relationships. Students are not encouraged, guided, supported, or confronted; they simply are not pushed or prodded in any way. Unlike Lewin et al., (who studied the laissez-faire leader in a scout troop of elementary school boys) Walberg did not find much friction or irritation within the high school classes of self-centered teachers. Walberg's finding was perhaps due to the unfortunate fact that high school students have usually learned not to manifest their boredom and frustration in open and direct ways.

Walberg's studies, along with other research that we will discuss in Chapter 5, indicate that teachers have the greatest potential power of all classroom members to influence the group climate. The teachers' personality styles, attitudes, information, and values help to shape their teaching behavior, to which, in turn, students must respond and with which they must cope. Even with high amounts of power, however, teachers do not operate alone. They are part of a nexus of professionals including the principal and other teachers that comprises their most immediate reference group. The pervasive spirit of the school—indeed the school's climate—does a great deal to influence how teachers enact their roles in the classroom.

c. The principal's influence on the school organization

Principals have been granted ultimate responsibility in most school districts for the many educational activities that occur in the school.

They are charged with helping to create the organizational conditions that will optimize student learning and with helping to construct an organizational climate that will aid rather than impede the work of teachers. In relation to the district office, they are responsible for efficiency, direct communication, financial acumen, and the maintenance of a smoothly running bureaucracy. They are expected, moreover, to keep parents informed and to involve themselves in school matters wherever they think it is appropriate. Being a competent principal requires the effective balancing of the diverse interests of these different groups. It is not simple to function effectively as a principal, partly because of the conflicts among the needs of students, teachers, district office administrators, and parents.

Naturally different principals work in different ways. Some effectively fulfill the requirements for a smoothly running bureaucracy by spending a great deal of time keeping careful records, filing reports, talking to district office administrators, and calming ruffled adversaries so that strife and discord do not become virulent and publicly prominent. Other principals focus less on the mechanics of running the organization, instead encouraging their staff to attempt specific curricular and instructional innovations. Still other principals emphasize developing warm, comfortable, and relaxed interpersonal relationships among teachers and students and between teachers and parents. For them, favorable interpersonal relationships are more important than bureaucratic efficiency or educational innovation. It is the rare principal who can perform all of the above functions equally well.

Knowing how the principal manages decision-making in the school is one key to understanding how the role is performed in general. The principal formally and traditionally carries more responsibility for what occurs in the school than any other single participant. The principal is responsible for basic economic matters, such as the distribution of the school budget; for the health and well-being of the students while they are in the building; and for numerous minor decisions, such as whether the north hall door should be locked or left open during the lunch hour. Even though this formal role delineation applies to most principals, the decision-making processes initiated or allowed by different principals can be very different. Most principals have considerable latitude regarding how decisions will be made in the school. For example, they may make most of the decisions themselves and hold teachers accountable for carrying them out, or conversely they can attempt to include teachers or students in the decision-

A human systems application

making procedure, thereby distributing influence more widely. We have found that *regardless* of what particular decision-making style is used by the principal, most other participants in the school, as well as the parents, are unclear about it. Indeed, school faculties seldom even discuss the ways decisions are made.

The principal's orientation to making decisions can have a significant impact on the school's climate. One useful typology for understanding different styles of decision-making and their effects was developed by McGregor (1967). He argued that managers base their decision-making procedures upon their philosophical view of man. For example, a manager who holds what McGregor called "Theory X" maintains that people are inactive, passive, and lazy and therefore must be pushed and prodded to action. Theory X managers believe that human motivation is extrinsic in nature, i.e., only when being granted rewards (as well as punishments) will people work diligently in their organizational roles. Theory X managers also tend to use a leadership style characterized by one-way, unilateral communication and high control, while at the same time promoting procedures for monitoring performance that are highly structured and restrictive. The Theory X manager makes most decisions alone or with only a few trusted parties.

The Theory Y manager, in contrast, views people as curious, active, and interested and also sees motivation as being more intrinsic. They believe that people take action when the activities satisfy needs of self-esteem and self-actualization. Theory Y managers employ participative patterns of leadership, characterized by equalitarianism and two-way communication. At the same time, they expect people to be responsible and hard-working once they have participated in decision-making and have recognized the relevance of performing a set of actions. The Theory Y manager tends to make decisions in concert with others.

Even though McGregor's conceptualizations focus on ideal types, and no principal can easily be characterized as exclusively one way or the other, many principals can be placed somewhere on a dimension line with Theory X and Theory Y at either end. We theorize that principals who are closer to Theory X emphasize smoothly running bureaucracies, build formal and distant relationships with most teachers and students, and foster impersonal and dehumanized relationships in the school. Emotional exchanges are suppressed; both love and hostility are generally held back. It is also quite likely that

Theory X behavior on the part of the principal will influence relationships between teachers and students. In imitating the leadership behavior of the principal, the teachers may try hard to maintain their positions of authority in the classroom. Bigelow (1971) found that classroom procedures reflected procedures among the adults; when the principal shared power with the teachers, similarly teachers shared power with students in their classes. The decision-making style of a principal thus has an important influence on what happens in classrooms. Teachers with Theory Y principals will allow students to become involved more in decision-making than teachers with Theory X principals. Conversely, teachers with Theory X principals will more likely be authoritarian in relation to their students.

Principals who are closer to the Theory Y end of the dimension will enter into face-to-face interaction more with many persons in the school. In their schools, there will be more informality at meetings, more collaboration and cooperation, and more involvement of students with teachers and the principal. With a Theory Y principal, teachers and students expect to share feelings and to risk getting emotionally close.

We are concerned that too few principals are aware of the creative power inherent in the group of teacher-colleagues in their school. Many principals try to influence their staff to adopt new practices either by memoranda or in faculty meetings or by chatting informally with individual teachers. Unfortunately, few principals view themselves as group facilitators, performing as conveners of small problem-solving groups of staff members. Often they fail to offer conditions conducive to the personal growth of teachers; indeed, the group conditions for creative synergy are almost nonexistent in most school faculties. Let us look more closely at four research studies demonstrating the power of the principal in shaping the school climate.

(1) *The Gross-Herriott Research.* Gross and Herriott (1965) constructed a questionnaire to measure the Executive Professional Leadership (EPL) of principals. Their research showed that high EPL principals differed from low EPL principals in expected ways. EPL was measured by asking teachers to make judgments of their principal's role behavior regarding such variables as supportiveness, collaborativeness, stimulation, knowledgeability, and helpfulness. The principals with high EPL scores talked more frequently with teachers about major educational problems, offered constructive criticisms, displayed strong interest in improving the quality of instructional programs, and

were responsible for making teachers' meetings a worthwhile activity. Teachers who credited their principals with high EPL were comfortable in their school work, and were stimulated and encouraged by the principal to improve. Teachers who felt supported and encouraged were not fearful of trying new educational procedures and, therefore, could provide a better academic learning environment for their students. Data indicated that the students of teachers with high EPL principals achieved more than students of teachers with low EPL principals.

(2) *The Chesler-Schmuck-Lippitt Research.* Chesler, Schmuck, and Lippitt (1963) studied associations between principals' behaviors and teachers' innovativeness. They found that teachers with principals who actively encouraged and supported new practices were more likely to try out instructional innovations. Teachers whose principals, on the other hand, were obviously not supportive of innovativeness or who were laissez-faire with regard to innovation tended to try out fewer new practices. Perhaps most interesting was the finding that new teaching practices were tried at the highest rate when the teachers saw both the principal and their colleagues supporting innovativeness.

Indeed, the principal can exercise indirect influence on teacher innovativeness by stimulating and encouraging staff members to talk about their goals and classroom practices. The principal's leadership position can be greatly strengthened by bringing staff members into active collaboration in solving problems. Typically, however, the principal relates to staff members only on a one-to-one basis and therefore limits his or her power to stimulate support for innovation. By encouraging teachers to collaborate in small groups, he or she can greatly increase the flow of knowledge and interpersonal stimulation among the staff.

(3) *The Schmuck-Runkel Research.* Schmuck and Runkel (1970) carried out a year of training in organization development for the staff of a junior high school. One of the central objectives of the intervention was to increase communication flow vertically and laterally among staff members. Assessment of the training indicated that communications on the staff were greatly improved in accuracy and quantity. One unexpected result was that the teachers applied insights and skills from organization development training to their classrooms. Transfer to the classroom was facilitated by the more open and accurate communication among staff members, by the staff's establishment of new collaborative relationships, and by the increase in teachers'

conversations about innovative ideas about classroom teaching.

(4) *The Willower-Eidell-Hoy Research.* Willower, Eidell, and Hoy (1967) studied the control ideology of educators in thirteen school districts and discovered that in general the principals were *less* control-oriented and *more* humanistically-oriented toward students than were their teachers. Although this finding agrees with our own observations and private conversations with many principals, it has been surprising to many people who view principals as authoritarian and control-oriented. Unfortunately, principals often do not behave according to their stated private values. For example, we seldom have heard a principal comment publicly about his strong concerns for the affective and mental health objectives of the school. Moreover, many principals do not encourage informality and openness at staff meetings even though they secretly value such democratic group processes. The cultural norms of schools so strongly support formality, interpersonal distance, and the indirect communication of affect that individual principals act in support of these norms in order to feel comfortable and legitimate in their roles. A principal's interpersonal distance from his teachers often is read by the teachers as support for a control orientation with students.

2. Impact of the learning group on individuals

The goals and norms that guide behavior evolve out of the prevailing attitudes, values, and interaction patterns of group members. These group goals and norms, in turn, strongly influence the members of the group. Much of the theory and research of social psychology emphasize the powerful influence of the group on its members. (See Collins and Raven, 1969.) Group members, more than persons working alone, have been shown to distort their perceptions of simple physical stimuli, to inflict pain on others under prodding, and to take unusual risks. Groups even can support the inhuman, immoral actions of an entire nation-state while applauding the members' courage and wisdom. In short, groups can call up individual strengths and weaknesses previously unknown even to the person who is suddenly called upon to exhibit them.

Learning groups also can have major impact on their members. It is impossible for any person to be a member of a classroom over a period of time without being influenced by interaction with others. Classrooms never remain mere aggregates of unrelated individuals

The procedures that are developed for the formal purpose of intellectual development can make significant differences in how the learning goals are set and in what the students learn. The ways decisions are made, which persons are viewed as sources of important information, whether students work in small groups or as individuals, the nature of the content to be learned, and how achievement is measured all can affect students' performances and the values they place upon learning and themselves as students. Formal classroom procedures set the boundaries within which each student must find his or her space for psychological movement and intellectual growth.

Classroom learning groups also develop interpersonal undercurrents of attraction and hostility. No matter how distant and impersonal classroom relationships may appear, teachers' behaviors toward students as well as students' interactions with their peers are replete with feelings. Often, because the open expression of feelings is not considered proper within the classroom, distortions, misperceptions, and fantasies arise about the affective undertones. A simple statement by the teacher such as "John, you did a good job" can be read with a variety of meanings by the students, ranging from "As always, you did a fine job!" to "For once, you did something well!" How the statement is presented and received depends upon the accumulated events of the past relationship, the nonverbal interactions accompanying it, and the norms that guide the communication of favorable remarks and feelings in the class. Any simple statement offered in the classroom can have multiple meanings, depending on the sender, the receiver, and the situation.

Within the learning group, a student must choose continuously between behaving as he thinks others expect him to behave or in ways that are contrary to others' expectations. The individual student can rarely avoid making such choices about the part he plays in relation to the norms of the group. He must make choices about such matters as how he will work and play with others, how he will relate to his teacher, and what he will do when frustrated and angry. Naturally, the teacher's expectations and behaviors will influence the sorts of behavioral choices that the students make. The following anecdote from Silberman (1970) shows, for example, how a teacher's behavior can create pseudo-stupid behavior in students:

Three children are in a special class—children with perceptual problems. The teacher insists on talking with the visitor about the children in their presence, as though congenital deafness were part of their difficulty. "Now, watch, I'm giving them papers to see if they can spot the ovals, but you'll see that this one"—he nods in the direction of a little boy—"isn't going to be able to do it." A few seconds later, he says triumphantly, "See, I told you he couldn't. He never gets that one right. Now, I'll put something on the overhead projector, and this one"—this time, a nod toward a little girl—"won't stay with it for more than a line." Five seconds later, with evident disappointment: "Well, that's the first time she ever did that. But keep watching. By the next line, she'll have flubbed it." The child gets the next one right, too, and the teacher's disappointment mounts. "This is unusual, but just stick around...." Sure enough, the child goofs at line five. "See, I told you so!" (Pp. 139-140.)

Students can exercise similar self-fulfilling processes in relation to other students.

Even though students start school with self-images that are already partially formed, their experiences in the classroom can have a decided impact on them, as this vignette from Silberman describes. Indeed, the self-concept is continuously being formed and reformed as new persons enter into one's life. During the school years, the peer group can have an especially significant influence on the individual's self-concept.

Students who bring insecurity and unfavorable images of themselves into the class tend to be disliked and rejected by their peers. Peer rejection often encourages a perpetuating and vicious cycle; students who view themselves as inadequate and unlikeable behave in ways that confirm these negative self-images. Their behaviors create interpersonal tensions and disruptions which lead to additional rejections, further confirming their negative self-concepts. Conversely, students with self-esteem tend to behave in attractive ways. They are rewarded by others and are successful in their work. Their positive self-images are bolstered through feedback from others.

Although most youngsters experience a blend of these two circular processes, there is a tendency for each student to experience one more than the other. The student who more often experiences the negative cycle feels under stress and is anxious about his adequacy. He frequently distorts and misperceives others' reactions, tending to distrust or to disbelieve favorable feedback. Such destructive misperceptions keep the student from breaking out of the negative cycle. As years go by and such experiences pile up, it becomes more difficult to make alterations in very negative self-concepts.

Intellectual performance itself is integrally related to the image a student holds of himself as a student. Students who are comfortable with themselves and pleased with their schoolwork and who have self-esteem tend to be realistic about their intellectual strengths and weaknesses. In contrast, students who dislike themselves and who view themselves as being disliked by others fail to recognize their capabilities accurately and tend to choose work that is either too easy or too hard. Students with high self-esteem tend to make good use of their ability, while students with low self-esteem do not.

A useful concept for understanding how group expectations and interpersonal interactions affect self-esteem and intellectual performances is the *self-fulfilling prophecy.* In an early and controversial study, Rosenthal and Jacobson (1968) found that teachers encouraged those students who they believed would flower and discouraged those they believed would not, even though the two groups of students did not differ in ability. To put their results in a different way, the teachers reaped what they had sown. Their expectations for the students' performances gave rise to teaching behaviors that eventually made the original expectation come true. Those students who were encouraged eventually performed better than those who were discouraged.

Because of several methodological flaws in the Rosenthal and Jacobson study (see Thorndike, 1968), Brophy and Good (1970) set out to study the self-fulfilling prophecy in more careful detail. In their research, the teachers were observed to demand better performance from those children for whom they had high expectations and were more likely to praise such performance when it was elicited. Conversely, they were more likely to accept poor performance from students for whom they held low expectations and were less likely to praise good performance from these students when it occurred. Brophy and Good interpreted their findings as supportive of the hypotheses of Rosenthal and Jacobson concerning teacher expectation effects and as indicative of the self-fulfilling prophecy.

Although individual student responses were the primary variables measured in these studies, additional studies indicate teacher expectations can also influence their own behavior and that within the student peer group. For instance, Brophy and Good (1970) demonstrated the quality of interaction between teachers and students differed according to teacher expectations; teachers who had high expectations for good performance from students praised them more frequently, allowed them more time to answer questions and offered fewer criticisms.

Another study by Flanders and Havumaki showed that expectations for performance can influence the climate of the classroom peer group. For example, teachers who praised randomly selected students and generally ignored others had a major impact on the emerging sociometric structure of the peer group. Those students who were praised by the teacher were more liked than those who were ignored. The emerging sociometric structure mirrored the reinforcement pattern exercised by the teacher. Thus, the teacher's behaviors were shown to influence the relationships and norms of the classroom peer group. These peer relationships, in turn, can take on power quite independent from teacher behavior after they are formed. Of course, teacher expectations can also have a reverse effect if the teacher is openly undervalued by the student peer group. There are many classrooms in which the norms and aspirations of the student group run contrary to the norms and goals of the teacher; a teacher's rewards in these cases may be viewed as demerits by the peer group.

Individuals do, of course, have some degrees of freedom in relation to their group, even within the most closely knit groups. Individual freedom increases, however, for students who have well-formed and secure self-concepts, for those who are older, and for those who have had more experience in various groups. Even though high school students come under strong influence from peers, they do have relatively greater leeway than elementary students to choose their friends or reference groups. The associations possible for elementary students, in contrast, are more limited. Elementary students do not have as many opportunities to move beyond their classmates or neighborhood peers to find alternative reference groups. Indeed, it is primarily through television, reading, and daydreaming that students can find relief from the pressure of the peer group. Usually students have little choice about their classmates or their teachers, but as they grow older and move out of school situations, they typically have more opportunities for relationships with others, gain more crystallized self-images, and are better able to resist negative influences of the group.

For schools to create individuals who view themselves as worthy human beings, teachers should be more concerned about their impact on students' self-concepts, both directly, as in the Brophy-Good study and indirectly through influencing the peer group, as in the research by Flanders and Havumaki. The old cliché of some educators that "I am not paid to make students happy, but to teach them subject matter" is not a justification for disrespectful and stereotyped behavior toward students, nor is it even a valid notion for teaching academic content. We believe that students will not easily grow in group situations that are characterized by I-It transactions, pervasive anxiety, and closedness. Some security, trust, and I-Thou interaction between participants in the classroom are ingredients essential to the humanization of our schools.

3. The impact of the school organization

Many innovations that are aimed at humanizing relationships in the classroom do not survive because the organizational setting in which they occur is not changed to accommodate them. Some features of the school's organization such as traditional norms, vested power interests, and formal budget restrictions often interfere with the viability of new practices. It would be difficult, for example, to implement an effective program of cross-age tutoring in a school where staff norms were in support of self-contained classrooms and where teachers were always supposed to be in control of students. In order for a peer tutoring program to flourish, staff norms about the boundaries of learning groups and student control, along with the definition of the roles of teacher and student, would have to be altered.

Vested power interests on the staff often come into play when attempts are made to change the patterns of participation at faculty meetings. There is little chance for basic changes in the group dynamics of staff meetings unless those in power are willing to change their own styles of influence. An overly rigid system of budget control also places high restraint on innovation. It may be more relevant, for example, for a teaching team to have a regular part-time aide in lieu of a budget for substitute teachers. If the formal budget category for substitutes cannot be altered to hire permanent paraprofessionals, the team's development and effectiveness could be impeded.

The organizational structure and psychological climate of the school are the stage on which the dynamics of its learning groups are played out. In particular, the school's formal goals, informal norms, staff relationships, and procedures for decision-making can have impact on the behaviors of teachers and students in the classroom. For example, these organizational processes provide a cultural framework in which the school's participants must find their own position. Second, the culture of the school subtly shapes each participant's view of schooling. It presents both teachers and students with a cognitive framework for defining proper teaching and learning. Third, particular behaviors such as smiling, pats on the back, or pushing take part of their meaning from the school's culture. Behaviors that are valuable and supportive in one school can take on negative meanings in another school.

The interface of the school organization and the classroom is experienced most intensively by the teachers, who simultaneously enact the roles of staff member and classroom leader. Teachers, being in continuous face-to-face interaction with students, are an integral part of learning groups while also participating as staff members within a professional culture with its own strong norms and procedures. They must attend to administrative directives, serve on committees or task forces in which the influence of colleagues is felt, attend staff meetings, interact in the teachers' lounge, and work full-time as classroom teachers. Achieving an integral professional self-concept is difficult for a teacher, especially when the norms of the staff are different from the typical values and behaviors of the students.

We believe that more humanized learning climates will develop in schools in which the teachers openly discuss their conflicts with students and with one another. Indeed, when the contemporary dilemma of living between the school bureaucracy and a learning community is discussed, the individual teacher can become more understandable to both colleagues and students. At some level of awareness, most staff members know about the pulls between formal role-taking and whole-person relationships. Unfortunately, current bureaucratic norms encourage teachers to collude informally in not admitting confusions and conflicts to one another or to their students. The result is staff relationships and classroom interaction which are in many respects artificial.

We can now be more specific about some features of the school organization that we think teachers should talk about with one another and with their students.

a. Educational goals

More than ever before, teachers are being exhorted to become more specific and precise about their teaching objectives. They are being encouraged, or pressured, as the case may be, to write their goals in behavioral terms. As long as affective outcomes are included in teachers' lists of objectives, we think that the emphasis on operational specificity can facilitate the humanization of learning climates. At the same time, we believe strongly that schools where administrators, teachers, students, *and* parents struggle *together* to list objectives will produce more humanized learning groups than schools in which the objectives are produced by the professionals only. It is unfortunate that in many schools the professional educators do not involve students and parents directly in the development of educational goals.

b. Procedural norms

In many schools, the rhetoric of educational goals is not matched by the behavioral routines that are actually carried out, and quite often both teachers and students know that these discrepancies exist. We believe that open discussion of these discrepancies will result in climates more supportive of humanized learning groups in schools.

For example, even though objectives such as "Students should learn how to carry out independent study programs" or "Students should learn to be responsible for themselves" may exist in the rhetoric of the staff, teachers may spend a great deal of time in maintaining very orderly behavior and restricting interactions within their classrooms. In many schools, teachers influence one another to pursue such custodial outlooks by reinforcing one another's controlling behaviors toward students. The new teacher, in particular, is the recipient of much advice from the more experienced teachers on how to control students effectively. Students also can communicate messages that lead teachers toward becoming more control-oriented. They may comment, "You certainly are a different sort of teacher" or "You probably won't last long here, you're too nice." Some students who have become comfortable and successful in the highly controlled classroom will encourage the teacher to restrain the deviant, misbehaving students. Other students who have adopted the traditional control norms of the school as their own will continue to behave in impersonal and restrained ways even as the teacher attempts to increase freedom.

We believe that such norms should be scheduled for discussion at staff meetings and within classrooms. We would like to see administrators, teachers, and students jointly diagnosing the discrepancies that exist between goals and procedural norms and attempting to reduce the discrepancies.

c. Staff friendship relationships

One of the most difficult organizational features for staff members to discuss is the way in which faculty friendships affect an individual staff member's feelings and energy levels. Clearly, friendships do affect adults and we believe that they can influence teacher-student interactions in at least two ways. First, the security, comfort, and stimulation that teachers receive from their colleagues increase the amount of personal esteem they bring to interactions with students and the amount of energy they have for working closely with students. Second, staff interactions offer models to students that represent the actual climate of the school. Some very observant students may attempt to emulate adult interactions in their peer relationships. Schools in which faculty relationships are tense, distant, and competitive also house isolated and anxious students. Even the relatively autonomous learning groups will reflect these negative staff relationships insofar as the teachers and students bring tension and loneliness into the classroom. Most important, teachers who do not share expectations for openness and trust among themselves are unlikely to try to implement such norms within their classrooms.

Consider an instance in which a teacher returns to the classroom from a committee meeting in which staff interaction has been tense and irritating. The frustration, anger, and dissatisfaction felt by such a teacher will undoubtedly affect his classroom behavior. Furthermore, it is unlikely that this uncomfortable teacher will easily reveal his negative feelings to the students. We believe, however, that the irritated teacher will encourage more I-Thou transactions in his class *if* he can reveal his feelings of frustration to his students. Unfortunately, in most schools norms that support such openness are not likely to be present in either staff or the student peer group.

We have gathered some empirical evidence to indicate that school staffs which learn skills of constructive openness and frankness translate these communicative procedures into their classroom teaching. Bigelow (1971) showed that teachers who begin to feel comfortable and collaborative with their colleagues can express feelings of insecurity and conflict, along with support, directly to their students. Moreover, the students seem to be encouraged to be more open within the

A human systems application

classroom after viewing improved friendship relationships among the teachers. Thus, it appears to us that school staffs that improve their friendship relationships are more likely to move toward more humanized learning groups than staffs that avoid working on the affective aspects of their interpersonal relationships.

d. Staff power relationships

Effective groups and organizations have members who think of themselves as having some power over what transpires. We believe that in schools, too, the equalization of power relationships is one means for humanizing both staff relationships and interaction in the classroom. Teachers or students who feel powerless will remove themselves from personalized encounters in the school and act out their frustrations and pleasures in fantasy or with others outside the school.

Generating a more dispersed decision-making pattern throughout a school can encourage more general involvement in school affairs. For example, the satisfaction of teachers with their principals is not simply associated with the help, guidance, and support that the principals offer. Teacher satisfaction is also related to their ability to influence the principal's actions and ideas. Similarly, students develop more favourable feelings about schools as they are able to determine more of what happens to them in the classroom.

In summary, we believe that specific features of the school organization influence the climates that arise in classrooms. Particularly, ways in which educational goals are set, procedural norms are confronted, friendship relationships are made public for problem-solving, and power relationships are equalized can have significant limiting or freeing effects on humanizing learning climates.

4. The impact of the school's environment

We believe that schools, more than most public organizations, are especially vulnerable to the pressures of their community. They are influenced by general economic conditions, prevailing cultural norms and values, salesmen from publishers, teacher-training institutions, community service clubs, local political organizations, and the mass media. Local community opinion, especially as it is understood by the school board, can greatly influence the curriculum offerings of the school. For example, courses in sex education or in Communism can be withheld from the school by a board if the board's members believe community opinion is strongly opposed to such courses. Indeed, the individual student's exposure to any innovative curriculum can be influenced by such forces from outside the school as the allocation of federal funds to the district, the school board's willingness to budget enough funds to continue the new curriculum, and a publisher's willingness to publish and market the new curriculum.

We wish to focus especially on three influences of the school's environment that we deem important: the rapidity of world-wide social change, the graphic presentation of news events by television, and the procedures for allocating funds for schooling.

a. Rapid social change

The pace of contemporary cultural change is so rapid that technologically, at least, American society has changed more in the past thirty years than in the 200 years preceding it, and current predictions estimate an even more rapid series of changes during the next thirty years. These rapid technological changes have been accompanied by deep cultural and psychological changes.

Significant cultural changes have occurred in the ecological and age distributions as well as the migration patterns of the American population, the nature of the economic system, the structure and operations of government, American international political activity, our religious and moral institutions, and many other areas of everyday life, including work, family life, and leisure activities. In fact, no segment of daily existence has remained untouched by these changes. Moreover, as we indicated in Chapter 1, these changes are not merely quantitative extensions of previous times; some are qualitative changes in the *zeitgeist* of our society.

The changing culture has demanded new forms of relationships for the individual, his small groups, and his larger associations. American society used to be more individuated; the individual and his small groups, whether in work, family, or leisure, were, politically and economically, largely autonomous. More recently, people have been called upon to accomplish tasks together; small groups and larger organizations have become interdependent. Projects for individuals are less easily available, so that the individual may more often feel protected as well as anonymous.

A human
systems
application

One result of this protected anonymity may well be an increased sense of bewilderment over the meaning and boundaries of the individual and his groups, and the resultant search for personal identity and human community. The blurring of interpersonal boundaries and the emphasis on work in larger and larger groups make it difficult to answer personal questions about meaning and direction, but at the same time these conditions seem to reassure the individual that he or she does not stand alone. The individual must depend to an extent on others for productivity, creativity, and social support.

An important feature of contemporary life is the rapid growth of scientific and technical knowledge. This tremendous knowledge explosion threatens to make cultural premises and standards of the past irrelevant and outmoded. The typical citizen is thus bombarded with evidence of new discoveries and continually forced to question his assumptions about man's social and physical needs, values, and behavior. These rapid changes have placed strong demands on young people to understand themselves, their society, and the physical world around them. As a result, more students are staying in school for longer periods of time, and more are entering college than did even a decade ago. In addition, fewer people completely drop out of schools of any kind now than a generation ago. For many adults, education no longer stops after formal schooling. Many industrial firms, for example, have their own extensive training programs, and many adult education programs are conducted by universities as well as private agencies. Continual increases in the numbers of students, along with changing individual goals and interests, put constant pressure on schools to change.

b. The impact of television

Television has now become the most prominent means of receiving information for young people. It has been pointed out, for example, that, on a yearly basis, television contact hours now generally exceed school contact hours, and that television can be much more influential than school. The cognitive gains shown in studies of children who view *Sesame Street* provide some backing for this estimate of the importance of television. And when the intense concentration of many children viewing television is contrasted with the boredom of many students in the classroom, the power of television is even more obvious.

Even the person who just casually watches television for entertainment can gain much incidental information about American society from it. Perhaps most significant are the ideas that young people acquire from television concerning the changing social structure, life styles, and ethics regarding interpersonal relationships. These television influences are prodding schools to change in concert with the changing culture.

A recent personal experience was illuminating to us about the importance of television in America. A few summers ago we traveled back to Patricia Schmuck's birthplace in Ontonagon, Michigan. Our first impressions, upon arriving, were that few cultural changes had taken place. There were no new roads or freeways, surprisingly few new houses, and the school not only was housed in the same building but also was the same size. At first glance, Pat's home town seemed to have maintained its 1940s culture.

The most prominent physical change was that virtually every house had a television antenna. And of course after talking with old and young alike, and reflecting on our conversations, we concluded that deep cultural changes had occurred even in this out-of-the-way place. The thoughts, concerns, and behaviors of its citizens were surprisingly similar to those of other Americans. We heard conversations over the Vietnam war, poverty, the problem of drug use among youth, and the lack of meaningful work. Whereas the Ontonagon of the 1940s, even with radio, was generally isolated and locally oriented, the Ontonagon of the 1970s was nationally and even internationally oriented. Television, with its vivid pictures, had come even to this seemingly insulated community and with it came the rest of the world.

c. Funds for education

Another significant external force on schools is related to the ways in which educational funds are distributed. Although the objective of equal educational opportunity is part of our rhetoric, the allocation of funds for schooling has typically been biased in our country. Primarily the rural and urban ghetto students have not received the same resources for schooling as wealthy urban and suburban children.

Today, the biased allocation of funds for schooling is being challenged before the courts. In Wise's book, *Rich Schools, Poor Schools* (1969), he argued that "the absence of equal educational opportunity within a state, as evidenced by unequal pupil expenditures, may constitute a denial by the state of the equal protection of its laws." Since Wise's study, several cases have been brought to the courts, and in California, in particular, Wise's position has received court support.

We hasten to point out that large per-pupil expenditures do not necessarily improve the quality of education nor facilitate more humanized learning climates. As we have written before, schools do not encourage more I-Thou transactions by focusing solely on introducing new resources from the outside. Unfortunately, some of our most dehumanized schools may also be the wealthiest and some of our most lively and humane, the poorest. The latter point is well explicated in Nat Hentoff's (1966) account of a very forceful and committed staff which operated an excitingly humane school in an inner city ghetto under very poor economic and physical conditions.

Although it is true that large amounts of money do not necessarily facilitate humanized interactions in schools, it is also true that insufficient funds can place major barriers in the way of improving a school's climate. Many underfinanced schools have inexperienced and insecure teachers, outdated curriculum materials, few special services, and students who have not learned to value intellectual competence. Sexton (1961) showed that schools with low levels of funding tend to receive few services, are overcrowded, experience many absences among both teachers and students, and have relatively low-quality teaching. Quite often in poor schools teachers feel harrassed, students feel disregarded, and nearly everyone feels negative toward academic learning.

The students who are now entering American schools are very different in their cognitive skills, concerns, and aspirations from those of just a few decades ago. The environmental influences discussed above have been most widely responsible for these changes in students. Our schools should take these student changes into account in their programs and curricula. After all, as we noted before, the most important task of a school is to produce "outgoing resources" in the form of psychologically well-integrated persons who have the skills not only to survive comfortably but also to contribute to others. Since the process of enabling persons to achieve such qualities is so extremely important, it is very important that our schools, in themselves, become more thoroughly and deeply humanized.

But if schools are to become more humanized, the persons who attempt to change them must take into consideration the complexities and nuances of school organizations. Too many valiant change efforts have failed because they did not take into account the systemic features of schools. For changes to be stable and viable at any one of the four system levels, changes will have to occur almost simultaneously at the other three.

Since most previous attempts to humanize schools have focused on changing the attitudes and skills of teachers, we will turn next to a discussion of the systemic barriers that keep programs of teacher change from humanizing the learning climates of our schools.

SUMMARY OF CHAPTER 3

Psychological applications have not humanized schools because they have been either too narrowly focused or piecemeal. A school's entire culture needs changing, not just the individual administrators, teachers, or students. It is the daily human interactions arising spontaneously and naturally within the school that must be the focus for improvement. Whole-person relationships and I-Thou transactions are likely to flourish only if comprehensive changes in interpersonal influence, attraction, communication, and norms occur simultaneously at the four system levels of school culture—the individual, the learning group, the school organization itself, and its social environment.

To be successful, modications must occur at all four of these system levels. Six networks of influence involving these four levels can be used as guides for making plans to humanize school cultures. These are: (1) student influence on the learning group, (2) teacher influences on the learning group, (3) principal influences on the school organization, (4) the impact of learning groups on their individual members, (5) the impact of the school organization, and (6) the impact of the school's social environment. Chapters 5 through 8 propose how to make changes in these six networks of influence. If schools are to become more humanized, those of us who attempt to change them should take these four system levels and six networks of influence into consideration.

ANNOTATED BIBLIOGRAPHY FOR CHAPTER 3

Backman, Carl, and Paul Secord. 1968. *A Social Psychological View of Education*. New York: Harcourt, Brace, and World, Inc.

A human
systems
application

This book discusses the various system levels of schools, from the psychodynamics of students to community influences, attempting to reveal how these levels of human activity relate and interact. While it emphasizes primarily the structure and function of classroom groups and neglects the larger school organization, it is a well written and a carefully documented presentation of the social psychological dynamics of schools and their effects on individual participants.

Buckley, Walter. 1967. *Sociology and Modern Systems Theory.* Englewood Cliffs, N.J.: Prentice-Hall, Inc.

This book is the most basic and comprehensive source of our conceptual thinking about the human systems application. It also forms the intellectual background for our thinking about school organizations and the theory behind training in organization development. (See Chapter 6.) Buckley does not write directly about schools but does discuss many kinds of organizations and group structures. We highly recommend this book to the serious student of the human systems application.

Guskin, Alan, and Samuel Guskin. 1970. *A Social Psychology of Education.* Menlo Park, Ca.: Addison-Wesley Publishing Co.

A basic text on the social psychology of education, the book's strength resides in its discussions of interpersonal perception and persuasion, group conformity and deviance, and intergroup conflict, all in relation to schools. Almost throughout, the emphasis is on explaining the dynamics of a school's social situation. Only the last chapter is devoted to demonstrating how such understanding may help to improve the school.

Johnson, David. 1970. *The Social Psychology of Education.* New York: Holt, Rinehart, and Winston, Inc.

Another basic text that explains social psychology to educators, this book applies examples and illustrations of the principles of social psychology to school situations. However, in total the book explains more about social psychology than it does about schools. The book's fourteen chapters are organized in terms of topics such as attitudes, leadership, norms, and cooperation-competition. The last two chapters are given over to explaining classroom climate and planned organizational change in schools.

Katz, Daniel, and Robert Kahn. 1966. *The Social Psychology of Organizations.* New York: John Wiley and Sons.

Already a classic in the behavioral sciences, this book applies theory and research from human systems thinking and group dynamics to large-scale organizations. Although the authors do not address school organizations directly, each of their chosen topics—organizational roles, power and authority, the flow of information, decision-making, leadership, and change—bears on organizational life in educational systems. Their discussion of organizational effectiveness is very similar to our concept of schools as resource-using systems.

March, James, and Herbert Simon. 1958. *Organizations.* New York: John Wiley and Sons.

The emphasis of this book is on industrial organizations rather than schools, but it does offer a thorough analysis of organizational life from a human systems point of view.

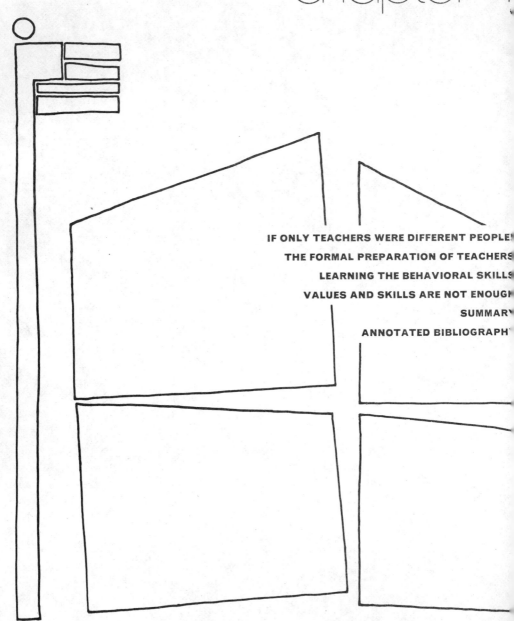

chapter 4

Barriers to
the influence
of teachers

Most attempts to humanize schools have focused too narrowly, taking into account only one or two important features of the school while ignoring other critical variables that continually influence and interact with the change effort. Indeed, the list of partial and incomplete change attempts is long and noteworthy.

Efforts of clinical psychologists to ameliorate certain student behaviors, for instance, have tended to accentuate the psychodynamics of the individual student or teacher and to ignore the dynamics of the classroom peer group. Similarly, mental health consultation with teachers has been aimed primarily at improving the teachers' knowledge of mental health and personality psychology without also helping teachers to analyze their relationships with students or to cope with the organizational circumstances in which they must apply their knowledge. Some consulting psychologists—especially those who lead personal growth and encounter groups—have focused almost entirely on the teachers' feelings *without* linking new teacher insights to revisions in classroom skills and instructional behavior. Even those T-group trainers who attempt to integrate the cognitive and affective features of teaching often have not taken into account the organizational procedures necessary to make classroom changes enduring.

Many of the change attempts of experimentally oriented educational psychologists have been even more narrow and partial. Curriculum innovators that champion the use of programmed instruction, for example, have often ignored the emotional and cognitive reactions of teachers and students to the required routines. Furthermore, psychologists who advocate behavior modification strategies have tended to ignore the important motivational differences among individual students and teachers. The 1972 edition of *A Consumer's Guide to Educational Innovation* (Smith *et. al.*) alphabetically lists and describes about fifty different innovations occurring in American schools. In the entire book there is no mention of altering the relationships between people in school as a focus for change.

Although efforts at modifying the organizational structures of schools seem on the surface to be more comprehensive than the above-mentioned innovations, these change attempts, too, have been limited in scope. For instance, proponents of the "multi-unit elementary school" (see Klausmeier, Quilling, and Sorenson, 1971) have made advances in modifying organizational structure and curriculum, but they have not paid enough attention to educating professional personnel to work comfortably and efficiently within the new organizations. They have given very little attention, in fact, to the emotional reactions of staff members grappling with innovative ways of working together. Conversely, many of the alternative or free schools have emphasized interpersonal feelings and reactions without paying enough attention to efficient organizational functioning.

The complexities of school organization are seldom fathomed by the intervener because schools are multi-leveled systems. The individuals who work together in tutoring pairs, classroom groups, committees, departmental units, cabinets, and boards learn to behave according to the traditional norms, rules, and procedures of those subsystems. These subsystems, in turn, are continually being influenced by the larger, more encompassing systems of the school district and the community.

Attempts to humanize learning climates fall short, then, because they do not encompass procedures for changing these various system levels at the same time. Change attempts, for instance, should consider both the cognitive and the affective aspects of the individuals involved, the small work groups through which the individuals carry out organizational goals, features of the organizational culture itself that encourage and impede change, and the larger organizational and community environments and how they relate to the change effort. Any major effort to humanize learning climates must include work on most of the system components and levels of the school and their relationships to one another.

This chapter discusses how specific kinds of barriers prevent the attempts of teachers toward humanization. Teachers are, at least potentially, the most powerful leverage point for changing other school system components. Teachers hold "link-pin" positions between the important components of the school—the students, the curriculum, and the administration. Moreover, they interpret and implement the curriculum for students and so implement the goals of the administration and the community. Students, administrators, and parents, in turn, respond to teacher actions in the classroom.

We will use a systems perspective to discuss the influences on teachers and the barriers that prevent them from creating more humanized learning environments. First we will discuss the common suggestion that schools would be healthier places if the kinds of people who teach in them were different. We do not agree with this point of view *as it usually is explicated*; we suggest *instead* that the socialization processes involved often discourage teachers from building whole person relationships and so from becoming *personally* involved with others in their classrooms and schools.

IF ONLY TEACHERS WERE DIFFERENT PEOPLE!

Teachers are the most frequent scapegoats for those who criticize public education. Although many essays and research reports have sought to specify the inadequacies of teachers and more than a decade of empirical research in educational psychology has gone into attempts to predict who would be "good teachers," most efforts have led nowhere. Many critics think of teachers as of inferior intelligence: they teach because they do not have the motivation or intelligence to find a better job. It is said, "If you can't do, teach; if you can't teach, teach teachers."

Teachers also have been characterized as anti-intellectual, as the bulwark of the middle class, and as the Babbitts of American society. Lieberman (1956), for example, presented the following account of the social background of teachers:

> The majority of teachers are coming from homes which are culturally unpromising if not impoverished. They are coming from homes in which light popular books and magazines or none at all are the rule. If the future teacher's family subscribes to any magazines, it is likely to be *Collier's, Saturday Evening Post* or the *Reader's Digest*. It is not likely to be *Harpers, Atlantic Monthly,*

Freeman, Saturday Review of Literature, American Mercury, Reporter, or any other periodical devoted to serious writing on political, social or cultural topics. The families from which teachers come are generally inactive both politically and in community affairs. Their social activities are likely to be confined to fraternal orders and lodges such as the Masons, Shriners, Order of the Eastern Star, Elks, Moose, International Order of Odd Fellows, or Knights of Columbus. Families in the upper-lower or lower middle class usually have rather limited experience in the fine arts such as music or painting. Attending movies, playing cards, listening to radio and watching television, and visiting the neighbors are the most popular recreational outlets for these classes. (P. 466.)

Lieberman has, we think, accurately characterized the home life of many teachers in 1956 (and even today); indeed his portrait describes well our own family background along with the backgrounds of many of our professional colleagues and friends. It is a mistake, however, to assume that teachers today are solely influenced by the anti-intellectual values of their lower middle class parents.

The defamation of teachers' characters dates from very early in educational literature. In 1911 Coffman conducted a survey of teachers because "the kind of people we have in teaching necessarily affects the kind of teaching we get." He proposed a genetic theory to explain who would become good and bad teachers, and advocated that more teachers should be recruited from the upper strata of society because upper class people, he thought, were intellectually superior to their lower class counterparts. Although Coffman's genetic theory is no longer a popular explanation for good teaching, the hypothesis that the teacher's social and personality characteristics make a significant difference to overall educational quality is still a prominent belief.

It is important to point out that the general characteristics of those who become teachers have changed somewhat over the years. The mean age of teachers, for instance, is decreasing; there are now more men teaching in America than ever before; teachers have more formal training than ever before; there has been a gradual increase of non-whites entering the profession; and the primary source of income for many families is now coming from the teaching salary (which has improved over the years), whereas previously a teacher's income was more often a supplement to the primary wage. As a group, American teachers are beginning to represent more closely American society in general. If our portrait of an emerging people-oriented culture is accurate, more persons will be entering the teaching profession who value other persons and relationships between people as much as academic subject matter and achievement. We believe that *who* teaches is more a *reflection* of our changing American society than it is a suitable *explanation* for the crises that face public education.

Another popular explanation for the failure of schools to change is the "resistance to change" on the part of individual professionals. This social psychological theory explains that professionals resist proposed changes because of such personal matters as insecurity about their positions, concern about revealing their inadequacies, and the fear of unknown consequences.

Gross *et al.* (1970) have criticized this theory as too narrow and simplistic to explain the variety of features that cause the failure of an educational innovation. In their study, they found that staff innovations failed not because of the emotional resistance of teachers but because of inadequate attempts to support the innovation at other operational levels. As examples, Gross *et al.* mentioned (1) the lack of professional behavioral skills to implement an innovative plan with which teachers *agreed;* (2) the lack of clear communication between staff members attempting to solve incidental problems; (3) inadequate leadership from the principal; and (4) incongruities in organizational arrangements: for example, continuation of the traditional ringing of bells to designate time periods when the curriculum was supposed to be fluid and open, and continuation of customary procedures when an innovation had been built around the idea of self-selection and self-direction for the students. The attempt to blame the failure of innovations on teacher resistance ignores the fact that very often the climate of school culture can defeat even the most committed individuals.

The belief that *individual* teachers can implement school change is further reflected in the emphasis on employing minority teachers to work with students of the same background. The assumption is that a teacher of the same social background as his students can better understand them, diagnose their educational needs, and avoid the cultural barriers that arise between persons of different background. Several studies have sought to find correlations between a teacher's social class and his educational values and teaching behavior, but reviews of such research have not shown that social class is an important variable in influencing teachers' ideologies or teaching methods. (See Charters, 1963.) Nevertheless, broader social goals are served by actively recruiting teachers from different ethnic backgrounds. We heartily support the current attempt in many American school districts to reduce institutional racism. Indeed, the hiring of more minority group administrators, teachers, aides, and paraprofessionals represents a desirable step toward increasing the ethnic pluralism in school staffs. However, we do not believe that recruitment of teachers of varying social classes or ethnic backgrounds will, *by itself*, humanize the learning climates of our schools.

It must be remembered that *many* kinds of students are descriminated against by teachers of all races, classes, and political persuasions. Many teachers react more harshly, for example, to boys than girls; they often have different expectations of students based on the student's I.Q. or Achievement Test scores; they enter into more overt conflict with students who disrupt classroom procedures; and they give more negative and punitive response to students who do not perform their academic work successfully or punctually, or to those who do not adhere to their image of the ideal student. We believe that a teacher's partiality to particular students cannot be explained entirely by his or her social background or personality characteristics. We look instead to those influences that have formed the standards and norms of the teaching profession itself: the formal and informal preparation and socialization that most teachers receive. These processes may wield the greatest influence over the values and behaviors teachers will employ in the classroom.

THE FORMAL PREPARATION OF TEACHERS

Some analysts agree that college tends to offer a liberating and humanizing experience; for example, persons who finish sixteen years of schooling tend to be less provincial in their views about politics, religion, and social relations than those who terminate their formal education with high school or before. Some analysts point to the formal curriculum as providing a broadened exposure to the world, while others are not so sanguine about the influence of the college curriculum. Sanford (1962), for example, wrote of the dearth of studies on the effects of college training and said, "It is as if there were a conspiracy of silence on this point, as if educators well know . . . that very little of the content of college courses is retained three or four years after graduation." (P. 806.) Sanford acknowledged that college students do alter their values and views of the world, but he pointed to factors of the college experience other than the formal curriculum, such as the interpersonal interactions within the university community, as the most potent influences on the development of student values.

Hughes *et al.* (1962) studied students in a medical school which has often been characterized as the most prominent illustration of curriculum rigidity and structured content in American education. They showed that the students themselves informally decided what they would learn and often ignored faculty decisions, especially when they did not reflect views of what was important to learn.

The influence of student culture has been noted by other observers of college campuses. For example, the social activists of the 1960s were often described as being in revolt against their parents' values and behavior, but Flacks's (1967) study of social activists presented a rebuttal to this assumption. He showed that many of the early activists came from homes in which the parents also were politically radical or at least liberal. He predicted, however, that the movement would spread to new recruits who had more traditional and conservative backgrounds as the liberal protest movements became the dominant culture of the college campuses.

An anecdote illustrates how Flacks's prophecy has been realized. Patricia Schmuck's sister, some eight years younger, entered the University of Michigan just after we had received our graduate degrees. During our undergraduate years the Students for a Democratic Society had been formed on the Michigan campus. We participated in some of the activities of SDS along with those of the then integrated Student Non-Violent Coordinating Committee. We also became involved in civil rights demonstrations when they were just beginning to be viewed as legitimate by citizens in general. During an evening with a few of Pat's sister's friends we were surprised to be placed in the role of "historians of the movement" of activities which had taken place only a few years earlier. To these young college students, social protest had always been present on the Michigan campus and it was virtually incomprehensible to them that the decisions we had made just a few years earlier—such as whether to picket or use the methods of civil disobedience—were necessary to make. For them, picket lines were prestigious, jail could be a badge of honor, the SDS was an established (even traditional) institution on campus, and issues of racial injustice, war, and peace were items for consideration by the student government, and not just the preoccupations of a few fringe groups of social activists.

The 1970s, we think, have ushered in an already somewhat different student culture, but conversions to a movement of greater radicalism still prevail. The dominant cultural norms on campuses now seem to be influencing students toward values of humanism, equality, human rights, the search for self, and the sanctity of the individual. These are the issues which college students confront daily, despite occasional retreats into their formal studies. Reich illustrated the process of rapid conversion in college clearly in *The Greening of America* (1971).

> What happens is simply this: in a brief span of months, a student, seemingly conventional in every way, changes his haircut, his clothes, his habits, his interests, his political attitudes, his way of relating to other people, in short, his whole way of life.... The clean-cut hard-working man who despises radicals and hippies can become one himself with breathtaking suddenness. Over and over again, an individual for whom a conversion seemed impossible, a star athlete, an honor student, the small-town high school boy with the American Legion scholarship, transforms himself into a drug-using, long-haired, peace-loving 'freak." Only when he puts on a headband and plays unexpectedly skillful touch football or basketball, or when a visitor to his old room back home catches sight of his honor society certificate, is his earlier life revealed. (P. 240.)

These same humanitarian and libertarian views are also found among students preparing to become teachers, although there are those who argue that teacher trainees are inferior by pointing to data which indicate that students in schools of education, along with other applied fields, have lower grade point averages and lower intelligence scores than students in more "theoretical" fields. In 1954 Wolfe presented contrasting data to show that schools of education share equally with other fields in attracting students who are ranked in the top fifth of their class. We expect the data would be similar in the 1970s. Furthermore, even though there may be some differences between students who attend colleges of education and those who are enrolled in liberal arts colleges, it should be pointed out that colleges of education do not prepare a large proportion of those who join the teaching profession anyway. Many students remain enrolled in liberal arts colleges while meeting minimum requirements for state certification. In fact, according to a survey by the American Council on Education conducted in 1967, less than half of the students who then planned to become teachers intended to enroll in colleges of education. It should be clear, then, that liberal arts colleges are responsible in large part for the formal education of persons entering the teaching profession.

But even if we focus on the types of students enrolled in schools of education, it is instructive to learn that they too hold libertarian, democratic, and humanistic values about the educative process. The data in support of this come from researchers using the Minnesota Teacher Attitude Inventory (MTAI), an instrument used in numerous studies to measure attitudes of teachers toward teacher-pupil relationships and to predict how satisfied a person might be in the profession of teaching. The manual for the MTAI states:

> ... the attitudes of teachers toward children and school work can be measured with high reliability, and they are significantly correlated with the teacher-pupil relationships found in the teacher's classroom. ... It [the test] is designed to measure those attitudes of a teacher and [predict] how well he will get along with pupils in interpersonal relationships, and indirectly how well satisfied he will be with teaching as a vocation. (Cook, 1951, P. 3.)

Trainees in education who took the MTAI preferred classrooms that were supportive and permissive and that allowed a great deal of student freedom in work and behavior. Unfortunately, other studies using the MTAI have shown that after students have taught in a classroom for awhile there is a dramatic change in their ideologies. Scores on the MTAI show a decrease in favorable attitudes toward students and an increase in concerns over discipline and meeting academic standards. The switch occurs sometimes during student teaching or more often during the first year of teaching. (See Charters, 1963.)

LEARNING THE BEHAVIORAL SKILLS

Why don't practicing teachers utilize the humanistic values that they bring with them from college? Is the university merely a stopping-off-place during adolescence, prior to taking on the harsh responsibilities of the working world? Is it inappropriate and unfeasible to believe that students can be trusted and worth knowing and caring about, and that the curriculum should be determined at least partly by students? Are these merely abstract ideas emanating from the isolation of a comfortable and secure university? Our answer is that humanistic ideas for education can be valid and practical, but that the preservice training of many teachers fails to provide them with the classroom skills to activate their humanistic values.

1. Traditional preservice education

Most teacher-training programs have been highly cognitive, structured, and impersonal; little experimental learning has been offered in them except for the short period of practice teaching which typically occurs late in the teacher's preservice experience. For instance, teacher trainees are taught that democracy is good and proper, yet in their training they experience few actual democratic educational procedures. They are taught to value helping students to become self-starting and self-determining, yet they receive few opportunities to implement this idea in the classroom. As early as 1904, Dewey wrote about such current deficiencies in teacher training. The teacher, he said, does not receive:

> ...the training which affords psychological insight—which enables him to judge promptly (and therefore almost automatically) the kind and mode of subject-matter which the pupil needs at a given moment to keep his attention moving forward effectively and healthfully. He does know, however, that he must maintain order, that he must keep the attention of the pupils fixed upon his own questions, suggestions, instructions, and remarks...for that, after all, was the way he was taught...[and] what he sees other teachers doing who are more experienced and successful in keeping order than he is; and the injunctions and directions given him by others.
>
> ...Here we have the explanation, in considerable part at least, of the dualisms, the unconscious duplicity, which is one of the chief evils of the teaching profession. There is an enthusiastic devotion of certain principles of lofty theory in the abstract—principles of self-activity, self-control...and there is a school practice taking little heed of the official pedagogic creed. Theory and practice do not grow together out of and into the teacher's personal experience.

Although what Dewey wrote almost seventy years ago is still true today, we should not simply place the responsibility on the teachers, at least without thorough analysis of the problem of translating theory into practice. Teaching is a very complex, challenging, and often arduous job. The demands of the students, their parents, the curriculum, and the administration are often overwhelming to the neophyte teacher.

First, it can be very tension-producing to face a group of students with the dual responsibilities of helping each of them to learn something important and maintaining adequate and reasonable control. Moreover, to complicate matters, young adults typically enter the teaching profession with high hopes and aspirations; they want to provide valuable experiences for students and at the same time to act in loving, supportive, exciting, and challenging ways toward them. But the teaching tasks are so demanding and complex that new teachers face serious ambivalence over how they should behave with their students and what they themselves need as developing young adults. A teacher's personal needs for support, security, and affection can become so paramount in the first days of teaching that he often fails to live up to his personal expectations and, as a result, feels inadequate to fulfill the needs of his students.

This view is supported by research done by Walberg (1967), who indicated that an important concommitant of a person's first teaching experience is a dramatic reduction in his self-esteem. Understandably, new teachers, with diminishing self-esteem, fall back on their own most primitive ideas about teaching (many of which come from their memories about their own student days) or they look to their colleagues as the models for optimal teaching and for survival in their new and seemingly demeaning professional life.

Apparently, the values that teacher trainees develop as a consequence of university studies and life experience are later gradually replaced by values and attitudes characteristic of their school staffs. The dynamics of this transition from the prevailing norms of the college culture to those of the "harsh realities" of the school are illustrated by a case study written by Iannoccone in the early sixties. He asked a university class of student teachers to keep a diary of their experiences in practice teaching and then he analyzed these diaries for the significant features of the transition revealed within them. His resulting analysis delineates several key transitional events. At the beginning of the program, for example, the student-teachers use the pronouns "we" when discussing the university personnel and "they" when writing about the public school personnel. By the end of the year of practice teaching, as we would expect, the referents were reversed: "we" referred to the public school personnel and "they" to the university faculty. Other more substantial signs of the transition were changes in attitude toward particular teaching methods. During her fifth week of kindergarten teaching, for example, one student teacher wrote it was difficult to "put down all the horrors or surprises I have felt," a reaction to experiences which ranged from seeing her supervising teacher shake a child into "behaving correctly" to seeing the teacher use valuable instructional time to clean up the children's paint equipment. By the end of the year, however, she was justifying those "horrors and surprises," as "being good for the children." Later in the year, the same student teacher wrote, "Now I understand how important it is to *force* some students to behave and to keep the room clean. These are important lessons for the students to learn."

Iannoccone ends by summarizing what values the student teachers had acquired during their practice teaching experiences. He believes that they learned how to ask questions so they would get the "correct answers," and, furthermore, that they learned how to arrange classroom activities so that their students would not get "out of control." He also wrote that the student teachers learned reasonable ways of justifying their punitive behavior of students who did not comply with school standards. Indeed, the student teachers believed, by the end of the year, that punishment for nonconformists was proper and good. Thus, according to Iannoccone, student teaching offers a powerful socialization experience for learning to appreciate and use teaching methods that help solve inconveniences of a lack of control and discipline in the classroom. At the same time student teaching moves future teachers away from the attempt to behave congruently with humanistic ideology.

The curriculum offered during preservice training typically does not help prepare future teachers to behave in ways that will facilitate the development of I-Thou transactions in their classroom. In fact, the curriculum as presented often mounts barriers to humanization because it omits experiences that could help teachers relate the values of democracy, self-selection, and self-determination to congruent classroom behavior. Unfortunately, much of the formal content of traditional college courses is mostly cognitive, and even when affective learning is offered, adequate links to instructional behavior are not developed and practiced.

Fortunately, there are a few alternative models of teacher education that do relate humanistic ideals to the behavioral skills necessary to implement them. It is in programs like these that formal training could enhance the skills needed to establish more humanized learning climates in our schools.

2. Alternative models of teacher education

At least three types of preservice training programs appear to be promising possibilities for realizing more humanistic teaching. These types are: (1) programs on urban education with new methods for training, (2) preparation for teachers within the "clinical school," and (3) university-based training programs in which humanistic concepts and experiential learning are linked in unique ways. Although the many on-going programs within these three categories have different purposes and methods, they are similar in providing some continuity among cognitive development, affective learning, and the behavioral skills that teachers need to humanize their classrooms.

a. Urban education

A primary assumption of many urban education programs is that the classroom itself is the most important training ground in preparing future teachers. The urban education programs we know about use classroom experiences as their focal point, with academic courses supporting such experiences but of secondary importance to them. Most urban education programs also emphasize a gradual and progressive movement toward taking over the teaching role. As a typical example, a program suggested by Rivlin (1965) advocated that college juniors work first as community service aides for from three to six hours per week and then as paraprofessional school aides for the same number of hours. Rivlin also advocated that during their senior year the trainees work for at least three hours per day as assistant teachers. Finally, to round out the preparation, Rivlin argued that the fifth year should involve an internship with full teaching responsibility accompanied by continuous supervision. Lectures and seminars were to run concurrently with these practical experiences. Although some of these academic experiences were to take place in the university, an important part of the program involved a teacher-education center housed in the public schools and staffed by both university and school personnel.

Urban education programs such as the one described by Rivlin have flourished since the late fifties. For additional information about such programs, see Reissman (1962), Cuban (1964), and Usdan and Bertolaet (1966). They have featured a training strategy which specifies that at each step of preparation the trainees should deal with their affective concerns about students and themselves, clarify their own values, and discuss and practice new behavioral skills. They also emphasize that most teacher preparation should take place in actual classrooms and that continuous feedback should be available to the trainees as they attempt new behaviors with students.

b. The clinical school

The second promising program, typically referred to as training in the "clinical school," also makes heavy use of the facilities of the public school for training. It is similar to the urban teacher education centers described above insofar as the responsibilities for training are given over to a clinical supervisor who has a joint appointment in the university and the public school. Adams High School in Portland, Oregon, has operated a clinical school. Dr. John Parker (1971), the clinical supervisor at Adams, viewed the program as being analogous to the "teaching hospital." Just as in the teaching hospital, many of the regular services of the clinical school are performed by trainees who are continuously monitored and supervised. During their residence at the school, the student-teachers participate in informal seminars and discussions with their supervising teachers, and they take part of their formal academic training right in the school building. At Adams, since differentiated staffing is a feature of the school, the regular teachers often meet in groups to decide on educational practices and procedures, and the teacher trainees also have an opportunity to be part of the team. This feature is important because it encourages continuous dialogue within the staff, in contrast to the isolation that arises in schools with a self-contained classroom organization.

At the very least, the clinical school could be a place where teacher trainees would spend one semester as student teachers, receiving their formal training during that term right in the school. This would represent some improvement over the separation that now typically exists between the public schools and the university. Variations on this basic concept of a clinical school are almost limitless. The clinical school could, for instance, serve as a context for training such future teachers as paraprofessionals who have not followed the traditional route to teacher certification and those such as teaching interns and participants in Teacher Corps who have completed college but have not taken the courses required for certification. The clinical school could also serve as a base for implementing cross-age tutoring. For instance, students could receive training for teaching other students under the guidance of a supervisor who might even be a teacher trainee. Finally, the clinical school could offer a practice ground for future counselors, administrators, consultants, curriculum developers, and educational researchers.

Unfortunately, the public schools have not been considered heretofore as settings in which to prepare future teachers. To create a school with the dual purpose of educating students *and* teachers requires new vision, planning, and action. Above all, it requires new norms regarding who does the teaching. For instance, it would take a major shift in thinking about instruction to view teaching as something all persons, including students, service personnel, and educators, should be doing. Indeed, we believe that students should be encouraged to act as teachers by tutoring other students as well as by giving feedback to adult teachers about their classroom practices. The clinical school of the future, if it is to be humanized, will require clearer and more authentic dialogue between staff members on the one hand and between staff and students on the other.

c. University programs

The third type of promising teacher training program is found in universities that provide for training experiences in public school settings and that provide a coherent theory of education based on the humanistic ideals of democracy, self-selection, and whole-person relationships. For example, the University of North Dakota's New School for Behavioral Studies in Education is modeling its training of teachers (many of whom have taught for many years but have not completed certification requirements) on the kinds of humanistic perspectives that the faculty advocates for the public schools. (See Resnick, 1971.) The faculty is attempting to prepare the teachers to manage open classrooms and, as one means to achieve this, has "opened" the college itself. The North Dakota innovators believe in the truth of the adage, "Teachers will teach as they were taught," by providing a living example of what can be done to humanize the classroom.

A different sort of program, designed primarily for undergraduates, is in operation at Weber State College in Ogden, Utah. It is similar to the urban education format described above insofar as it is designed to introduce students gradually into the public schools with incremental increases in responsibility and a continuous emphasis on instructional experiences as the primary basis of cognitive learning. Many other universities, such as Harvard and Massachusetts, offer fifth-year programs for teachers who have completed their traditional college requirements in liberal arts colleges. Generally these programs, like the one at Weber State, make use of sequential instructional experiences starting with observing and moving through tutoring to managing an entire class alone.

In our brief description of these new programs we have attempted to show that a teacher's formal training does not have to stand as a barrier to implementing humanistic values. Formal preservice training, in fact, can be an effective vehicle for teaching future teachers to implement humanistic values. The successful programs, from our point of view, do not advocate anything different for teacher education than we are advocating for the education of young people—that students of any age are respected, that their rights are considered, that their psychological needs and desires are important, and that they are expected to negotiate and collaborate with their teachers in determining the goals and methods of their education. We believe that future teachers who have experienced these kinds of humanized teacher-training situations will have a head start in feeling competent and comfortable in entering into whole-person relationships and I-Thou transactions with their students.

3. Continuing education

Teacher education does not end after the Bachelor's Degree is gained, nor is it complete at the point of official certification. Virtually all teachers continue some form of advanced training after they have been teaching. Many states, in fact, specify that a required number of credit hours beyond the Bachelor's Degree must be completed before permanent certification is granted. Moreover, many school districts provide monetary incentives for teachers so that they will acquire additional formal training. Most school districts provide some inservice training days for their teachers, and many large school districts have their own inservice programs. Unfortunately, many programs in continuing education for teachers have weaknesses comparable to those of preservice courses in that they are primarily cognitive, have little realistic connection to actual classroom problems, and are often designed for administrators, curriculum specialists, or outside experts who are not very empathic with the daily problems of classroom teachers. Teachers usually have little to say in determining what will be studied, how they will study it, or how such courses will be evaluated.

Some of the training programs that were designed during the widespread dissemination of the "new math curriculum" in the 1960s are apt examples of the lack of involvement of teachers in their own training. During this innovative push, the teachers implicitly were viewed only as conveyors of the new curriculum: instruments that required retooling in order to convey the rudiments of the new curriculum. The new math was hailed as the greatest single innovation of the 1960s; as a so-called "teacher-proof" strategy, it was supposed to help young people think like mathematicians and to help preserve America's international position in the "science race." Some critics did argue that the new math curricula had been insufficiently evaluated or claimed that these were only old techniques in new packaging, but such critics wielded little influence and most school districts nevertheless moved to adopt a "new math" curriculum. Inservice workshops were devised, pamphlets were written and disseminated, and summer college courses were implemented to help prepare teachers to use the new curriculum. What teachers already knew, or believed they knew, was considered both irrelevant and potentially detrimental to implementing the new math effectively. Teachers were instructed in different base number systems, in the arbitrary nature of rules concerning computation, and most importantly in the idea that mathematics was both a logical and a creative process. Teachers were presented with statistics about the many students with poor understanding of math; they were told about how the schools had been deficient in their math curricula; and they were paid, warned, and cajoled to adopt the new methods and procedures.

Just as there is a dearth of studies that evaluate what teacher trainees gain from any training program, there is also a dearth of research about how teachers actually made use of the new math in their classrooms. At the same time, there is sufficient informal evidence that the mathematical skills of elementary teachers are not strong and that the new math curriculum, if properly implemented, could have been superior to other arithmetic programs that emphasize computational skill, rote, and drill. However, we believe that continuing education programs such as the one on new math should rely more on the ingenuity and creativity of the teachers who participate in them. More respect for teachers needs to be built into inservice education programs.

Attempts to implement the new math curricula reflect the implicit dehumanization and inconsistency so prominent in teacher training programs. The rhetoric in support of curriculum innovations implies that teachers are the most important persons in the educative process, and that a student's life will be enriched and made more meaningful if he has contact with effective teachers. Yet although teachers are granted almost total responsibility for the care and education of their students, it is nonteaching experts or administrators who decide on what is good and proper for teachers to learn and teach. It is inconsistent, it seems to us, to give teachers full responsibility for their classrooms and to expect them to encourage independent thinking and work on the part of students, while at the same time withholding from them the responsibility for their own continued education and development. The implicit message communicated by many inservice training programs is that teachers are not really valued and that they are considered to be unmotivated and incompetent. This has led to neurotic self-hatred on the part of many teachers, as is illustrated in some succinct comments by teacher Larry Cuban.

Cuban tells of the difficulties he had in deciding to return to teaching after writing a book and several articles on teaching. He was required to take a course on "Teaching in the Secondary Schools" before he could teach in a high school classroom, even though he had taught many similar courses to secondary teachers. In an open letter to Bill Cosby, who had just decided to join the teaching profession, Larry Cuban (1971) wrote:

> The reward system—dollars, status and time away from kids—supports the real value, not the stated one. As presently established, teaching is grubby work. The gifted teacher either burns himself out—just like a 100 watt bulb—and leaves or moves into administration.... The continual seduction of teaching talent into administration is scandalous because, sadly, the kids suffer.
>
> I write this not to further expose the public schools, God knows, no one can write anything more to reveal or indict the failings of

our school system. All of it has been said before.... Until tangible efforts are taken to prove concretely to teachers that they count, that teaching is—indeed—important, all the Clark plans, Passow reports, community school ventures, open classrooms, and decentralization schemes will be wisps of straw in the wind. This system needs bricks, not straw.

"Bricks" will be made, we think, by making more effective use of the human resources already available on our school faculties. Many teachers already possess the knowledge and skills to determine what they need to learn to improve their own classroom performance. Moreover, the personal involvement and participation of teachers in determining how they will deal with their own professional growth are important foundations for cognitive growth. One study, for instance, compared the effects of two different teacher training designs in the new math on the growth of the participants in mathematical concepts. The workshop that produced greater cognitive gains in the participants was designed by the participants themselves. Making use of their own knowledge and the help of a consultant, they determined the goals and primary procedures for the training session. In contrast, fewer cognitive gains were made in a workshop that was designed by administrators in the district office and implemented entirely by an outside expert (Dutton and Hammond, 1966).

We believe that the very procedures by which teachers are trained to teach constitute salient models for how they will teach later on. The emotional experiences that teachers have during training can have strong effects on their subsequent interpersonal behavior within their own classrooms. The theories and ideas that are communicated to teachers, on the other hand, are much less important in relation to their classroom performance.

As an interesting example of the ways in which teachers learn to teach, we wish to point to some unanticipated effects of a program of training in organization development (OD) for the entire faculty of the Highland Park Junior High School in Beaverton, Oregon. The training emphasized improving staff relations in the school, in terms of their communication patterns, modes of decision-making, role clarification, and affective concerns. The training was *not* designed specifically to stimulate new classroom behavior of teachers, nor were relationships ever drawn between the OD training and classroom group processes by the trainers. Yet, to the surprise and delight of the trainers, the training experiences provided models and processes that teachers did apply later in their classroom teaching. (See Schmuck and Runkel, 1970.)

Another important point about the organizational training at Highland Park was that the teachers were treated as intelligent, reasonable human beings who naturally had difficulties and hang-ups but who were expected to define the nature of their own problems and, with help from the trainers, to find solutions. The teachers later began to treat their students in similar ways, as intelligent and curious human beings who needed help and guidance but who also had many strong resources of their own for solving problems. (See Bigelow, 1971.)

4. Supervision

Another type of inservice education for teachers is presented in the form of supervision. It has been a formal part of the operation of school districts since the eighteenth century. During that period lay committees had the authority to inspect and monitor the school's performance, enforce rules and regulations, and determine the competencies of teachers. Generally, the lay committees were more concerned about dismissing inadequate or immoral teachers than in helping teachers to improve the quality of their instruction. Gradually school personnel took over the supervisory functions; first as superintendents, next as principals, and most recently as specialists in curriculum and instruction hired especially to serve as supervisors, or, as they are more often being called, consultants.

Supervision, in fact, has become a specialized area in public education. There are numerous graduate programs in educational supervision and many states now require formal certification for the role of supervisor. The processes of supervision, however, are gradually changing from enforcement and inspection to consultation and facilitation. Contemporary texts in educational supervision increasingly view the primary function as consultative and stress the guidance function of supervisors. Supervisors are being urged to collaborate with teachers in finding solutions to individual or classroom problems. This consultative orientation grants the teacher his own instructional goals and aims at helping him to achieve those goals. The supervisor is to enhance a teacher's continued growth and development in ways that are important to the teacher. (See Goldhammer, 1969.)

Research on supervision has been ambiguous with regard to its benefits for teachers. Few studies, for instance, indicate that supervisors have helped teachers to humanize their learning groups. The studies do show that the job titles, functions, and tactics of supervisors vary enormously from district to district and even within districts; and that most of a supervisor's work time is taken up with administrative details rather than consultation with teachers. (See Bradford, 1959; Landry, 1959; Savage, 1952; and Savage, 1959.)

Frequently supervisory functions are carried out by the building principal but many other district personnel may also carry out specific functions. There may be coordinators or supervisors for special academic subjects such as math, music, or language arts. There may be supervisors (or consultants) for special services such as counseling and guidance, testing, and nursing. Sometimes cooperating teachers serve as supervisors to student teachers, and department heads (or team leaders) may be expected to supervise some of the nontenured teachers in their units. However, even though the possibility for much consultative help is great, very little actual facilitation seems to take place.

We think that it is fair to say that supervisor-consultants have *not* facilitated humanistic changes and that earlier emphasis on inspection and enforcement persists. In fact in some cases supervisors stimulate and encourage depersonalized and custodial care in the classroom as indicated by the following quotes (Herndon, 1965).

> ... Mrs. A. [the principal] had said I was incompetent, and the consultant (Mrs. X) had come down to talk to me. Neither she nor the principal had been satisfied; they couldn't quite decide, so the language supervisor (Mrs. Y) arrived in a couple more days to observe me and my class. It was a catastrophe.
>
> ... and although Mrs. Y was still there in the back of my mind, I thought she'd see what the panic was all about and it might even be a useful demonstration. I got ready to begin cooling everyone off, thinking that perhaps we should have two, maybe three more reading leaders which would take the pressure off of Wade and the group, too, planning how to explain it for all of us. I moved over to deal with Alexandra first, who by this time was angrily claiming that Wade was trying to start a fight with her so's she would get in trouble and how she didn't let nobody pick on her.... but all of a sudden everyone shut up and saw that Mrs. Y was standing in front of the class.
>
> In all my life, said Mrs. Y, I have never seen such a rude, disorderly, disgraceful class. (P. 121.)

After this event, no supervisors visited Mr. Herndon for the rest of the year. Even the principal no longer bothered him. Herndon was fired before the academic year was over.

In this example, and in others, supervisors are presented as primarily interested in control and discipline instead of in excitement, stimulation, and a humanized classroom climate. Part of this problem, as in the Herndon illustration, is the differing values and goals of the supervisor and teacher. The major part of the problem, however, lies in the nature of the role relationship and status differences between supervisor and teacher. The supervisor, even if he is called a consultant, usually has superior status and higher authority than the teacher, and has control over the rewards or punishments a teacher may receive from the district. Supervisors have potential coercive power over teachers by virtue of their position of authority, and such relationships do not stimulate dialogue and discussion about new ideas or teaching practices. We would like to see more attempts to distribute the supervisory functions to the teaching peer group or even to students as a way of overcoming some of the current deficiencies in supervisory positions.

Jack Nelson (1971) tried out an intervention that he called "collegial supervision." To implement this sort of supervision, teachers collaborate with one another to specify instructional goals, to devise ways to diagnose where they stand in relation to these goals, and to help one another through discussion and problem-solving to move toward their goals. After a team of colleagues has helped one another to determine personal goals, observation times are arranged so that the teachers can watch one another teach. The observations are followed by feedback sessions during which the observer tells the teacher what he saw. (See DeVita, 1963.) In Nelson's program, the teacher being observed and the observer agreed on the categories of observation prior to the observed period. Feedback from students can be even more powerful than feedback from colleagues; we will discuss this in more detail in Chapter 5. (See Tuckman, and Oliver, 1968.)

Forming clusters of teachers to perform supervisory functions with one another is not merely a theory. It is happening right now and tentative results indicate that it can flourish. For instance, in Kent, Washington, and Eugene, Oregon, there are cadres of teachers (along with administrators and staff specialists) who have been trained in consultation skills. They have full-time teaching jobs but are granted about ten to fifteen days a year to serve as consultants to other schools that request their services. In both districts, the demand for their consultation exceeds the cadres' time and energy. In Kent, when the cadre was being formed and trained, the schools used the resources of outside experts (from The Center for the Advanced Study of Educational Administration) until the cadre was ready to take on that function. Evidence (see Schmuck, 1971) indicates that the subsequent help rendered by the cadre of teachers was superior in some ways to that of the outside experts.

We hope that continuing education programs for teachers will more and more enhance rather than impede the growth and development of more humanized instructional practices. To accomplish this, however, teachers will have to be valued more as competent professionals and as whole persons. It is the teachers' values, skills, knowledge, and feelings that should constitute the foci of continuing inservice programs of learning how to humanize classrooms. At the same time, we would warn the eager administrator that he cannot initiate effective programs of collegial supervision, student feedback to teachers, and cadres of teacher-consultants through administrative fiat alone. In fact, destructive results may arise if movements toward more involvement of teachers in supervision do not also flow out of teacher interests and concerns. Collegial supervision will fail in a school where the norms of the staff emphasize secrecy, emotional distance, and distrust. Indeed, the influence of a peer group of teachers expected to regulate teaching practices is perhaps the most important element of dynamics in moving schools toward or away from a humanized learning climate and should be taken into consideration and altered if necessary before any major change in supervision is tried.

VALUES AND SKILLS ARE NOT ENOUGH

Very few new teachers start their teaching careers within a faculty that has no history of working together. They typically enter a school which has an already formed network of on-going relationships involving the principal, his assistants, the counselor, the teachers, the students, and even the custodians and cooks. This social structure has its own culture and its own specific norms. Interpersonal behaviors within a school culture are governed and maintained by the norms through the verbal and nonverbal messages that are communicated from day to day. New teachers, if they are to become comfortably integrated as full staff members, must learn how to relate to fellow staff members in ways compatible with the school culture. Often this socialization process changes the attitudes and values of the new teacher.

1. The influence of colleagues

The faculties of many public schools do not have norms that support whole-person relationships and I-Thou transactions. Instead, professional distance, control of students, and academic standards are typically emphasized, and the new teacher is pressed to take his part dutifully in disciplining and controlling students. The neophyte teacher who is enthusiastic about his own humanistic ideas soon will hear that "he is naive and will see how a school and classroom should be run after he has taught for a while."

Willower and his colleagues (see Willower and Jones, 1967; Willower, Eidell, and Hoy, 1967; Willower, Hoy and Eidell, 1967; Willower, ERIC; and Appleberry and Hoy, 1969) have done extensive empirical research on some of the prevailing norms of public schools and have presented evidence about the mechanisms by which new personnel are socialized into the prominent norms. Their primary instrument, a questionnaire referred to as *Pupil Control Ideology* (PCI), was designed to measure an educator's values regarding education. The end-points of a conceptual dimension measured by the questionnaire are labelled "custodial" and "humanistic." Most educators do not score at either of the extreme ends; rather most scores indicate that an individual's values lie in one direction or another.

A teacher who scores on the custodial side tends to think about students as in need of control and training; students are viewed as lacking responsibility and self-discipline. The school is viewed, moreover, as being responsible for the behavior of the students and it is believed that authority should be hierarchically organized with administrators and teachers at the top, giving students little opportunity to make their own decisions. The teacher with a humanistic orientation, in contrast, views the school as a community of persons engaged in learning through their interactions with one another. He believes that power should be shared by all participants, including the students, and that decisions should be made by those who are affected by them whenever possible. Also, Dobson, Goldenberg, and Elsom (1972) have shown that teachers who score high on the humanistic side use significantly more verbal behaviors classified as indirect and supportive in their teaching than do teachers who scored more custodial. Perhaps, most importantly, the teacher with a humanistic orientation views all persons as responsible for their own behaviors and learning.*

The questionnaire asks for a reaction from "agree' to "disagree" on a five-point scale regarding items such as: "Pupils can be trusted to work together without supervision," or "A few pupils are just young hoodlums and should be treated accordingly." The validity of the instrument has been questioned as a "straw man" kind of questionnaire. It is argued that there is an evident bias toward the humanistic orientation. One would expect that teachers have learned some "test wise" behaviors, that many of them have heard—and even espouse—the lofty rhetoric of humanistic values and consequently might answer in the humanistic direction even if it did not represent their actual behavior. However, teachers typically do not favor the humanistic side in their answers.

Results of the research on teachers show that generally they score closer to the custodial end of this dimension. Moreover, the research shows that teachers become increasingly more custodial the more years that they teach. For example, teachers who were tested both at graduation from college and again at the completion of their first teaching year significantly changed in the direction of a more custodial orientation. In contrast, the control ideology of future teachers who had completed four years of teacher preparation but who did *not* teach their first year out of college did *not* change over the one-year period.

Willower, Eidell, and Hoy (1967) described how the new teachers of a junior high school were socialized into the prevailing norms of custodialism. As new teachers, their ideas about what was good teaching were quite different from many of the ideas of the more experienced teachers in the school. Basically, the new teachers differed from their more experienced counterparts in placing more value upon a humanistic orientation emphasizing student freedom and choice. At the same time, the new teachers were striving to feel at ease,

---

*McGregor's Theory X and Theory Y, discussed in Chapter 3, in many ways are analogous to custodial and humanistic values. The primary difference is that the former concepts refer to what leaders believe motivation and behavior to be like while the latter concepts refer to what leaders believe human relationships should be like.

secure, and accepted by their more experienced colleagues, both as fellow teachers and as persons.

The researchers pointed out that there were essentially three alternative courses of action open to the new teachers. First, they could accept the differences in ideology and simply remain separate from the more experienced teachers. Second, they could confront the older teachers and, through discussion, attempt to find ways of diminishing the value differences or co-existing with them. Third, the newcomers could gradually succumb to the prevailing custodial values in the school. Most new teachers followed this last course of action.

Acculturation into the prevailing custodial norms occurred mostly within informal gatherings of teachers. For example, in the teachers' lounge—at lunch time or before school—there were frequent instances of "tough talk" about formidable students, boasting about the vigorous, uncompromising ways in which a teacher had handled an unruly student, gossip about students' families, and even criticism of teachers who were not present for being too "soft." Formal gatherings, such as school assemblies and athletic events, were prominent settings in which older teachers could display to their neophyte colleagues their toughness with students. The new teachers observed these displays and often actively participated in them, both in the informal discussions and in the formal gatherings.

Socialization into custodial values often involves a painful and frustrating course for the new teacher. As one new teacher put it, "No matter what I try to do or say, they (the older teachers) still think I am soft." A common rationalization is that the university teacher-training program is to blame because it is unrealistic and ineffective. New teachers come to view their university professors as naive do-gooders while simultaneously coming to see their more experienced colleagues as realistic and practical. After a period of actual classroom experience, many new teachers come to see humanistic values as mostly unrelated to the "harsh realities" of the real school. Like many student teachers, new teachers come to accept the custodial treatment of students as necessary to keep the school running smoothly.

It is not hard for us to empathize with the challenges that both new and experienced teachers face. It is difficult to teach effectively and humanistically when one is continually struggling with the pressures of one group of students who continually test the limits of acceptable behavior while others expect "control," of parents asking for increased control over their youngsters, and of administrators expecting teachers to keep the school "running smoothly." Under pressures like these most teachers need some support and comfort from others, and usually such gratifications can be found only with colleagues. The influence of the colleague group can therefore be extremely powerful. Back in 1932, Waller wrote:

> The significant people for a school teacher are other teachers, and by comparison with good standing in that fraternity the good opinion of students is a small thing and of little price. A landmark of one's assimilation to the profession is the moment when he decides that only teachers are important.

New teachers who attempt to debate value differences with their colleagues find that such discussions can be time-consuming, energy-sapping, and often very frustrating. Moreover, heated intellectual discussions about values and teaching strategies are usually not considered appropriate in most schools. Faculty norms often emphasize distance from and control of students, and smooth, unruffled, and distant relationships with fellow teachers. After all, teachers who are involved in challenging interaction with students for most of the day do not want their lunch-hour or after-school discussions filled with divisiveness and argumentation. The teacher colleague group becomes a context in which to find comfort and sympathy for the difficult job of classroom teaching.

In another study on humanistic values and faculty norms, Appleberry and Hoy (1969) correlated the scores of staff members on the Pupil Control Ideology questionnaire with a measure of the "climate of the school." School climate—the quality of relationships among the adult staff—was measured by the *Organizational Climate Description Questionnaire* of Halpin and Croft (1963). Tabulations of this questionnaire can be used to characterize school climates as more or less open or closed. In schools with open climates, relationships among staff members are more truthful and straightforward, faculty members disagree with one another openly, and the norms of the staff support a wide range of teachers' beliefs and behavior. Closed climates, on the other hand, have staff relationships that are formal, distant, and mostly role-related; faculty members do not disagree openly; and the norms of the staff specify a narrow range of acceptable teachers' beliefs and behavior.

Appleberry and Hoy collected climate and pupil control scores from forty-five elementary schools in thirty different districts. Their analyses showed significant associations between scores from the two instruments: openness and humanistic ideology on the one hand and closedness and a custodial ideology on the other went together. The further significance of these results lies in the tie between norms governing relationships among the adult staff and the values that are deemed acceptable for relationships between teachers and students. Teachers who behave openly with one another tend also to be open with their students. When teachers respect one another's beliefs and behavior, they tend also to respect the beliefs and behavior of their students. When teachers value debating one another's ideas and attitudes openly, they also tend to be willing to accept differences in the students' perceptions and attitudes. Teachers teach as they were taught; they also teach in ways that reflect the kinds of relationships they have with their colleagues.

Findings of the Willower group support the view that one effective way to move teachers toward a more humanistic orientation is to intervene into the culture of the school itself. Instead of calling for additional training in teaching methods or psychology, these findings call for training programs aimed at *organizational change*: opening up faculty communication, helping staff members to confront and discuss differences in values and methods, and exploring new group agreements that will allow for and even encourage a wider range of professional differences.

It is important to emphasize that such organizational change cannot be accomplished by simply placing a few more teachers with humanistic values into a "closed" school. Indeed, the research by Appleberry and Hoy (1969) showed that planting a few humanistically oriented teachers in a closed staff can be disastrous, especially for the humanistic teachers, who must undergo confrontation with strong custodial norms and at the same time face a staff culture that discourages talking out professional differences. The pain of this sort of confrontation for the neophyte humanistic teacher is perhaps the major reason behind the growth in the number of disillusioned teachers leaving the schools. These dropout teachers in general do not name students as their primary source of disillusionment but rather the adult professionals in the school. The many studies that have made use of the Pupil Control Ideology questionnaire tend to substantiate our belief that the social and personality characteristics of those who teach are less important for humanization than a school's cultural traditions and organizational procedures.

2. The principal

It is common among education critics to focus on the principal's importance in influencing school organizational dynamics. We believe that principals do have enormous influence on the staff climate and can either help or hinder the effort of teachers to become more humanistic. Perhaps the best research done to substantiate these beliefs is that of Gross and Herriott (1965), who showed empirically that a principal's leadership behavior is associated with staff morale, staff norms about innovation, the professional performance of a staff, and even student learning.

However, though a principal can be very influential, it is important to note he or she is only *one* participant in a network of staff relationships and that the prevailing norms of a faculty are always stronger than the influence exerted by even the most competent principal. Several studies have shown, for example, that principals tend to hold *stronger* humanistic orientations than their teachers. Moreover, on tests of dogmatism, principals have scored as significantly less dogmatic than their teachers (Willower, Eidell, and Hoy, 1967). Other studies have shown that principals are *less* conservative than teachers about innovative changes in the school program. Indeed, although the available research does *not* portray the typical principal as rigid and conservative, it is true that many school faculties continue to emphasize closedness and the tight control of students.

One study sheds light on the way both the principal and his staff play a part in encouraging or discouraging innovative instruction. Chesler, Schmuck, and Lippitt (1963), in attempting to isolate the factors that contribute to great amounts of innovation in a school, found both the norms of the teacher peer group and the principal's leadership behavior to be critical. Schools in which the staff peer group and the principal supported and encouraged more humanistic practices had many more new and creative practices actually underway than schools in which the teacher peer group did not support the principal's interest in instructional innovation. The principal's most significant influence seems to be in *setting the stage* for the interpersonal relationships and climate that staff members are capable of providing. Their major impact lies in the way they facilitate the development of a humanized staff climate through the example of their leadership behaviors. They do not influence teachers very much by communicating their values and beliefs about instruction.

SUMMARY OF CHAPTER 4

Since schools are complex, multi-leveled social systems, any attempt to change them must at least take into account individuals, small groups, the total school organization, and the surrounding social environment. In such a complex organization, the barriers to change are numerous and bewildering. One frequently selected lever for change is the classroom teacher. In this chapter we attempt to show how particular influences prevent teachers from humanizing learning climates.

The major barriers that teachers confront in trying to humanize even their own classrooms arise from two general sources: first, their formal preservice and inservice training, and second, the formal and informal socialization of teachers during their first few years in the public schools.

While the college experience tends to be liberalizing for teacher trainees, they are affected primarily intellectually, not attitudinally or behaviorally. The college curriculum tends to emphasize cognitive awareness and idea accumulation, and typically does not help trainees to match new behaviors with the new concepts. Although, there are some promising alternative training designs for teachers, these have not yet had wide enough impact to be decisive.

Even with these alternative training programs, the norms and procedures that trainees face as new teachers tend to be strongly custodial, with emphasis on control, discipline, and the striving toward academic standards set by other adults. The permissive values and skills learned in college tend to give way to norms and behavior that are more in tune with the so-called "harsh realities" of the school. The staff's norms have strong influence on a neophyte's values and instructional behaviors. He quickly leaves his ideology of freedom, growth, and self-expression on the doorstep of the "ivory tower."

To modify this custodial influence means to change training programs as well as the professional climate of the control. The latter is especially critical. Schools that have open staff climates do tend to be humanistically oriented, but such staffs are too few in number. Most school staffs have norms which support distant, impersonal behavior and discourage dialogue, encounters, and I-Thou transactions. We believe that humanistic changes in schools will not occur until norm-changing, problem-solving procedures are used to train entire staffs for open dialogue concerning values, goals, and methods of teaching.

Charters, W. W. 1963. "The Social Background of Teachers," in N. Gage, (ed.), *Handbook of Research on Teaching.* Chicago: Rand, McNally and Co., 715-813.

Charters's contribution to this encyclopedic volume is a comprehensive review of social psychological research on teachers. He summarizes research on who teachers are, what influences them, and what happens during their preservice training. We have relied heavily on this excellent article in the preparation of this chapter. His review shows data-based support for the informal socialization of teachers as a major influence on their values and professional behaviors.

Fuchs, Estelle. 1969. *Teachers Talk: Views from Inside City Schools.* Garden City, N.Y.: Anchor Books, Doubleday and Co., Inc.

This book presents the common, everyday problems that face new teachers—problems involving both students and colleagues. Each chapter has several diary-like accounts of the experiences of new teachers in inner city schools. The author provides detail on the general social dynamics involved.

Knoblock, Peter, and Arnold Goldstein. 1971. *The Lonely Teacher.* Boston: Allyn and Bacon.

Although not a thorough systems-analysis of the influence on teachers, the book does offer an analysis in depth of the psychological dynamics of individual teachers. The authors maintain that the separateness and loneliness of teachers can be ameliorated by their entering into close interaction with colleagues and students. In this way they strongly advocate that the group dynamics application can be used more often with teachers. They give most space to suggesting ways to create open and honest exchanges between teachers and students.

Miles, Matthew. 1964. *Innovation in Education.* New York: Bureau of Publications, Teachers College, Columbia University.

This fine compendium contains twenty-five articles illustrating the many barriers that confront any program of planned change in schools. Miles includes chapters on small-group and organizational theory, case studies of specific innovations in curriculum and organization, and a broad perspective on the influences of the external environment, from state departments to the mass media. The book's examples and analyses apply a human systems perspective to educational innovation.

Patterson, C. H. 1973. *Humanistic Education.* New York: Prentice-Hall, Inc.

This book offers a positive plan for helping teachers to humanize their classrooms. The suggestions center on experiential curricula involving observation, intensive group experiences, and expanded practice teaching and supervision.

Runkel, Philip, Roger Harrison, and Margaret Runkel. 1969. *The Changing College Classroom.* San Francisco: Jossey-Bass, Inc.

This book is a collection of case studies of innovative teaching within college classrooms. The editors chose contributors who had experimented with changing the traditional role relationships between teachers and students, and most of their innovations inevitably also involved changes in the curriculum and the microorganization of the class. While the examples are all taken from college classrooms, many are directly applicable to high school and even elementary classrooms. Each example is an inspiring and realistic example of what can be done by a creative and energetic teacher.

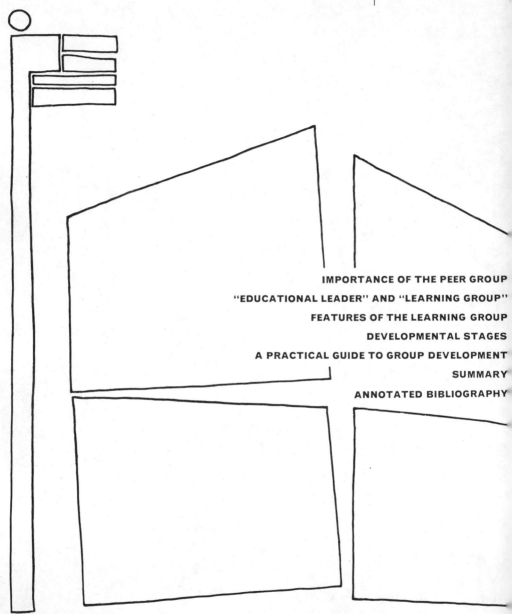

chapter 5

Humanizing
learning groups

We have argued that more open buildings, individualized curriculum materials, sophisticated teaching procedures, and even more knowledgeable teachers will *not* in themselves bring humanized schools into being. Further, we have said that the routine, day-to-day interactions that students, teachers, and administrators carry on should be the primary targets of change if schools are to become truly humanized. Since most such interactions take place in learning groups or within the surrounding organizational context of the school, we believe that these are the two chief settings for change in a school's culture. This chapter focuses on the climates of learning groups and offers suggestions for humanizing relationships within them. Chapter 6 deals with some general aspects of school climates and specific organizational interactions involving faculty and students.

Any group—regardless of size or type—that exists for any length of time develops predictable patterns of interaction. We have used the terms "climate" and "culture" to characterize such patterns as they influence individual attitudes and behaviors. Such groups forces can be powerful even when some members disagree with the prevailing norms or try to move their fellows in new directions. Indeed, it is the climate of learning groups, not the administrators, teachers, and students taken separately, that must be humanized.

IMPORTANCE OF THE PEER GROUP

For students, the peer group constitutes one of the most important social forces. Peers come to have enormous power in a student's life and they can strongly influence his or her general attitudes and behavior development. Of course students also interact frequently with teachers, administrators, and the formal curriculum, but their most salient and meaningful rewards and punishments come from their peers. The influence of the family, though also quite significant, gradually decreases in magnitude as the student grows older. Starting in about the third or fourth grade, the peer group becomes influential in determining how young people will crystallize their identity, what attitudes they hold about school, and what their aspirations and academic goals will be. During adolescence the peer group can have even deeper influence on virtually every important decision that the student faces. One key to humanizing learning groups lies in understanding and dealing with the power of the peer group.

One particularly dramatic illustration of the power of the peer group was presented by David Hargreaves (1967) in his study of streaming (dividing students—in this case according to their scores or examinations) in an English secondary school for boys. Hargreaves studied the psychological impact of several different types of peer group cultures. Although the extreme differences that he found among the several peer group clusters were obviously heightened by the traditional British custom of streaming students according to their examination scores, nevertheless his research is very instructive for Americans. Even though it is true that American schools typically do not make quite such blatant distinctions on the basis of a student's achievement level, Hargreaves' results show how deeply a peer group climate can affect individual behavior. Moreover, the norms of the British peer groups obviously operate in many American schools, too, and have, we believe, effects similar to those noted by Hargreaves.

Hargreaves focused his analysis of social relations in the peer group on the fourth (or last) year boys because at almost fourteen years of age they represented the "final products" of required schooling and had spent the longest time being initiated into the values of the school. The fourth year class, like all others, had been divided into five streams upon entry into the school. Hargreaves studied only four of the streams, excluding the fifth stream, which was composed mostly of retarded or minimally educable students.

He showed that each stream had an unique climate, complete with its own special norms, values, dress codes, attitudes, and expectations about teachers. Furthermore, he discovered that the climates of these streams persisted even when the boys were shifted among them.

The highest stream, labeled A, had a climate that was consonant with the school's formal goals: boys valued academic achievement, looked down upon "mucking around" in class, discouraged fighting, thought that teachers should be obeyed, and thought that plagiarism and cheating should be strictly against the student code. Their informal social organization was characterized by a strongly hierarchical clique structure.

Stream B had quite a different culture. For one thing, the clique structure was more diffuse and there was less agreement among the individual members on personal values. For another thing, the boys in stream B most often did not go along with the academic goals and procedures of the faculty. The following quote from a high-status student within B illustrates how the climate in his peer group differed from the climate in stream A.

We don't like boys who don't mess about. We don't like boys who answer a lot of questions. If you answer all the questions, the lesson goes all the quicker, doesn't it. I mean, say you have two periods and you start having all these questions, right then it would take a period to do, and then you have another period and then you'd have to do some new work. If they start asking questions and we don't answer them they have to start explaining it all to us and it takes two periods. So we don't have to use the pen. (Hargreaves, 1967, P. 27.)

Stream C was actually composed of three subgroups. It was similar to B in that most of the members strongly devalued academic work, but whereas in B fun was valued more than work and "messing around" was encouraged for its own sake, the high-status clique members of C apparently were primarily interested in behaving contrary to school values and defying the school administration. In other words, the C group was negatively oriented toward the establishment of the school, while the B group was more fun-loving. Group C also had very different interpersonal relationships from those of the other groups. Whereas the A and B groups were led by strong individuals and cliques, the C group had a fragmented influence structure and was less cohesive than the other two groups. In fact, one low-status clique in C was rejected by and isolated from the other C boys and it continued to maintain norms very different from the rest of the C group. This deviant C subgroup, for example, valued work, obeyed teacher demands, dressed well, and attended school regularly.

Stream D had an even more diffuse leadership than the C group. Boys of great power in D vigorously opposed the norms of the school; in fact, one criteria for status seemed to be doing poor academic work. Truancy was encouraged, physical violence was used against the low-status boys who went along with the teachers, and delinquent acts of all sorts were frequent and highly valued by the high-status clique.

Members of the four streams entered into very little interaction with one another except when students were switched from one stream to another or when there was some mixing while participating on the school's rugby team. Most participants in the school—both students and staff—held stereotypic conceptions of members in the different groups. For example, the A's were viewed as snobby while the D's were seen as delinquent. Hargreaves also showed that the students' identification with their own group was very strong. For example, at times the boys in the lower streams would decrease their performance on tests purposely so that they would not be moved up to a higher stream.

The thoughts, attitudes, and behaviors of teachers also differed in relation to these various peer groups. One obvious difference was in the teachers' expectation of achievement for the boys in the four streams. It became apparent to Hargreaves that the self-fulfilling prophecy was very much at work. One student reported:

> If you're in 4A, the teachers expect you to set a standard, you know. But if you're in 4B the teachers almost expect you to be that bit more stupid, you know what I mean? (P. 30.)

A finding that was not so obvious, however, was the number of rewards (house points given for good behavior or academic performance) that the teachers gave to members of each group. The two highest streams received less house points from their teachers than the two lower streams. In a given period of time a mean of 47.2 house points was given to streams A and B, while a mean of 101.1 house points was given to streams C and D. The increase was even greater with stream E, which received 178.9 house points in the same period. Hargreaves explained that the teachers of the lower streams gave rewards more freely in hopes of inducing good behavior and increasing academic performance.

Although Hargreaves did not indicate the procedure by which the house points were given—presumably at a teacher's discretion—it is interesting to note that the reward system seemed to work against the values of the teachers. We hypothesize that boys of the higher stream needed fewer rewards from teachers because they already received many implicit rewards and encouragement from their peers for behaving well and achieving highly. On the other hand, the lower stream boys, whose cultures were quite different from that of the faculty, remained relatively uninfluenced by the teacher's rewards (even though in the form of house points such rewards were frequently given) because their peers were informally rewarding them more strongly for behaving contrary to the interest of the teachers.

Hargreaves concluded:

> ... that the streams exert a powerful influence on the extent and form of interaction between age-mates in the same neighborhood school. Boys tend to interact with and choose friends from boys in the same stream and only rarely from streams more than one removed from their own. As the predominant norms of each form become differentiated and the various barriers to communication between streams are erected, negative stereotypes develop. These serve to reinforce the normative differentiation and inhibit further cross-stream interaction, and thus the incentive value of the "promotion" system is undermined for the low stream boys. (P. 82.)

Hargreaves's results bring into bold relief one of the limitations of a behavior modification strategy solely engineered by teachers: the peer group can also present very powerful and sometimes competitive rewards. We have little doubt that teachers can have a powerful influence on students by using careful reward strategies; however, if a student peer group maintains a standard that defines those who succumb to teacher influence as "square," no form of "soft" reinforcement or logically ordered stimuli on the part of the teacher can compete successfully with the social reinforcements of the peer group. Of course, teacher threats and ridicule can be employed to confront the peer group's strength, and Hargreaves noted that such means were used in the lower streams—but without success. Assignment to teach lower stream students was disconcerting, so that teachers often took out their resentment upon the boys they had to teach. The lower stream teachers even unwittingly contributed to the peer group's devaluation of academic work by their expectations of and interactions with those "unintelligent louts."

Too often, learning groups, such as these described by Hargreaves, develop haphazardly without teacher planning and in ways that are inimical to humanized relationships and intellectual growth. In the face of such evidence, teachers should hold as one of their top priorities helping students to build a peer group climate that encourages I-Thou transactions and involvement with learning tasks, rather than unwittingly perpetuating a climate of rejection, distrust, and defeat. We believe that if students and teachers will openly share their knowledge of the group processes at work in developing a normative structure, and will frankly discuss the issues that confront them, they can form learning groups that are liberating rather than restrictive. The formal distance between teachers and students in the school studied by Hargreaves—a pattern not unlike that of many American high schools—banished the sharing of thoughts and feelings about the school from the classroom.

We believe, however, that students and teachers can gain control over the climate of their group and chart its course together deliberately if they can break through to work collaboratively and democratically.

In the rest of this chapter we present concepts and practical suggestions to help students and teachers to humanize their own learning groups in this way. We will first clarify the terms "educational leader" and "learning group," which we use throughout the chapter, next define the essential features of a learning group, then discuss a sequence of developmental stages in learning groups, and finally suggest specific practices that can be employed by students and teachers alike to humanize their learning groups.

"EDUCATIONAL LEADER" AND "LEARNING GROUP"

We deliberately use the labels "educational leader" and "learning group" instead of the customary terms "teacher" and "classroom" to encourage a fresh, nontraditional terminology about schools. We are concerned that the terms "teacher" and "classroom" may invite a limited and standard view of teaching and learning. Typically, of course, the educational leader is the teacher, but there is no sound reason—except for that of tradition—why the educational leader should *always* be the teacher. Humanized schools make use of their inherent resources, whether they are held by teachers, students, principals, parents, or other persons in the community. "Educational leader" is a generic term which can cover all persons who function from time to time as facilitators of learning.

The term "learning group" refers to a collection of people working together, at least in part, on learning tasks. It encompasses an array of potential organizational patterns for learning, ranging from the stable, long-term, self-contained classrooms to the fluid, ad hoc groupings of people who come together to learn specific things during a limited time period. The variety of learning groups can be virtually unlimited. There are ungraded classrooms in which students are tentatively grouped according to their level of skill; instructional groups, based primarily on interest, that may last from two days to two years; long-term extracurricular groups such as career guidance and student government groups, and groups formed for specific short-term purposes, such as special seminars or drama groups.

FEATURES OF THE LEARNING GROUP

We think of learning groups as possessing interaction, interdependence, shared goals, and an organized structure. Classrooms do not necessarily contain learning groups. For example, students taught in a classroom by a program of Individually Prescribed Instruction (IPI) are not required to interact with one another to carry out their learning tasks. Indeed, interpersonal interactions are intentionally underplayed in many IPI formats. Moreover, although the ultimate learning goals for the students may be similar, the students do not function interdependently in attempting to reach those goals: each student acts more or less autonomously, in fact. Of course, even the most individuated IPI classrooms are influenced by some aspects of group life. The mere physical presence of other students does have some effect on a student's performance even as he or she engages the simplest tasks. Furthermore, despite a teacher's attempts to discourage interaction between students, they still carry out some informal interchanges both in and outside the classroom.

Indeed, physical proximity and extended time together are really primary ingredients for the formation of any group. At the same time, proximity and time are not sufficient in themselves for the formation of a learning group. Some students meet together for a whole academic year in the same room, ostensibly working toward similar goals, but they still may not know the first names of some of their peers. As an example, in the month of May, a six-year-old friend of ours was talking about a boy who had been in his class since the previous September. His mother said, "I didn't know he was in your class —you never mentioned him before." His retort was, "I just met him today." This sort of class, along with the IPI classes described above, would be on the low end in a measurement of "groupness." On the other hand, a collection of students can work together for only a short period of time, such as in rehearsing a play, in raising funds for the school, or even in a seminar, and while doing so display most of the features that would place them at the high end in a measurement of "groupness." As a collection of school participants comes to display the features of a group, it becomes more relevant and important for its members to apply the concepts and skills offered in this chapter.

We believe that all students should have some school experiences in a fully functioning group. Interaction and interdependence are facts of life in the 1970s and students should learn to cope effectively with these conditions. Moreover, although alienation is prominent in schools, it does not follow, even in our largest schools, that learning groups must be impersonal or inhuman. Collective life can introduce a multitude of new issues and conflicts to individuals who have lived primarily in small, low-tension, primary groups, but these conflicts can be solved creatively and constructively only if the participants have had some experience and practice in learning how to work effectively together to cope with group problems. Students should receive such learning experiences in the family, in their friendship groups, and in their interactions at school. Just as students learn the basic cognitive skills of reading, writing, and arithmetic, they should also learn the behavioral skills of relating to others. Students need to learn how to exert positive influence in groups, how to confront the conflicts that inevitably arise between interdependent persons, and how to preserve their own individuality and integrity without destroying those of others.

We now will elaborate on the three key features of learning groups, showing the form these take in many contemporary schools and also how they might appear in a humanized school.

1. Interaction and interdependence

A learning group can be defined partly as a collection of persons who communicate face-to-face and who have some reciprocal influence in relation to one another. This definition deliberately excludes mere aggregates of people such as fans at a football game, the audience in a lecture hall, or people who sit near one another in a study hall.

During the historical period of entrepreneurship in America competition was stressed more than interdependence and the norms in the schools of that era stressed that a student's performance should be pitted against that of every other student. In schools reflecting this entrepreneurial philosophy it was *not* in a student's personal interest to interact with another student in helpful ways since the other might thereby surpass the helper's performance level. Although later the theme of cooperation and interdependence was accentuated, in schools with the bureaucratic philosophy, the emphasis was on dependence upon the formal organization (planned primarily by the administrator and teachers) rather than upon functional interdependence with fellow students. In bureaucratically oriented schools it was in a student's personal interest to cooperate with the school administration and to interact congenially with the teachers to receive rewards and to reach academic goals. Collaboration by teachers and students to learn together was discouraged. Even though now in many schools the social studies curriculum, for example, has gradually broadened to emphasize the interdependence of community and world resources, students are still not being encouraged to share their skills and knowledge with each other in the learning group.

Even now formal communication between students in many schools continues to be de-emphasized and sometimes discouraged. Helping another student still can be defined as cheating (or at least as inappropriate) and teachers continue to control most of the verbal airtime in the class. (Some researchers have estimated the typical amount of teacher talk in the classroom as 80 percent.) Sharing affective concerns and expressing affection for others also continue to be out of place in many schools. And expressions of anger along with direct statements of irritation are even more out of the question.

There is, however, some evidence emerging which leads us to be optimistic about the future of American schooling. Some indications of increased interdependence among teachers and students are occurring. Interdependence is increased, for instance, in some alternative or urban schools as they attempt to cope with the problems of economic deprivation, inadequate physical space, and inadequate curriculum materials by providing opportunities for staff and students to work in close, collaborative problem-solving. Furthermore, some schools are building formal mechanisms to help students to learn from one another in the form of mini-courses, cross-age tutoring, and multi-unit arrangements. The very act of rebuilding or creating a new curriculum or organizational arrangement can involve a great deal of helpful interaction and interdependence among students and teachers.

Some alternative schools have been in the forefront of building more humanized learning groups. The staffs of many alternative schools have brought affective concerns, support, and caring among faculty and students to a high level of priority and focus. In such schools, students are valued as persons in their own right and as powerful resources for teaching one another. The amount of support, concern, sharing, and teaching of others in some of the alternative schools we have visited is gratifying in comparison to the stilted and nonaffective relationships we have seen in many of our public schools.

However, there are several features of these avant-garde schools which lead us to be cautious in claiming that most of them encourage whole-person relationships. One important problem is the disrespect that some free school students show for adults. In fact, in some of these schools, adults are granted far less leeway to express their wishes and concerns than the students. Moreover, in many of these schools adults who are known to have earned credentials or taught in public schools are rejected out-of-hand by the students. In other words, I-Thou transactions may be normative but often adults are treated more as objects than as living feeling people.

Sylvia Ashton-Warner, noted writer and teacher, discussed student disrespect for adults in a recent article entitled "Spearpoint" (1972), in which she told of some of her experiences with the students of an American free school. She was struck by how the students and staff carefully encouraged one another to distrust the "evil of authority." As an adult, she felt alien to the culture of the school. Time and again she would attempt to enlist student help for some learning activity only to be met with rebuff and rejection. Her conclusion was that adults were supposed to relate toward students on an equalitarian basis, but that students, in turn, were *not* obliged to reciprocate the norm of equality. Indeed, students seemed to be granted immunity from relating respectfully toward adults, regardless of how the adults treated them.

Furthermore, while support and concern are present in many alternative schools, norms often exist to discourage open verbal expressions of anger, frustration, and interpersonal annoyance. It is as if one's newly formed community and friendships are too fragile to withstand emotional criticism. Such reactions appear similar to the distaste and discouragement shown toward the expressions of anger or hostility in many public schools. The main difference seems to be that in most alternative schools negative feelings are submerged by an informal consensus of members, whereas hostility and anger are most often repressed by administrative fiat or the didactic moralism of teachers in public schools.

Kozol's recent criticism (1972) of the free school movement—that it puts creative basket-weaving for middle class students ahead of survival skills for the poor and disenfranchised students—may be an early indication that at least the alternative school movement is now ready to undergo criticism, debate, and dissension within the ranks. We believe that public schools should follow suit by allowing and encouraging a full complement of communication, both favorable and unfavorable, among the staff and students. Both groups should openly share information, opinions, and feelings about what goes on in their learning groups.

2. Interaction around common goals

Group goals define a preferred or desired state which guides the behaviors of group members. The pursuit of subject matter learning is an example of a common formal group goal in public school classrooms. Other school goals have to do with maintaining cohesiveness and identity as a culture by doing well in such events as fund-raising drives, performing well in athletic competitions, or dressing attractively and behaving properly on a field trip.

Inevitably two issues for disagreement arise in all groups that have work to accomplish. The first involves reaching an effective balance between group goals and individual interests. In most groups, for example, there is a conflict over the time needed to accomplish the group's work and the time that individuals want for personal activities. The second issue involves conflicts between working on the group task and exploring the feelings of individual members. A common example of this conflict occurs when a group is working vigorously to reach a production deadline while at the same time some of the members are experiencing frustration, mistrust, and hostility. The question arises: does the group forego work to discuss these negative feelings, or do the members attempt to "shelve" the feelings until the group's work has been accomplished? When these two differences are used to construct a matrix, four categories emerge: *task-group, task-individual, social emotional-group,* and *social emotional-individual.*

During the entrepreneurial era the emphasis was on the *task-individual* category; the interests of individuals took precedence over system goals, and accomplishing work was more important than openly discussing one's feelings about the work. Indeed, feelings were supposed to be subordinated in the service of productivity. Success was measured in terms of performance output rather than by peace of mind, serenity, or exhilaration. Ayn Rand, writing during the bureaucratic era, revived the values of the earlier entrepreneurs. Her protagonists took on large-scale organizations, treating them as the enemies of individuality. Personal success had its foundation in hard work, intelligent action, and toughness. Interpersonal tenderness or the open expression of affection were fatal to the antagonist, who would then easily succumb to the group pressures of organizational life. The prototypical student of this period was competitive and hard-working; his success was measured by how well he performed *in competition with* his peers.

During the bureaucratic era, people looked at life goals in a new way. Individual interests were submerged for the sake of organizational achievement (*task-group*). The organization, in return for the individual's commitment, offered him security and peace of mind. More humane management procedures were introduced in industrial settings, but primarily to increase productivity and to solicit greater commitment to organizational goals. In schools, educators began to pay more attention to the psychological needs of students because they came to believe that academic achievement could be enhanced if the students had good feelings about themselves and school.

If the burgeoning counterculture and the alternative school movement are signs of a new era, American society seems to be refocusing on the individual (*social-emotional-individual*), while at the same time playing down system goals. Work and productivity have also taken lower priority in relation to individual feelings and interpersonal relationships (*social-emotional-group*). And, as a significant departure from both the entrepreneurial and the bureaucratic periods, individual feelings are being emphasized, not so that people will work harder or produce more, but so that they can reach emotional gratification and self-realization.

The issue of finding a proper balance between (1) system requirements and individual interests and (2) productivity and emotional satisfaction can never be finally resolved. We believe that these conflicts eventually produce tension, especially in modern, urban, highly populated societies. It seems inevitable, regardless of the social class, age, and experience of group members or the structure of the organization, that groups will swing back and forth between the polar points of these issues. As the members grow and change so will the group also develop and gradually modify its goals.

Learning groups are confronted with these issues continuously. In a humanized learning group the members will view solutions to these issues as inevitably temporary and will diagnose signs of new tensions and conflicts so that new procedures can be employed to deal with them. From our point of view, learning groups are not truly humanized if they avoid dealing openly with these natural tensions. Humanized learning groups will work to find ways of matching individual interests with group goals; they will focus on members' feelings; and they will have room for both shared purposes and individual aspirations.

3. Interaction through structure

After a short period, all human interactions achieve some regularized and predictable patterns; they take on form and structure. Interaction is called "structure" when it becomes to some extent repetitive and predictable by the participants. Most groups take on structure both at the formal level of role relationships and at the informal level of friendship and influence patterns. Some groups, such as large bureaucratic organizations, industrial plants, hospitals, government agencies, and high schools, emphasize the formal type of structure. Rules, roles, and regulations usually take precedence over the interests, goals, and wishes of the individual participants. In large schools, for example, where formal rules are abundant, most successful students learn to adjust to the formalities and regulations. One student aptly put it this way:

The main thing is not to take it personal, to understand that it's just a system and it treats you the same way it treats everybody else, like an engine or a machine or something mechanical. Our names get fed into it—we get fed into it—when we're five years old, and if we catch on and watch our step, it spits us out when we're 17 or 18. (Noyes and McAndrew, 1968, P.58.)

Unfortunately, most schools have become so formally structured and are characterized by so much repetitive and regularized impersonality that they do not have much room for individuals to relate genuinely and closely toward one another. Indeed, the foremost impetus for the rapid growth of the alternative school movement has been rejection of formally structured schools that dehumanize and devalue individual participants. In virtually all of the alternative schools of which we know, the individual is proclaimed as of supreme importance. Often formal, non-human aspects of the school structure, such as curriculum materials and designated times for classes and meetings, are very much underplayed and sometimes avoided entirely. Of course, those alternative schools that have survived beyond their first year do develop some formal rules. No organization, even the most humanized school, can remain viable without some division of labor (and consequently some differentiated role-taking), some formalized rules and regulations, and some routines expected of everyone.

4. The humanized learning group

In summary, we wish to review how the group characteristics that we have just described would operate in the humanized learning group. The interaction patterns would be active, intimate, and personal. Group members would talk about their own feelings and encourage others to talk about their feelings. For some tasks, interdependence would be important but not binding on the members. Thus, individuals would be free to participate in certain tasks and at other times free to work on individual projects or just "get their heads together." Since the group goals would be collectively determined, enough participants would participate to accomplish such goals together. At still other times, the group could divide into subgroups to work on different tasks and to reconvene at a later time to organize their separate products.

Common goals would be established, yet there would be a great deal of leeway for individual expression and diversity of interests. Group and individual goals would overlap often, although some individual interests would never be completely integrated into the group's missions. A comfortable balance would be found between producing something and getting a kick out of doing it and working together. Sometimes the group would be very task-oriented; other times it would focus primarily on the members' feelings. Anger and irritation would be just as easy to discuss as pleasant feelings, and the group would share the expectation that analyses of the interpersonal relations among them would be regularly discussed.

Finally, the group's relationship structure would be predominantly personal and informal. First names would be used, the role of convener or educational leader would be rotated from member to member, and important group functions would be assumed interchangeably and be rotated around the group. Ad hoc task groups would be formed and reformed but seldom with the same members every time. Rules and regulations would be developed out of decision-making procedures involving all members of the group. Although all decisions would not necessarily be by consensus, group agreements would be binding on all the individuals. The minority would have their say but would not interfere with the final decisions.

DEVELOPMENTAL STAGES*

Groups, like individuals, develop systematically and progressively. Individual members have power to choose the course of their group: they can give it a freeing and fluid structure or an inhibiting and closed structure. In this section, we will explore the developmental stages that a learning group might go through on the way to becoming a mature and humanized group. We will start by presenting a theoretical discussion on the formation of learning groups and follow this with some concrete suggestions for the way in which a learning group might proceed toward becoming a humanized and self-renewing group. We believe that almost any learning group, regardless of the

*This section is adapted from Richard Schmuck and Patricia Schmuck, 1971, *Group Processes in the Classroom*, pp. 114-120. For a provocative article with an analogous perspective see Kohlberg and Mayer (1972).

ages of the members or how much time they spend together, will be able to use some of the procedures we recommend.

Just like individuals, groups move through stages as they develop. Erikson's theory (1950) of an individual's psychological development presents some hints for understanding the growth of learning groups. He states that the individual faces a series of problems during his lifetime that must be resolved before he can achieve maturity. He views psychological development as being sequential and successive; each stage follows another in time, and solutions to problems at any later stage are dependent on the resolutions that were made during prior stages. We think that learning groups also pass through sequential and successive stages as they develop. Similar to the individual, a group's growth can be arrested at one stage of development, as, for example, when a learning group cannot effectively carry out an activity requiring cooperative behavior because it has not yet established interpersonal trust and open, two-way communication. Indeed, if a learning group never develops basic interpersonal trust, it will have difficulty developing to more advanced stages because distrust will close off communication and thwart progress.

While both individual and group development are sequential and successive, they also are cyclical, with the same development issues arising in new situations. Even though certain types of psychological problems seem to relate more to specific times in life than do others, individuals continually face many of the same problems throughout their lives. Erikson points out, for example, that the development of trust is the first problem faced by the young infant; however, trust is confronted again when a child begins to have friends, again when adolescent dating occurs, and again when the marriage vows are made. To some degree the interpersonal trust pattern learned during infancy always remains with the developing individual as he enters new relationships. Likewise, group development is cyclical; issues of trust and clear communication continually arise as the group deals with issues of leadership, friendship cliques, and norms.

In attempting to accomplish their academic tasks, learning groups are faced with a vast inner world of emotional life. The social dynamics of both the emotional and task aspects of group life develop simultaneously. Among the many theories regarding group development, three appear to be especially revealing and useful. Each focuses on different aspects of group development and all three have contributed to our understanding of the developmental stages of learning groups.

Schutz (1958, 1966) developed a theory about the emotionality of group members which was based on the members' expressed needs for *inclusion, control,* and *affection.* Schutz's theory emphasizes the personality dynamics of individuals. Parsons and Bales (1955) proposed a theory of group development that emphasized the roles or functions that members must perform in problem-solving groups; their theory is closer to a social level of analysis than a psychological one. The Parsons and Bales theory is helpful for understanding the activities that members must perform in order for learning in a group to occur. Finally, Gibb's (1964) theory of individual and group development contains essential ingredients of both emotionality and problem-solving and therefore has been most useful to our understanding of learning groups.

None of the three theories has been used directly in research on learning groups in schools. Schutz's research included teacher-student dyads and sensitivity groups with educators but was not carried out in public schools. Parsons and Bales made use of simulated problem-solving groups and real families. Gibb conducted experimental and field studies in several industrial and organizational settings. Even though these three theories certainly have limitations in understanding the school learning group, we believe that each presents useful ideas concerning possible developmental stages.

1. Schutz's theory

According to Schutz, individuals naturally express the three interpersonal needs of inclusion, control, and affection to different degrees. His theory states that in the beginning of a group's development the predominant theme of interpersonal interaction is inclusion; this is followed later by control, which, in turn, is followed by affection. This cycle may recur several times prior to the termination of a group's life. The final three stages of a group's history, according to the theory, occur in reversed order, with affection preceding control and inclusion. These stages of group development are viewed as sequential but also as overlapping and continually intertwining.

Issues of interpersonal inclusion characterize the beginning of a group's life. In any kind of learning group, the students and educational leader confront one another's presence and raise implicit questions such as: How will I fit in here? Who will accept me? Who will reject me? What do I have to do to be accepted? Academic work cannot easily be accomplished until these questions of inclusion are answered satisfactorily. Each person—student or teacher—cautiously reveals aspects of himself, while gathering information about others in the learning group. Schutz called the content discussed during this period "goblet issues," because he visualized persons figuratively picking up their goblets and gazing through them to size up others without at the same time revealing themselves. Issues related to inclusion in the peer group may revolve around having friends in common, where one lives, what one's hobbies are, or clues about whether one is pleasant and considerate. Students reveal themselves bit by bit and issue by issue until most of them feel a part of the learning group. Unfortunately, some students never achieve such a feeling of inclusion.

Schutz then views groups as moving on to struggle with influence, which involve the development of decision-making norms and the sharing of responsibility. He calls this the stage of control. It appears inevitable to us that students will test their degree of influence with the designated educational leader as well as with other students. This period of testing for control finds each person attempting to establish a comfortable level of influence for himself within the group.

Next, group members begin to face the emotional issues surrounding affection and closeness. "Who will like me?" and "Whom do I like?" are characteristic questions of this third stage of development. During this period of group growth each person strives for the optimal degree of intimacy with others to suit his personal needs.

Basic to Schutz's theory of group development is the variable of interpersonal compatibility, which he defines as the amount of comfort that exists between two or more persons by virtue of their satisfying each others' needs. Compatible groups have members whose desires for inclusion, control and affection are complementary. For Schutz, groups will develop optimally only when the members are psychologically compatible.

Most educators already know, as the Hargreaves study showed, that simply grouping students according to similar ability or achievement levels does not lead necessarily to cohesiveness in work groups. While it may be difficult for schools to form student groups solely on the basis of psychological needs, on some occasions psychological compatibility may be the best criterion to use. Letting students organize their own ad hoc or task groups may be one way to organize around personality characteristics—students often are accurate judges of their own competence and who they can work with best.

2. Parsons and Bale's theory

This theory specifies that group members must perform certain roles so that the group can solve its problems and remain viable. The two major clusters of roles are designated as *task* and *maintenance* functions; if both functions are not performed, the group will not be effective. We have seen the dilemma discussed by Parsons and Bales occur in several alternative schools which have *not* survived beyond the first year. Members of such schools typically did not perform the task functions needed to keep the organization going. We think this may have been because the participants were often reticent to assume leadership roles or to try to persuade others because such actions might be viewed as inappropriately dominating and consequently as a violation of the autonomy of the individual.

Potentially any member can perform task or maintenance functions, but in most groups particular individuals engage in certain behaviors to a greater degree than others, and usually interpersonal expectations become set about who should perform which roles. According to Parsons and Bales, personality characteristics are important determinants of group life only insofar as they explain why particular persons may take particular roles. Their theory specifies that groups develop in a predictable fashion regardless of the personalities within them.

Research on the Parsons-Bales theory of group behavior was carried out on four-to-eight-person groups with specific problems to solve. The research illustrated the development of a group over a series of meetings as well as its development during one period of time. Stages labeled "phase movements," for example, were shown to occur within a single meeting of two or three hours. Three phases were noted. The first phase generally involves giving and receiving information. During this period of time, information about the problem, background information, and possible solutions are presented. Usually, the solutions are tentative and not well developed. The next (or middle) phase is characterized by the exchange of opinions and evaluations. Members test out ideas, criticize one another's ideas, and jointly develop new ones. Decision-making about what actions to take also occurs during this period. Finally, during phase three, there is an increase in pleasant feelings and a decrease of criticism. Joking, the release of some tension and jovial laughter are typical during this final phase; members attempt to increase their solidarity and to turn their attention to emotional support of one another.

Particular learning groups will go through different phases in one session and other stages over a longer period of time. A single meeting is in some ways, however, a microcosm of total group development. For learning groups to gain strength and momentum, they should be encouraged to move through all three phases during a single meeting. Lippitt (1940) showed an instance in which a group of youngsters failed to reach the third phase of group development but remained instead at the stage of argumentation. In Lippitt's example, the group of students was floundering without direction, decisions were hard to make in the face of interpersonal conflict, and the leader, with his controlling, dominating behavior, could not successfully intervene to move the group onward. The group ended on a note of devisiveness, with a large number of negative interpersonal feelings. In considering this example, we think large amounts of negativism occur in learning groups, especially when the leader has given the group freedom to solve a problem but then steps in prematurely to control and alter the group's decision-making process.

In most school situations which we have observed, the beginning period of a learning group is, for the students, fraught with ambiguity and unclear direction. The way in which the resulting feelings of frustration and insecurity are resolved is critical to the question of how involved the students will become in the group. Educational leaders who suppress the students' resources and feelings and who take over in an authoritarian fashion may lead their learning group in the direction of impersonality and I-It relationships. A leader may not even realize he is doing this, especially when the ideology he or she holds for schools is humanistic. Witness the contradictory thinking of the director of a free school who was bent on maintaining a loose and open school. In speaking about demands on the part of the parents and students for more influence in the school, she seriously commented:

> There was sudden insurrection. There was a demand for a "democratic" structure instead of the autocratic one I had. I insisted on maintaining this control because I knew that as long as I was in control we would have a democratic school. (Carbaga, 1970, P. 7.)

Systematic developmental patterns also arise over the course of a series of meetings, according to research by Heinicke and Bales (1953). They found that over the span of four meetings, members gradually spent less time doing work and more time carrying out social-emotional functions. Although the first meeting was mostly character-ized by cautious and polite behavior, a great deal of negativism arose during the second meeting. The researchers characterized this nega-tivism as "status struggles," (parallel to what Schutz labeled as the control phase), noting that interpersonal conflicts arose mostly when the group was faced with making decisions. The groups that were unable to resolve their status struggles did not move on to become effective in problem-solving, nor were the members happy with the group. Groups which did move successfully through this stage went on to make action plans and did develop favorable feelings and sup-port among their members.

One of the most important revelations of this research is that groups tend to alternate in a cyclical fashion between emphases on task and social emotional concerns. When groups of students are asked to work together on classroom projects, it is realistic to expect that they too will spend nearly half of the available time dealing with emotional aspects of their interpersonal relationships. All groups, both student and adult, spend *a great deal of time* granting emotional support to their members. Learning groups that do not solve their emotional problems also have difficulty in accomplishing academic learning tasks.

3. Gibb's theory

Gibb's ideas (1964) are highly relevant to humanizing learning climates because of his description of personal and group growth as occurring interdependently. His major themes are that groups grow into maturity only after they develop interpersonal trust, and that groups in which trust is not established do not help individual mem-bers to develop self-esteem.

His theory proposes that group members have four basic concerns while their group is developing. The first concern involves interper-sonal acceptance and the formation of trust and confidence in oneself and the group. One's feelings of adequacy and self-esteem are at stake. For the group, concerns of membership and trust in others are most prominent.

The second concern involves what Gibbs calls "data-flow." During this stage, individuals think less about themselves and more about the group. They become aware of the ways in which the group is functioning and begin to evaluate whether they like what the group is doing. Norms begin to emerge about how the group will make decisions. If some degree of acceptance and trust has *not* already been established, decision-making will be hampered by closed and guarded communication, and decisions will be made without much deep commitment on the part of the members. Moreover, solutions of less than optimal quality will be chosen if the closed and guarded communication prevents individuals from contributing novel or appropriate data.

The third stage involves the achievement of goals for both the individuals and the group. Individuals want to achieve something in order to feel successful and competent. They will feel independent and autonomous, provided earlier concerns have been successfully resolved. At the group level, norms will be established about goals and procedures; if there is open communication, goals can be determined to complement those of individuals and the group will develop a comfortable and flexible task structure.

The final concern presented by Gibb is described as the control stage. Individuals feel independent and autonomous provided earlier concerns have been resolved successfully. For the group, norms are formalized, interpersonal behaviors are agreed upon, and the group is able to change itself.

We believe that these four developmental concerns are present in learning groups. Students cannot directly express their own ideas and opinions until they have learned that their peers and the teacher will not reject them. Those students who do not feel accepted will tend to withhold their ideas from discussion. They will feel alienated from academic learning, will be directionless and poorly motivated, will suppress their feelings, and will not abide by the academic norms of the school. Students who learn to trust their peers will become more involved in pursuing their own goals within the learning group, and in abiding by learning group norms.

Learning groups naturally differ in these aspects. In one group, the development may halt and the interpersonal relationships may become formalized and distant. Students do not get acquainted with one another very well in such classes because they do not communicate openly and personally. Some of the students become afraid to express their ideas; discussions, when they do occur, are awkward and lack spontaneity. Typically, the learning goals are presented to the students by the teacher, rewards are extrinsic, and the direction of the group is determined by the evaluations of the teacher. Classroom organization becomes routinized, norms are characterized by a narrow range of tolerable behavior, and the teacher enforces classroom rules. This picture, unfortunately, represents the majority of public school classrooms that we have observed.

In a humanized class the same developmental concerns are confronted, but because of different ways of working with the issues, the group develops differently. As the students cautiously reveal elements of themselves, the teacher accepts a variety of student behaviors. The students learn that their peers are also afraid to reveal themselves but they gradually imitate the teacher's behaviors of acceptance. The students begin to reward one another for the expression of ideas, information is more freely exchanged, and joint decision-making begins to occur. Later the students begin to direct themselves and to establish things they want the class to accomplish. Norms are discussed and changed by the teacher and students as they are no longer helpful to what the learning group wishes to accomplish.

A PRACTICAL GUIDE TO GROUP DEVELOPMENT

The ingredients necessary for the development of whole-person relationships and I-Thou transactions in a group are the skills and abilities of members to communicate their thoughts, feelings, and impressions directly. Because effective communication is so crucial to the development of humanized learning climates, we will begin by summarizing the important skills and exercises that can be used in schools to maximize effective communication. Next we will briefly review the four developmental stages that learning groups move through on the way to humanization and suggest exercises and procedures that can be used to highlight the issues of group development at each stage.

An "exercise" (or simulation) is a structured game-like activity designed to produce group processes that participants can then easily understand *because* they have just been experienced in the game. Each exercise is designed to make salient a certain type of group process. The exercise is not intended to match the complexity of reality but rather to enable members to learn the advantages or disadvantages of specific forms of group behavior. In brief, each exercise has a particular content and product.

The term "procedure," on the other hand, refers to a group activity that does not, in itself, entail a specific content to be learned, but rather allows a group to accomplish its work more effectively. A procedure can be used for a variety of tasks or purposes. For example, certain forms of decision-making (such as majority vote) or problem-solving sequences are procedures. Whereas exercises typically are carried out only once or twice by a learning group, procedures can and should be used regularly throughout the life of a learning group.

Although our ideas are presented in a sequential format, we wish to emphasize that group development is also cyclical. Thus, exercises that are used at the beginning of a group's life to resolve membership issues, for instance, may also be appropriate at a later time because of the fact that questions about belonging can arise repeatedly during the life of a group. The suggestions we present are meant only to be examples. We have not set out to prepare a comprehensive catalogue of activities, although we have tried to include a variety of techniques for humanizing learning groups. Some of our ideas are treated in detail; others are described only briefly, with a reference to where the reader can find additional details. The annotated bibliography at the end of the chapter includes still more ideas.

Our primary criteria for including the activities here are three: first, that the techniques relate primarily to issues of on-going group processes and development, and not to curricular material to be learned; second, that the techniques may be used by anyone—administrator, teacher, or student—with a small amount of previous experience in working with learning groups and a modicum of time and energy; and finally, that the techniques require only materials easily found in most schools. All of our suggestions can be tailored to fit learning groups of all ages.

1. Skill training in verbal communication

The main purpose of the skills that follow is to enhance the clarity of communication between persons. Such skills can also help a group in achieving closeness, interpersonal acceptance, shared influence, and collaborative decision-making. These skills should prove invaluable in helping the learning group to become collaborative and cohesive.

We think that the skills should be practiced one at a time, first as exercises and later as recurring procedures. Initially, the skills should be practiced in a game-like atmosphere; later the same skills should be used as part of the regular class interchange and monitored by student observers to see whether they are being used appropriately and effectively.

Below are brief synopses of five different verbal communication skills, some ideas on how to use them in exercises, and an observation sheet that can be used when the skills are being tried out as part of a group procedure. All students should be shown the observation sheets and given some practice before the skills are used as a learning group procedure. A student's initials can be recorded whenever he performs one of the basic skills. After the learning group has had some experience with both the skills and the observation sheet, student observers can be selected to monitor any class discussion. The student observers should report their findings and the student participants should discuss their own effectiveness in using the skills.

a. Paraphrasing

Paraphrasing is the skill of reiterating the essence of what another person has said in one's own words. If performed properly it shows a regard for what the other person has said and a desire to mirror the other's thoughts accurately. Useful lead-ins to paraphrasing are "I understand you said. . . ." and "Did I read you to say . . . ?" The functions of paraphrasing in a learning group are twofold: to insure that one has understood the communication, and to demonstrate to the other that he has been understood.

One paraphrasing exercise can also be used to achieve feelings of inclusion. In this exercise one student talks to another on his own feelings about coming into the group and the second attempts to paraphrase him. After paraphrasing to the first student's satisfaction, the second student discusses his own feelings on the same topic and is likewise paraphrased. This exercise works very well during the first meeting of a learning group and can be extended in various ways to help create a more accepting atmosphere. For instance, the pairs can be collected into foursomes and, after further discussion and paraphrasing, into eight-person groups, and so on, until the whole group is discussing feelings of acceptance and practicing paraphrasing. The educational leader should participate equally as a member of the learning group.

b. Behavior description

The skill of behavior description involves noting some of the overt behaviors of another person *without* impugning motives and without trying to generalize about or interpret the other's actions. Looking beyond behavior for psychological interpretations often is a cause of miscommunication and defensiveness. Some differences between behavior description and the assignment of motives are clarified by the following examples. "Paul and Mary have talked most during this discussion," and "That is the third time you have interrupted," are behavior descriptions. "Paul and Mary are the only ones who understand the idea," or "Why don't you listen to what I'm saying," are not behavior descriptions but *interpretations* of behavior, and are likely to create defensiveness and to close off dialogue.

Members of a brand new learning group can practice the skill of behavior description in an exercise in which they try to list all those behaviors at the first meeting which made inclusion and involvement easy. They can also list those behaviors that seemed to get in the way of achieving feelings of inclusion and membership. These listings can be done by pairs or small groups, or by the entire group. All three group formations can be used in sequence.

Practice in behavior description generally only works well in regard to recent and relevant behaviors. One should be careful not to use behaviors that were performed too long before, since memories are faulty and too often the actual behaviors have been lost, with only the interpretation remaining. The ideal procedure is to discuss behaviors that have just occurred.

c. Description of own feelings

The direct statement of one's own feelings is probably the least used skill of communication, and its lack of use can cause considerable misunderstanding in a group. It is true that a direct statement of one's feelings places a person in a vulnerable position with others, especially if there is little trust between them. Because trust is an unknown quantity in many learning groups, feelings tend to get expressed in indirect ways and so are often misunderstood. The following examples illustrate differences between direct and indirect expressions of feelings. Direct expressions of feeling are: "I feel embarrassed," "I feel pleased," or "I feel annoyed." These same emotions are often indirectly (and thus ambiguously) expressed by blushing or giggling, or saying, "That's OK" or "Forget it!" Anger, which can be directly expressed in such statements as "That makes me angry," (or annoyed or hurt) is often indirectly expressed by simply withdrawing or by characterizing the other person, as in the statements, "You're mean" and "Why do you do such awful things?"

A poignant instance of the indirect expression of feeling occurred when Allen, our four-year-old son, went to receive a gamma globulin injection against hepatitis. He was well prepared and, at the beginning, not very afraid. His composure broke down, however, when he saw the needle, and he broke into tears. The nurse quickly administered the shot before he could become very agitated, but his immediate response was an angry and teary "You're a bad lady." Such an indirect expression can be accepted and understood from a four-year-old; when it occurs between adults or between a teacher and a student the results may not be as amusing.

A useful exercise early in a group's existence is to ask students to express in various ways their feelings regarding inclusion and then in general discussion to practice making the distinction between direct feeling descriptions and indirect feeling expressions. The exercise begins as each student jots down on a card a description of the feelings he has at present about his place in the group. He then sets the card aside. The leader should explain the entire exercise to the students so they will know how the cards will be used. The next part of the exercise utilizes nonverbal expressions of feeling about one's part in the group. The group stands in a large circle and each student (and the educational leader) in succession places himself in relation to the circle according to how he feels about his membership in the group. A student can also direct the group to move so that his feelings will be expressed clearly. For instance, a focal individual might get in the middle of the circle and direct the members to crowd in closely around him. By contrast, a student might direct the circle to move to one end of the room while he goes to the other end. Next, the nonverbal indirect-feeling expressions are discussed in small groups. The discussions should emphasize the direct description of one's feeling about inclusion. Finally, the students share their previously prepared descriptions of feeling by taping them to the wall for all to see. After some conferring about these responses in twos and threes, all the members of the group discuss how they might enhance one another's feelings of inclusion and membership.

d. Impression-checking

This skill involves checking one's impressions of another's psychological state in a tentative fashion. It is similar to paraphrasing, except that it concerns the interpretation of the *feelings* and *internal processes* of another rather than his words and overt behaviors. Impression-checking is inevitably tentative; it should be used to free the person described so that he will respond by describing his *own* feelings directly. The students and leader should avoid implying disapproval when checking impressions. Some effective impression-checking statements are: "I get the impression that you are angry with me. Are you?" and "You appear uninterested in your work today. Is that right?" Some ineffective impression checks are: "Why are you angry at me?" or "Why don't you like to do what you're supposed to be doing?" These questions make assumptions which may arouse defensiveness and dishonesty.

The most appropriate time to practice impression-checking early in a learning group's life is soon after an exercise on behavior description has been completed. Students can then use their perceptions of one another's behavior as grist for forming their impressions. For example, after some listing of behaviors that were helpful and unhelpful to the development of feelings of inclusion, small groups can discuss their estimates of the feelings that might have been behind such behaviors. In this way, the practice is theoretical and relatively non-threatening. Immediately after, members of the small groups can pair off and practice actual impression-checking by seeing whether they have accurately read some of each other's feelings as aroused by the discussion.

e. Feedback

Feedback involves the giving and receiving of information about how people are affecting one another. It may involve any of the four communication skills, such as *paraphrasing* ("Did I understand you to say that....?"), *behavior description* ("This is the fourth time you've asked me that. Can you say more about your question?"), *descriptions of own feelings* ("I felt very good when you asked my opinion."), or *impression-checking* ("You seem to feel very strongly about the point you were making. Do you?"). The person who receives feedback should be free to use it or not, as he or she chooses. In a learning group, feedback should be given only after careful assessment of the needs of the student receiving it. If feedback is to communicate and engage the student in thought and dialogue, it should arise from a concern for him and not from a need for catharsis on the part of the sender. Feedback is instructive and useful when it is specific and concrete rather than general. Often we do not realize the consequences of our behavior: feedback makes people aware of such consequences. For instance, many students (and adults) often interrupt others. Specific feedback such as, "This morning I have been annoyed because you have cut me off two times—once when I was . . . and then when I . . ." can help others become aware of the consequences of their behavior and provide an opportunity to try to change. It is also important that the sender check to see if the message has been received correctly ("Do you understand why I have been annoyed?").

Feedback should be given after all the four previously mentioned communication skills have been practiced and can be used routinely. Perhaps the best time for feedback regarding issues of inclusion and membership is at the end of the learning group's first two weeks. It is important, of course, that the feedback is constructive and helpful and not traumatic or damaging at this early stage of the group's development. The leader might ask students to write down a few questions about themselves and then choose individuals from whom they would like to receive feedback. Each group should have a student observer whose job is to make sure that all participants are following procedures for constructive feedback.

Feedback should become a routine procedure in the learning group. It is especially important that the educational leader take an equal part in the process. It is good practice to set some daily or at least weekly time aside for discussions. Not only do such discussions help to build feelings of inclusion and membership in the group, but they are also ideal occasions for practicing the four communication skills.

Figure 5-1 is an observation sheet that can be used to monitor communication skills during the regular activities of the learning group and to remind students of their importance.

2. Developmental stages and practical suggestions

We turn now to a discussion of four stages of learning group development, offering exercises and procedures that may be used to highlight the important issues of each stage and to facilitate the development of humanized relationships at each stage.

FIGURE 5-1
OBSERVATION SHEET FOR COMMUNICATION SKILLS

Jot down in the boxes the initials of those who use the skill.

Time

EVIDENCE OF LISTENING:										
A. Paraphrases.										
B. Makes a point relevant to the discussion.										
CONTRIBUTIONS:										
A. Makes a direct description of feeling.										
B. Describes another's behaviors.										
C. Contributes an idea or suggestion.										
IMPRESSION-CHECKING:										
A. Checks the feelings of others.										
B. Paraphrases to understand.										
FEEDBACK:										
A. Tells how others affected him.										
B. Asks others how he is affecting them.										

a. Stage 1: establishing feelings of inclusion and membership

A friend we knew well was very ambivalent about the birth of her first child. Since she had hoped to accomplish many more tasks before becoming a mother, she did not look with favor toward the birth of the child. While she continued to feel resentful and unhappy after the birth, she also gradually grew more fond and attached to the baby. She resolved her ambivalent feelings in a unique manner, surprising especially to those who did not know her well. She openly expressed her resentment to the baby with words, "You messed up my life," "You're a little nuisance," or even "I hate you," while at the same time communicating love and care nonverbally. All of her hostile statements were emitted in tones of endearment and tender affection. She soon settled her ambivalence and accepted the baby both verbally and nonverbally. There is a happy ending to the story: the baby is now a happy healthy child. What the mother uttered apparently was not as important as *how* she said it or the nonverbal cues that she emitted.

At the first stages of group development the specific verbal statements of members are often not as important as the feeling tones and the behavioral patterns that take place. While we do not advocate that leaders should dump their inner conflicts and psychic turmoils verbally onto members at the first meeting, we do think that the way in which the educational leader behaves does have a stronger effect than what is said. A teacher who begins by saying, "You are important and I want to hear what you have to say," but who at the same time curtails discussion among the students will have communicated a different message from that of the words.

Consistency between an educational leader's verbal and nonverbal behaviors is especially important during the very first meetings of a learning group. At the beginning, most students are reticent, anxious, and very concerned about the impressions the teacher and their peers will have of them. Since this new interpersonal situation is at least somewhat ambiguous, the students look to their educational leader for cues on how they are expected to behave. Thus, typically the students scrutinize the leader's behavior very carefully. Most first meetings of a learning group do tend to go smoothly and harmoniously, at least on the surface. All students and the leader attempt to present the best possible images of themselves.

During the first period of group development, by virtue of the traditional position of authority, the educational leader takes on extraordinary power for setting the tenor of the group's future. The leader can set the stage for whole-person relationships, I-Thou transactions, and close collaboration; or for distant role relationships, I-It transactions, and one-way influence; or for something in between. Not until later in the group's development do the members have sufficient information to decide whether the educational leader's behaviors are worth following, ignoring, or rejecting. What is crucial for humanization, then, is that the educational leader take the initiative to help the members of his learning group toward establishing feelings of inclusion and membership.

Herbert Kohl (1969) illustrated two ways in which teachers view their role in the first stage of group development by telling of two classrooms on the first day of school. The first teacher had spent much time arranging her classroom room to appear attractive. On the first day of school, she explained her rules and regulations to the students and informed them of the classroom procedures they would follow. Contrastingly, in the second classroom the teacher had not prepared any particular presentation. She had decided to leave the classroom as she found it the week before and to spend the first day encouraging students to decide how to arrange the physical space. Kohl argued that a year-long pattern for student involvement was already being established on the first day of school in each class. We concur with his view.

The primary theme of the first stage of development in a learning group involves "belongingness": membership. Questions such as "Will they accept me?" "Will they like me?" "Who are they?" and "Can I get close to them?" are asked implicitly and preconsciously by all students. Some learning groups, of course, never do develop past this stage, so that such questions remain unanswered throughout the life of the groups. In such groups the students remain formally distant and unconnected; interaction is subdued; goals usually are not discussed, except perhaps when the teacher announces what they should be; and the group structure is characterized by isolated students taking separate turns to interact with the teacher.

We cannot be precise about the length of time it takes for learning groups to achieve feelings of inclusion and membership. The intensity of the striving for inclusion and its eventual resolution depend on the amount of time the students spend together, the past familiarity of students, the ages of the students, and their previous experience in working out some of the developmental issues in a learning group. However, we believe that every learning group must first resolve the basic issues of membership in some way, even though the resolutions will take on quite different forms and patterns.

The following six suggestions provide what Schutz refers to as the "goblets" through which teacher and students size up one another and cautiously reveal parts of themselves. These exercises and procedures emphasize the kind of interaction between teacher and students and among students themselves that we believe will help build more whole-person relationships and I-Thou transactions in learning groups. They may be used during the launching period or at anytime during the life of a learning group when tensions about belonging and membership arise.

(1) Where do I belong?

Members stand up and mill around the center of the room. Without verbal communication they are asked to divide up into subgroups of four people each. The rule of four to a subgroup is very useful unless the number in the entire group does not allow for this kind of division. As a subgroup becomes too large, members are asked to leave it to form another one. The educational leader should not talk or suggest where students should move; he should just remind them of the rule of four to a group. After the groups have been formed, the students discuss how this entire process felt, how it felt to have to leave one group and join another, and in general their reactions to forming and reforming groups. The educational leader might ask: Was it easier to move toward some groups and not others? Were there verbal or nonverbal messages of acceptance or rejection given? If so, what were they like?

After the subgroups have had a chance to discuss each individual's experience, the entire group should then discuss what the exercise means for the whole learning group, insofar as the group will be working together for a long time. The students should be encouraged to construct a list of behaviors that communicate acceptance of others and those that communicate rejection. The group might also make a list of feelings that students have when they are not accepted or when they do not feel part of a learning group. Finally, the students can discuss what they might do to help new student members feel more at ease and become a part of the learning group.

(2) Finding ways to communicate

This exercise is carried out by pairs of students. The students in each pair begin by sitting back to back, so that they cannot see each other. In this position, they are asked to get to know each other. This activity usually is frustrating because nonverbal facial expressions and bodily motions are generally very integral to communicating verbally with another person. Discomfort often arises when the two students do not know each other very well. Next, the two turn around and face each other and are told to communicate nonverbally— primarily with their eyes, facial expressions, and bodily motions. Feelings of embarrassment and silliness are typical emotional responses. Finally, the two are asked to communicate, still without words, by touching each other while at the same time keeping their eyes closed.

We think that it is mandatory to spend considerable time debriefing these activities because they may leave students confused and embarrassed. Questions raised for discussion might be: What were some of your feelings during part 1, part 2, and part 3? Which form of communication was most conducive to getting to know the other person? Which was least conducive? What other things can we do to get to know others?

This exercise can be useful especially during the first days of a learning group, but can also be employed usefully even after the learning group has been in existence for some time. Remember that when students have already communicated with one another their means of communicating will be different from when they are essentially strangers. At no time during this exercise should the students be pushed into participating or be criticized for what they have or have not done.

(3) Communication by touching

This exercise is done nonverbally. Participants begin by focusing on themselves; they are asked to become acquainted with themselves by touching their face, trunk, legs, arms, etc. Next, pairs are formed, and they similarly become acquainted by nonverbal touching. Both members keep their eyes closed. Finally if crayons, chalk or other supplies are available, each student draws a "feeling portrait" of himself and his pair-mate.

(4) Interviewing

Since this technique can easily be integrated into the work of a learning group and used recurrently throughout the group's life, we define interviewing as a procedure. For the purpose of achieving feelings of inclusion and membership, students count off in pairs to interview each other. Each student within a pair acts as both an interviewer and interviewee. The interviewer is responsible for finding out about the other student and eventually introducing him to the learning group.

This procedure works most efficiently when questions in the interview are decided on beforehand. A discussion in the whole learning group about the questions relevant to getting to know another student can be a very useful prefatory experience to the interviewing. Each interviewer can also be encouraged to construct his own questions. Those students who have writing skills can prepare summaries of the interviews and gather them into a class book. Both the educational leader and new students who enter the group should be interviewed, introduced, and added to the book. Periodically, interviews on other aspects of the lives of the students or about their opinions and ideas on a specific topic can be carried out and added to the class book.

(5) Clearing the air

Interaction in a learning group is most often characterized by studying and producing. However, between these activities many things happen among students which go unnoticed or are ignored because the time seems inappropriate to discuss them. In pursuing the tasks at hand, even very intense irritations may be submerged. Avoiding open discussion of interpersonal tensions is quite natural in work-oriented groups of any kind.

"Clearing the air" offers the learning group a formal period of time for dealing with those events that have created tensions or caused ill-feelings that otherwise would remain submerged and potentially troublesome. Often merely venting one's grievances or irritations publicly can be sufficient to handle them. At other times, however, problems may be of such importance or complexity that steps must be taken toward new understandings and agreements in the learning group. These more serious problems should be earmarked for formal problem-solving (the techniques of which we will discuss later).

Depending on the students' age and experience, the procedure of "clearing the air" can be carried out in various ways. One way is for the students to plan for a specified time of day to hold such discussions. Learning groups with students who have not experienced such discussions should be highly structured, at least until the procedure becomes comfortable and seems legitimate to the students. Another way is to move into a "clearing the air" discussion whenever tension is brought to the surface. If such a norm is established, any time is appropriate for such a discussion; however, some sort of regular structure probably will be preferred by most students.

The following four steps exemplify a design that might be used for clearing the air: (1) *Identify what you liked or did not like about what happened in our learning group today.* The criteria of effective feedback as enumerated above should serve as guidelines for this discussion. The educational leader should emphasize the use of communication skills. Students should be encouraged to specify the behaviors or circumstances that gave rise to their feelings. Perhaps allowing students some time to write out their behavior descriptions and feelings will leave more time for seriously considering the feedback. (2) *Identify what things left you disinterested or bored today.* Again, the students should be encouraged to be concrete, specific, and behaviorally descriptive. (3) *What problems should we work on?* Here, the students should be encouraged to brainstorm a list of problems. After the list is generated, a few can be earmarked for immediate work. Small subgroups of students can be formed to brainstorm proposals for solving the problems. Each small group can later report its proposals to the entire learning group, which in turn can decide on the course of action to be taken. (4) *How is our proposal working?* This question should be asked after some proposals have been tried. For most educational leaders and students this sort of discussion will be a brand new experience, so it is reasonable to expect an initial period of cautious distrust and testing of the limits of risk. Most students will not have a clear idea of what to bring up at first, so it is probably best that someone, probably the educational leader, actively guide discussion. It should also be expected that there will be a few radical statements, such as "School ought to be abolished," "We don't want to do any school work," and "Why do we need to learn arithmetic?" At times like these whoever is leading the discussion should behave with patience but also with directness. If the educational leader is unwilling even to explore a particular proposal, he or she should rule discussion on that point out of order. Of course, on most very radical proposals, the leader can wait for other students to respond or ask other students how they feel. Usually the more reasonable proposals will prevail unless the students have some emotional irritations and tensions to work out with the educational leader or the school.

The least productive thing that the educational leader can do, in discussions like these, is to act accepting of the proposals at first but then later to ignore them or rule them out of order. If educational leaders have nonnegotiable points, they should openly and honestly mark out the boundaries. For students inexperienced in "clearing the air," limiting the boundaries of the discussion can be confusing and tension-inducing. Limitation is important, however, for the eventual development of trust and openness between students and the formal leadership of the school.

Finally, it should be noted that the time provided for "clearing the air" need not be given solely to making grievances public. Just as negative feelings often get submerged, so do positive feelings. Too often, for example, "I liked when you helped me" is not said in learning groups. This kind of discussion is also appropriate for voicing unspoken favorable feelings.

(6) Diagnosing feelings about inclusion and membership

The term "diagnosis" denotes the formal gathering and analysis of data for the solution of a problem. Here we wish to describe some simple diagnostic strategies that can be used to achieve increased feelings of inclusion and membership in learning groups.

One simple method of uncovering feelings in the first stages of a learning group's development is to ask each student to jot down (on an index card) his current feelings and thoughts. These can be read off anonymously by a student while another student records them on the blackboard. Then small subgroups of students can be formed to list the behaviors and circumstances that may have given rise to those feelings and thoughts.

Another simple diagnostic method is to ask the students to check their reactions to the first day of class on a five-point scale such as: (1) strongly favorable, (2) favorable, (3) neutral, (4) unfavorable, and (5) strongly unfavorable. Using the same sort of scale, they might in more detail complete these statements: When I entered the room this morning I felt _____, After being with this learning group for one hour I felt _____, Toward the educational leader I felt _____, etc. Answers can be put on the board immediately for feedback and review the next day. The students can then discuss what aspects of interaction made it favorable or unfavorable. For very young students the verbal five-point scale can be replaced by a three-point or five-point scale of smiling, indifferent, and frowning faces drawn on the board with numbers under them.

b. Stage 2: establishing shared influence and collaborative decision-making

After the students and educational leader have built some sense of security and belonging, two kinds of "power struggles" typically become prominent in a learning group. One has to do with testing the formal leader's power limits and typically involves the psychodynamics of dependency and counterdependency. The other concerns the pecking order of the student peer group and involves the psychodynamics of domination and autonomy.

Traditionally the pattern has been for the teacher to maintain *all* important power in the classroom. Beneath the surface of a controlled classroom, unresolved interpersonal conflicts and tensions exist between the teacher and students and also within the student peer group. Teachers of such classes have been warned, "Don't smile before Christmas." This means that if they can maintain formal control during the first four months of school, they have a good chance of avoiding disruptions or attempts to gain control. They also prevent the development of a humanized climate in the learning group, however.

Those teachers who manage to "keep the lid on," not only waste energy in policing students' interactions, but also tend to miss the excitement—as well as the pain—of getting genuinely close to their students. Conflict over how things will operate and who will make decisions is very natural. After all, such conflicts arise in all human relationships: between child and parent, friends, and spouses, and also in churches, communities and communes, and nation-states.

Attempts to control can be seen clearly at certain stages of child development. There are the invincible and incorrigible two- or three-year-olds who struggle with their parents as they discover ways to be autonomous and independent. "I do it myself" the child says, as he or she persistently and incapably tries to button a shirt, or "You go away" as the child touches a forbidden object. The child hears the word "no" over and over as he or she attempts to establish an independent position in the world. Of course, the child's attempts at autonomy and influence are mixed with wishes for love, acceptance, and security. Part of the control issue for the youngster involves testing the limits of love and acceptance.

A similar development of acceptance and control occurs in learning groups. One common question among T-group trainers is whether the trainer has managed to "stick it out" with his group or if he has been kicked out. In learning groups a similar issue arises. How the leader's role in the group will be resolved depends in part on how the group has developed during its first stage. The educational leader who has maintained all power by "not smiling before Christmas" will most likely produce a well ordered, formal (possibly even pleasant) classroom where no student makes an obvious attempt to gain power. Such classrooms, however, also tend to produce students who feel alienated from classroom life and school. There will not be many public influence struggles, except for a few attempts to test the authority of the leader.

We do not intend to imply that educational leaders who have encouraged closeness, "belongingness," and shared leadership in the beginning stages of the learning group's life will have an easy time during this second stage. After all, their norms support public discussions of conflict and "clearing the air," and the movement toward collaborative decision-making and shared influence can produce a great deal of tension. An example of the difficulty comes from the innovative Adams High School in Portland, Oregon. From the beginning great effort was made at that school to increase dialogue and collaborative decision-making between staff and students. Apparently these efforts were successful in bringing a feeling of community to the school: While other schools were suffering from delinquency, drug problems, racial conflicts and the like, Adams stood out for its cohesiveness and high morale. Yet, during its second year of operations, there were several attempts—both from students and faculty—to write and rewrite a constitution and to change the governmental structure. Apparently the difficulty was not in establishing collaborative power as much as in defining the structures to maintain it. In other words, the logistics of shared influence and collaborative decision-making are extremely cumbersome even when the norms and attitudes support them. Even if successful structures for collaboration can be built, they will not be utilized without some conflict and interpersonal struggles. The important criterion for humanization is that this struggle is carried on openly and honestly, and that the individual students and staff members are heard and respected. The following eleven procedures and exercises can help learning groups to deal with the inevitable difficulties of arranging for shared influence.

(1) The learning group steering committee

The steering committee is a procedural structure for implementing representative democracy; it is one way of trying to disperse influence among the students. The primary purpose is collaboration in decision-making; the primary procedure is for a small group of representatives to solve problems and propose innovative actions to the entire learning group.

The very first arrangements for implementing such a group should be decided upon either by the educational leader or by the learning group as a whole. However, since many students will not have a very clear idea of what is possible, the educational leader should be the most active in launching the steering committee. Successful examples that we have observed have provided for a rotating membership with the terms of some students overlapping for purpose of continuity. If the membership is rotated, eventually all students in the learning group will have an opportunity to take part. The terms of service should not be shorter than two weeks nor longer than two months. The steering committee is charged with suggesting goals, rules, and procedures, and final decisions are made by the whole group. Naturally, the educational leader should decide whether to reserve veto power and should announce that decision to the steering committee at its first meeting.

The educational leader should remember that the communication skills of paraphrasing, behavior description, description of feelings, impression-checking, and feedback are very useful, and perhaps necessary, for successful participation in the steering committee. Also, some practice in "clearing the air" and in collecting diagnostic data will be useful prerequisites to the group. In short, some maturity of understanding and skill about inclusion and membership is basic to effective collaboration among the students.

One teacher met with the steering committee three times a week during lunch hours. She actively trained the students beforehand in communication skills and reminded them to use the skills in the group. She also helped the committee establish agendas and clear decision-making procedures. Later in the school year, she gave still more power to the committee and became much less involved as the initiator and prodder. Students became group conveners and began carrying virtually all of the discussion.

As an example of committee influence on learning procedures, let us consider a high school general science class studying plants. The steering committee has gathered information that students are bored and disinterested in this topic and the teacher is concerned that students are not mastering the material. The steering committee may have made a diagnosis of the problem after several students complained to them about the topic. They may then have gathered more information by having each student fill out a short questionnaire and by talking to the teacher. The problem posed to the steering committee is: How can we make the study of plants more interesting and at the same time help the students to master the information prescribed by the teacher or curriculum guide. The steering committee may think of several alternative plans: (1) have more field trips so students can see plants in their natural habitat, (2) have the teacher make up a list of specific competency requirements so that students know what is expected of them, (3) have speakers from conservation groups of local nurseries come in to discuss the importance of plants, (4) set up a simple plant laboratory in the school so students can conduct their own experiments. The steering committee could bring the statement of the problem and the list of alternatives to the entire learning group concerned with plants. The entire group would decide which, of any, of the options they would pursue. The final procedure for decision-making would depend on the learning group; if it were a class involving several hundred students and several teachers, the decision might be made by majority opinion; if the group were small it might strive for consensus: everybody is willing to go along with the plan decided upon, even if some were in disagreement with it.

Although the establishment of a learning group steering committee may be a complex procedure for achieving shared influence and collaborative decision-making, it is the sort of structure that we believe will be useful in humanizing schools. Prior to establishing a steering committee, however, it may be necessary to help the students gain knowledge and skill in using influence processes. Exercises 2, 3, and 4 are helpful for this purpose.

(2) Hand-mirroring

Pairs are formed, and the two students in each pair are asked to face each other but not to talk or touch. They then put their arms and palms up facing those of the other person. At a signal, one student moves his arms up, down, sideways, or diagonally, and the second student follows the movements as if he were a mirror. After a short period, the roles are exchanged and the second student leads. Finally, the two are told to exchange the leadership in any way they wish, but to find agreement and share the leadership nonverbally. It can be effective to let each student carry out this exercise with four or five others before final discussion. The exercise should close with a discussion about reactions to hand-mirroring. What feelings did the participants have? Was it easier to lead or to follow? How did each feel when the leadership was unspecified? What implications are there in this exercise for the learning group?

(3) The influence line

The influence line exercise allows potential power struggles between members of a learning group to surface. The learning group members —including the educational leader—are asked to line up according to their own perceptions of who is most influential (first) to who is least influential (last). The basis on which they line up, of course, is very important. The way the students make decisions about who should be placed where in the line constitutes information for subsequent discussion.

In some groups a final line-up of influence may never occur because of continued disagreements about who should be where. The line-up itself should take no more than twenty minutes. If the line has not formed by that time the leader should intervene and begin discussion about the processes. The important element in this exercise is the discussion about what behaviors are influential; the exercise should *not* focus on the qualities of the individual students. For some groups physical prowess is the most important factor leading to influence, for other groups high intellectual abilities may lead to influence, and for others how pleasant and "nice" a person is to others may constitute an importance influence. Students should be able to see the qualities that they, as a group, value and which are therefore influential. They should *not* end up merely with the fact that because Joe is the most influential member in the group he is therefore better than the other members. Students may also carry on this discussion by asking themselves what an ideal influence structure would be like; what qualities or traits or behaviors are valued highly enough to influence others.

(4) Tinker toys

Another effective exercise for exploring influence in a learning group involves a common set of tinker toys. The students are divided into about three subgroups, each receiving a box of tinker toys. Each subgroup then is asked to use half the toys to construct a model of the learning group's influence structure as it currently exists and the other half for a model of an ideal influence structure for this learning group. Afterwards each subgroup describes to the other two what they talked about while they were constructing the models and finally all the students try together to summarize the generalizations.

The six procedures that follow (numbers 5 through 10) can also help to disperse interpersonal influence in learning groups.

(5) The chance to listen

Although discussions in a learning group can allow everyone to have a say, there is often little regard for whether what is said is understood or persuasive. One procedure facilitating clearer and fuller communication is for participants, before they speak, to paraphrase what the previous speaker has said. The rule should also apply to the educational leader. Before a proposal is decided upon, also, several students can paraphrase the terms of the proposal so that everyone is clear about what is being decided on. The educational leader can also be charged with insuring that all participants are granted, along with their right to be heard, the right to understand completely the group's communications. This procedure may first be tried as part of a paraphrasing exercise, later attempted within the steering committee, and finally employed during discussions of the entire learning group.

(6) Tokens for talking

This procedure, as well as item number 7, can be used to encourage all students to participate in discussions and decision-making. For instance, when only a few students talk during discussion, the time tokens can be used to ensure wider participation. At the start, each student is allotted the same number of tokens. When making a verbal contribution, he must give up one of his tokens to a spot in the middle of the learning group. He can speak only as long as his tokens last.

(7) High-talker tap-out

Another method to prevent domination by only a few students is the "high-talker tap-out." A coordinator (either the educational leader or a student) monitors the group to see if any participant seems to be dominating the interaction. If one or two are dominating, then the coordinator hands them instructions to refrain from further comment, except perhaps on the group process. In this way, the balance of participation can be made more equal.

(8) Buzz groups

Another device that can be used to increase participation in a large learning group is the buzz group. The class meeting is temporarily interrupted while subgroups of from four to seven students form to discuss a developing issue for a short time. This can be done especially when important decisions have to be made and some students hesitate to express contrary views in front of the entire learning group. When feelings are difficult to bring out, the buzz groups can have reporters summarize the ideas and feelings of each group without indicating which students expressed them. Such summaries also make it difficult for any one group of students to dominate the flow of interaction.

(9) Fishbowl

Since the problems of participation in a large learning group are much more complex than those in a small one, tap-outs and time tokens may not be very useful or practical. One procedure that uses some of the advantages of small-group discussion within the setting of a large meeting is the fishbowl or theater-in-the-round. In the fishbowl arrangement, a small group is formed within a circle made by the larger group. The small group (which may be the steering committee, for instance) discusses whatever is on the agenda while the other students observe. Empty chairs can be provided in the fishbowl, so that any observing student can *temporarily* join the discussion, thus insuring wider participation.

(10) Clarification of norms about decision-making

The following procedure (which can also begin as an exercise) can be used to help a learning group to clarify its norms about how decisions should be made. The educational leader should first present some information about what a norm is. He can say, for instance, that a norm is a sort of "rule of the game." A more formal definition is that a norm is a shared group attitude about how members ought to behave. A distinction should be made between formal and informal norms. Formal norms are usually open and clear and sometimes written out; for example, "Everyone should turn in assigned work on time." Informal norms, on the other hand, are usually not stated and are held only implicitly by the group. Such norms, for example, would govern the way in which one talked to the educational leader and would dictate that one followed the behaviors of some peers and not others.[*]

After definition, students are asked to write what they think the formal and informal norms are that govern the behaviors of their learning group. They are asked to describe what the norms are, not what they *should be*. Small groups of five students each can then assemble to pool their ideas of the norms and to write them on large pieces of newsprint so that all others can see them. The small groups then come together into a total body, which considers these lists and then makes up its own list of the formal and informal norms that govern the learning group. The next step is to determine whether some of these norms should be changed. Steps can then be taken to modify them.

One reason for starting this activity as an exercise is that norms are rather difficult to understand. Students may come to understand them more easily if they first attempt to describe the norms of some fictitious groups, such as a typical football team. Furthermore, it is

---

*For more information about norms see Chapter 5 in Schmuck and Schmuck, 1971.

very important for students to understand that norms are those shared expectations about behavior that actually govern the actions of a group, and *not* concepts of behavior that students or teachers regard as ideal. For instance, students usually do not think that interrupting another person is a good thing to do, but in many learning groups it is a frequent and common occurrence. If interrupting occurs frequently and is not rebuffed or punished by the members, it is actually a part of the informal normative behavior of the group.

(11) Diagnosing the influence process

Just as diagnosis can be valuable as part of stage 1, it also can play an important part in helping a group to become more knowledgeable and skillful about its influence processes. Students (and the educational leader) might be asked: "How satisfied are you with your level of influence in the group?" The choice of answers could range among (1) highly satisfied, (2) satisfied, (3) neutral, (4) dissatisfied, and (5) highly dissatisfied. Or they might be asked, "In what part of this learning group do you think you personally stand with regard to influencing others?" (1) upper half or (2) lower half. Or each member might be asked to complete a sentence such as, "When this group makes a decision, the part I play is _____," or a paragraph beginning, "The following list describes some of my feelings when our learning group is holding a discussion."

The answers to any of these queries are useful, of course, only to the degree that they are categorized and fed back to the group. It is an appropriate function for the steering committee of a learning group to collect such data intermittently and to create meaningful ways of feeding it back and using it.

c. Stage 3: Pursuing academic and individual goals

We have friends who helped establish the New School, an alternative school located in Spokane, Washington. In the beginning stages, the staff, parents, students, and consultants spent hours in seemingly endless talk, making decisions about running the school, until all were on edge, frustrated, tired, and feeling as if the talk had been fruitless. These feelings lasted almost until Thanksgiving vacation, when a student finally noted a breakthrough. "At last," he exclaimed, "We have come to a decision. We have finally decided who will empty the ash-trays."

To some people, analysis of such an "unimportant" decision may seem belabored and inconsequential. For the New School in its first months of operation the decision was monumental in the importance of its implications. This seemingly unimportant decision was the first one in which all the decision-making processes had taken a visible and concrete form. In fact, this decision set a precedent for many later decisions. By implication, the decision meant (1) that all people should be involved in making certain decisions, (2) that some maintenance chores had to be accomplished, and (3) that somebody had to be responsible for carrying out necessary maintenance chores. In working out this seemingly unimportant decision the group had developed a crude sense of responsibility to establish a division of labor to maintain the organization itself. The New School is now in its fourth year; it has rules and regulations about emptying ash trays and community meetings no longer focus on such concerns, except when members are not doing their jobs. However, the school has kept the precedents set down by its first decision. Learning is carried out when an inventory of individual's objectives is taken, plans of action are decided upon, and someone is assigned responsibility to make sure those plans are carried out.

Learning groups within public schools are not in the position of creating a new institution; consequently many of their concerns are not the same. Public schools operate within a framework of "givens" laid down by the school board, as well as community or fiscal concerns, and they usually do not include "ash tray" issues. Yet humanized learning groups within the public schools do take time to discuss issues of procedure and decide on precedents for how they will function.

Teachers who are concerned about finishing the formal curriculum may ask, "But aren't such discussions a waste of time?" Learning groups are not ready to work diligently and productively on academic and personal growth until they have settled the issues of group membership and interpersonal influence at least to some degree. This does not mean that learning groups have merely to "sit and rap" for their first few months of existence. Some academic work, of course, is done during the early stages of group development, but not so much as during this third stage.

One third grade teacher in a public school put the case very neatly when she described to us her three-stage design for the year. The first stage generally lasted from the beginning of school until December. Students carried out the usual tasks of skill development and reading but her primary goals were helping the students to feel comfortable with one another, to work independently, to make collaborative decisions, and to learn how to be cooperative. She visualized January through May as the period of high academic productivity. During these months, students set their own goals and developed many projects that emphasized various academic skills. May and June were primarily given over to evaluating progress by students and teacher, setting goals for the students' next year at school, and getting the students ready to work with their next teacher.

One frequent complaint we hear from teachers in traditional classrooms is that they waste too much time policing interactions in the learning group. To us, such complaints of unruly and undisciplined students indicate that the first two stages of group development have not been resolved to a sufficient degree to allow academic work and personal growth to become predominant themes. In our experience, students who have achieved feelings of membership along with the skills of shared influence and collaborative decision-making do not have the great number of discipline problems that plague traditional classroom groups.

The third stage of group development is a "high production" period; it is the time when the norms and procedures established during the first two stages come to fruition in the attainment of academic and personal goals. This stage is most closely visible in a learning group which comes together for a short time to fulfill a specific function, such as a project. By the third stage the students should know each other well and have an understanding of one another's resources. They have settled some of the leadership questions and are ready to set clear goals, divide tasks, and set deadlines for completing the tasks.

During this stage the antagonistic pulls between the production goals of the group and the students' feelings will become obvious and persist as a problem intermittently. As we indicated before, research by Bales and Parsons showed that groups tend to swing back and forth between a focus on task and a focus on the social-emotional issues. Some meetings are almost totally given over to individuals' feelings while others are directed toward production.

We believe concerns about students' satisfactions and feelings should take up a good deal of time in learning groups, and that the time taken is not wasted in terms of academic learning. It is imperative that social-emotional issues are handled if learning groups are to work productively. Learning groups that ignore the basic pulls and tugs between members' goals and class academic goals will not be successful in their production efforts and will be missing a significant part of their productivity—the personal growth element.

The third stage is by no means all "sweetness and light," with students diligently and efficiently working on their goals. Group development is cyclical as well as linear. Some hours or days, even at the height of productivity, will be filled with intense conflicts between students about improper participation or incompleteness. Also, a learning group may come to a collective decision with which a minority disagrees strongly. Such conflicts, of course, should be publicly dealt with immediately. It should be kept in mind that short-term groups which are part of a larger body will themselves reflect in microcosm the developmental sequence of the larger group.

For students who have already developed some trust and skill in communication and group decision-making, the key problems of the first two stages can be resolved quickly and easily. Unfortunately, public schools do not usually provide opportunities to learn about group development, so that teachers with a group-skill orientation must spend much time developing students' decision-making skills—even for deciding such simple issues as who will empty the ash tray.

The third stage of group development focuses upon the pursuit of academic goals as well as individual student growth—the two primary reasons for which students should go to school. The six exercises and procedures that follow present ways in which these two very important goals can be pursued simultaneously.

(1) Students as educational leaders

The surest way to combine the pursuits of academic goals and personal growth is for students to assume the role of educational leader part of the time. There are several reasons why student teaching can be beneficial. For instance, teaching a body of knowledge requires more involvement and commitment than merely being presented with it. Also, teaching encourages the individual student to display and build upon his own resources. Furthermore, teaching presents the student with experience in being responsible for others and can thereby increase the student's feelings of inclusion and influence within the learning group.

There are several procedures for putting students into the teaching role, described in items 2, 3, and 4 below.

(2) Cross-age tutoring

In this procedure an older student tutors a younger one in some academic area. The actual tutoring procedures can vary considerably; for instance, the older can take the younger student to the library, read to him, or teach him specific lessons, such as in reading or arithmetic.

Most of the research on cross-age tutoring indicates that it is the *older* student who gains more from the tutoring relationship; an older student, for example, who has trouble with reading may well be assigned to a beginning reader, or an older student who has problems in math may benefit from teaching simple mathematical skills. Patricia Schmuck, for example, used a group of junior-high-age boys with severe reading disabilities to tutor elementary students in reading, and found that the reading skills of the older boys, as well as their understanding of personal problems, were greatly enhanced.

(3) Teaching mini-courses

Mini-courses (short courses with a specific curriculum) can be ideal mechanisms for encouraging students to teach. Short courses involving arts and crafts, special hobbies, or social problems can be created in nearly any kind of school organization. The main administrative issues are (1) identifying the strengths and interests of the students and (2) scheduling such a program. The first of these calls for a diagnostic questionnaire, prepared and scored by a team of students. Scheduling difficulties can be worked out by the principal and a few teachers and students in a problem-solving session.

(4) Teaching the formal curriculum

In some instances students can do a better job of teaching the formal curriculum that the regular teacher. One third-grade teacher, for instance, who was confused and insecure with the New Math decided her students had fewer hang-ups about the mathematical concepts than she did. Consequently, she gave up her information-giving function and replaced it with the functions of advisor and helper. For two weeks, two students were assigned the role of math teacher. She worked closely with them in developing lesson plans and practicing their presentations. The students would present the information, give the assignments, and then evaluate the class's progress. Her class did about the same as other classes in math achievement tasks; however, her students expressed more liking for math, compared to students of other classes.

Before students teach the formal curriculum, however, they should gain some knowledge and skill in how to be helpful participants in a learning group. Few people can execute facilitative leadership without some training and practice, and students are no exception. If students are to be successful as educational leaders, there must be considerable previous discussion clarifying the rationale, norms, and procedures for everyone. The following exercise (number 5) and procedure (number 6) can increase students' awareness and skills in group discussion and open the way to increased skills in tutoring and teaching.

(5) Goal-directed leadership

This exercise helps students to learn about the functions needed to make a group discussion effective. About half the group acts as discussants while the other half, acting as observers, surrounds them in the fishbowl arrangement discussed previously. The observers are given some instruction and practice in how to use observation sheets. (Figure 5-2 presents an example for elementary groups. Figure 5-3 is more appropriate for secondary students.)

The exercise can achieve high student interest when a real problem is discussed. Examples of such problems are: What can we do to learn a lot, work hard, and still have fun? How can we make sure that everyone in our learning group is learning? How can we help one another learn? If we could make this an ideal school for learning, what would it be like?

The time allowed for discussion, especially on the first occasion, should be limited to about ten minutes for younger children and twenty minutes for older students, to enable the observers to practice and to allow ample time for their feedback afterward. During the discussion, the observers mark their sheets by writing the initials of whomever performs one of the leadership functions listed. At the end of the discussion the observers report their observations to the entire group.

FIGURE 5-2
OBSERVATION SHEET FOR GOAL-DIRECTED LEADERSHIP
(Elementary)

Jot Down Initials of Students

Task Jobs	Time 1	Time 2	Time 3	Time 4
Giving Ideas:				
Getting Ideas:				
Using Someone's Idea:				

Jot Down Initials of Students

People Jobs	Time 1	Time 2	Time 3	Time 4
Being Nice				
Saying How You Feel				
Letting Others Talk				

Humanizing
learning
groups

FIGURE 5-3
OBSERVATION SHEET FOR GOAL-DIRECTED LEADERSHIP
(Secondary)

		Time				
		1	2	3	4	5
TASK FUNCTIONS	1. Initiating: Proposing tasks or goals; defining a group problem; suggesting a procedure for solving a problem; suggesting other ideas for consideration.					
	2. Seeking information or opinions: Requesting facts on the problem; seeking relevant information; asking for suggestions and ideas.					
	3. Giving information or opinions: Offering facts; providing relevant information; stating a belief; giving suggestions or ideas.					
	4. Clarifying or elaborating: Interpreting or reflecting ideas or suggestions; clearing up confusion; indicating alternatives and issues before the group; giving examples.					
	5. Summarizing: Pulling related ideas together; restating suggestions after the group has discussed them.					
	6. Consensus testing: Sending up "trial balloons" to see if group is nearing a conclusion; checking with group to see how much agreement has been reached.					
SOCIAL EMOTIONAL FUNCTIONS	7. Encouraging: Being friendly, warm, and responsive to others; accepting others and their contributions; listening; showing regard for others by giving them an opportunity or recognition.					
	8. Expressing group feelings: Sensing feeling, mood, and relationships within the group; sharing own feelings with other members.					
	9. Harmonizing: Attempting to reconcile disagreements; reducing tension through "pouring oil on troubled waters"; getting people to explore their differences.					
	10. Compromising: Offering to compromise his own position, ideas, or status; admitting error; disciplining oneself to help maintain the group.					
	11. Gatekeeping: Seeing that others have a chance to speak; insuring a group discussion rather than a one-, two-, or three-way conversation.					
	12. Setting standards: Expressing standards that will help group to achieve; applying standards in evaluating group functioning and production.					

The educational leader should set the ground rule that no one should talk until the observers' report is finished. There is bound to be some disagreement or clarification needed on the way observers have decided upon the relevant categories. After the observation reports are understood and issues of disagreement are resolved (paraphrasing is an excellent device here), the whole group should hold a general discussion about the typical processes of their group. Do some students take all the initiative? Do some students perform only one function? Do all students have a chance to perform some function? What have we learned from this?

One variation on this exercise is for the discussants to determine privately before the discussion begins one or two leadership functions that they will emphasize. The observers are then charged with trying to determine what function any particular discussant was performing. The primary purpose of their observations is to supply feedback to the discussants on how their behaviors in the group came across. An alternative is for the educational leader to give to every discussant a card with a leadership function printed on it. The discussant then tries to act out that function during the discussion. Either of these exercises gives students practice in new types of behavior for facilitating effective group processes.

It should be warned that objective use of observation sheets takes time and practice. It is useful if some skills of observation and recording can also be taught as part of the academic curriculum prior to the use of this specific exercise. Indeed, if fishbowl observations are to become regular procedures for the learning group, the build up of additional knowledge and skills is very important. One teacher we know regularly designated three observers for almost every group activity. The observers' reports served as a source of data for students and were learning experiences in themselves. Observing became a regular procedure and turned out to be a rich activity for learning—especially learning about oneself.

(6) A problem-solving procedure

A systematic problem-solving procedure can help learning groups work out new ways to reach their academic and personal growth goals. The procedure calls for a group to organize its discussions about goal-striving within the framework of a problem-solving sequence. A problem, in this application, is defined as any discrepancy between a goal and present reality—between what ought to be and what is. The problem-solving procedure emphasizes making clear statements about goals, diagnosing the situation as it is now, and establishing plans and commitments for future action.

The formal sequence of questions in the procedure is: (1) What are the goals? (Distinguish between academic areas and personal desires.) (2) What, to date, has been done to move us closer to our goals? (3) What is our present condition in relation to those goals? (4) If our here-and-now condition is not desirable, (a) what forces are keeping us from moving?, (b) what plans or solutions seem appropriate, and (c) what other things do we have to know about before making a plan or proposing a solution? (5) What should our proposed activities be and what should our schedule be for completing them? Finally, (6) Who will do what, and what should the outcome be?

d. Stage 4: Keeping the learning group adaptive

Healthy learning groups, like healthy students, eventually reach a condition of adaptive maturity. For the healthy student reaching such a state is not synonymous with completion, but rather a state of heightened readiness for continuous growth and for the regularized broadening of competencies, skills, and interests. Adaptive maturity involves confronting the options in one's life, the ability to respond with choices, and the courage to accept the consequences of one's decisions. John Gardner (1963) applied the term "self-renewal" to this kind of adaptive procedure. Self-renewing groups can continue to form new purposes and procedures out of their own internal resources and they have the competence to adopt new processes when the old ones are no longer functional. They are termed "mature" because the members accept the responsibility for their life as a group and are continuously striving to improve it.

Although this description may sound appealing, self-renewing learning groups are not easy to live in. They face a continuous array of human problems such as intermittent feelings of exclusion and alienation, power struggles and resentments, and frustrated goal-striving. While they afford much satisfaction and comfort to the members, they do not allow for complacency. While they support individual growth and insight, they also are confrontative and challenging.

Indeed, from one point of view, adaptive learning groups can be seen as having many contradictions. They are always the same, but yet they are changing. There is no end, no point of completion. Each day, like every other day, brings its miseries and frustrations along with its small joys and miracles. Allan Watts (1961) said it well:

> The people we are tempted to call clods or boors are just those who seem to find nothing fascinating in being human; their humanity is incomplete, for it never astonished them. (P. 130.)

The following two exercises are examples of the kinds of activities that can greatly strengthen a learning group's ability to remain astonishing to its members and therefore adaptive as a group.

FIGURE 5-4
JOHARI MODEL OF AWARENESS IN INTERPERSONAL RELATIONS*

	Known to Self	Not Known to Self
Known to Others	1. OPEN Area of sharing and openness	2. BLIND Area of blindness
Not Known to Others	3. HIDDEN Area of avoided information	4. UNKNOWN Area of unconscious activity

(1) The Johari model

The Johari Awareness Model, named by combining the names of its authors, Joe Luft and Harry Ingram, assumes that every person has elements that are known and unknown to the group. It should be used late in the life of a group. Its purpose is to help strengthen the learning group by increasing the openness of the members and by decreasing the hidden, blind, and unknown. The educational leader presents a picture of the so-called Johari Window (as shown in figure 5-4) to the group. Students should draw the chart and fill in quadrants 1 and 3. Pairs or small groups are formed to give feedback about quadrant 2. An example of what a completed form might look like is illustrated in figure 5-5.

FIGURE 5-5
COMPLETED JOHARI MODEL

Example: How I Feel About This Class

1	2
I don't like to read out loud. I like to have class discussions. I think this class is "cool."	You act mean when you get a score. You say "ah" a lot when you talk out loud in class.
3	4
I am afraid of making mistakes. I like to work with Joe.	

(Reproduced from p. 111 of Schmuck and Schmuck, 1971)

(2) Strength-building exercise

This exercise aims at building self-esteem and identification with the learning group by publicly sharing students' favorable characteristics and identifying the group's resources. This exercise can be used several times during the school year to keep students informed of the group's resources as well as their growth. It should not, however, be introduced too early, because it requires a modicum of basic trust. We have found that it often is difficult for students to express openly to one another their strengths. Young children and even many adults respond to this exercise with "It's not nice to brag." It must be clear, however, that the exercise is important in keeping the learning group's ability strong.

Students are given a large sheet of newsprint paper and asked to put their name at the top and to list at least three things that they consider as personal strengths. Sample items are: I obey the rules, I listen to others, I help, I can blow a bubble, I don't get angry fast, I can tie my shoes, I'm pretty smart, I get good grades, I like people, I read a lot, I can build a motor, I know about dinosaurs, I ski well, etc.

Each student then tapes his or her paper to the wall for all to see. The students move about reading the papers. Each student lists at least one additional strength on everyone else's paper. Written statements may be repeated or not, depending on the group's decision. Next, the learning group divides into subgroups to discuss how each student's strengths can be used in the group. One student, for example, may be a resource for another student or for the entire group. The exercise may lead to a new project or it may mean nothing more than a new appreciation of the various strengths of students. The strengths of students, once they are shared as a resource, can be used at various times during the life of a learning group.

A variation on this exercise is to list weaknesses next. The same method can be followed but the discussion can include ways in which students' strengths can be used to help others with their weaknesses.

SUMMARY OF CHAPTER 5

Educators often overlook the strong influence that a student's peer group has on his or her attitudes about teachers, the curriculum, administrators, fellow students, and the school as an institution. In most schools, neither curriculum designs nor many instructional strategies take into consideration the power of informal interpersonal relationships. Indeed, many teachers never plan to use the energy of peers in interaction with one another to achieve educational goals.

We believe that school participants can work collaboratively to design the course of life for their learning group. Since group members can alter their normative climate—if they work at it together—they can humanize the traditional learning group climate of formal role relationships and I-It transactions, developing interpersonal norms that support warm and encouraging whole-person relationships, public discussion of tensions and conflicts, collaborative decision-making, and the development of a view of learning as an exciting and joyful adventure. The primary step in gaining power over the group climate is for the educational leader and students to recognize how the dynamics of learning groups work.

Groups develop through stages, just as individuals do. Learning groups, in particular, face a series of interpersonal problems that must be resolved if the groups are to develop humanized climates. Learning groups develop in a sequential manner; each stage of development must be passed through and the tensions of it resolved before the next stage can fully begin. The resolutions developed at one stage are important for the way in which the interpersonal problems that arise in the next stage will be resolved. Like individuals, learning groups may be thwarted or arrested in development. If successful resolutions are *not* made during any given stage, further resolutions at later stages will be difficult, if not impossible.

We note four stages of development for learning groups. Resolutions must be made first on tensions that concern inclusion and membership; second, on issues involving authority, influence relationships, and the way in which decisions are to be made; third, on the establishment of and agreement upon goals; and finally, on the challenge of building an adaptive, self-renewing group. To facilitate learning group development at each of these stages, we present some exercises (simulations designed to examine group processes) and procedures (methods for handling current tasks or problems) that learning groups can use to confront the complex dynamics of each developmental stage.

We maintain that unless the primary issues at each stage of learning group development are publicly confronted and resolved, the emotional and intellectual development of the students in them will be frustrated and limited.

ANNOTATED BIBLIOGRAPHY FOR CHAPTER 5

Brown, George, 1971. *Human Teaching for Human Learning: An Introduction to Confluent Education*. New York: Viking Press.

Reporting on the results of the Ford-Esalen project, Brown applies ideas of humanistic psychologists (drawing strongly from Fritz Perls) to affective education in general and to actual classroom situations. The book deals with students of all ages and gives concrete lesson plans on subjects ranging from planning a first grade curriculum to teaching an English class in high school. Brown puts emphasis on showing how personal growth experiences can be incorporated into the classroom.

Chesler, Mark, and Robert Fox. 1966. *Role-Playing Methods in the Classroom*. Chicago: Science Research Associates.

This is a practical step-by-step guide for using role-playing in teaching. The book deals with the functions of role-playing and its advantages and pitfalls.

Fox, Robert, Margaret B. Luszki, and Richard Schmuck. 1966. *Diagnosing Classroom Learning Environments*. Chicago: Science Research Associates.

This is an introduction to the rationale of diagnosis and to the concept of formative evaluation. Most of the book presents specific diagnostic instruments that can be used to measure features of classroom group life, such as climate, social relations, norms, student-teacher interactions, and self-esteem. The text is replete with specific and practical suggestions.

Gorman, Alfred E. 1969. *Teachers and Learners: The Interactive Process of Education*. Boston: Allyn and Bacon.

About half of this book is given over to an interpersonal analysis of teaching and learning. The other half offers concrete exercises and practices that can be employed within a learning group, such as role-playing, communications activities, buzz groups, etc. An entire chapter is devoted to diagnosis and evaluation.

Institute for Development of Educational Activities, Inc. (IDEA). 1971. *Learning in the Small Group.* Suite 950, 1100 Glendon Ave., Los Angeles, Ca. 90024.

This pamphlet reports a conference on learning in small groups. It describes and analyzes twelve different small-group instructional projects and shows how they might be used in learning groups or larger school groups.

Lewis, Howard, and Harold Streitfeld. 1970. *Growth Games: How To Tune in Yourself, Your Family, Your Friends.* New York: Harcourt, Brace, Jovanovich, Inc.

This is a collection of games for personal awareness and development, including sensory experiences, consciousness-expanding activities, and games for building interpersonal relationships. The collection is not designed specifically for schools but it constitutes a rich source of ideas for educational leaders. It also includes a useful bibliography of humanistic psychology references and a listing of growth centers in the United States.

Miles, Matthew B. 1959. *Learning to Work in Groups: A Program Guide for Educational Leaders.* New York: Bureau of Publications, Teachers College, Columbia University.

Miles's book includes group training theory and practices for both classroom and school settings. It focuses primarily on the behavior of the educational leader and what things he can do to make group life productive and satisfying.

Schmuck, Richard, Mark Chesler, and Ronald Lippitt. 1966. *Problem-Solving To Improve Classroom Learning.* Chicago: Science Research Associates.

This book describes how a problem-solving sequence can be applied in the classroom. It has sections on diagnosing problems and taking action, showing how the dynamics of learning groups can be constructively altered.

Schmuck, Richard, and Patricia Schmuck. 1971. *Group Processes in the Classroom*. Dubuque, Iowa: Wm. C. Brown Company.

This book is a theoretical, data-based analysis of the basic interpersonal processes of learning groups—leadership, attraction, norms, communication, and cohesiveness. It is designed to increase an educational leader's level of understanding and to suggest teaching practices to enable the development of healthy classroom climates. The text typifies the group dynamics application.

Simon, Sidney, Leland Howe, and Howard Kirschenbaum. 1972. *Values Clarification: A Handbook of Practical Strategies for Teachers and Students*. New York: Hart Publishing Co.

This book contains seventy-nine lesson plans or strategies that deal with clarifying values. Each is described in a standard format and can be adapted to many different purposes and group situations. Any of these strategies could be employed rather easily by students and educational leaders in most learning groups.

Stanford, Gene, and Barbara D. Stanford. 1969. *Learning Discussion Skills Through Games*. New York: Citation Press.

This booklet is a useful, practical guide for educational leaders. The Stanfords give suggestions on how to communicate effectively while teaching. They also suggest solutions to fifteen common interpersonal problems in learning groups.

Thelen, Herbert, 1954. *Dynamics of Groups at Work*. Chicago: University of Chicago Press.

One of the earliest group dynamics applications principally devoted to the schools. A rich source of theory and of practical suggestions, the book applies the laboratory method of learning to classrooms and school organizations.

Zahorik, John, and Dale Brubaker. 1972. *Toward More Humanistic Instruction*. Dubuque, Iowa: Wm. C. Brown Co.

Although this book has a short conceptual analysis of humanistic education, it forcuses primarily on teacher behavior, teaching strategies, and the content of curriculum. About half the book offers concrete lesson plans, with Gestalt games and ideas for course content in human relations, ecology, race relations, and population control. The book also includes a rather lengthy section on interaction analysis.

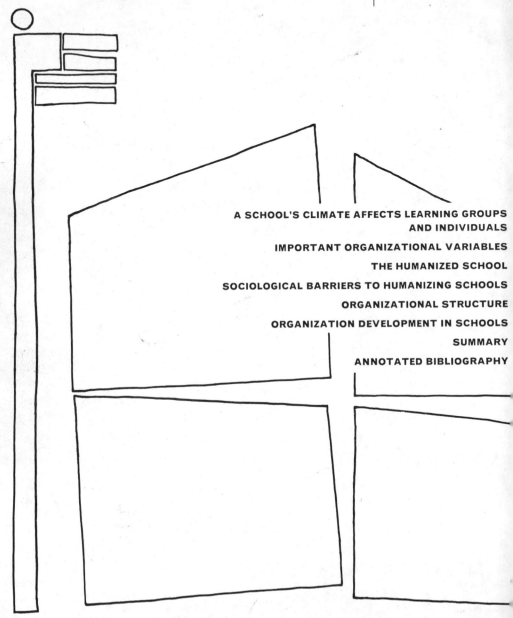

chapter 6

Humanizing school climates

The human organization of the school, especially the affective relationships of the staff and their methods for solving schoolwide problems and making decisions, sets the stage for the climates of its learning groups. Just as the learning group influences the behaviors and attitudes of its members, so does the climate of the school organization affect the groups within it. Even though research in social psychology has often demonstrated that the properties of social settings can be more powerful determinants of behavior than the personal characteristics of an individual, many critics of schooling have tended to simplify or even neglect the power of the school's organizational milieu. While some teachers remain creative and energetic despite the inimical regimen of the organization, too often such teachers simply become tired, or else their accomplishments in humanizing their own classrooms are annulled by the forces of an inhospitable school organization. To endure, improved relationships in learning groups must be strongly supported by healthy school climates.

In this chapter we make a case for the importance of studying school organization. We show how a school's climate can have a direct impact on learning groups and how relationships among the participants in a school can affect the students' academic performance. Second, we discuss four organizational variables—norms, roles communication, and power—and third, we show how these four variables can operate in a humanized school at both the organizational and the individual levels. Fourth, we discuss some inevitable obstacles that confront schools as they attempt to humanize their organizational climates. Fifth, we present a number of promising organizational structures already in existence in some schools, along with a proposal for how a school can build a more humanistic organization. Finally, we describe the theory and techniques of Organization Development (OD), a change strategy that appears to be the most promising vehicle for humanizing the climates of schools.

A SCHOOL'S CLIMATE AFFECTS LEARNING GROUPS AND INDIVIDUALS

The ways in which a school's climate influences its learning groups and the behavior of individual teachers and students often are subtle and covert. Although there has been little systematic empirical research on this relationship, so that we can cite only a few studies to support our analysis, our experiences and observations have corroborated our impression that the school's climate has a subtle but powerful impact on classroom behaviors. The following elements of a school's climate appear to be the most relevant:

1. Trust and openness

The level of trust and openness among faculty members can affect the levels of trust and openness among teachers and students in learning groups. The mode of relating between the members of a faculty largely fashions the ways individual teachers respond to their students; whole-person relationships among staff members, for example, offer the best soil for planting humanized relationships between teachers and students. When teachers experience feelings of comfort and rapport with their colleagues and when they are supported in their feelings of worth, they are then better able to respond positively and openly with students. Unfortunately, many teachers feel insecure, isolated, and competitive in relation to colleagues. Feelings of hostility, guardedness, or alienation in relation to colleagues create anxiety in teachers, which in turn lead to low levels of tolerance and openness with students.

We have found only a few schools in which the level of trust and openness among staff members is high. In schools where trust and openness on the faculty are great, teachers frequently visit one another's classrooms, for example, and ask one another for help or suggestions. In most schools, however, teachers act as though they never need help from their colleagues. A fiction is maintained that a "professional and highly trained teacher" has already achieved sufficient competence and skill to handle all exigencies in the learning group. The actual result, however, is that innovative and creative teaching is stifled by the insecurity, anxiety, and competitiveness typical of these staff relationships. In such schools, feedback is neither solicited or offered, so that inventive ideas, for example, remain the property of a single teacher, either because there are no avenues of communication or because other teachers fear to "copy someone else."

2. Communication skills

The level of skill in communication between faculty members is also associated with the level of such skill in the classroom. Even when attitudes of trust and openness exist in a staff, helpful and supportive relationships do not automatically develop. These attitudes must be accomplished by similar *behaviors* before they can be productive. Thus, some staffs are comfortable but not collaborative; some are secure but not innovative; and some are confrontative but not constructive or creative. Faculties that have developed *behaviors* that are constructive and open can be collaborative, innovative and helpful. The skills of communication that we discussed in Chapter 5 (paraphrasing, behavior description, feeling description, impression-checking, and giving and receiving feedback) constitute the essential means of increasing constructive openness. But these skills alone, without some initial degree of trust, can produce phony and detrimental results. Constructive openness emerges from staff norms emphasizing trust between people as well as from skills in communicating clearly and accurately.

We have observed that open and trustful faculties frequently and easily criticize one another's classroom performance and offer help when it is needed. To be critical and helpful at the same time is not necessarily destructive; on the contrary the effort can *support* a teacher's feeling of worth and need not threaten his or her feelings of competence. Faculties that have such skills can be confrontative and creative, and can do more to help one another than simply provide a "soft shoulder" or a "sympathetic ear."

The informal setting of the faculty lounge is often where teachers let off steam, for example, about a student who is making their teaching life uncomfortable. If the staff shows trust and skill in its interpersonal relationships, the comments of others may help the teacher view the relationship in a new and constructive way. The use of constructive openness between teachers also can be formalized in a program of collegial supervision. In collegial supervision, one teacher observes another with the intent of giving feedback to the observed teacher. Usually such observations are preceeded by a collaborative planning period during which the two teachers determine what observation categories should be used. In this program, teachers also bring problems to faculty meetings for the perceptions and suggestions of others. The key to success seems to be a combination of norms of trust and openness and the skills of communicating directly.

3. Interpersonal power

Staff members' feelings of power within the faculty can affect their performance in the classroom. Research done by social psychologists has shown that people who participate within authoritarian organizations often feel passive and sometimes incompetent and hostile toward their formal leaders. Among teachers, powerlessness seems to be a typical feeling; they often feel powerless not only in relation to the school's administration, but also in relation to the school board, the parents, and, increasingly, their students. Despite this general feeling, individual schools differ considerably in how the teachers feel about their influence positions. In many, the administrator is seen as making most organizational decisions; in a few others, teachers see themselves participating equally in running the school.

There is some research indicating that teachers' satisfactions with their role in the school are strongly associated with their perception of how they can influence the school's decision-making processes. Findings by Hornstein et al. (1967) showed that teachers report greatest satisfaction with their principal and their district when they perceive that they and their principal have been mutually influential, and especially when they view the principal as a competent person. According to Hornstein et al., as teachers feel more influential and see their principal as an educational expert, they feel better about school and behave more supportively toward students. As teachers become more involved in school decision-making, they take more initiative in designing innovative programs and in getting feedback and criticism from their colleagues to improve their plans before bringing them to the principal. We have already pointed out that teachers' relationships with the principal set a model for teacher-student relationships (Bigelow, 1971). Equalization of power between administrators and the staff can lead to more nearly equalized power between teacher and students, and in turn improve the quality of teacher-student interaction in learning groups.

4. Leadership behaviors

The principal's style and skills in carrying out the leadership in a school have a direct bearing on a teacher's performance in the classroom. Just as the behaviors of teachers have strong effects on learning group processes, the principal's behavior can affect the staff dynamics and in turn the learning group climate.

In a classic study, Gross and Herriott (1965) showed that principals' leadership behaviors influenced staff morale, innovativeness, professional performance in the classroom, and even student learning. They created a program of evaluation called Executive Professional Leadership (EPL) to describe the principal's leadership. Principals' EPL scores were determined by asking teachers how supportive, collaborative, and helpful they were to them. The principals with high EPL scores were characterized by teachers as: having constructive recommendations to offer teachers in dealing with problems; showing strong interest in improving the quality of educational programs; giving teachers the sense that they could make significant contributions to the improvement of student performances in classrooms; and making teachers' meetings a valuable educational activity. These attributes obviously can be instrumental in creating a more humanized school, since the teachers who credited their principal with high EPL scores were comfortable in the school work and felt stimulated and encouraged by the principal to improve. Teachers who felt supported and encouraged by their principals were not fearful of trying new educational procedures and could provide a more supportive academic learning environment for their students.

5. Interpersonal relationships

We believe that the students' view of relationships among their teachers and with the principal affects their own style of interaction in the learning group. When students see staff relationships as congenial and supportive, they feel more comfortable in the school and are better able to focus their energies on learning tasks. When they see the teachers experiencing tension and conflict, an anxious climate arises which can interfere with their learning. Since teachers serve as adult models, students may also tend to imitate them by emulating their conflicts within the learning group. Often this can lead to increased tension between teacher and students and even within the peer group.

IMPORTANT ORGANIZATIONAL VARIABLES

An organization consists of interpersonal relationships formed to reach established goals. These relationships are expressed in interactions between participants which include performing their roles and functions, harnessing physical resources for use, utilizing interdependence, and establishing friendship patterns and networks of communication. In order to diagnose this complex web of interactions, we must establish some guidelines for understanding it. The four clusters of variables discussed below can serve as one framework for the planned diagnosis and modification of a school climate.

1. Norms and goals

Usually when we refer to the climate of a group or organization, we are actually discussing the norms that characterize it. Norms are group agreements, generally implicitly established and maintained, that help to guide the perceptions, thoughts, feelings, and behaviors of the group members. They influence the interpersonal relationships of a staff by helping the members know what is expected of them and what they should expect from others. Organizational goals are thus one kind of norm. A school's goals are those objectives that the members believe *are* shared by most participants or at least *should be* shared by most. School faculties are notoriously unskillful in formulating goals and norms in a planned way.

2. Roles and functions

When the condition of a school organization is diagnosed, repeated use should be made of the concepts of norm and role. While norms are strong stabilizers of organizational behavior, roles represent the organization in action. Roles are constituted of the functions that staff members perform in their positions with the school. A teacher acting in the instructional role, for example, performs the functions of calling on students, asking questions of them, and giving information to them. Roles are patterned primarily by organizational norms.

Perhaps the most important insight of social psychology, often overlooked by personality psychologists, is that role-taking is done in *interaction with other role-takers*. For this reason we think it misleading to focus on the psychodynamics of a role-taker without also considering the situation in which his or her behavior takes place. When it is said, for example, that a given staff member is doing a poor job, what is meant is that the interaction between the individual and other role-takers is creating difficulties within the organization. As the popular song of the 1950's put it, "It takes two to tango!"

3. Communication networks

To understand how a particular school organization works, it is important to learn who communicates on a regular basis with whom. Networks of interpersonal communication may be either formal or informal; the two quite often are significantly different and only partially overlapping. Schools traditionally have had hierarchical formal communication networks and more lateral, clique like informal networks. In Chapter 5, we discussed the importance of centralized and diffuse sociometric structures for learning groups. Such a structure can also be applied appropriately to the school organization.

4. Power and influence

A very important feature of school organizations, involving norms, roles, and communication networks, has to do with power and influence. Power is the potential influence that a particular member or cluster of members wields. Influence is power in action and it emanates from particular social psychological bases. French and Raven (1959), for example, divide the bases of influence into expert, referent, legitimate, reward, and coercive categories. Legitimate power is given to principals and teachers by the school board and the community. It is invested in their role and enables them to use rewards and coercion in the form of grades or school expulsion. The traditional school has based much of its influence on legitimate reward and coercive influence and has typically neglected the other two categories—expert and referent bases for influence. These bases are earned; they are not invested within the role. They are earned when others see a person either as possessing knowledge or expertise or as so charismatic that they identify with and want to be like him.

These four clusters of organizational variables are useful constructs to bring more humanized schools into existence; they stand as benchmarks against which we can compare any school organization to see what changes it should make.

THE HUMANIZED SCHOOL

The primary building blocks of a school organization are the normative structure (norms and goals), the organizational task structure (roles and functions, formal power patterns), the informal structure (communication networks, influence patterns), and the competencies, skills, and attitudes of the administrators, teachers, and students. The humanized school has normative, task, and informal structures that support whole-person relationships. Thus, it has norms of openness and authenticity, roles of helping and facilitating, and informal interactions that are intimate and gratifying. As we have described before, humanized schools can also be thought of as human-resource-using systems; they use their human resources to establish organizational structures that offer personal fulfillment, encourage cognitive growth, and provide opportunities for all participants to apply their skills.

We wish to emphasize the interdependence and reinforcing relationships between a school's organizational structures and the attributes of the individuals who compose the organization. On one hand, organizational change in schools cannot occur without individuals having behavioral skills. Too many alternative schools that we have visited have attempted to modify their organization radically only to be thrown into chaos because the participants lacked the know-how and behavioral skills to cope with the changes. On the other hand, too many public schools have failed to make proposed changes because they have relied only on individual administrators or educational leaders and have ignored the power of the organizational structure and the strength of its traditions.

In this section we describe the norms and goals, the roles and functions, the communication patterns, and the power and influence patterns of the humanized school. We also point to the competencies and skills required of the individual participants to make such an organization viable and effective.

1. Group processes in the humanized school

The social climate of the humanized school is characterized by feelings of caring, trust, warmth, openness, confrontativeness, informality, and closeness. It houses relationships considerably different from those of the traditional school, which is more task-centered than person-centered, more impersonal than intimate, and more formal than informal. Interpersonal relationships in the traditional school are often cold, reserved, and suspicious; competition is high; and hostile feelings are carefully guarded. The norms of the humanized school place value on persons and interpersonal relationships above any particular subject-matter or task.

The philosophies of management of these two protoypical schools also differ significantly. In the humanized school, for example, the principal's primary task is to direct the energy, creativity, and ingenuity of the staff by using power supportively and collaboratively; the educational leaders manage their learning groups in a similar fashion. No administrator or educational leader is expected to be a complete expert or totally responsible (or, as educators are so prone to say, "ultimately responsible") and roles are flexible and changing as demanded by the exigencies of a situation. Particular school members are called upon to perform functions according to their competence and interests. So, for example, students may take over the function of information-giving at times, while educational leaders become listeners and recipients of new information. Thus the faculty of a humanized school is supportive of doing things in new, even radical, ways; it supports variety, heterogeneity of ideas, and diversity of pedagogical applications. Having a norm in support of risk-taking, they view errors as experiences from which to learn and they can tolerate a great deal of ambiguity. At the same time, they emphasize working interdependently and cooperatively to enhance the cognitive and personal growth of both the adult staff and the students. Their dual support for diversity and collaboration is buttressed by group skills in uncovering and working with conflict.

The staff of a humanized school, furthermore, has a perspective on management similar to what McGregor (1967) referred to as Theory Y about human motivation. Theory Y specifies that people are curious and active; consequently, they should be allowed freedom to find their own best ways of doing things. People are not lazy or just motivated by extrinsic rewards and they will not let you down if you build a trusting relationship with them. School faculties with a Theory Y orientation allow for student freedom and are collaborative, confrontative, and flexible. Although their perspective allows for permissiveness and autonomy, it also includes the construction of rules and regulations through two-way communication and consensus decision-making. As such, the humanized school supports norms of both permissiveness and confrontation.

In contrast, traditional schools are run from a perspective similar to what McGregor referred to as the Theory X orientation to human motivation. Theory X stipulates that people are lazy and passive, and must be pushed, prodded, and extrinsically reinforced to behave in certain ways. Staffs with Theory X orientations tend to employ traditional modes of leadership, characterized by authoritarianism, one-way communication, and restrictive norms. The function of management essentially is to control personnel through incentives or coercion and to monitor work behaviors carefully. Errors must be avoided or covered up, so that as a consequence personnel are cautious and refrain from taking risks. Less emphasis is placed on the continued cognitive and personal growth of existing staff than on selecting new highly trained staff members. The traditional school is both cognitively restrictive and emotionally closed.

Communication and decision-making patterns in humanized and traditional schools also differ significantly. In the former, communication is open and multidirectional, going up, down, and laterally. Information is relatively easy to retrieve and feelings are just as prominent as ideas in the flow of communication. The traditional school is characterized, on the other hand, by more restricted flows of formal information, mostly traveling downward, but also by a great flow of private informal communication between people in similar role positions. However, information is difficult to get from personnel at different hierarchical levels: especially information about feelings and critical thoughts, which are hidden especially from superordinates. As Robert E. Thompson wrote of the traditional, static organization:

> There is no real trick to establishing an organization without problems. One needs only to let it be known that no problems will be tolerated, and none will occur—at least none that become evident

With the slightest encouragement, subordinate levels of supervision can act as effective insulators between the manager and the problem.

What Thompson described as a phenomenon of life in traditional organizations also has its analogue in learning groups. A fourth grade teacher we knew sincerely maintained that her students did not experience angry or hostile feelings in the classroom. All was calm, tender, supportive, and pleasant. Hence, she did not have to deal with unpleasant feelings in relation to her rules for classroom behavior or the curriculum. And indeed it was evident when observing her class that the public display of negative feelings was not a problem. Negative feelings were not tolerated; they were submerged until students were privately asked their feelings about the class.

In the humanized school or learning group, public discussions of negative feelings, conflicts, and irritations are expected. Since decision making grows out of a problem-solving orientation, the surfacing of differences is inevitable. Before decisions are made, those who are affected by them analyze the situation, share their feelings about it, specify their own goals, and attempt to clarify any proposals for action that they have in mind. Thus, differences of opinion are bound to arise. Even after decisions are reached, they continue to be treated as hypotheses to be tested and decisions are seen as revocable, future events may call for more problem-solving and decision-making.

In the more traditional school, decision-making usually does not involve many participants; it is carried out by specified administrators or teachers who retain legitimate power. Typically, individual teachers retain power to make decisions about what will transpire in their learning group, but the broader organizational issues of scheduling, discipline, curriculum change, and communications with the community are carried out by nonteaching administrators. Perhaps the most dehumanizing feature of decision-making in the traditional school is its blatant lack of real democracy, as revealed in the clear distinction made between the functions of policy determination and policy execution. Typically, policy decisions are made by top-level administration personnel (even at the district level), while implementation is expected from less powerful personnel, such as teachers and students. Usually decisions made by district office administrators are final—at least until changed *at that level*—and the obedient execution of policy by teachers and students is expected. The lack of integration between policy-making procedures and the day-to-day work of the school tends to alienate teachers and students and to close off the upward flow of communication, in the manner described by Thompson.

Democratic decision-making requires shared trust among the staff members. The level of trust directly affects the degree of defensiveness in an interpersonal relationship. Gibb (1961) found that members of small groups that developed a defensive climate had difficulty concentrating on the content of messages, perceived the motives, values, and feelings of others inaccurately, and distorted messages. Meadow *et al.* (1959) similarly found that defensiveness induced a lasting decrease in problem-solving effectiveness. But the most conclusive results come from a recent study by Zand (1972), who studied trust and problem-solving effectiveness among industrial administrators. Groups of business executives were given identical factual information in order to solve a difficult manufacturing-marketing policy problem. Half the groups were briefed to expect trusting behavior among themselves, and the other half to expect untrusting behavior. Zand found highly significant differences in effectiveness between the high-trust groups and the low-trust groups in the clarification of goals, the reality of information exchanged, the scope of search for solutions, and the commitment of managers to implement solutions.

Along with high levels of trust, the humanized school supports norms of growth and autonomy. Flexibility for individuals is built into the organizational structure in the form of ad hoc task forces and short-term special interest groups. The structure of these groups changes as the individual members change; as old problems are solved, new problems emerge and so new problem-solving groups must be formed. In contrast, the traditional school is rigid; groups, classes, and project units remain intact throughout the year or even for several years at a time. A great deal of energy goes into simply maintaining and preserving self-contained classes, departments, committees, and the like. There is very strong adherence to a hierarchical chain of command and to the tradition that the staff perform as custodians while the students adapt themselves to adult-made procedures. In many schools, traditional forms and procedures seem "natural" and are preserved without question or experiment.

To summarize, the climate of a school is gauged in terms of its norms, roles, and patterns of communication, power, and influence. A humanized school has the following attributes:

Norms that show members valuing:

(1) Collaboration and confrontation between educational leaders and students and between staff members and student peer groups.

(2) The rights and integrity of all participants.

(3) The cognitive and affective growth of educational leaders as well as students.

(4) The freedom of participants to pursue their own goals.

Norms that encourage the behavior of:

(1) Direct, open, and authentic communication.

(2) Creative risk-taking to find new ways to solve problems.

(3) Public discussion on the dynamics of the group itself.

(4) Critical assessment of school operations by both staff and students.

Organizational roles that are:

(1) Publicly defined, so that participants know what others expect of them.

(2) Flexible, so that participants' functions are consonant with their interests and capabilities rather than only their status.

(3) Changeable from time to time, so that students may teach, teachers may learn, and all are seen as potentially helpful to one another.

Communication that is:

(1) Free-flowing between all participants in the school, moving up and down as well as across status positions.

(2) Encouraged, so that there are both formal procedures, such as confrontation meetings, and informal gatherings for discussion, such as in staff lounges.

(3) Personal and direct.

(4) Skillful, utilizing the learned procedures of listening, paraphrasing, and impression-checking, among others.

Power and influence that are:

(1) Clearly defined, so that there is general understanding of who makes what decisions.

(2) Shared, so that all persons affected by a decision are involved in making it.

(3) Dispersed, so that all persons perceive that they can have some impact upon the affairs of the school.

(4) Negotiable, so that procedures are available to appeal what appears to be the unjust use of power.

2. The individual's behavior in the humanized school

We have tried to show how the organizational climate of a school can affect the learning groups and individuals within it. Indeed, a school cannot remain directed toward its goals unless the administrators, educational leaders, and students adapt themselves to organizational patterns and norms which are congruent to those goals. However, while it is true that schools can be studied as organizations—as social systems alone—it would be sheer folly to believe that the behaviors and attitudes of individuals do not make a great difference in how an organizational structure will emerge and function.

If a school is to be truly humanized, its structural and normative changes must be accompanied by interpersonal behaviors which are skillful and helpful. Administrators, educational leaders, and students must make every effort to humanize their relationships also, and yet too often they are forced to retreat, for lack of skill, to traditional, formal, and closed relationships. They exclaim, "We tried it but it didn't work!" For new ideals and procedures to be shared, the individuals must have skill in accurately communicating and in reaching consensual decisions. They must take hold of the organization—not just reside within it—and make it work for them. For the normative structure of a school to support openness, effective-problem solving, and collaborative decision-making, the individuals must be responsible for their own behavior.

In humanized schools, individuals act as follows:

(1) *Speak for themselves.* Administrators, educational leaders, and students alike publicly admit their own opinions and feelings. Staff members do not speak for or make decisions on behalf of others on the basis of "hunches" or vague impressions of what the others think. When they do explain another's thoughts or feelings, they first check his point of view carefully.

(2) *Use communication skills both to speak directly and openly and to understand the messages of the other person.* People in a humanized school are, above all, true to themselves and others; they do not attempt to hide their feelings, they try to understand others, and they can give both constructive criticism and praise.

(3) *Work collaboratively to reach goals and solve problems.* The cliché, "Love it or leave it," is detrimental to a school striving to improve itself. Constructive criticism, public statements of frustration, and collaborative problem-solving are the responsibility of everyone to keep a school on its target. In a humanized school, participants feel that school goals overlap closely their own personal interests.

(4) *Regard conflict as inevitable and even necessary.* Conflict is dealt with publicly, not informally behind the scenes. Annoyance is expressed directly and not to a third party, rumor and gossip are at a minimum, and people expect others to disagree with them at some time or another.

(5) *React to conflict or criticism with a minimum of defensiveness and closed-mindedness.* Because the norms of the humanized school encourage pluralism and variety, individuals expect that there will be conflict and that their views or opinions will be "called on the carpet" at one time or another. People accept the responsibility for their own opinions, explain their stand to others, and expect that any goal or problem has to be worked out collaboratively to satisfy the various beliefs and interests of the people in the school.

(6) *Are responsible for themselves and initiate the getting and giving of help.* People in humanized schools do not blame others for their own lack of initiative, motivation, or commitment to follow through. When a person needs help he asks someone else for assistance and also freely gives his help when it is asked for. Teachers are not viewed as having the sole responsibility to teach something to students; students accept a great deal of responsibility for their own learning. Students often act as education leaders in learning groups.

(7) *Accept the responsibility for performing their functions.* Administrators, teachers, and students do not abdicate their formal responsibilities. Even if they do not agree with a final decision they do their part in implementing it as concerned and responsible individuals.

(8) *Take responsibility for sharing decision-making with one another.* They accept the principle that all persons want to be involved in making decisions that affect them, but that there will also be individual differences with regard to how much participation is appropriate. Administrators, educational leaders, and students exert

influence on one another and in turn expect others to wield influence on them at times.

SOCIOLOGICAL BARRIERS TO HUMANIZING SCHOOLS

Even when organizational variables and individual behavior are humanized, organizational changes still may be inhibited by the larger socio-cultural environment in which a school exists. Even if we improve the existing conditions within the school itself, its encompassing community may present formidable barriers to creating a school climate that is personally intimate, intellectually stimulating, and functionally collaborative. We wish to emphasize three basic sociological variables which are of special importance in blocking humanistic changes in schools. They are the school's sheer size, the socio-economic characteristics of its members and community, and the degree to which its internal subsystems and individual members are functionally interdependent.

1. School size

It seems axiomatic that as the size of a school increases, possibilities for closeness among the administrators, teachers, and students decrease. This *can* occur if the members do not take initiative in creating new forms and procedures to cope with the school's bigness. The careful research of Barker and Gump (1964), along with the followup work of Baird (1969), indicated that although small and large senior high schools had approximately the same ratio of facilities and activities in which students could participate, a much higher proportion of the students in small schools actually did participate than in large schools. The mean number of extracurricular activities participated in by each student was twice as great in small schools and the variety of activities participated in was also much greater. Moreover, a greater proportion of students in small schools held formal positions of importance and responsibility. Students in small schools reported more personal kinds of satisfaction: for example, developing competence, being challenged, participating in activities they considered important, and becoming clearer about their values. In contrast, students in large schools reported more satisfaction with impersonal items such as availability of courses and laboratory facilities but indicated very little joy in close interpersonal relationships.

These studies run counter to the argument that large schools can concentrate resources, develop more activities, and stimulate more learning than small schools. The findings suggest that the use made of facilities is more important than their magnitude. Students in small schools make more efficient use of their facilities, at least in terms of group participation. The data give clear evidence that involvement and participation are not encouraged by large and impersonal schools.

However, large school buildings can be so organized that students will receive the benefits of a large school and still also obtain the psychological gains from participating in a small-school setting. For example, a large school might be housed in a multistructure consisting of many smaller schools or units. Even in a conventional building, school programs can be geared to allow for small-group seminars, while at the same time offering large-audience lectures and individualized instruction. Small learning groups can be organized as followups to mass instruction, as reaction panels, or as committees with specific objectives. Small cohesive learning groups can be organized on the basis of shared interests, abilities, or friendships.

2. Socio-economic characteristics

Research indicates that schools made up primarily of lower class students have climates less hospitable for *academic* learning than schools with a preponderance of middle class students. This is the case partly because the norms of the peer group play an influential role in relation to a student's academic achievement and the values and rewards of American schools essentially are middle class. We think that the schools that serve lower class communities could and should be modified. The intellectual challenges, emotional reinforcements, interpersonal styles, and educational alternatives should be shaped in concert with the culture of the school's community. Thus, a school in an urban ghetto necessarily must be different from one in a wealthy suburb; the students have had quite different experiences, have developed different attitudes and skills, and often hold different expectations about the purposes of the school and their place in it.

Aside from peer group influences, which we think are extremely important, several studies have shown that the quality and quantity of teacher competence, physical resources, and general services of schools in lower socio-economic neighborhoods are inferior to those of middle or high socio-economic neighborhoods. In a classic study, Sexton (1961) showed that in a single large city district the money spent for schools in each neighborhood, as well as the quality of education offered, varied in direct proportion to the average family income in that neighborhood. These differences in expenditure and quality clearly set the stage for differences in interpersonal relationships in the classrooms. Herriott and St. John (1966) corroborated Sexton's findings by showing that both teachers and principals in schools of low socio-economic status were less experienced and less satisfied in their jobs than were the teachers in high status areas. Moreover, principals in the highest status areas were considerably more satisfied with their teachers. In the lowest status schools poor physical conditions, overcrowding, outdated curriculum materials, and inexperienced or harsh and punitive teachers were characteristic. In schools of the lowest socio-economic status, most measures showed teaching performance and the quality of classroom group processes to be poor.

Unfortunately the student of low socio-economic status seems in general to receive less of all that is offered by most middle class school districts except punishment. One welcome exception from this generalization was described by Nat Hentoff (1966). In his account of a school in a black neighborhood in New York, he wrote of a staff that provided learning alternatives and interpersonal relationships needed by and appropriate to those children. To produce more such schools, we need to put much more effort into creating additional educational alternatives, training teachers to realize how their own values affect their teaching, training entire staffs to be more perceptive and confrontative about discrimination and unconscious prejudice, and hiring more personnel from lower socio-economic backgrounds. In these efforts, the guiding principle is to increase the skill of teachers in building whole-person relationships with others who are different from themselves.

3. Internal interdependence

Interdependence in an organization is related to the functional interaction occurring regularly among the members. We believe that as the formal interdependence of staff and students increases, the possibilities for humanized relationships also increase. Thus in an elementary school with self-contained and autonomous classrooms, interaction among the teaching staff is low, so that the possibility of close or whole-person relationships among colleagues is also low. In such an atmosphere, the teacher alone really gets to know his students, and acts with very little communication from his colleagues. Relationships between teachers and students in different classes tend to be distant, impersonal, and superficial.

In the matter of interdependence, the team teaching structure differs strikingly from the above "self-contained" structure. The team teaching structure has high interdependence within the team and moderate interdependence across teams, directly as a result of team leaders forming a group with the principal. In a team teaching school, the students also tend to be more interdependent, since they are likely to be involved in more projects that require collaboration.

Although interdependence within school organizations presents an opportunity for humanized interpersonal relationships, it does not in itself assure that humanized relationships will actually arise. At the same time a structure of low interdependence restricts closeness and openness, a condition which in turn prevents participants from recognizing interdependencies that *do* exist. When low levels of interdependence are required, the structure of the school is individuated and fragmented. Very close relationships do, of course, form between teachers and their students in self-contained classrooms, but these occur rences are not frequent, and when they do take place, they are out of joint with the more impersonal relationships that prevail in the rest of the school. The Sherifs *et al.* (1961) have shown that the interdependence required by certain tasks may serve as an important means of developing cooperation between groups that have a history of competitive or hostile relationships. In a school we think it is important for the staff and students to be interdependent in planning and implementing instruction if whole-person relationships and I-Thou encounters are to flourish.

ORGANIZATIONAL STRUCTURE

The structure of an organization is in one sense, the arrangement of interdependent relationships established to achieve organizational goals. Thus, in factories the assembly line was established as a structure to facilitate the maximum production of machinery. Of course, as an organizational structure the assembly line has undergone great changes as the importance of worker satisfaction and the ill-effects of repetitive work have been realized. Schools were once organized in ways believed to help young people attain skills required of them as "productive citizens." Since adults were believed to be in the best position for passing on the wisdom and skills of the past, children were organized into clusters with one adult as their teacher.

In organizational theory a distinction has been made between the structure for a *continuous producing* technology (such as an automobile assembly line, where several people work on one product) and that for a *unit production* technology (such as a carpenter making a cabinet). Whereas the continuous producing technology requires supervision of the many people working on a product, unit production does not require as much supervision because people are not working collaboratively. Schools are structured more like unit-production technologies; the teacher is responsible for the education of the child—or some apparently autonomous aspect of his education. Supervisory activities of the school are in general relatively superficial, as are collaborative efforts among teachers to do the best job. It is possible even today, especially in elementary school, for a child to spend an entire school year under one teacher.

The one-room schoolhouse typified the unit-production technology to the greatest extent. A student studied all subjects with one teacher and the same peers. Because of this very high *internal* interdependence, the one-room school has been treated romantically by some critics, who advocate that we return to it for its intimacy and closeness. No doubt, some one-room schools were exciting and joyful places while others were as harmful psychologically as some of our present-day schools. So while we do not advocate a return to the unit-production of the one-room schoolhouse, some of its features may be valuable for contemporary schools.

Since the lock-step arrangement of age and grade did not exist, cognitive growth and skill mastery tended to occur when the student was ready. Even though advanced testing procedures and sophisticated concepts about psychological and cognitive development did not exist, the teacher, students, and parents knew each other well enough and cared enough to help each other learn. Today there is probably less collaboration between parents, teachers, and students about what they are ready to learn—even with sophisticated testing procedures—and most schools are set into the lock-step relationships of age, grade, and subject matter. Moreover, the one-room school was characterized often by intimate relationships between families who were functionally and socially interdependent in the community. There was an abundance of opportunities for students to work in the "real world" to apply their new skills; school was a focal point of the community and students were usually involved in the actual work of the community.

It may be possible to establish technical structures in today's complex schools that include the desirable characteristics of the close and personal one-room school, while at the same time taking advantage of psychological knowledge and technology not available to educators in the earlier days of American schooling. Indeed, there are some promising signs that indicate a return to some of the favorable features of the one-room school: the close relationships, the interdependence of students and community, and the abolition of the lock-step approach to learning. First, the professional roles of school faculty members are becoming more varied; some schools are using people formerly excluded, such as highly trained specialists, aides, parents, businessmen, older students, and retired people. Second, in many schools teachers, aides, and other personnel are forming into teams to use their talents in more complementary and collaborative ways. This movement toward increased interdependence has in turn a better likelihood of fostering I-Thou interactions than the present self-contained classroom organization. Third, mass instruction is gradually and slowly being replaced by more individualized instruction or instruction in small seminar groups. More accurate and sophisticated testing procedures, more curriculum alternatives, and more flexibility in learning and teaching will set the stage for more personalized interaction. Furthermore, the criterion of age is increasingly being supplemented by interest, ability, and personal compatibility levels in the formation of learning groups.

1. Examples of promising organizational structures

A number of innovative technical structures are currently being tried in schools which show great promise for creating humanized school climates. They are based on the premise that the emotional development is just as important as cognitive development. The magnitude of interest in these new school structures is indicated in a recent analysis of the literature issued by the ERIC Clearinghouse on Educational Administration—more than 150 references are cited on "alternative organizational forms." Although no single technical structure can guarantee that school climates will be humanized, some structures create more opportunities for close, emotionally facilitative and affective relationships. The following examples of current technical structures support our cautious optimism about the future of schooling in the United States.

a. Preschool arrangements

Several promising arrangements currently are underway for educating four- and five-year-olds; the most widespread of these is the Head Start Program. Head Start aims to help youngsters from relatively deprived urban and rural settings develop some basic cognitive skills that will facilitate their learning to read. In turn, cognitive growth in relation to the demands of regular schooling is seen as helping the youngster to develop a positive view of himself as a student.

In the most successful programs, parents have been included so that they can support at home those skills that are introduced and practiced at school. Success also seems to be occurring in Head Start programs in which retirees and high school students are employed as tutors of the preschoolers.

Along with a large number of public programs, many private nursery schools have been established where preschoolers are learning skills in human relations as well as developing cognitive mastery. Prominent among these are day care centers that involve the parents as participants in program planning or others who serve as surrogate parents. Such programs aim primarily to help youngsters to feel secure with others, good about themselves, and excited about learning.

A preschool program that shows some promise for humanizing relationships within schools is the Human Development Program (HDP) described by Bessell (1972). It was designed to foster the healthy emotional development of preschoolers and youngsters of primary age. The basic structure of HDP consists of a daily meeting of an encounter group, referred to by some practitioners as the "*magic circle*" the purpose of which is to stimulate and support openness, exploration of feelings, and the development of empathy. The interpersonal processes that take place in the magic circle roughly resemble the group dynamics of sensitivity groups. Discussion is aimed at revealing the humaneness of the teachers to the young students and to increase the closeness and rapport between teachers and students.

Curriculm materials, including a manual of theory along with specific curriculum guides, were developed by Bessell and Palomares (1967). These spell out recommended teaching techniques and provide a set of tested sequential verbal cues for daily use in preschool classes through the third grade. Bessell (1972) reported that at the time of writing (probably 1971), teacher training institutes had educated more than 25,000 teachers in HDP techniques and methods, exposing, indirectly at least, some 5,000,000 children to the program. While quantitative evaluation is still incomplete, Bessell writes that teachers report reduced discipline problems, greater personal involvement, increased verbal expressiveness, higher motivation to learn greater confidence, and more constructive behaviors among their students. Teachers have also reported that their personal styles of working with their classes have changed. Bessell wrote, "They find themselves more flexible and able to cope with teaching problems, more comfortable, and less hostile and distrustful toward children." HDP techniques still should be thoroughly and carefully evaluated, however, by objective outsiders.

b. The informal primary school

Many elementary schools are becoming more informal, relaxed, secure, and supportive. Some have patterned their technical structure after the British Infant Schools. Other changes in the direction of increased informality are associated with open architectural arrangements. In many communities, elementary schools constructed during the past five years are open-space schools, which typically means they are arranged with a large modern resource center at the center, surrounded by places for classrooms. Free movement from classrooms to resource center is facilitated by the absence of wall and hallways. Open structures also make it easy for students of different ages to mingle with one another and for teachers with different specialties and interests to interact and work together. Even schools built as the old egg-carton type of self-contained structure have made moves toward more informality. In some older schools, for example, the corridors are used for small group work, tutoring and individual study. Doors to classrooms are left ajar and hallways between rooms have become a learning area for students to use.

In North Dakota educators have gone into informal education in a major way. A few years ago the leadership of the North Dakota State Department of Education recognized the need for advanced training among the state's elementary teachers, a considerable proportion of whom had never obtained bachelor's degree. Instead of developing additional programs at the state's colleges of education, a decision was made to build a new center for teacher retraining. The new center, called the Institute for Behavioral Studies in Education, was initially led by personnel convinced of the value of informal education. This statewide innovation represented a courageous major step toward humanizing schools. Although revised teacher training in itself probably will not bring about increased humanization, institutes like the one in North Dakota can perform a significant part in bringing about productive change in education. This is especially the case as educators, parents, and students become more knowledgeable about alternative procedures in schools.

c. Team teaching arrangements

With the trend toward more informal elementary education there has been another toward more collaboration and cooperation among staff members. Increasingly, teachers are expected to work together and share their strengths so as to provide a broader range of opportunities for children. The assumption of this move is that the total impact of the team will be greater than that of its individual parts; teachers can work within their strengths and interests while colleagues of various kinds can make up for weaknesses. As previously noted, such increased informal interdependence also enhances the potential for more fully humanized relationships.

One prominent example of a technical structure to implement team teaching is the multi-unit elementary school (Klausmeier and Pellegrin, 1971). The typical multi-unit school has three teaching teams, each made up of a team leader (master teacher), three or four regular teachers, several aides, and an intern or practice teacher. Each team generally works with about one-third of the students in the school; the teaching team and students together are referred to as a unit. Most often one team takes the six- and seven-year-olds, another works with the eight- and nine-year-olds, and the third team works with the ten- and eleven-year-olds. Some schools have wider age or cross-interest structures; many kinds of grouping are possible.

In the multi-unit school, the leadership group is made up of team leaders, the principal, the resource librarian, and the counselor (or human development specialist). This group coordinates the school program, keeps communication between teams open and accurate, and maintains contact with resources outside the school. The multi-unit school's technical structure is similar to the kind of arrangement advocated by Likert (1961) to increase an organization's resourcefulness and potentiality. Likert points to the importance of an organizational arrangement in which a communicative link exists between each level in the hierarchy and each formal subsystem. Thus the leadership team has the principal as the link-pin connecting the central office with the school; and team leaders connect the leadership team with the teachers and students. Everybody knows someone who can directly communicate with the leadership team.

Among the various multi-unit schools where we have worked, consulted, observed, or interviewed, we generally discovered great excitement and stimulation, but at the same time we found that staff members were overloaded with responsibilities and commitments, tired, and frustrated over being unable to accomplish more. One multi-unit school had two large posters in the teacher's lounge. One poster read, "I am young and strong and living a great adventure." The other poster said, "When you're up to your ass in alligators, it's hard to remember your original objective was to drain the swamp." These two posters nicely typify the joys and pains that teachers feel when working collaboratively. We have found no easy ways to make transitions from self-contained schools to multi-unit arrangements. During the great adventure, some alligators are bound to appear, but there is no doubt in our minds that adult professionals working in teams holds a considerable potential for creating humanized school climates.

One special example of an exciting team teaching structure is a school that has supplemented its regular teams of teachers with an extra team of art specialists who are experts in music, art, dance, and drama. They work with the regular teams to facilitate more art-oriented programs as well as to offer programs of their own for students. Schools like this one are especially fertile ground for integrated curricula which focus on more than just cognitive skills.

d. The middle school

The middle school is another technical structure being tried in some urban settings to help educators deal more effectively with the intergroup tensions and prejudices that exist in the community. Since the neighborhood school is typically constituted of a homogeneous population, young students generally receive few direct learning experiences to help them cope with intergroup tensions and prejudices. Indeed, the homogeneous neighborhood school in many ways helps to perpetuate and perhaps even exacerbate these cross-group tensions and prejudices. The middle school receives youngsters from a variety of neighborhoods and, by bringing heterogeneous clusters of students together for the middle years in school (typically grades 5-8), attempts to teach skills necessary for coping with complex community life.

The middle school offers several exciting possibilities. For example, it could be organized as a multi-unit school. The curricula could be oriented toward issues of growing up, awareness of self, building self-confidence, and training children in social interaction skills as well as academic skills. It could house several small schools, each with a different pedagogical emphasis. One house, for instance, could emphasize individualized instruction; another could focus primarily on human relations knowledge and skills; another could emphasize teaching basic cognitive skills from a traditional perspective; another could focus on the arts; and still another could be a very permissive school-within-a-school based on a Summerhill philosophy. Whatever the particular arrangement, a school between the elementary school, in which basic skills are taught, and the high school, in which future careers are fashioned, could provide a unique and important step toward humanizing the education process.

e. Innovative high schools

Unfortunately, too few senior high schools have been able to change their cultures to become more relaxed, informal, and open. Some, it is true, have innovated in scheduling, number and comprehensiveness of courses, counseling services, and the like, but very few have involved staff members and students together to build a more humane climate.

An outstanding example of a school that *has* made major inroads in teacher-student personalness and collaboration is Adams High School in Portland, Oregon. The Adams technical structure is highly innova‑ tive. At the present time, the school has several houses. Each house has a somewhat different philosophy, program, and culture because of the different interests and skills of students and staff comprising it. All houses attempt to involve students directly in house governance. A student is a member of one house for most of the day; however, he or she can work in others part of the time. Some of the houses take retreats several times each year to assess how the interpersonal proc‑ esses and programs are going. Several houses hold planned "process discussions" (see Chapter 7) at least once per week.

The most striking as well as the most restricting, aspect of the Adams experience is that it is a public school in a working-class area with a heterogeneous racial and ethnic population. Adams's problems have originated not primarily from within the school but from without. The larger community has not supported the Adams innovation; some people have viewed it as noneducational, while others have seen it as downright subversive.

Although most of the original innovators have left, Adams still maintains some of its innovative structures. Although the school is now administered by local professionals who have not been noted for innovation it is being managed very capably. It is true that Ohme in his article (1972) and many others verbally have cited the replace‑ ment of the highly innovative principal by a capable local man as evidence that the Adams program has failed. *We do not agree with that assessment.* The current administration and staff, while perhaps less interested in getting new programs started than their predeces‑ sors, are nevertheless working out some of the disorganization prob‑ lems inevitable in new programs, improving Adams's image in the Portland community, and strengthening many of the beneficial pro‑ grams commenced by the former leadership staff.

Another innovative organizational arrangement is the Governing Board of Staples High School in Westport, Connecticut (Jacoby, 1972). The Staples Governing Board (SGB) has shown how effective a staff-student legislature can be in a large public school. The board operates under fairly simple procedures: student representatives are elected by the students, teachers by the staff, and administrators by the administration. Board meetings occur once a week, and one eve‑ ning meeting is held every month to attract parents.

The SGB has a rather complex committee structure, through which much of its work is carried out. A 60 percent majority vote is required before a bill is passed; however, the principal does hold veto power over all decisions, which can be overridden by a seventy-five percent majority vote of the SGB or by the school board. The principal, for example, used his veto power on a bill calling for major changes in the school's method for final examinations. The bill had also aroused considerable opposition from faculty and students. The SGB resumed its work in developing an alternative bill that was agreeable to all. No plan had been finalized at the time of the writing of the article. The SGB has made some important decisions; students may now select one course a year on a pass no-pass basis and the SGB was also instrumental in establishing a new ecology course. At the time Jacoby visited the school, the SGB was working on a bill giving students the right to study their high school transcripts and plans to develop better communication with parents.

According to Jacoby the SGB has worked very well. Many parents, staff members, and students have been pleasantly surprised with its success. Meetings run smoothly, communication is open, and staff and administrators participate equally with students rather than dominating them. The major problems are in maintaining two-way communication with the student body and the parents.

f. Open schools

The open-campus school is one more technical structure that could pave the way for changes in the traditional relationships between the faculty and students of senior high schools. In its most limited form, the open campus offers nothing more than a cafeteria of resources from which the student chooses what is best for him. In its most ideal form, the open campus provides not only student choices about a variety of educational options but also student-faculty discussions to decide what the goals of the school should be and what educational alternatives should be offered. After all, it is primarily the hierarchical power arrangements within senior high schools that help to maintain impersonality, alienation, and withdrawal; the open-campus senior high school plan could offer a way to modify this power structure, making the power ratio between the professional educators and students more nearly equal.

The Parkway Plan, a "school without walls," is a good example of one kind of open school. The school actually does not exist as a physical plant but exists in the community of Philadelphia at large, more specifically on the Parkway, a boulevard with many valuable resources—the main library, museums, parks, hospitals, a detention home, and other community sites which the students use as their classroom. The curriculum is decided upon jointly by students and faculty; and while there is a great deal of group activity, many programs are also designed for the benefit of one or two individuals.

2. A proposed organizational structure

Traditionally schools have stressed the academic and intellectual development of students. Today in our crowded and complex world that view is too narrow. We believe schools must also play an instrumental role in helping all students cope with emotional issues and personal life concerns. This has been done to some extent by some understanding and caring teachers and also done formally by counselors and psychologists to help students in serious trouble. Schools should also teach students how to apply their knowledge and skills; the "storehouse of knowledge" is not useful to students who cannot apply what they have learned.

We propose a school organization constituted primarily of three different learning settings. Each student and faculty member would spend time in a group focused on guidance or personal growth, in groups oriented toward academic and intellectual development, and in other groups which aim to help students apply and use their knowledge. We refer to these three types as the guidance group, the instructional group, and the application group.

Although some aspects of these groups are now found in most schools, few schools give equal attention to each type. Most public schools, for example, are structured around instructional groups. We agree, however, with Coleman (1972) who pointed out that contemporary students tend to receive too much information and too little chance to apply it. We also think that students need more opportunity to work through personal and emotional concerns. Public schools, in other words, need to structure more educational experiences around guidance and application and fewer around formal instruction. Many alternative schools stress personal growth experiences, thus offering learning experiences within what we call guidance groups. However, we also agree with Kozol's criticism (1972) that many free schools have failed to provide adequate opportunities to learn basic skills needed for survival. Vocational schools traditionally have focused on the practical uses of information, but have emphasized skills required for specific jobs. Most young people will have a number of jobs and many other tasks and problems before their careers are completed. Attempts to help students to cope only with specific job skills are inadequate.

We will explain in some detail how we view the operation of each of these three groups in the context of a humanized school.

a. The guidance group

Experience in guidance groups would help students develop a basic core of self-esteem and develop ways to strive for self-knowledge. The central philosophical goals are self-oriented—to know, to accept, and to continue to improve oneself. The group interaction would be designed to build awareness of individuals, to gain self-confidence by learning how one's behaviors affect other people, and to increase understanding and acceptance of others.

The kinds of activities to reach these goals would include teaching how to distinguish among personal thoughts, personal feelings, and perceptions of others; teaching how to gather valid information about one's strengths and weaknesses in relation to others; and encouraging group members to discuss the interpersonal impact of each person's behavior.

The overall task of the guidance group would be to provide emotionally meaningful experiences to facilitate the personal growth and psychic integration of the members. Merely providing the time, space, and membership for such a group would not, of course, be sufficient. The behavior of the formal leader of the group, initially at least, would be crucial. They must themselves be open, direct, sensitive, empathic, and skillful in facilitating constructive openness. They must share their own feelings, check their impressions of others' feelings, paraphrase the thoughts of others, ask for clarification when there is confusion, and summarize the position of the group when its activities begin to bog down. Above all, they must share with the students their own feelings of anxiety, incompetence, and fear of rejection. The suggestions offered in Chapter 5 about personal growth should be heeded especially by the formal leaders of guidance groups.

Obviously the traditional role of teacher as instructional leader will not work in guidance groups. Although, as the formal leader, the teacher should take responsibility for initially convening the group, for making suggestions about how the group should proceed, and for offering particular activities to guide the group's learning about self and interpersonal relations, we believe that gradually the teacher should move out of the focal role of leader. The teacher must eventually act more as a member of the group than the dominant person. Thus, as the group progresses, its goals should be determined increasingly by the interests and concerns of the students. There is, after all, no standard curriculum for the teacher or students to finish, nor is formal evaluation of student progress required. The curriculum is what the members set out to do and the evaluations of their work are formative—i.e., can we do this better?

We know that the task of facilitative, social-emotional leadership will be challenging for many teachers. However, we are confident that, given the opportunity, many teachers will discover they have the flexibility and skill to perform effectively both as the leader of an instructional group and as the facilitator in a guidance group. Moreover, when they experience these two types of leadership and groups side by side, they will see real changes in student behavior.

It has been our experience that many discipline problems have been greatly relieved in schools that offer some form of guidance group as part of the standard program. Moreover, we think that instructional groups can be greatly strengthened if the members periodically discuss among themselves their emotional stresses, interpersonal attractions, and individual irritations. As educators, we must come to realize that the interpersonal processes of living are just as important as the development of our cognitions.

b. The instructional group

Instructional groups would be aimed toward helping students develop cognitive skills. They would deal with traditional subject matter such as reading, writing, arithmetic, science, and a category of integrated subject matter with a problem-oriented approach. Such groups would be organized in many ways with many curriculum aids, materials, and instructional procedures. We think that the most prominent norm for instructional groups should be in support of a continual process of inquiry; thus curiosity, spontaneity, logic, experimentation, and creativity all would be valued. Expectations would be in support of clarifying the issues of study, seeking information from many sources, compiling the information systematically, and helping one another to learn about the salient points of the subject matter. The educational literature already is replete with discussions and arrangements of the instructional group, so we will not explore it in as much detail as the other two types. Chapter 5 presents several ideas about exercises and procedures that can be used in making instructional groups more effective.

c. The application group

Application groups are action-oriented groups; they are neither as introspective as guidance groups nor as devoted to academic disciplines as instructional groups. Students and faculty apply their knowledge, insights, and skills to find out what will work and what will not work in solving real problems. The problems chosen for concentration can come from inside specific classrooms, from the school organization, or from the community outside the school.

Application groups would be more fluid and flexible than guidance or instructional groups; several ad hoc groups might exist simultaneously for a short time, disbanding as soon as their purposes are accomplished. For example, a small group of students might attempt to build a communication structure between two instructional groups, both of which wish to test out the advantages of cross-age tutoring. The application group probably would disband when the structure was going well or when it was dropped. As another example, an application group concerned with school functioning (such as the student-faculty group at Staples High School) might organize for a semester or full year to help build a collaborative governing system for the school. Still other application groups could analyze new sorts of curriculum offerings, compile helpful information about instructional materials, or arrange for problem-solving meetings in which school conflicts could be discussed. The basic assumption behind the establishment of these application groups is that school functioning is everybody's responsibility, so that all members should take some part in keeping the school adaptable and effective.

Application groups developed to deal with community problems may likewise tackle various issues and organize in different ways. Some of the issues could be racism, crime, pollution, school budget votes, park and playground needs, and the lack of dialogue between segments of the community. They could be tied organizationally to an instructional group, such as civics or sociology class in which city government or community relations are studied. Like the student groups of the "school without walls" in Philadelphia, these groups might use the resources of the city, such as libraries, museums, hospitals, and police stations, as settings for learning and action. Many times they could simply organize on an ad hoc basis to study and act upon lively and important issues facing the school or community.

Like guidance groups, application groups will not work if offered merely the time, space, and opportunity. The skills of educational leaders are critical at first. Students must also learn skills for collaborative work and for systematically and sequentially solving problems. Their tolerance for conflict both *within* the application group and *with* their target groups must be high. For instance, an application group may be working on a school issue in which real differences exist between the subgroups concerned. The application group can learn how to handle the resulting tensions by using their own processes of direct communication and by trying continually to be objective and open about all difficulties. Usually, when appropriate channels for anger and frustration are allowed and when the members of application groups try to follow a systematic, objective plan of action, the difficulties that occur offer valuable learning experiences and are not disruptive.

Application groups provide opportunities for students to find ways of linking personal values and academic information to their own behavior as responsible and intelligent citizens. We believe that the student is better equipped to cope with the exigencies of his future when he has practical experiences as well as academic knowledge. Application groups can provide behavioral experience that will help students to see the practical relevance of what they learn in the guidance and instructional groups.

The role of the educational leader in the application group differs somewhat from his role in the other two groups. In the guidance group, leaders strive to facilitate closeness and openness by being honest and informal themselves and often describing their own feelings as an equal member of the group. In instructional groups leaders take on more formal leadership functions; there is cognitive material to be mastered and the leaders often are more resourceful than the students in initiating a sequence of learning steps and choosing learning materials. In instructional groups leaders should assume an active influence relationship with students. The application group calls for a blend of these two types of teacher roles.

Application groups deal with personal values, academic information, and behavioral tryouts. The educational leader should attempt to be facilitative and personal when values are being described and shared. On the other hand, the information to be provided about problem-solving and the academic content of specific problem-solving activities call for leaders to be more directive and structured in their approach. Planning for, executing, and giving feedback about new behaviors all call for a blending of the directive and the facilitative. As an example, when working with an application group concerned with city management, the educational leader might try to teach and promote the procedures of objective research, but if the group moves to *act* toward improving some aspect of city management the leader might act more as an equal member of the group, so that the values and concerns of *all* participants can be communicated and worked on. In the matter of "taking action," each individual—whether student or educational leader—should be urged to make decisions for himself.

ORGANIZATION DEVELOPMENT IN SCHOOLS

Regardless of how creative and potentially exciting the organizational structure of a school may be, the school will not be thoroughly humanized unless both staff and students share the behavioral norms and skills to make the structure truly live. Although norms and skills of competence in interpersonal relations do not by themselves insure that school relationships will be humanized, without them even the most ideally organized school with the richest curriculum and finest instructional materials will lack real human substance. The skills of communicating directly, openly, and authentically are crucial as building blocks of the humanized school. Unfortunately, the good intentions of many staffs are too seldom accompanied by effective skills.

Furthermore, if a school is to continue to have a vital and self-renewing climate, it must go beyond just skills in communicating. The staff and students must be capable of attacking problems openly and jointly by using the skills of rational problem-solving; and they should also have norms and skills in support of thorough evaluation so that they can determine how they are proceeding. Unfortunately, it is very rare to find a school where all these elements exist—especially one in which joint evaluation is carried out by staff and students. Such schools do not exist primarily because norms for openness and collaboration have been slow to develop between staff and students

Behind this lies the fact that both staff and students generally have a low level of knowledge and skill in communicating effectively, solving problems systematically, and evaluating their contributions collaboratively.

Training in organization development (OD) appears to be the most promising vehicle for establishing norms, structures, and skills to facilitate clear communication and effective problem-solving and evaluation among staff and students. The overall objective of OD is to build *self-renewing schools*—schools that are able to adapt to current changes within the student body, community, and world while continuing to maintain an effective educational program. Self-renewing schools are continuously adaptive; hence, they are changing and not restricted to any single organizational structure or set of procedures. While there is typically some formal status hierarchy, form follows function instead of tradition. Staff members and students are organized into groups to solve specific problems; both the organizational structure of the school and the methods used in the group change to fit the nature of the current problems. Through OD interventions we believe that it will be possible to establish schools that not only are self-renewing but also have norms in support of listening to the individual (whatever his status), using communication skills naturally, and working efficiently and systematically while still remembering the importance of feelings.

OD offers the kind of consultation that encourages the members of a school to collaborate with one another to solve their own problems. In emphasizing system change rather than mere attitudinal changes in individuals, OD aims at modifying the culture of the school, and not just some of the feelings of the staff and students. To accomplish this cultural change, OD involves the school participants themselves in the assessment, diagnosis, and transformation of their own goals, the development of their own newly acquired group skills, the redesign of their own structures and procedures for achieving the goals, the alteration of the working climate of their school, and the assessment of results.

Continuous training in OD can be useful for any school. The reason for this is that *no* school, no matter how well adapted to the current needs of its community, can stay the same and still remain adaptive in the long run. A school that strives to have significant impact—and especially a humanistic influence—must be able to change its modes of operation as it discovers that it is ineffective in coping with its changing environment. We believe that OD can help a school develop the capabilities for humanistic change.

1. How organization development works

The OD intervention aims at increasing the effectiveness of work groups and attempts to teach school personnel how to function more humanistically while at the same time carrying out the required tasks of the school. The measure of a successful OD intervention is that a school has developed the capacity to solve its problems by using the staff and student resources already present. These resources include, besides information about different curricula, empathy for the feelings of others, willingness to take risks, and supportiveness of others. Thus, staff resources are not simply ideas residing in filing cabinets, nor are student resources simply the zealous energy reserves available at football games. The true human resources of the school become available only when teachers and students call upon one another for fresh ways of looking at things, when each staff member or student is unafraid to offer his own ideas and feelings, and when a group moves a new idea into action.

Organization development carries a humanistic mesage: in this way OD differs from the type of help offered by traditional management consulting firms. Most management consultants look at the problems as defined by organization administrators and then later recommend solutions to these problems. Rarely does the consultant remain with an organization long enough to help carry the recommendations into practice. Organization development consultants, in contrast, do not accept the problems as defined by the administration but rather explore the perceptions of all segments of the organization. Recommendations for change do not come from the consultant alone but also from the relevant parties. The consultant then works directly with the organization in designing *and implementing* the recommended changes. Training sessions in OD help a school staff to carry out the changes which often they themselves have recommended and designed.

Most OD interventions move through three sequential stages, described below.

a. Stage 1: Improving communication skills

Training in OD aims first to build increased openness and ease of communication among staff and students by developing their skills in paraphrasing, describing behavior, describing feelings, and giving and receiving feedback.

b. Stage 2: Developing humanistic norms

Organization development training builds new norms which support the idea of mutual help between staff and students and which lead to the uncovering of interpersonal conflicts in the school so that they can be worked on constructively. The process of OD builds on the already existing reservoir of staff and student interest in school improvement to help ameliorate some of their real problems.

Once communication skills have been introduced and practiced, staff and students are encouraged to state some frustrations they encounter and are taught to use a sequence of problem-solving steps. The collaboration required to complete the problem-solving steps reduces frustrations and also brings the satisfaction to most individuals that they have participated in the solution. Changes in school norms occur only when the staff and students actually behave in more open and honest ways. In other words, the problem-solving does not become effective and the OD process is not completed until plans are implemented.

c. Stage 3: Structural changes

As stated above, an intervention in OD is not complete until new functions, roles, procedures, or policies are built. New organizational structures such as guidance, instructional, and application groups must become part of the basic design of the school. The new structures must not be just ideas; they must be formal, institutionalized, and budgetarily supported. Humanized schools cannot exist only on the good intentions of staff or students; they must also have organizational structures to support the humanized climate.

2. Organization development applied to the schools

The goals and methods of OD are related to problems that beset most school organizations—clarifying communications, establishing norms, and developing organizational structures and procedures to facilitate healthy learning climates. While these are the overriding aims of OD, the specific designs and the particular training methods used take on different emphases depending on the school and the problems it has.

Organization Development has already been applied to schools in many different ways and its real adaptability in dealing with even more situations has yet to be tested. Following are three examples of how it has already been used.

a. Training for a school faculty

An entire junior high school faculty, including secretaries, cooks, and custodians, participated in a six-day summer workshop followed by several sessions during the following school year. The intervention was aimed at improving the organizational problem-solving of the school faculty. The school was not faced with any critical crisis or extraordinary difficulties; the principal and his staff used the services of the organizational consultants because they felt generally thwarted and frustrated about their working relationships and believed that their group processes warranted some critical investigation.

The first stage of training was aimed at improving communication skills. Group exercises were focused on interpersonal organizational processes—especially those involving trust and openness. Second, the faculty outlined three problems which were impeding the faculty's functioning and then divided into subgroups to work on these problems. The three problems were (1) confusion about roles, especially among those in authority positions, such as the principal, vice principal and departmental coordinators, (2) the ineffective use of staff resources, and (3) low staff involvement and participation in meetings and committees. Each of the subgroups followed a systematic procedure of problem-solving in its area of concern and then made recommendations for solution. The entire faculty then discussed the recommendations and made specific plans for change. Later in the school year there were three training events with the consultants, during which the faculty looked at its problems, evaluated its progress, and made new plans. Certainly the school staff did not solve all its problems, but there were enough individual, normative, and structural changes for the training to be considered successful in increasing the staff's ability to function together as a unit (Schmuck and Runkel, 1970).

b. Self-renewal for a school district

As part of a two-year project, OD consultants worked with the Kent, Washington, school district. During the first year organizational training was carried out with key district people and groups, such as the superintendent and his cabinet, the principals, educational personnel in the central office, and leaders in the local educational association. This training was aimed at increasing the collaboration and decreasing the competitiveness of district staff members. For this purpose confrontative meetings were held to increase understanding of the grievances and frustrations among people whose work was interdependent. After training these groups to a certain level of skill, the consultants worked with some individual school staffs. The training in the various schools lasted for different periods of time and focused on concerns of special interest to the school being trained (Schmuck and Miles, 1971).

c. Cadre of organization consultants

One of the major purposes of Organization Development is to assure that changes in norms, communicative processes, and organizational structures will be enduring, i.e., self-renewing. One characteristic of any organization is that individuals and groups are comfortable doing things in the same old way—*even if* that way is no longer adequate to the situation. Although OD helps to create new organizational procedures, those procedures must change as the problems of the surrounding community environment change. A cadre of OD consultants is a permanent organizational structure within a school district to monitor the behaviors of individuals and the processes of subgroups to make sure they are helpful and adaptive behaviors. A cadre is composed of people from within the district itself—teachers, counselors, and principals—who have received training in developing communication skills, diagnosing problems, designing training events, acting as third party mediators, and implementing training for schools or groups in their own district. The cadre is a formal part of the school district, with assigned personnel and budgetary allocations to monitor organizational procedures and to help district subsystems to continue developing healthy and personalized climates for learning (Schmuck, Runkel, Saturen, Martell, and Derr, 1972).

3. The progress of organization development in schools

Although interest in OD for schools has been rising rapidly, research and development on it still is rather meager. The program of Richard

Schmuck and Philip Runkel at the Center for the Advanced Study of Educational Administration continues to be a focal point for research on OD in schools. Most of the important data-based research has been described in detail in Schmuck and Miles (1971) and the development work on OD designs, techniques, and evaluation procedures has been thoroughly summarized in Schmuck, Runkel, Saturen, Martell, and Derr (1972). The latter volume contains much information helpful to school participants who may wish to get involved in OD. It contains chapters on such topics as clarifying communication, establishing goals, uncovering conflicts, improving meetings, solving problems, and making decisions. The ideas and empirical evidence published in the above two volumes along with our own continuing consulting experiences suggest strongly that the techniques of OD are a plausible and useful vehicle for humanizing schools.

Perhaps the most limiting feature of OD in schools, as it has generally been practiced, is its dependence on its philosophical base of trust and truth. The trust-truth model specifies that shared expectations of trust, honesty, and supportiveness will form as members of a working team gain confidence and skill in communicating clearly and openly. These norms and skills, in turn, support working collaboratively to solve problems and to make rational decisions. This model assumes that the real work of schools is carried out through members' interpersonal interactions and that new norms for open communication and support are necessary to develop skills for collaborative problem-solving. Thus the development of *trust* makes it possible, in simple terms, for *truth* to emerge and be used effectively.

Research on successful OD interventions in schools indicates that virtually all of the projects have been carried out with middle-class and suburban schools. While middle-class white schools have their fair share of problems and the techniques of OD should be helpful to them, it is unclear how well the trust-truth model will work in other situations. Some critics justifiably have pointed out that perhaps the trust-truth model will work best in schools where value conflicts and community stress is minimal. They ask how well the trust-truth OD intervention will work in urban schools which are fraught with racism, low operating budgets, centralized and bureaucratic decision-making, and widespread despair, frustration, and loneliness.

An alternative model, the *power-conflict* model, has been well described by Chesler and Lohman (1971). Although often conflict is uncovered and used in the trust-truth OD, the power-conflict model calls for conflict to be employed deliberately to increase tension and to force negotiation of differences. This model calls for an intervention design that teaches groups with vested interests to fight with one another for their own goals. The model stresses the inevitable conflict between particular groups, such as students, teachers, paraprofessionals, service personnel, parents, and administrators. The intervention is designed to build new organizational power structures, roles, norms, and procedures. Negotiation rather than collaborative problem-solving is the main lever for organizational improvement. An effort is currently underway by Richard Schmuck and Philip Runkel to test the respective benefits of trust-truth and power-conflict OD in attempting to bring students, teachers, and parents together for deciding on how their school should be changed.

Regardless of the model used, a key feature of OD training is the focus upon the processes of the organization. In other words, OD calls for process consultation, not help in specific matters involving instructional methods or the curriculum. In the next chapter, we discuss the role of a process consultant in schools, showing how school buildings and districts can derive humanistic benefits from such help. The purpose of the process consultant is to help groups solve their own problems by guiding them through a systematic plan of diagnosis, proposing alternative plans, taking action, and evaluating the results and the processes.

This chapter has focused on the role of the outside consultant; the next chapter will show how the techniques of OD and the skills of process consultation can be used by anyone in the school with the interest and energy to do so. Humanized schools cannot depend solely on the efforts of outsiders. Students, teachers, counselors, principals, central office administrators and parents can effectively use the skills of process consultation to strive toward changing alien and inhuman interactions into personal and caring relationships.

SUMMARY OF CHAPTER 6

The human organization of the school sets the stage for the climate of its learning groups. In order to understand and change the complex web of dynamic interactions in school organizations, we note four important variables upon which their climates are dependent. They are: norms and goals, roles and functions, the networks of communication, and power and influence relationships.

Humanistic schools have norms and goals that stress the importance of individuals; at the same time these schools are pluralistic organizations with a variety of goals, values, and interests that will sometimes be in conflict. With all these differences, the participants collaboratively strive to create an organization in which every individual has some influence and can play some important part. Humanistic schools also have communication channels which allow the participants to express their thoughts and feelings directly. There is a heavy responsibility placed on individuals in humanistic schools; they must think and act and speak for themselves, but they must also continually take others into consideration.

These good intentions, individual skills, and group norms are *not* sufficient, however, to develop and perpetuate schools that are truly humanistic and self-renewing. The formal organization of the school must also be structured in ways that will enhance close relationships between the participants. The traditional physical structure of schools —the egg-carton architecture—emphasizes the isolation of one teacher and one group of students with one specified subject from other learning groups. This organizational structure is not likely to provide the events that will give rise to widespread humanistic relationships in schools. Many new promising organizational arrangements are now being tested in elementary, middle, and senior high schools. We propose especially one structure that gives particular attention to equalizing the time spent on three central curriculum issues: the emotional dynamics of students (guidance groups), their intellectual development (instructional groups), and the application of students' knowledge to goals that are important to them (application groups).

To change schools is very difficult and many efforts have failed. One method showing promise, organization development (OD), is a systematic training intervention for building organizational goals, norms, and structures to create new and humanized schools. It asks people to use their resources, try out their strengths, and risk their ideas to create organizations that truly reflect their own feelings, information, and goals. Research on OD is limited, yet the available evidence indicates that it shows promise as a powerful and important method to help create humanized school climates.

Argyris, Chris. 1970. *Intervention Theory and Method: A Behavioral Science View.* Menlo Park, Ca.: Addison-Wesley.

Designed for action researchers and consultants who intervene in living organizations, this book is for advanced students of behavioral science. The first nine chapters deal with the theory and methods of organizational intervention, while the last seven describe specific examples of intervention. Although the book is about industrial organizations, it is easily applicable to schools.

Foster, Marcus A. 1971. *Making Schools Work.* Philadelphia: Westminster Press.

Sometimes rambling but always interesting, Foster presents insights gained from a variety of experiences in the Philadelphia schools. He focuses especially upon his experiences as the principal of an inner-city school, indicating ways in which he was able to bring about change. Unlike many of the contemporary chronicles of despair in education, this book is inspiring and hopeful. Foster uses many concepts from group dynamics and organizational theory, couching them in a very personal and readable style.

Fox, Robert S., Charles Jung, Richard Schmuck, Miriam Ritvo, and Elmer Van Egmond. 1973. *Diagnosing Professional Climate of Schools.* Fairfax, Va.: NTL Learning Resources Corporation.

This book offers ideas about how a school's climate affects students' learning experiences. A series of detailed guides to diagnosis, based on experience, makes up the major part of the book. Actual problem-solving models also are developed in the areas of staff responsibility, behavior, and resources.

Katz, Michael B. 1971. *Class Bureaucracy and Schools: The Illusion of Educational Change in America.* New York: Praeger.

In unflinching words, Katz attempts to prove that American schools are mirror images of American society. He explains the discrepancy between the popular educational rhetoric of "education serves the people" and the common practices that seem to belie such rhetoric. Katz's special contribution is his argument that the basic structure of schools has essentially remained the same since 1880. He describes the development of schools during 1800-1885, when problems had begun to be identified, and demonstrates how reform movements have failed since that time. A well ordered and clearly written book, it should be of interest particularly to educational reformers.

Minuchin, Patricia, Barbara Biber, Edna Shapiro, and Herbert Zimiles. 1969. *The Psychological Impact of School Experience.* New York: Basic Books, Inc.

This is a carefully done research project concerning the effects on children of two different kinds of school climates—the traditional and the "modern." The modern schools are closer to our image of a humanized school than the traditional schools. The findings tend to support our theory that whole-person relationships between teachers and students help the students to understand themselves and to attend more to here-and-now interpersonal relationships.

National Elementary Principals' Journal. Vol. 52, No. 3 (Nov. 1972).

This issue is entirely devoted to the dynamics of open education. It contains an article on the new School of Behavioral Studies in Education of the University of North Dakota and one by Lillian Weber on the open corridor. There are several articles about the British primary schools and some practical articles about implementing an open classroom.

Price, James L. 1972. *Handbook of Organizational Measurement.* Lexington, Mass.: D. C. Heath and Co.

This volume, intended primarily for researchers in the behavioral sciences, promotes the standardization of measures used in the study of large-scale organizations. It can serve as a useful source of examples of measurement tools for the educator who wants to diagnose school climates.

Schmuck, Richard A., and Matthew Miles. 1971. *Organization Development in Schools.* Palo Alto, Ca.: National Press Books.

This book summarizes all of the theory and data-based research on organization development in schools up to 1971. Several contributors present descriptions and evaluations of their interventions. The book presents many practical programs and suggestions for school districts interested in implementing organization development.

Schmuck, Richard A., and Philip J. Runkel. 1970. *Organizational Training for a School Faculty*. Eugene, Ore.: Center for the Advanced Study of Educational Administration, University of Oregon.

This monograph describes the details of OD training for the faculty of a junior high school. It can be useful to educators at several different levels of sophistication about organizational theory and practice; for the beginner, its detailed description of the OD events shows what happens during an organizational change effort, and for the advanced educator, the presentation of the OD rationale, design and evaluation procedures will be of interest for implementation in various educational settings.

Schmuck, Richard, Philip Runkel, Steven Saturen, Ronald Martell, and C. Brooklyn Derr. 1972. *Handbook of Organization Development in Schools*. Palo Alto, Ca.: National Press Books.

This is a comprehensive and practical book about organizational improvement in schools. Designed for educational practitioners or consultants, it presents theory, research, diagnostic tools, and a large number of exercises and designs for humanizing school climates.

Thelen, Herbert. 1960. *Education and the Human Quest*. New York: Harper and Brothers.

This book, annotated previously in Chapter 1, is also included here because the new school organizational structures which Thelen suggests to stimulate inquiry are very similar to our guidance, instructional, and application groups.

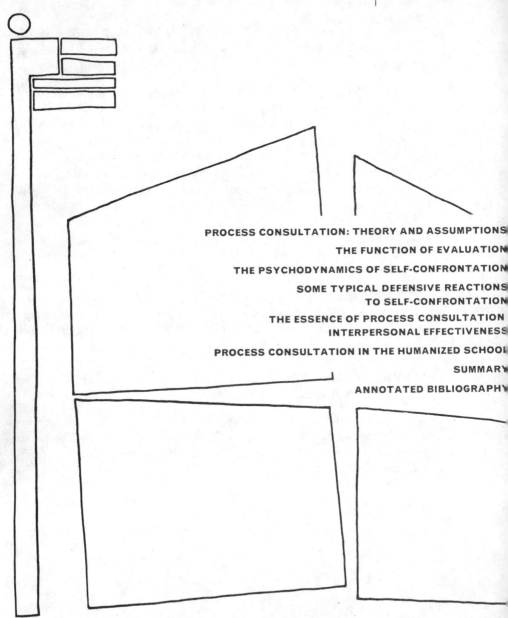

chapter 7

Using consultation to humanize schools

Consultation is one avenue for educators to collaborate with one another and other professionals to humanize learning climates. In fact, collaborative help among educators and noneducators is virtually required to cope with contemporary complexities in our schools.

During earlier periods in America there was perhaps less need for consultative help; educators concentrated their efforts on a narrow range of subjects, there was little pressure from parents to modify schooling, and the students tended to learn "the most important things," such as vocational skills and standards of behavior, in the community or home. Now, however, the courses and services offered by American schools have grown to be so diverse that professional educators alone do not (and cannot) possess all of the skills and competencies necessary to run such broad-based programs. Schools now are responsible for continuous expansion of the formal curriculum as well as a multitude of other activities such as vocational training, psychological guidance and counseling, health services, athletics, and hot lunches. If we add to this long list the continuous pressure for change from critics, researchers, developers, parents, and students, the need for professionals to help one another becomes obvious.

Consultants can perform in countless ways to help the schools, but three primary approaches are most prominent. The first type of consultation comes in the form of *assistance*; consultants are used to implement a particular function—as, for instance, when an expert is hired to design a new educational program in testing or reading, or when a specialist is hired part-time to teach a particular course to students. Another example of consultative assistance occurs when a management firm helps a school district to decide upon the optimal procedure for spending money on, for example, needed space. Some business firms are currently offering assistance to schools by contracting to take over aspects of the instructional program, with the guarantee of student mastery. This consultative approach helps the school to fill a temporary gap or to get over a contemporary hurdle, but typically it does not change the skill levels of educators within the district or affect the interpersonal relationships that are occurring in the schools.

A second type of consultation aims at educating the professionals in a particular substantive area so that they will perform more capably. This type of help is called *content consultation*. The most typical mechanism for content consultation is the inservice course or workshop; an expert is hired to train educators in a substantive subject such as reading, mathematics, social studies, or the arts. Examples of content consultants also include the psychologist who teaches educators about child development, the mathematician who helps teachers develop new instructional strategies, the mental health consultant who helps teachers cope with students who have problems, and the specialist in precision teaching who helps teachers to use various reinforcement strategies. Usually consultants like these are either employed by another organization, such as a university or educational laboratory, or are in private practice, and are contracted with by the district for their services.

More and more school districts are hiring their own full-time consultants, however. Consultants in such domains as language arts, science, music, or early childhood education are typically based in the central office, have district-wide responsibilities, and are expected to maintain contacts with outside experts in universities and educational laboratories. They design and arrange inservice workshops for teachers, help to determine the instructional materials that are purchased, and often are available to individual teachers for consultation.

Content consultation of this type can be an invaluable resource for the schools. If the internal consultants are performing effectively, they serve as the liaison between specialists in the forefront of knowledge and educators charged with transmitting the knowledge to students. Although the potential for change is always present, the content consultant typically does not alter the mode of relating between people in the school; hence we do not believe this type of consultation is very effective for humanizing American schools.

The third type of consultation, called *process consultation*, is the primary topic of this chapter. We believe that it has the best chance for helping to humanize American schools. We already have discussed one kind of process intervention in Chapter 6, in our discussion of organization development. Process consultation aims at improving the interpersonal procedures used by school personnel to reach their educational objectives. It focuses on the *how* of interpersonal interactions rather than on the *what* of their content. Process consultants thus deal with such phenomena as the patterns of communication, leadership attempts, underlying tensions, and decision-making procedures. They do not deal directly with the subject matter of the interactions.

The success of process consultation is measured in terms of how effectively school personnel work together subsequently in reaching their objectives. The consultant's success is determined by how effective the school personnel are in defining their problems and goals (which may, for example, have to do with the content of a program of remedial reading), how resourceful the educators are in devising ways to reach their goals (which may include conferring with a content consultant in reading methods), and how stable, adaptive, and effective the groups products are over time (as shown, for example, by measuring the long term effectiveness of the reading program with the students). Thus, the process consultant provides help with methods of communicating and problem-solving and procedures for planning, decision-making, and implementing; the educators provide the substantive issues, problems, goals, and plans for action.

Persons skilled in process consultation have not generally been employed directly by school districts. Working in universities, research centers, educational laboratories, and behavioral science institutes, process consultants have typically been contracted for by school districts primarily to teach inservice workshops on group processes. There are now several programs in operation to train process consultants for schools. The University of Chicago* has a graduate program in educational psychology to train social psychological specialists for schools (Lighthall, 1969); the Center for the Advanced Study of Educational

---

*For information write: Dr. Frederick Lighthall, Department of Education, University of Chicago, 5835 Kimbark Ave., Chicago, Ill. 60637.

Administration (CASEA)* hires and helps to train graduate students in education and psychology to perform as process consultants; the Northwest Regional Educational Laboratory (NWREL)** is prominent in developing training designs and preparing process consultants; and the National Training Laboratories Institute of Applied Behavioral Science*** is in the forefront of the postgraduate professional development of process consultants. Although a few school districts have shown active interest in using process consultation as part of their ongoing work, most schools have not yet been touched by process consultation. Even though there are cadres of organizational process specialists in Eugene (Oregon) and in Vancouver and Kent (Washington) and even though the Louisville, Kentucky, district has been actively involved in OD, the movement toward using process consultation extensively in schools is still in the very beginning stages.

The primary advantage of process consultation is that its methods can be used by *all* school personnel, regardless of position. Process consultation is concerned with the communication skills of listening, questioning, clarifying, and confronting, and with systematic problem-solving to help an individual or group move toward its goals. Such skills can be used by students, principals, parents, counselors, secretaries, cooks, and custodians whenever they are placed in the role of helping a group to move more surely toward its goals. We think that a school will become more humanized to the extent that process consultation becomes an integral and widely used part of the organizational procedure. Process consultation can be used by many people; there is nothing sacred or elitist about it.

However, we also believe that a school's interpersonal processes are important enough to warrant formal and specific positions of process consultation. Self-renewing schools must have particular persons in the district who have formal responsibility to give their time and energy to improving the human condition of the schools. Without responsible monitoring of the school's human interactions, even the best-intentioned staff will gradually give higher priority to such daily custodial chores as collecting money, organizing schedules, and keeping track of people and equipment. It happens over and over again—

---

*CASEA, University of Oregon, 1472 Kincaid Ave., Eugene, Ore. 97401.
**NWREL, Lindsay Building, 710 S.W. Second Ave., Portland, Ore. 97204.
***NTL-IABS, P.O. Box 9155 Rosslyn Station, Arlington, Virginia 22209.

organizations with the best of intentions gradually begin to give more importance to efficient and smooth operation than to monitoring interpersonal processes. For this reason, specific individuals must be charged with redirecting attention toward the school's real goals and confronting the appropriate people when those goals have been bypassed or forgotten.

In this chapter we first discuss how process consultation relates to the systematic procedures of problem-solving. We will especially emphasize two steps in the problem-solving procedure: the use of *evaluation* to assess performance and to provide diagnostic information for further procedures, and the use of *self-confrontation* to keep an individual working toward his objectives. Second, we discuss the functional skills of process consultation (the basic communication skills of listening, clarifying, questioning, and confronting) and how they can be used by anyone in the school regardless of his position. Third, we show ways in which process consultation can be used with individuals, small groups, or large organizations, pointing out some typical defensive reactions during self-confrontation and what the consultant can do to move the defensiveness in constructive directions and to harness its energies. Chapter 8 goes on to discuss the skills inherent in process consultation and how the skills can be incorporated into the activities of students, teachers, principals, counselors, and parents.

PROCESS CONSULTATION: THEORY AND ASSUMPTIONS

Process consultation helps individuals and groups to solve their problems in a rational, organized, and sequential manner. It is facilitative behavior enabling individuals or groups to agree upon a set of goals, to brainstorm alternative paths to achieve those goals, to decide on a plan of action, to implement the plan, and finally to evaluate its effectiveness.

Problem-solving as we define it here is not a mere academic procedure; we all use problem-solving methods informally in daily life. Educators use problem-solving techniques in making most educational decisions, although their use may be informal and largely unconscious. The job of the process consultant is to make this process more consciously rational and public so that the participants recognize their procedures and consequently gain more control over their goals and behavior. The functions of evaluation and self-confrontation are important in that they help individuals or groups to move toward those goals.

THE FUNCTION OF EVALUATION

Rational thought involves taking accurate readings of the real world. Teachers face the challenge of accurate assessment every day. They must diagnose, for example, the ambient of knowledge or skill a student has in order to prescribe instructional procedures for improvement. Consciously or otherwise, teachers also constantly evaluate their effect on students: are students listening and excited or simply bored and passing time? Indeed, being human involves such evaluative perceptions and reactions; for this reason, we believe, they should be made more explicit and open if a school is to become humanized.

1. The need for objective evaluation

Although evaluation, as a critical component of problem-solving, is performed automatically, it often lacks objectivity and accuracy. Many evaluations—especially of our own behavior and especially when we lack objective evidence—are distorted, biased, or even irrational. Of course, we do not deceive ourselves knowingly, and for most of us no planning goes into self-deception. What we want most of all is to believe in ourselves; the deceptions occur to help us maintain an optimal level of self-esteem.

For example, the teacher who hopes that his students will attain a high level of academic performance may actually behave so as to produce a stress and tension among students which will actually *reduce* their performance level. No doubt such a teacher's self-esteem is associated with his or her ability to help students learn academic subject matter. Indications that teachers are not achieving their objectives may be difficult for them to acknowledge. Likewise, principals who have invested time and energy in innovative programs may bypass or ignore altogether certain negative effects of the new programs.

Indeed, educators should not be expected to assess all the complex phenomena in their schools—especially when they are themselves heavily involved in particular plans. Administrators, teachers, and students naturally tend to protect their interests by selecting data to confirm those interests. Given this problem, there is great need for objective methods of evaluation. For us, the humanized school is characterized by distortion-free flows of information and more accurate estimates of the effects of various behaviors.

A major part played by the professional process consultant is to provide such objective feedback on organizational and individual processes, so that the school's participants can gather objective information. A sheet of facts about ourselves can be an enlightening and humbling experience. In a humanized school, however, the participants must be able to evaluate themselves objectively and, as a consequence, must be prepared for frequent confrontation with disconcerting and dissonant feedback.

2. Summative and formative evaluation

Two ways of thinking about educational evaluation have become prominent; they are referred to as summative and formative evaluation. (See Bloom *et. al.*, 1971, for detailed discussion.) Summative evaluation, perhaps better known to practicing educators, involves assessing what finally has been accomplished. For instance, a grade ostensibly reflects the level of mastery a student has reached in a particular subject, and a supervisor's report may represent the summing up of a teacher's classroom performance. Final research reports on experimental projects in the district are another example. Summative evaluations are helpful primarily to policymakers and decisionmakers: Should the student be allowed to move on to more advanced work? Should the teacher be retained or given a raise in salary? Should the experimental program be continued?

Formative evaluation, on the other hand, is more useful to teachers, counselors, curriculum developers, and principals. It helps to inform practitioners about the next steps to be taken toward a goal. The astute educator continuously sizes up the present social situation to see what his next move should be. Informally, at least, most teachers and administrators do collect formative data as they are performing their daily functions. However, formative evaluation has *not* been used enough in schools in formal and deliberate ways.

There are a number of effective methods of formative evaluation that can be used in inservice training. For example, as a feedback medium video taping is a useful vehicle for formative evaluation of teachers or administrators. The video tapes can be viewed either by the subject alone or perhaps with a consultant who helps to identify strengths and weaknesses. The technique known as micro-teaching, in which a teacher receives feedback on a brief simulated teaching performance, also employs video taping. In both cases, the tapes are viewed in order to improve the behavior of a teacher or administrator.

Another example of formative evaluation is a diagnostic performance test used with young students in particular skill areas, such as reading. Test results give the teacher information about how to proceed in developing reading skills; its purpose is not to evaluate summatively but to pinpoint the skills the youngster lacks and to indicate the appropriate kind of instruction. Formative evaluation provides objective information to identify problems and to suggest alternative paths of action to solve the problems.

3. Evaluation and problem-solving

Both summative and formative evaluation are basic components of problem-solving. Stufflebeam (1971) has written extensively on the interface between objective evaluation and problem-solving. His analyses offer useful tips to process consultants who are striving to help someone work toward his or her own goals.

Stufflebeam points out that useful evaluation in education involves four basic steps; the first three steps are phases of formative evaluation and the fourth step is summative evaluation. First, one specifies and claries the problem; second, one thinks of alternative actions to solve the problem; third, one monitors the chosen actions; and fourth, one evaluates the results of the actions. We will now elaborate each of these four stages, indicating how they relate to problem-solving. In discussing each stage, we will include examples demonstrating how both teachers and students with little scientific training, and highly trained behavioral scientists can use these kinds of evaluations when working as process consultants.

a. Specifying the problem and evaluating the reality

The first step entails collecting data on the immediate situation. Often referred to as baseline measurement, this step involves diagnosing the problem objectively. For example, a teacher may sense that the relationships between students in the classroom are not going well, yet she may be unable to specify exactly the nature of the problem. She

Using consultation to humanize schools

could then use some general measures of classroom climate, such as sociometric inventories or questions on group norms, to help her understand the classroom situation more clearly.* She might also ask a colleague to observe the class and for feedback about student interaction. In addition, she might interview students on their views of the group's problems.

Let us suppose, in this example, that the data collected indicate clearly that there is a lack of peer group cooperation and helpfulness, that many youngsters are being neglected and rejected, and that peer group cohesiveness in the classroom is very low; furthermore, the students are evidently reluctant to share opinions because they have little mutual trust and fear rejection if they reveal their true ideas and opinions.

One effective way for the teacher to begin problem-solving would be to present some of problems directly to the students, engaging them in a sort of group confrontation. The teacher and students could determine whether they wish to alter the negative or unhelpful relationships among themselves. At first the students generally have some difficulty in talking about their relationships in this manner; however, such discussions can be very important steps for building a humanized school.

Teachers should encourage students to discuss their goals and ways in which they would like the class to change. By so doing they show their supportive interest in the students, their perception of the problems, and their commitment to improve the situation. At the same time, humanized relationships mean that teachers, themselves, have an obligation to state their feelings and values, and cannot merely occupy a distant position as formal leaders of the group. Such confrontations as suggested above may also be uncomfortable for teachers, but one of the most significant values of a humanized classroom is that all of the persons in it, including the teacher, can express their feelings and thoughts—uncomfortable or not—about their own group processes. Working through such discomfort by discussion is in itself part of the humanizing process.

To continue our example, let us say that the teacher and students agree that certain interactions ought to be improved. If the subsequent problem-solving effort is to be effective, the terms of such an agree-

---

*For a few examples of such tools of measurement, see Chapter 5; for much more detail, see Fox, Luszki, and Schmuck (1966).

ment should not be left vague. The objectives for improvement should be written out concretely and clearly so that all class members understand them. Moreover, in this group confrontation, considerable time should be spent discussing examples of what classroom interactions would be like if the objectives were reached, so that class members can visualize concrete examples of goals. Such discussions of goals can in themselves facilitate changes in classroom interaction.

The process consultant or teacher who attempts this sort of discussion should expect the dynamics to be tense and uncomfortable. From our experience, this initial step in problem-solving is not without pain, anxiety, and anger. The development of behavioral objectives can also be arduous, time-consuming, and tiring. For groups with difficult and complex issues, problem identification and clarification sessions should take place right in the work setting during regular work time; they should not take place informally or during a lunch hour. Indeed, we would expect weeks or months of short meetings before a problem would be clarified within a school district.

An example of a highly complex educational problem is racial friction within a school. Even when most teachers and students recognize the dangers, there is still need for the collection and presentation of objective diagnostic information to bring the problem into shared focus. Indeed, by insisting on objective diagnosis and the sharing of data, process consultants can introduce more reasoned thinking into the conflict. Their initial step, for example, could include administering several attitude questionnaires which when made public might legitimize the need for problem-solving and new action. They could also arrange for diagnostic presentations from others. For examples, the administration could present reports on actual incidents of racial disturbances in the school or students might report on discriminatory behavior on the part of the faculty.

As another complex problem for diagnosis and clarification, suppose that an assistant superintendent believes that the central office staff, because of its inability to work together as a group, is blocking district progress. For various reasons, she is quite reticent to mention it. Some assessment of a formal sort—perhaps even a periodic evaluation of central office interpersonal relations—could be quite useful. Here, outside process consultants would be appropriate. First, their assessments could be presented at an administrative meeting, following which the central office personnel themselves could decide whether they had in fact tapped an important problem.

b. Brainstorming alternatives and evaluating ideas

The second phase of evaluation, discussed by Stufflebeam (1971), provides evidence on the consequences of the specific plans suggested to reach stated objectives.

This sort of evaluation of ideas works best if it follows a period of creative and freewheeling listing of alternative actions, often referred to as brainstorming. Brainstorming encourages the free, spontaneous creation of ideas for moving from the current situation to a target. During brainstorming, the participants should allow and even encourage unusual and even wild ideas *without evaluation*. Judgments of how good or bad an idea is should be withheld; too often ideas are rejected before they get a fair hearing because they are not the "tried and true."

Following the brainstorming period, each idea is scrutinized and evaluated for feasibility and potential effectiveness. Naturally, some of the ideas will be rejected quickly, but delayed scrutiny at least allows time for reasonable thought. As a consequence, after evaluation is carried out, a target has been specified and an action idea or two have been proposed for reaching it.

To continue with our previous examples, in the classroom the students would brainstorm about how to increase cooperation and helpfulness in the peer group. For this, one could divide the class into small buzz groups, which would allow for the production of many more ideas than if the whole class brainstormed together. One student in each buzz group could be appointed to note the ideas presented. Perhaps the ideas could be written on a large piece of paper taped to a wall where all group members could see it. Examples of ideas generated are: (1) get involved tutoring younger students in the school; (2) pair up all students for tutoring each other; (3) have students teach lessons sometimes; (4) list all the things we know and share the lists with one another; (5) develop a community cleanup project; and (6) have all students in even-numbered seats tutor other students in arithmetic and students in odd-numbered seats tutor others in social studies.

Evaluation would take place after this period of brainstorming. The classroom group would scrutinize each idea for its feasibility and potential effectiveness. The class might want to call on outside people or material for evidence regarding specific ideas. If an idea involves activities outside the classroom, the principal or other teachers may have to become involved. In Schmuck and Schmuck (1971), in the sections entitled "Action Ideas for Change," we have gathered together a number of actual classroom practices which have proven useful.

This stage of evaluation may take a great deal of time. In complex, multi-leveled situations, for example, numerous committees may have to be formed to explore the implications and potential ramifications of ideas before real action can be taken. In the example of a school facing racial conflict, the problem might require not only extended brainstorming of various kinds but also an even longer period for sifting through the ideas suggested. For example, the teachers and students might first brainstorm together, teachers and administrators might brainstorm further at staff meetings, and perhaps a meeting of parents, teachers, and students could offer a further opportunity for brainstorming. Whatever the brainstorming methods used, we believe that subsequent evaluation of the ideas presented should be carried out first by a small group and later checked with other participants. In our example of the school with racial conflict, a special evaluative committee, composed of educators, students, a community representative, and a process consultant, could test the feasibility of the ideas suggested by interviewing resource people, reading relevant literature, and visiting other schools or districts. They could then bring their findings back to larger groups for discussion.

Evaluation of brainstormed ideas is not simple and straightforward. Information about alternative actions, especially in the case of an organizational crisis, is generally not readily accessible. Although information from many sources may be desirable and even necessary, the data available may well be inconclusive or contradictory so that the attitudes of the committee members may largely influence their decisions. The evaluative process is also lengthy. Indeed, in issues of any complexity, evaluative problem-solving cannot be both quick *and* effective.

The interpersonal tensions in the central office example might be handled by brainstorming ideas ranging from firing personnel to involving the entire district in an organization development program with an outside process consultant. The evaluation of ideas for this problem would require a great deal of study, partly because most of the ideas would involve a major financial outlay for the district. New ideas about such activities as cost accounting, scheduling, and inservice training require planning, altering priorities, and approving new expenditures. School districts are more likely to do this sort of "problem-solving" when the physical plant, curriculum materials, or supplies are involved than when the problems have to do with the interpersonal relationships.

c. Monitoring the new actions and evaluating the process

The person taking the role of process consultant is very active during the third stage of problem-solving. After the brainstormed ideas have been evaluated, a plan of action is designed and first steps are taken to implement the plan. During the ensuing period of implementation, the process consultant monitors the action plan by performing what Stufflebeam (1971) refers to as "process evaluation." Process evaluation helps to determine whether short-range, interim objectives are being reached. The process consultant looks for unexpected pitfalls and gives feedback about ways in which the original plans are preventing the group from achieving its goal.

In the classroom, the logistics of group process evaluation are fairly simple. In our example, the class interested in becoming more cooperative might set aside ten minutes each day to check on progress and "clear the air," as discussed in Chapter 5. Students and teachers could periodically prepare a brief questionnaire for completion and discussion. Hindrances and pitfalls would no doubt arise during implementation of any plan that would call for some changes.

The school with racial tensions would not be able to expedite process evaluation quite so easily. Since the participants would undoubtedly have developed several very different courses of action, the process evaluation appropriate for each would be different. For example, let us say that a decision was reached to begin a new curriculum in black history. Short questionnaires or interviews might be employed periodically to see how the students and faculty were reacting to the course. Students' reactions to the teaching and relevance of the course content could be measured in this way. Perhaps the school also has decided to invite more black speakers to assemblies, and several teachers have discovered that after each assembly the students want to discuss the speech at length in their classrooms. After discussion of this fact with one another, the teachers might then take steps to begin a formal period of discussions after each assembly. This kind of evaluation and action probably would not have developed from a student questionnaire.

Finally, the example involving interpersonal tension in the central office would require periodic checks within small groups of administrators, along with questionnaires and interviews collected by outside process consultants for a more objective measure of the solutions being attempted.

d. Product evaluation

At the end of a problem-solving effort, its success should be estimated. Product evaluation tells us to what extent long-range targets have been reached. This is summative evaluation; the results are often used to decide whether the program should be continued, modified, or terminated.

Typically, some sort of a pre- and post-test design is used in product evaluation. For instance, in our classroom example, the teacher or process consultant could use for the final test another form of the instrument used previously during the context evaluation, or they both could involve the students in some behavioral activities to test their degree of cooperation and helpfulness. For the school in racial turmoil, attitudinal measures might be taken before and after, using standardized instruments. Also, information about performance after the intervention might be assessed by noting achievements within the new courses. In the example of district office friction, product evaluation could be implemented by asking central office administrators to write short evaluations of their new arrangements or by administering questionnaires and interviews before and after changes.

4. The status of evaluation and research methods in education

Many educators are ambivalent about evaluation and research in schools. While they sometimes voice respect for it, practicing educators do not typically study educational research, nor do they carry out systematic evaluation of the sort we have just described.

An example of this ambivalent attitude toward research occurred when Patricia Schmuck served as a curriculum associate during the planning of an innovative middle school. The rhetoric used to describe the school's innovativeness placed great emphasis on integrating evaluation and research procedures into everyday operation of the school, and yet when a displaced team-teaching leader was given a position as "director of research," the predominant view among the staff was that the new research person had "lost out." Research was viewed, in fact, as peripheral to the "real events" of the school.

Using consultation
to humanize
schools

This inconsistency of view keeps the use of objective evaluation and action research at low levels in schools. Yet, if the problem-solving model is to help humanize our schools, objective evaluation must become an integral part of the operation. Evaluation should no longer be separated from the ongoing events of teaching and learning, group discussion, and curriculum development. Continuous evaluation of programs and practices, whether it is implemented through simple discussion or more complex measurement procedures, enhances accuracy of communication, thereby increasing the potential for openness, directness, and authenticity in the school. Because of this, we hope that process consultants, principals, counselors, and teachers will work toward a new respect for evaluation and the collection of objective information in general. Systematic evaluation will teach students much about the practical use of the scientific method and at the same time provide a mechanism for increasing the number of whole-person relationships between school participants.

THE PSYCHODYNAMICS OF SELF-CONFRONTATION

A second important part of process consultation is self-confrontation. We find a useful analogy to the process of self-confrontation and evaluation in the events of track and field. In this sport, athletes strive to improve upon their own performance. They strive to move closer, each time, to an *ideal* which is determined usually by their own athletic history or sometimes by the record performance of others. As the event commences, they must be in top physical and psychological condition, have their particular plans worked out, do their best to execute the plans faithfully, and use all the extra energy they can muster. Finally, the event is over and very specific information (measured in the hundredths of a second) on their performance is available. This concrete feedback informs athletes about how closely they have come to their ideal. The observations and feedback from their coaches and teammates help them to train in new ways, to trim their movements, and to gauge their pace differently so that the next time their performance will come closer to their ideal.

The track event offers a good analogy to the use of evaluation in education and the strategy of self-confrontation in process consulting. Even though the stopwatch and the measuring tape offer very specific data about the performance (as product evaluation), the trained observations and skillful verbal feedback of a coach are necessary for the athlete to plan improvements for future performances. Athletes need objective data both on the final outcome and on how they moved as they were performing; in other words, data on the product and the process. Many athletes and coaches are convinced that the "sport" of it all is in the process.

The process consultant who works with groups and individuals in schools similarly attempts to present an objective mirror in which reflections of performance can be seen. In self-confrontation, the process consultant confronts the group with data about how well it is doing in relation to its goals. We use the term self-confrontation because it is carried out in the context of the group's goals, and not the goals of the consultant. But just as the coach knows that certain of the athlete's movements are more dysfunctional than others, so the process consultant knows that certain behaviors can block the group from reaching its own goals. He confronts the group not with hostility, but with his knowledge and objectivity.

It is true, of course, that most educational aims—especially those that involve personal goals—cannot be stated so concretely as the goal of the runner who wishes to break the four-minute mile. But the process consultant should strive to help members to be as specific and concrete as possible about their objectives. Also, the behavior of a group in action is considerably more complex than the movements of a single runner, yet the process consultant should strive to make his descriptions of behavior as accurate and as free of his own private biases as possible. He should use assessment tools that are objective and reliable. Basic both to track and field and to group dynamics is the assumption that when a person or group is confronted with discrepancies between actual performance and an ideal, the person or group will be motivated (or energized) to reduce those discrepancies.

1. The theory and assumptions of self-confrontation

Leon Festinger (1954, 1957), along with many other social psychologists, has argued that all people are motivated to evaluate their own abilities. In other words, people seek continually to appraise how competently they are functioning. People either seek cues from their environment to test how well they are performing or directly ask other people for feedback. Along with this "need for evaluation," Festinger also posits that people want to improve themselves continuously. That is to say, they want to perform better than the last time, they want to feel better about themselves, and in general, they want to grow beyond their present condition. Thus, people are never completely satisfied with where they are because even as they are improving they are striving to improve even more.

Although this theory of motivation probably does not fit every cultural group in the world, it does seem to apply to American society. And in the American context, it seems to apply very well to highly educated professionals working in schools.

Festinger goes on to argue that when someone receives feedback about his own behavior that is discrepant from his image of himself he feels tense and uncomfortable. Festinger labeled this tension as a condition of *dissonance*. He further argues that the individual experiencing dissonance will adopt behaviors, thoughts, and feelings to eliminate or at least reduce his or her discomfort. Naturally—and of course this is the point at which self-confrontation can function constructively—the new behaviors may be adaptive, such as when the runner who changes his stride and pace to gain his objective, or the new behaviors may be unhelpful, as in the case of defensiveness and withdrawal. Self-confrontation takes place when people note discrepancies between where they are now and where they would like to be and then behave in ways that they hope will reduce the gap. During the process of confrontation, anxiety plays a major part.

2. Anxiety—its role in behavior change

When a person is confronted with discrepancies between his ideal and actual states he usually experiences discomfort and the urge to change. Think of occasions when someone has said to you, "Yes, it was good, but...." Even though your stomach tightens and you experience some discomfort, you usually want the person to finish his statement. Anxiety is what you are experiencing. It is a psychological condition that is usually accompanied by observable physiological reactions such as sweating palms, dryness in the mouth, heart palpitations, tightening of muscles, increased eye movements, or stammering speech. The urge to change involves the desire to reduce these unpleasant reactions.

For the psychoanalyst, anxiety is viewed as a signaling function, enabling the person to take preventative measures to avoid intense pain. Thus, anxiety triggers off defensiveness which, in turn, saves the person from being overcome with tension. Neurotic behavior is characterized by anxiousness; although the defenses are still relatively operable, they are usually maladaptive. Psychotic behavior occurs when the person is so overwhelmed by anxiety that he or she is unable to function effectively.

While there are several conceptual and technical differences between psychological treatments of anxiety, psychologists of most every persuasion agree that anxiety is a universal experience, usually pushing people to behave in ways to reduce it. Two prototypic reactions are *flight* and *fight*. Individuals vary in their responses to anxiety, depending at times upon the situation that has given rise to it. This dynamic view of anxiety stresses the interaction between the social situation and the psychology of the individual. Many psychologists have treated anxiety as a stable personality attribute; *i.e.*, some persons are generally more anxious and others less so. Sarason *et al.* (1960), in one of the most definitive studies of anxiety in children, showed that highly anxious children have a negative self-esteem whereas children with low anxiety have a more favorable image of themselves and are more self-confident. Indeed, one's self-esteem and confidence are critical factors determining how one will behave in anxiety-provoking situations. For instance, in one study, Benjamins (1950) showed that when forty-eight high school students were asked to rank their performance on an intelligence test, and then were given false reports one level above or below the individual predictions about how well they had actually done, they performed *in the direction of the falsely reported results* on the second test. That is, students who thought they had done better than they expected to do on the first test actually did better on the second test. Conversely, students who "did" more poorly than expected on the first test, in fact did more poorly on the second test.

This finding is one among many which supports the concept of a self-fulfilling prophecy; *i.e.*, individuals perform according to their expectations for performance. One's self-esteem and predictions for performance are inextricably linked with how one will respond to an anxiety-provoking situation. This means that when a person is confronted with discrepancies between his ideal and actual behavior, he will experience some anxiety, and that his reactions likely may be defensive and nonadaptive. It follows that confrontations with persons who believe themselves to be incompetent and who lack self-confi-

Using consultation to humanize schools

dence will lead to more anxiety, increased confusion, and even more maladaptive behavior.

Persons who experience high anxiety are more likely to behave in adaptive ways if they are encouraged to talk about their tense feelings. McKeachie *et al.* (1955), for example, found that highly anxious college students performed better on multiple-choice exam items when they were given the option to comment on the questions in the margin of the paper. Such catharsis clarified the students' thoughts and helped bring them to a more relaxed state so that they could perform more effectively. Similarly, in a classroom, highly anxious students have been shown to perform better when gripe sessions are introduced (Hoehn and Saltz, 1956).

Evidently, the gripe sessions reduce the students' anxiety to a functional level. In contrast, students characterized by low anxiety levels performed less well with gripe sessions. We assume, therefore, that the gripe sessions served to reduce the anxiety levels of these low-anxiety students below an optimal point for effective performance.

3. Anxiety—its optimal level for performance

The classic Yerkes Dodson law in psychology specifies that there is an optimal level of motivation (or anxiety) for learning. When that optimal level is either not reached or surpassed, one's performance, especially on complex mental tasks, is decreased. There seems to be a relationship between the anxiety state and the difficulty of a task with regard to performance. A person in a state of high anxiety will perform better on simple motoric tasks than on more difficult mental tasks. Sprinters, for example, with a rather simple motoric task to execute are facilitated by high levels of tension, while chess players who are attempting to decide on their next move may be severely hindered by high amounts of anxiety. In other words, a given degree of anxiety facilitates some kinds of performance but not others. The exact point of facilitation or hindrance depends upon the nature of the task and the confidence that the individual brings to that task. This can be seen in the performance of the distance runner, who must not get so anxious that his muscles tighten and his pulse becomes too active. With confidence in his own ability he probably will maintain an optimal level of anxiety that will prove functional for his performance. If he becomes too relaxed, he may not do as well because of his lack of constructive tension.

For self-confrontation to be effective, feedback about a discrepancy between the ideal and actual must be proffered so that it issues forth an optimal level of anxiety. The exact nature of the confrontation and the particular responses of people being confronted depend on many factors; their general level of anxiety, their image of their own competence, and the complexity of the task apparently are the most important factors. People who use self-confrontation must learn that for some individuals an abrupt, direct, and even harsh confrontation is appropriate, while for other people or in other situations a softer, gentler confrontation will be more beneficial.

SOME TYPICAL DEFENSIVE REACTIONS TO SELF-CONFRONTATION

Anxiety and dissonance inevitably result from a person's confrontation with discrepancies between his ideal and his actual performance. The anxiety thus leads to behaviors to reduce or eliminate the uncomfortable feelings. Sometimes the new behaviors are constructive in pushing the person to behave in adaptive and functional ways; other times attempts to reduce psychological discomfort are maladaptive. Defensiveness is one usual and common reaction to confrontations of the self. In this section we explore some typical defensive reactions that may occur when individuals, small groups, and large organizations are confronted with the disquieting information that their behavior is not congruent with their stated goals; we also offer some suggestions about how a person acting as process consultant might deal with such maladaptive behaviors.

1. Face-to-face situations

There is an unending array of face-to-face interactions in school where the skills of process consultation (listening, questioning, clarifying, and problem-solving) can be used. There are many face-to-face situations that can be useful in helping a person to arrive at his goals; students can formally help another student, teachers can collaborate with another teacher on teaching methods, and the meetings in general between people, can, with training and practice, be more productive.

The self-confrontation process is not a head-on clash between people who have different objectives. It is not the attempt of one person to persuade another, nor is it an attempt to manipulate the environment so that another will behave as one wishes. Self-confrontation involves knowing the goals of the other, having some idea of where the other is in relation to them and confronting the other with apparent contradictions between aims and performance. Self-confrontation is the teacher saying to a student, "You set out to finish by 3:00, but it doesn't look now as though you will make it," and not the teacher saying, "I gave you an assignment to complete by 3:00 and you are not working hard enough to be finished by then." Self-confrontation is the principal saying to a teacher, "You said that you wanted to talk less in class discussions, yet when I observed, you spoke three-quarters of the time," and not the principal saying, "According to my observations, you are not doing well in classroom discussions." Self-confrontation is the students saying to the principal, "You said that you wanted students to become more involved in school decision-making, but students have never been invited to faculty meetings or to meetings you have with department heads," and not the students bringing a list of demands to the principal. Such self-confrontations are not typical in most schools, and when they do occur they are generally between persons with different objectives or between those who are working on their own private agendas. Typically, people criticize or gripe behind the scenes but rarely in a self-confrontative way.

Being confronted with discrepancies between one's actual performance and one's aim is bound to lead to feelings of anxiety. The person who provides discrepant feedback should be prepared for reactions of defensiveness, such as incredulity, rationalization, or withdrawal. Among defensive reactions, the following three are common:

(1) *Perceiving ideals to be unrealistic.* When an individual is confronted with failing to accomplish a personal objective (such as a student's wish to carry out a project, a teacher's desire to individualize instruction, or a principal's interest in more student participation), he may defend himself by arguing that such an objective is "impossible to achieve at this time." Students may say that, although they would prefer to complete the project, other demands make that impossible. Teachers may say that they cannot begin individualized instruction yet because the class involved is still undisciplined enough to need more teacher-directed activities. Principals may argue that because the school board or parents would object strongly to increased student involvement in school decisions they must wait until their attitude changes.

In the face of this, the process consultant should help the person to set a new objective which "takes in" the original objective without entirely altering it. For instance, students might be encouraged to reduce the size of their project, or to seek an "incomplete," giving themselves more time to finish it. Teacher might be helped to see alternative ways of individualizing instruction for selected students or to see new ways of using individualization to *decrease* classroom discipline problems. Principal might be encouraged to list both those activities in which students could be involved without angering the board or parents, and also the activities in which the students should not be involved.

(2) *Believing discrepancies between the ideal and the actual are inevitable.* We have heard many times that "it sounds great but schools could never really be that way." People who use that justification are struggling to restrain their anxiety; such a resigned view enables them to maintain the status quo. The very act of self-confrontation contradicts this resigned view and may be strongly resented. Usually logical arguments and evidence have little impact against someone convinced of the impossibility of a plan. In that case the process consultant may take the stance that "Yes, that may be so, but we can at least move in the right direction. What kinds of things can be done now to move closer to the ideal?" The task is then to help the client to design new instrumental goals—small steps enabling him to move closer to the larger goal.

(3) *Working toward objectives not previously stated.* Another common defensive reaction is to argue that what one is doing is worthwhile in light of new objectives, even if it does not help to accomplish one's original objective. For instance, many educators agree that competitive behavior is not a high-priority objective and yet they behaviorally encourage it. When confronted they might retort, "Well, I don't especially like competition, but knowing how to handle it will help students face the real world. After all, we should be helping students to adapt, shouldn't we?" We knew a principal who agreed it was a good idea to teach young children skills in communicating, but later rejected the new curriculum because the youngsters might "turn off" their parents. "After all," he said, "the school should be trying to make family relationships more amicable!" The process consultant accepted both goals—student skill in communicating and family amicability—as important and urged the principal to consider how the communication curriculum could be modified to accomplish both.

In other instances of this sort, the process consultant should be sure to paraphrase, question, and probe until clients are clear about their own priorities. When the priorities are clear, at least both the consultant and the clients understand what objectives are being worked toward.

2. Process consultation with small groups

Many school activities take place in face-to-face groups, ranging from classroom learning groups to departmental faculty meetings. As we have noted previously, the functioning of small groups in most schools leaves a great deal to be desired. Because working with groups introduces many more complexities than working with individuals, we believe process consultation for them should occur on a more formal and deliberate basis than with individuals. In addition, the skills and techniques needed by a person working with group self-confrontation are considerably greater and more varied than those needed in face-to-face situations.

People acting as process consultants to small groups in schools need some training and practice in communication and problem-solving and skills in evaluation and self-confrontation. They also should have confidence in themselves and be relatively aware of their own defenses. With adequate training, principals, counselors, teachers, and even students can serve as consultants to other small groups in their own school. The services of district consultants (such as the Cadre of Communication Consultants) and of course outside consultants trained in the behavioral sciences can be used. We think, in fact, that every school district should have easy access to people trained in small group processes, to help school participants cope with the interpersonal stresses that can hinder individual satisfaction as well as group productivity.

Small groups in which the process consultant's skills can be valuable include tutoring pairs, helping trios, small project groups, whole classroom groups, teaching teams, departmental groups, curriculum committees, student governments, staff meetings, and school leadership teams. In most of these groups, the designated formal leader is in the strongest position to set the tone for procedures adopted by the group. Therefore the process consultant may spend considerable time helping the leader to develop group convening and discussion skills. In effect, the consultant should try to teach the formal leader some of the skills of process consultation. Within the groups, the leader can then take the initiative in exhibiting the interpersonal skills of listening, clarifying, questioning, and confronting.

Just as with individuals, process consultation with groups occurs in stages. First, the groups should come to some consensual agreement about the problem being faced, the current state of affairs, and the group's objectives. Problem identification and clarification can be implemented through such activities as having everybody write up problems or objectives on newsprint so that others can later see them, and interviewing everyone or having them fill out questionnaires and then sharing the results in a group discussion. When the group has uncovered a number of different views, surveys of the entire group should be taken during subsequent discussion until agreements have been reached about the problem and goals. Then the group should look at the most important facilitating and restraining forces that are impinging on the problem. Then the group can brainstorm alternative actions for reducing restraining forces and moving toward the goal. Next, the brainstormed ideas must be scrutinized, refined, and modified so that only the feasible and realistic ones are selected. The group can then use these ideas to build a plan for action and can subsequently commence with the first step. The process consultant monitors the group's actions as it implements the plan, presenting the group with feedback whenever appropriate.

The defensive reactions typical in small groups include the three previously mentioned responses: (1) perceiving the group's goals to be unrealistic, (2) believing discrepancies between the group's current state of affairs and its goals are inevitable, and (3) working toward group objectives not previously stated. In groups a fourth reaction also often occurs: noting that the process consultant also has weaknesses.

In groups, individuals can try to get support in attempts to oppose or sabotage the efforts of a leader or process consultant. One way to undermine the strength of a confrontation is to call into question the legitimacy of the person doing the confronting. The focus is on the human frailties of the process consultant and is evidenced by questions about the consultant's personal life, professional life, or competencies. Such questions are frequently asked regarding external consultants not viewed as part of the educational profession. One sort of defensive statement is, "He (she) really doesn't know much about schools or students; I'll bet he's (she's) never even taught in a public school classroom." These group efforts are aimed at diminishing the significance of the consultant's feedback. Students do this when they criticize teachers for having forgotten the problems of the young, and teachers do this when they belittle administrative actions by characterizing the administrator as having been "kicked upstairs" after an ineffective teaching career.

In some cases, of course, such accusations are not so much defensive reactions as they are accurate reflections on competency. Such reactions should be considered primarily defensive, however, when they deal with the personal characteristics of the consultant and lack descriptions of personal feeling or analysis of the consultant's behaviors. The consultant who is confronting others should try not to become defensive himself about challenges to his competency or personality. He should call on others in the group to see if his perceptions and feedback can be corroborated. Usually another group member or two will support the consultant's point of view and sustain the impact of the self-confrontation. After all, the consultant's first mission is to get the group moving toward its own targets and only secondarily to be fully accepted by the members. Ultimately, he will have to challenge the group to recognize discrepancies between its present position and its goal. Usually such confrontation will bear fruit if the consultant is persistent.

An example of how persistence on the part of the consultant can be helpful may be illuminating. At a meeting of parents and faculty in which the problem of a school program unrewarding for some children was being discussed, the principal argued at length about the dangers of giving students opportunities to evaluate the adult professionals who were running the school. The consultant probed to solicit more details about the principal's concern. The principal presented extensive arguments about respect, discipline, and control. When the consultant mentioned the possibility of using objective questionnaires and interviews to open up communication between students and faculty, the principal spoke about the faultiness of questionnaires, the inadequacy of the ones he had filled out in the past, and the difficulty of tabulating such measurements. At each step of the way, the principal called into question the legitimacy of any method to bring students into closer and more critical interactions with the faculty.

The consultant next pointed out, however, that students continually evaluated teachers, and most teachers in the group agreed that students did informally talk a lot about the faculty. Next the consultant asked if hidden conversations were preferable to "getting things out in the open" and again most agreed (including the principal) that openness was better. The principal began to alter his position significantly when one influential parent commented that private evaluations were probably more distorted and harmful than public ones. The principal then admitted that there might be some place for a questionnaire for students. At this point the principal remembered that an attitude inventory taken two years previously at the school showed that the students were highly satisfied with the program and teachers. The principal's initial fears were reduced; by the end of the session he was viewing objective survey feedback as a useful vehicle for increasing student-faculty dialogue about the school. This turn-about would not have occurred without the persistence of the process consultant.

3. Process consultation with the larger organization

Rarely does a process consultant within a school district work with the entire district as his target. He typically aims his interventions at one or two subsystems, such as a school staff or a central office team, and attempts to articulate communication and problem-solving between them. The consultant should understand, however, that even though he is not working with the total district, his consultation with key parts of it will have reverberations throughout the district.

When consultants do work with a large collection of personnel from the central office or with a large high school faculty, most aspects of problem-solving naturally become more complex and involved. The meaning of "self-confrontation" also takes much more complexity. For sixty or seventy persons to develop a set of common goals is an extremely complex and difficult procedure taking a considerable amount of time, energy, and planning. Also, in working with large groups involving several subsystems, consultants typically meet in all kinds of interpersonal situations: they meet with some people on a face-to-face basis, they encounter small groups, and they work with large numbers of people at one time. Consultants will probably meet most, if not all, of the common defensive reactions to confrontation that we have already discussed.

One common reaction to humanization programs from central office personnel is, "That sounds great but we don't have the money to pursue it." Given the uncertain financial position of most school districts, we are in sympathy with those who have budgetary decisions to make. Yet, as we have repeatedly pointed out, increased expenditures of money are not usually necessary for dealing with the human culture of the schools. The primary expenditures we have been discussing are those of time, energy, and commitment, and the willingness to follow a difficult and painful course involving anxiety and uncertainty. For school districts the expenditures we have in mind have to do with time—time for training, time for talking, time for working together, and perhaps some released time for teachers.

In Kent, Washington, the entire school district received process consultation from the Center for the Advanced Study of Educational Administration in exchange for serving as a research site for the center. The district provided released time for its professional staff and a conference center for the meetings. After the CASEA staff had worked with the district on an external consulting basis for two years, the Cadre of Communication Consultants was established and has since carried out all process consultation in the district. The cadre has lived through some significant financial crises; Boeing, the primary source of community income, was beset by financial peril with the collapse of the SST project, and at the same time a large deficit was uncovered in the district budget. Yet the cadre remained.

Indeed some evidence indicates that the Kent cadre performed even more effectively as process consultants than the CASEA "experts" did. For instance, although tradition argues against subordinates acting as consultants for superordinates, we found that teams of teachers acting as process consultants helped the superintendent's cabinet and the curriculum division to improve their interpersonal relations. Again, although tradition says it is almost impossible to act as a consultant in one's own school, the cadre found that by rotating the role of process consultant among faculty members that interpersonal interactions at meetings were greatly facilitated. The Kent experience lent support to the concept that school participants can develop methods of process consultation with virtually no new expenditures of funds. The money argument is often, in fact, a defensive reaction; it means in reality that there are items of higher priority than human culture. We do not imply here that any district rejecting the techniques of this book is rejecting the idea of the importance of human culture. We do mean, however, that schools that do not deal with their human culture problems in some direct and meaningful way are ignoring the very aims of education. How a district allocates its resources and spends its time and money is a good indication of what it thinks is important—regardless of the rhetoric.

THE ESSENCE OF PROCESS CONSULTATION: INTERPERSONAL EFFECTIVENESS

As we have previously noted, there is nothing sacred or elitist about the behavior of a process consultant. Any person with some degree of interpersonal skill can facilitate the growth of an individual or a group by using problem-solving techniques and the methods of evaluation and self-confrontation. The effectiveness of a process consultant lies mainly in his own interpersonal behavior. As the old adage has it, "What you do speaks so loudly that I cannot hear what you say."

1. Trust and rapport

A person's helpfulness depends in large part on the sort of trust he is able to build with others. Some degree of trust and rapport, along with a norm of equalitarian reciprocity, is especially important when one person confronts another (or a group) with discrepancies between his actual performance and his ideal. If the relationship is very formal, distant, and one-way, the dialogue between them will be stilted, biased, and incomplete. For example, there must be enough reciprocity for a teacher to challenge a principal with, "I don't agree with what you concluded; can you present more evidence?" or, in another example, enough personal concern on the part of the person doing the confronting for him to say, "I know this will hurt some of you but I think I must tell you anyway...."

The process consultant's effectiveness is also related to how skillfully he can help create new plans after confrontation. We have in mind here a skill in communicating optimism, and a sense of urgency to others. Clearly, self-confrontation should involve a *constructive* shakeup, encouraging new behavioral trials and innovative action. The effectiveness of confrontation is defined in part by the readiness of others to explore alternative actions and the consultant's adeptness in arousing enthusiasm for some of these alternatives.

2. Friendship

From another point of view, the interpersonal behavior of the process consultant is similar to that of one friend interacting with another. A

Using consultation to humanize schools

friend understands something about one's ideals and where one wishes to go; and he also cares enough to support or confront one in his striving to get there. Friendship is a kick in the pants as well as sympathy and support. Friendship is a whole-person relationship, and as such it humanizes the participants.

Even though school participants do not typically have a history of friendship with all others in the school, the process consultant can take the point of view that all participants will react similarly to self-confrontation—that a kind of common humanity prevails. Therefore, to relate early as if one were interacting with a friend need not be phony or strange. The process consultant can attempt immediately to show that he is human; that he has feelings, concerns, values, and ideas. He should show that he wants to listen, clarify, understand, and confront. He should allow others to challenge and confront him; he should make himself available to the same kind of probing that he is doing with others. The consultant's behavior can also be discussed by the participants from the point of view of his helpfulness.

3. The helping relationship

Even with the best of intentions, a friend can sometimes behave in very ineffective ways, and so, of course, can the process consultant. The function of process consultation requires more than good intentions; equally important are skills, knowledge, and perceptiveness.

As Jack Gibb (1964) has so aptly pointed out: "To have the intention of helping does not mean automatically that one's behaviors will be helpful." Gibb (1964b) noted that the helper is often thinking about his *own* objective of being helpful rather than about the effects of his behavior on the *client*. The effective consultant will not so involve his own self-concept in the relationship that he wants others to do things only in his way. His mission is to help others to arrive at *their own* solutions to their problems.

Many times those very behaviors that tend to make us feel competent, important, and helpful are those which are unhelpful to others. For example, behaviors such as giving advice, doing it the "right" way under the guise of demonstration, arguing rationally and logically, or pressuring and cajoling a person to follow a certain path tend to raise the giver's self-esteem, while not providing real help for the other to move toward his (her) own goals. Kolb and Boyatzis (1970) found that ineffective helpers had greater tendencies to display their power and achievement within the helping relationship; they talked more, were more self-conscious, gave more negative feedback, and were more impatient than persons who were effective in helping others. It seems clear, in fact, that the function of the process consultants should not be to display his own competence nor to demonstrate his own skills. Process consultation should allow individuals and groups to arrive at their own objectives or goals and should disclose procedures for finding the ways to achieve those objectives.

4. Skills in communicating

The behaviors of process consultation are the essential communication skills of listening, probing, questioning, interviewing, clarifying, and confronting.

a. Listening

Listening calls for the consultant to be attentive to the messages being sent by others. As a rule of thumb, the process consultant should attempt to listen more than talk, but he should keep in mind that listening does not always mean being quiet. Active listening involves paraphrasing what another has said to see if the message is understood (*and* to show the other that the consultant is listening) and checking impressions of the other's feelings to see if they are being read correctly. Attentive and active listening communicates that the consultant believes the other's messages to be important, and that the consultant will take the other's messages into consideration in later phases of the consultation. Listening also means keeping an open mind, waiting until the other is finished before preparing a reply, understanding the others clearly before evaluating what they have said, and not projecting one's own experiences onto the others' messages.

b. Probing, questioning, and interviewing

Often when school people are discussing a problem, their topic evokes so much anxiety that they digress into irrelevant matters. The consultant's behaviors probing, questioning, and interviewing are aimed at keeping the participants at the task at hand and increasing the information available for problem-solving.

For example, a team of teachers may set out to discuss the climate of their learning groups but soon get bogged down in talk of one or two problem students. One implication of their discussion may be that only a few students are responsible for the poor climate and that they, the teachers, are not culpable in the matter. The process consultant in such a meeting might ask if it is true that the problem does indeed rest with one or two students and then probe to see in what ways the teachers see themselves as being responsible for poor climates in the learning groups.

c. Clarifying

Clarifying involves both active listening and probing. The process consultant should attempt to clarify another's comments when the other's messages seems to have multiple meanings. Such clarification involves not only listening for hidden meanings, unrevealed feelings, and unconscious thoughts, but also checking one's impressions of the other's feelings.

For example, the teacher who is discussing the adoption of a new program with a seemingly resistant principal may hear, "The superintendent won't allow any new programs until the budget is passed— and that's final." If the relationship involves some trust and openness, the teacher might very well act as a process consultant by checking out several potential impressions—that the principal is angry with him or at something else, that the principal feels insecure in relation to the superintendent, or that the principal does not like the new program. Clarifying the principal's inner thoughts could perhaps bring the principal and teacher closer together and at least could avoid leaving each filled with frustration over this exchange.

d. Confronting

The skills of listening, probing, and clarifying are incomplete without the skill of confrontation. Confrontation shows others that someone will "keep them honest." For the confrontation to be effective, the goal stated and chosen paths of action should be clear. The process consultant confronts others when they deviate from what they have previously committed themselves to do.

PROCESS CONSULTATION IN THE HUMANIZED SCHOOL

In the humanized school every participant, regardless of his job description or status position, can use the interpersonal skills of process consultation at one time or another to help an individual or group move more surely toward its goals. Ideally, even students, aides, and unclassified personnel should be viewed as appropriate helpers of others. Indeed, one hallmark of a humanized school is that lower-status persons help higher-status persons as much as the other way around.

Traditionally, schools have been organized so that assistance is defined as appropriately coming from someone of higher status than the person in need. In most schools, when a student needs help, he approaches a teacher, a counselor, or perhaps the principal. Students generally seek help from other students only on an informal, irregular basis and then only with friends. Moreover, when teachers need help, they most often turn to their department head, supervisor, or principal. Asking fellow teachers for help occurs seldom and then only informally. For teachers to approach students for help in solving a professional problem is indeed rare and in many schools would be frowned upon as unprofessional behavior.

Likewise, evaluation of one's performance is always formally done by a party of higher status and then is usually summative evaluation. Students are evaluated by teachers, teachers by principals, and principals by district office personnel. In fact, one of the key elements of a status position in schools is control over the fate of participants of lower status. We believe that such interpersonal power distinctions lead to distance and inauthenticity between participants in the school. Status distinctions based on power and position rather than on specific competence can restrict the sort of help people will ask for or give.

We believe that a much more equalitarian power structure can offer a much more potent environment for academic learning and human development. Some recent evidence supports this point. Tuckman and Oliver (1968) found that student appraisals of teacher performance constitute much more powerful feedback, as measured by the amount of subsequent teacher change, than the appraisals of supervisors or principals. In other words, the teachers were more affected by the reaction of their students than by the reactions of higher-status personnel. Margaret Nelson (1972) showed a similar phenomenon in a study of change among substitute teachers. She simply supplied the substitutes with systematic feedback from students about their classroom behavior and subsequently showed major behavioral changes among the teachers in a very short time. Given the evidence offered in these studies, it is difficult to envision the extent of positive impact on a faculty if a student body were trained in giving constructive feedback to its teachers and administrators.

Studies of cross-age and same-age peer tutoring have also shown that students can be potent helpers and tutors of one another. Students can help one another overcome some of their anxieties about school, they can help interpret the expectations of faculty members, and they can support one another when problems become difficult. We have found that the impact of peer criticism—especially during adolescence—can be much more powerful than feedback from teachers or even parents.

For self-confrontation to function effectively, feedback must be given on the basis of the person's own goals. Schools are not organized to support self-confrontation as a helping method. They are organized hierarchically; goals are handed down from a higher status level to a lower one. Teachers cannot use self-confrontation effectively with students when the students are being prodded to work toward the teacher's goals. Principals cannot use self-confrontation effectively with teachers when the administrators are judging teacher performance in their own terms. Higher-echelon personnel get caught in the restraints of persuading, pushing, rewarding, and punishing; they cannot be helpful process consultants until the goals are established and "owned" by those being helped.

Imposing goals on students, of course, is done for many reasons, some of them noble, some of them Machiavellian. Since the imposition of goals has been the general practice in education for many years, we should not expect that a change will come easily. Indeed, if students were suddenly given the opportunity to write their own goals and to make their own decisions about what to study, we should expect them to be confused and anxious; likewise, teachers would also be confused in their relationships with administrators, and so on up the ladder. The process consultant can help clarify such confusions and help both individuals and groups to work through problems to autonomy and the "personal ownership" of goals. When goals and purposes are unstated or unclear, process consultants will have to spend considerable time helping participants to establish their own priorities. Only after this will self-confrontation and problem-solving be successful.

We are not suggesting that professional educators abdicate their expert power. The teacher should not, for example, allow a student to opt out of school work completely. Laissez-faire leadership on the part of the teacher in the face of student challenge would not be helpful to either party. The teacher should take student challenges as just what they are; tests of the power relationships, of how much trust can be built, of how phony or authentic the teacher is. Tentative listening, clarifying, and probing—at first even acceptance without evaluation—often will change the nature of the relationship and help the student to see that the teacher really wants him to identify his goals. When a stalemate exists for too long, the teacher should try to establish a contract for learning which, in part, at least seems to satisfy both the student and teacher.

In our experience, we have been struck by the great amounts of cognitive work students will do when they are "turned on" by it. Students are not loafers, nor are they lazy. They are turned off by formal rules, uncaring people, inattentive ears, and bureaucratic procedures that seem to place them in depersonalized positions. We and they ask no more than that all participants in the school be granted some modicum of respect and support from others. Such a request, of course, carries certain disadvantages; closeness and caring bring responsibilities that take time and absorb energy; they require patience and steadiness.

Regardless of how skillful persons are, they do not easily incorporate the interpersonal skills of listening, questioning, clarifying, and confronting into their personal styles of relationship. Training and practice in helping skills are necessary for all process consultants and we believe that such training should involve students, teachers, and administrators together as fellow learners. Certainly, the goal of learning how to help others to learn is a legitimate function for schools. Why cannot the learners come from all status levels? Such courses could have secondary benefits; they could bring together persons of different roles in the district into close communication. Such closeness could have far-reaching effects for humanizing the schools.

Also, special courses could be given at different levels in the school organization. The students who tutor other students could congregate occasionally to discuss helping skills. Teachers might use a faculty meeting or two for giving process consultation to one another. Administrators might meet to discuss how they could convene their faculties more effectively for group problem-solving. All could be set up to give feedback to individual process consultants about their performances in a particular setting.

The humanized school is guided by the assumption that everybody wants to develop more adaptive ways of coping with life. Humanized schools have norms that legitimize asking for help from anyone to facilitate one's growth. The norms support asking for help and giving feedback across status levels in both directions. Students legitimately give feedback to teachers, teachers to principals, principals to students, etc. Such interpersonal relations will not strip high-status personnel of power; they will grant them *more* influence because of the rising trust, rapport, and cohesiveness in the school.

SUMMARY OF CHAPTER 7

Consultation is a key method by which educators can collaborate in helping one another to humanize the schools. It is traditionally car ried out in two ways—in the form of consultative assistance (when the consultant himself solves the client's problem) or as help with the content of the tasks at hand (when the consultant helps with the curriculum or with particular instructional procedures). Instead of these, we focus on a third kind of help, called *process consultation*, which is aimed at improving interpersonal interactions and to enhancing the joint efforts of educators to solve problems.

Process consultation is constituted of a number of facilitative behaviors designed to move an individual, a small group, or an organizational unit toward its own objectives. All school participants (including students) with some training and some awareness of their own behavior can serve effectively as process consultants. While we think that most participants in a school can learn process skills, we also advocate that some people should be designated to pay attention formally to the interpersonal processes of the school. The important point is that the school designate time and people for the implementation of process discussions.

Two interrelated features characterize process consultation; one involves using objective evaluation, and the second, the strategy of self-confrontation. Although judgments are made informally in schools on a daily basis, we strongly encourage school personnel to become more publicly explicit about their procedures of evaluation. When they do, self-confrontation and its attendant pressures for improvement inevitably will follow. The process consultant's role is to enhance both objective evaluation and self-confrontation.

We especially emphasize the value of formative evaluation; i.e., assessing the state of a problem, determining how well the plans to solve a problem are working, and establishing a means for changing those plans if necessary. Becoming involved in such a process—especially when data are objective and undistorted—can be disconcerting and disquieting for even the most open and well-intentioned person and groups.

Self-confrontation can occur when the data indicate discrepancies between one's ideals and the actual current state of affairs. Process consultants facilitate the occurrence of these events. They should be skilled in collecting and feeding back objective data; they should also know how to use self-confrontation to urge educators to act in new ways. The major challenge for the consultant is to help clients to harness the tensions they experience during self-confrontation for productive action. Indeed, these very process norms and skills are essential to a humanized school.

Humanized schools have strong norms for people to help one another to be more authentic and honest in both defining and striving for goals. The degree to which such norms can be actualized depends upon the amount of trust and personal concern, to be sure, but it also depends upon the process skills that exist among the staff. Process consultation is one way of assuring that process norms and skills will be a part of the daily life of the school.

ANNOTATED BIBLIOGRAPHY FOR CHAPTER 7

Bloom, Benjamin, J. Thomas Hastings, and George F. Madaus. 1971. *Handbook on Formative and Summative Evaluation of Student Learning.* New York: McGraw-Hill Book Co.

This book, a comprehensive and scholarly work, follows the earlier work of Bloom and his colleagues on the cognitive and affective objectives for school learning. It provides well delineated theory along with some practical suggestions and solutions to the problem of assessing what students have learned. The authors view learning from a wide perspective, discussing evaluation from the points of view of different school curricula. This book is written and organized well; it will serve as a useful reference book and as a helpful guide to the neophyte educator and is also invaluable to the serious student and practitioner of education.

Using consultation
to humanize
schools

Klein, Donald C. 1967. "Consultation Processes as a Method for Improving Teaching," in Eli Bower and William Hollister (eds.), *Behavioral Science Frontiers in Education.* New York: John Wiley and Sons.

A pioneering article on process consultation in schools, this work shows how the mental health and group dynamics applications relate to consultation. In particular Klein focuses on the similarities and differences in mental health and process consultation methods. An excellent introduction to the function of process consultation in schools, this piece is short and well written.

Kolb, David, Irwin Rubin, and James McIntyre. 1971. *Organizational Psychology: An Experimental Approach.* Englewood Cliffs, N. J.: Prentice-Hall, Inc.

This text—a kind of handbook of group dynamics—contains fifteen learning units covering topics such as problem-solving, organizational decision-making, power, affiliation, and personal growth. Each unit discusses purposes, simulations, and evaluation tools, and lists recommended readings. While the book focuses primarily on industrial organizations, its simple graphic layouts, teaching strategies, and practical information can be very helpful for the educational consultant.

Northwest Regional Educational Laboratory. 1971-1972. *Research Utilizing Problem Solving* and *Preparing Educational Training Consultants.* Portland, Ore: NWREL.

These two packages can be very useful to the educational consultant. The first can be employed by the consultant to help teachers to use problem-solving techniques in their learning groups. The second is in itself a training device for educational consultants. The concepts and skills taught in this second package relate very closely to process consultation as discussed in this chapter.

Schein, Edgar H. 1969. *Process Consultation: Its Role in Organization Development.* Reading, Mass.: Addison-Wesley.

This book presents a conceptual and practical guide to process consultation. It should be studied by every serious educational consultant.

Schmuck, Richard, and Matthew B. Miles. 1971. *Organization Development in Schools*. Palo Alto, Ca.: National Press Books.

This book—annotated previously in Chapter 6—is included here also because it includes a list of over one hundred people, from all parts of the United States, with experience in organization development in schools. Each of them can serve effectively as a process consultant in schools.

Schmuck, Richard, Philip Runkel, Steven Saturen, Ronald Martell, and C. Brooklyn Derr. 1972. *Handbook of Organization Development in Schools*. Palo Alto, Ca.: National Press Books.

This book is one of the most complete volumes now available for guiding process consultation within school organizations.

chapter 8

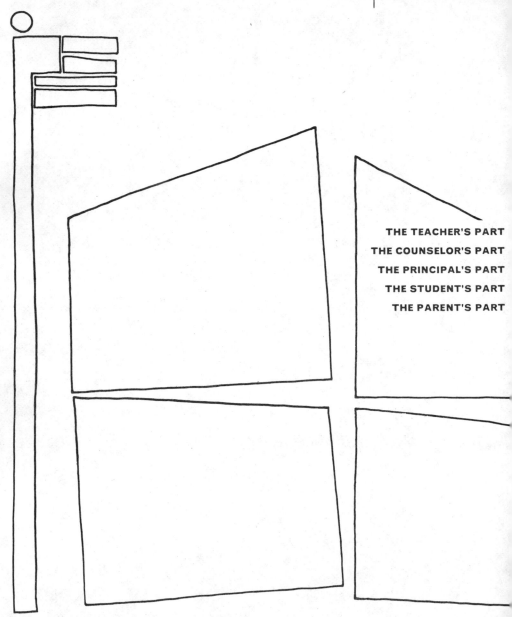

THE TEACHER'S PART
THE COUNSELOR'S PART
THE PRINCIPAL'S PART
THE STUDENT'S PART
THE PARENT'S PART

Everybody's part in humanizing the school

Throughout this volume we have drawn attention to the need for *cultural* changes in schools, in contrast to mere *cognitive* and *attitudinal* changes on the part of *individual* staff members and students. However, we do not view individual participants merely as cogs in an ongoing school bureaucracy. It is true that the cultural change we have recommended will be sustained only by *systemic change*, which means that long-term organizational interventions must involve all school participants, or at least most of the functional subsystems of the school. It must be remembered, however, that these activities are performed by *individuals.* Norms and social systems are a strong influence on individual behavior but in the final analysis, involved and committed administrators, teachers, students, and parents will be the ones to humanize our schools. *A school which is "everybody's house" means that individuals take their respective parts as concerned, well-intentioned, and skillful participants.*

We believe that many people are ready to take bold action to humanize our schools. If we are correct, our society is moving toward a new era—an era when the happenings of daily living will be cherished as highly as the material products of life; where emotional maturity will be appreciated as much as the accumulation of knowledge; and when wisdom may be defined in terms of an optimal balance between awareness of self and the rewards and demands of living with others. The message of our times is, however, that each individual must take part in helping this new day emerge.

For the schools it is especially important that educators take an active part in supporting these humanistic trends. It is critical that teachers do not "stand in the doorway or block the hall." The teacher's age-old functions as paternalistic guide, transmitter of information, and guardian of traditional customs must give way to a more equalitarian helping and sharing relationship with students. Knowledge and societal problems are changing far too rapidly for any single professional group—however well educated and well intentioned—to have all of the power.

But it is not just the educators who must change if this new era is to come about. Each person will have to take part. Everyone's responsibility lies in accepting others, in helping to build learning communities in which whole-person relationships are valued, and in working to develop school cultures in which the norms support openness, directness, and empathy for others. In this chapter we discuss those activities that we believe should become integral elements in the behavior of teachers, counselors, principals, students, and parents. Since this is the final chapter, we will also summarize the key concepts and suggestions made throughout the book.

THE TEACHER'S PART

While we advocate major changes in the traditional role of the classroom teacher, we do not believe the role of the educational leader will ever become obsolete in learning groups. On the contrary, in the kind of school we have in mind, formal leaders will be actively and thoroughly involved in facilitating and stimulating interpersonal exchanges within guidance, instructional, and application groups. They will act more as diagnosticians and conveners for learning groups than prescribers and dominating leaders. Perhaps most importantly, teachers will be regarded as persons in their own right, with feelings, opinions, and information to be shared with students, rather than manipulators who hide their feelings and attempt to "psych out" students.

Teachers will be viewed more as real people who are personally and emotionally involved in the interpersonal interactions of the school. They will also be viewed as continual learners, even though they may have more skills, experience, and resources to offer than any other member of a learning group. Teachers will be expected to make mistakes and to exercise poor judgment sometimes; these are features of being human.

In relation to students the humanistic teacher's special function will be in greater acceptance of and broader responsibility for the psychological development of students. Emphasis on a student's accumulation of information and acquisition of skills will continue, but the teacher we have in mind will place just as much emphasis on students "getting their head together" or crystallizing their identity and gaining a deepened awareness of their emotional nature. Finding applications for knowledge and understanding one's own emotionality will take on as much importance as learning facts and accumulating information.

1. Teachers in relation to students

In the most general terms, the teacher has been charged with providing opportunities for students to become knowledgeable and responsible citizens. This responsibility has been defined in different ways in various periods of American history. At one time, for example, the teacher's fulfillment of that responsibility was measured simply by whether students had reached a given standard of literacy. Later teachers were expected to provide a broader array of competencies; they taught science, social studies, speech, physical education, and many other skills along with the three Rs. The expanded curriculum was used to provide students with more comprehensive knowledge of an increasingly complicated environment. Today, the basic skills of reading, writing, and arithmetic—although still extremely important —are not sufficient in themselves to allow individuals to find satisfaction in our very complex world. Large amounts of information about the world are in themselves no longer sufficient tools to operate effectively in it. Students need to learn more about who they are, where they wish to go, and how they can get there.

In Chapter 6, we proposed that schools should take on the task of providing opportunities for the personal and emotional growth of students (*all* students—not only those in trouble). We proposed, more specifically, that guidance groups should be developed for this purpose and that they should become a regular, institutionalized part of school life. We also proposed that school is an appropriate setting for students to learn how to use new information to solve practical problems and how to apply newly developed skills to everyday life. We suggested that such attempts at application could be discussed and perhaps rehearsed in application groups.

In each of these three kinds of learning groups, the teacher plays a major part. While it is obvious that each required different sorts of behavior from the teacher, we view four basic functions as necessary for teachers to perform in each of these groups: (1) providing objective diagnoses of the current state of affairs, (2) helping students to make personal contracts for learning, (3) confronting students with discrepancies between their own ideals for learning and their actual behavior, and (4) managing the human and nonhuman resources of the learning group, whether inside or outside the school. Each of these functions is an aspect of process consultation as discussed in Chapter 7. Teachers need the skills and orientations of process consultation to facilitate the emotional and intellectual growth of students.

a. Teacher as diagnostician

As we indicated in Chapter 7, the term "diagnosis" refers to the first step of formative evaluation; it is a way to assess the current state of affairs. Diagnosis is applied to a particular system level—such as the individual or the small group—to prepare to overcome obstacles that are getting in the way of reaching goals. As leaders of instructional groups, teachers traditionally have used standardized tests to measure academic achievement on a regular basis in order to discover the skill levels of individual students. Although many teachers have used such achievement data primarily for grading (summative evaluation), skillful teachers also have made use of test scores to design future sequences of learning activities, to help determine the most appropriate learning materials for a given student, and to determine the content of instruction for a particular period of time. Diagnostic measures should be more widely applied by teachers for formative evaluation.

(1) Diagnosing group climate

In addition to providing data about instructional matters, diagnostic instruments can also help teachers and students to view the climate of their group objectively. In Chapter 5, we presented a short review of diagnostic instruments and how they can be used. Assessments can be made to see if the norms of a learning group are congruent with the individual student's stated goals. As an example, the teacher might use diagnostic tools to see if the norms support and encourage academic excellence or if they support mediocre performance. In guidance groups, the question might be asked: Is there a climate of support and acceptance and a wide range of tolerance so that students are free to express their personal concerns and feelings? In application groups, the question might be asked: Is there a climate in support of the exploration of ideas and for trying out plans jointly? The interpersonal norms of a learning group, regardless of the group's specific goals, can help or hinder its progress; teachers and students should know about the kinds of dynamics that are implicit in their own groups.

(2) Diagnosis to establish individual goals

Diagnostic procedures can be used to help students determine their own goals. In traditional classrooms, teachers set goals for each student based on what they, the teachers, believe are the appropriate objectives for a particular age group or for particular students within the group. But if goals are to be set by the students themselves, then the diagnostic inventories should be made for joint teacher-student use. Teachers can help students to define their own goals by guiding them through a personal diagnosis; they can also help by asking students to share their goals with some of their peers. In these ways, teachers and students can help one another to reach personal objectives collaboratively.

(3) Diagnosis for problem-solving

Having a firm grasp of the current state of affairs is absolutely crucial for successful problem-solving—for moving progressively closer to a goal. In guidance groups, for example, students become involved in setting objectives for their own personal growth, but they must know where they are at the present time in order to plan how to move toward those objectives. In application groups, a problem-solving scheme is used to show students how to use knowledge and skills to take action; thus collecting data about the current state of affairs is also basic in application groups. For instance, if students are studying the city government and decide to become involved in aspects of it, they will need accurate information about the current realities of the local government. Indeed, diagnosis as a means of assessing situations is a process necessary for any sort of group problem-solving.

b. Teacher as helper with learning contracts

Academic goals of students traditionally have been set by teachers. The typical pattern has been that at the beginning of the school year many conscientious teachers study their students' past performances. They look at accumulated records, recent achievement and intelligence test scores, and students' performances on prescribed curricula in order to judge each student's knowledge and skill levels and to decide upon alternative strategies of instruction. For many teachers, this is the only time of the year when goals are considered seriously and deeply. Unfortunately, for most traditional teachers, the conclusions drawn during this diagnostic period do not significantly influence the sort of instructional procedures that they actually implement. They will teach very much as they always have taught. For many of these teachers— regardless of the particulars of the diagnosis—seats are assigned, rules are presented, and the instructional program proceeds much as it did the year before. A distinct status difference between the teacher and students is maintained, emotional closeness is discouraged, and the students quickly fall into a comfortable, or uncomfortable, routine.

Helping students develop their own learning contracts works quite differently from this. Teachers and students mutually determine the learning goals: some goals are set by individual students, others by the teacher (or the school district or the state), and still others are determined by the entire learning group. We believe that unilateral goal-setting by the teacher should be underplayed because it often keeps students from becoming involved and committed to their own learning programs and it places the teacher in the uncomfortable position of having to act as the monitor of behavior. In such a position, the teacher becomes the primary person to police the academic performances of all the students. Also, the teacher must devise persuasive techniques for convincing the students—and perhaps himself—that the time and energy expended on a particular lesson will be well spent.

When contracting is used, students become involved in determining their own goals for learning, and manipulative strategies are not needed for persuasion. Contract-making involves the willing consent of the student and the teacher to work toward particular objectives. Contractual agreements for learning put the responsibility for learning on the learner, allowing the teacher to facilitate rather than monitor a student's attempts to fulfill a contract.

Helping students to develop their own contracts for learning is a natural way to proceed if shared decision-making is valued over hierarchical and unilateral decisions. Both teachers and students should be involved in determining goals because each has something different to bring; teachers have more knowledge and skill in the subject-matter and students, as learners, understand at least partially what their own interests and proclivities are. Of course, teachers should take an active part in helping students to decide on what should be learned, how the learning process will occur, and how evaluation will take place. Also, some students naturally will require more involvement from teachers than will other students.

As an example, contract-making within instructional groups might call for the use of standardized tests as diagnostic aids. Students would have an opportunity to study the test results to discover their strengths and weaknesses in particular skill areas. Students and teachers together would decide on a program of learning to improve the students' skills. They might decide on programmed instruction, receiving tutoring from another student, doing some particular reading, carrying out some library research, or using the help of someone in the community. In short, this program would be designed to eliminate discrepancies between students' goals and their current performance levels through the cooperative efforts of the students and the educational leaders.

Helping students to develop their own contracts for learning also seems natural when we remember that students learn different things in different ways; what is to be learned and who aims to learn it both should be taken into consideration before working on a particular instructional format. Although at times all students of a learning group might pursue the very same learning activity, much of the time individuals will be proceeding differently from one another.

Individual differences in goals will be especially prominent in guidance groups. For example, some students may wish to learn how to talk more in groups; others may want to learn to express themselves succinctly. Some students may want to work on their self-confidence; others may work toward expressing anger constructively. Some students may want to work on their relationships in the family, others with the peer group, and still others with their teachers. Although undoubtedly there will be some interpersonal skills that all members of a learning group will want to develop, the main purpose of the guidance group is to help all students to work on those objectives that will help them toward self-actualization.

Finally, helping students to develop their own contracts for learning is also helpful when the teacher encourages the students to gain control over their own peer group dynamics. In Chapter 5, for example, we wrote about a group procedure for bringing into the open the formal and informal norms that operate within a learning group. The procedure included a phase during which the students decide for themselves the norms and processes that are worth keeping and those that ought to be changed. By encouraging the group to build agreements (group contracts) about how they wish to work together, the teacher enables the students to exercise more influence over what happens to them in school.

c. Teacher as confronter

Confronting people with discrepancies between ideal states and current performance can be effective only when the one being confronted values the ideal condition. When teachers prescribe learning goals and procedures unilaterally, their confrontations can be seen as authoritarian power plays and actively resisted or passively resented unless the students already share the teacher's goals. Teachers often attempt to persuade, reinforce, cajole, or punish students into pursuing particular goals in specific ways. Helping students develop their own learning contracts places more responsibility on the student to determine goals and the means for achieving them; and teachers are then better able to confront the student about behaving on his own terms.

We are suggesting that part of the teacher's role in contract-making is to help monitor the students' fulfillment of their own contracts. No matter how well-intentioned any of us may be, we often stray from our plans. The teacher can help students to stay on course by regularly reminding them of the details of their contracts. Such confrontations obviously should be given skillfully and with tact; they should be direct and serve to help students get back on course, not to humiliate or punish them. Ultimately, the decision to fulfill the contract is up to the student—as it always has been in the final analysis.

d. Teacher as manager

Teachers traditionally have tried to manage virtually every event in the classroom. They have set the learning goals, devised the instructional procedures, developed rules for conduct, and taken up most of the verbal airtime with their own talking. Our concept of the teacher as a manager is quite different. We use this term to refer to management of resources for learning.

As manager, the teacher coordinates the learning resources that are brought into the class, the curriculum materials that are used, and the physical aids and arrangements for learning. This kind of management encourages the participation of students; it does not involve the issuing of rewards or punishments without the full knowledge and participation of everyone. It has been our experience that groups which do not have someone to take over the jobs of managing logistics and procedures waste a great deal of time and energy.

We indicated in Chapter 6 that flexibility should be a key feature of the humanized school. We realize, however, that achieving an ideal level of organizational flexibility in schools is very difficult. We have worked with staffs and met many teachers and administrators who are reticent to loosen up the school because they fear a resulting disorganization and even chaos. They are concerned that equipment would be ruined, that students would get lost in the confusion, and that the public might look critically at the resulting professional profile of the school. There is no doubt that considerations of organizational efficiency are important for schools, but it is also very important that students and teachers become stimulated and active. These favorable behaviors are more likely to arise in schools that are flexibly organized.

In order to keep schedules, use of space, movement of people, availability of curriculum materials, and availability of audio-visual aids flexible, some designated person or group should be responsible for planning and monitoring the logistics of the school: helping the professionals, the students, and other learning resources to flow together effectively and efficiently. This can be handled, for instance, by the educational leader of each learning group and by a cadre of professionals and students for the school as a whole. The details of such management can be worked out in many different ways. But the logistics and management should serve educational needs—not the other way around.

Managing the flow of people and other resources in the informal and open learning environment can be especially difficult. In working to achieve a structure to facilitate individualized instruction, for instance, open classrooms typically are made up of a variety of activity centers to which students go to work at their own discretion. The availability of choices for learning can result in some of the activity centers being overcrowded, some being underused, and others not being used at all. Physical crowding in particular corners of the room can lead to frustrating disruptions and wasted time. This problem has been solved in some informal schools and classrooms through a simple counting system to which the students can easily adapt. Each student has a cardboard name card with a hole, and every activity center has an allotted number of hooks for hanging the name cards. A student puts a card on the hook while working at that center. When all the hooks in a particular learning center have name cards on them, additional students must go elsewhere. A simple procedure like this one requires minimum effort, yet without something like it some learning groups have been unduly disrupted.

Schools that are open and informal also run into difficulty keeping track of where students are located at any given time. We knew a principal who was eager to develop more openness and informality in her school, but was embarrassed and frustrated on more that a few occasions when a student was wanted by a parent, a counselor, or a teacher but could not be found except by searching from room to room. The principal and staff worked out the following procedure to keep track of everyone. The students met every day for the first forty-five minutes in a guidance group where logistics problems as well as personal growth issues were handled. On Mondays each student filled out a standard class schedule in duplicate, indicating where he would be, what activities he would be involved in, and what educational leader he would be near. Daily changes were made in the schedule as needed. One copy was kept in the guidance group, while the student carried the other copy with him. On some occasions, of course, students were not in their scheduled place, but with repeated explanations by the principal on the need for keeping track of students, the practice was successful.

Managing the flow of students, teachers, and other resources can be especially challenging in team-teaching situations. Some teams of teachers have developed elaborate charting methods for matching times, physical space, teacher resources, and student needs. They design schedules for a one- or two-week period showing all students in a particular place at a certain time with a specific teacher. Some students remain in a single learning group for a long period of time; nonreaders, for example, meet together over several months for remedial reading activities but they also participate in other groups for other activities. The use of such chartkeeping involves considerable time in the beginning; however, after such scheduling procedures operate for several months, the rearranging of people, places, and times can become routine.

2. Teachers in relation to colleagues

In Chapter 4 we discussed some of the ways teachers are socialized into their roles and indicated that informal interactions in the faculty lounge may have more impact on a teacher's instructional behavior than formal preservice training. At the same time, teachers are often physically and psychologically isolated from one another and from their students. Many teachers and students find school a lonely, alienating place and are in need of enriching contact with one another.

In a humanized school, faculty members have many formal and informal ways of sharing the joys and burdens of teaching. This relieves the isolation and loneliness of teachers as well as the students. In contrast, schools in which the adults are distant, formal, and distrustful of one another will also have classes where the same sorts of relationships occur. Some interpersonal trust and support must exist among the adult professionals before such qualities occur between teachers and students. There are programs in the school's instructional areas or within the organizational procedures which can be used to bring about increased collaboration among teachers.

a. The teacher and instructional innovations

One example of an instructional innovation that inspired collaboration among teachers was Lillian Weber's open corridor plan. Her main objective was to present a visible demonstration of how an open and informal classroom might work within a very traditional inner-city school that was physically organized in the self-contained, egg-crate fashion.

The staff of the corridor plan did not strive to influence the teachers of the school directly; rather they set up extracurricular activities and displays of materials for educational enrichment in the corridors of the school. Each teacher was left to decide how, if at all, his students would use the resources in the corridors. A few teachers never made use of the corridors; however, the majority of the teachers were stimulated to modify some of the procedures in their own classroom, often modeling the new teaching procedures on activities and exhibits they had observed in the corridors.

Many teachers also began to combine their teaching efforts by using their rooms and the corridors between as the total space for learning. Using the corridors meant that the teachers left their rooms more often and consequently interacted more with one another. Team-teaching arose among several clusters of staff members as a natural consequence of the open-corridor program. In a similar fashion, many instructional programs growing out of the behaviorist, mental health, and group dynamics applications that are new to a school can be used to increase teacher collaboration and sharing.

b. The teacher and organizational innovations

A school searching for ways to change will usually develop increased collaboration among its staff members. Furthermore, when the process of change is accompanied by training in organization development, new levels of staff collaboration are virtually certain. Organization development training helps a staff to communicate about goals and procedures; it encourages joint problem-solving and cooperation decision-making. As we indicated in Chapter 6, the OD process can help a faculty to discover the stimulating and supportive friendships that are missing in so many schools. The OD process can be used for any organizational arrangement; it assumes that no single organizational plan will work effectively in all schools. Only through open communication and deliberate planning can faculties determine what is best for them and their students.

Even in the most traditional schools, opportunities are usually available for teachers to team up with colleagues to share some of the problems and excitement of teaching. Of course, the ease and extent of such planning depend on how supportive the staff norms are for teacher collaboration, how flexible the scheduling and room arrangements are, and the degree of encouragement and direction offered by the principal. Either of the two plans that follow can be implemented in some form by a single teacher within almost any type of school.

(1) Collegial supervision

Collegial supervision is a plan in which professional peers—instead of higher-status administrators—are responsible for monitoring one another's professional behavior. It is based on the assumption that peers can help one another to improve, especially if they are given some skills in analyzing instruction and giving feedback. The process is most effective when there is administrative support and time is allowed for teachers to work together, but pairs of teachers can meet informally to improve their teaching even in schools where little or no formal support is offered.

Small groups of teachers can be organized in several different ways to implement collegial supervision. They might come together to deal with specific learning group problems or schoolwide issues, to learn about new teaching methods, or to explore new curricula. Within such groups, teachers set their own goals, procedures, and methods for evaluating what they do. The core of a program in collegial supervision involves teachers observing each other in the classroom and giving feedback about their observations.

(2) Formal staff sharing

We noted in Chapter 3 that schools are resource-using human systems and that in humanized schools the participants learn to appreciate the variety of resource and skills that are at their finger-tips. Unfortunately, in traditional schools it often occurs that, for example, an outside "expert" is brought to a faculty meeting to discuss an instructional innovation with which a couple of teachers in the building are actually experimenting at that time. Few faculty members are aware of the variety of teaching expertise available on the average staff.

Also, it is often the case that teachers confront a problem that could be solved with the help of another teacher; however, they do not know whom to call on for assistance. An English teacher who has a nonreader in class, for example, may in desperation call in an outside consultant, read up on techniques in remedial reading, or continue to plod through with the problem. In most schools there is somebody with the skills to help a teacher with a nonreader, but quite often such resources remain unknown and unused.

In most schools, the backgrounds, special skills, and interests of the professional staff and students are insufficiently publicized and shared. A formal procedure should be instituted for the sharing of such information. The principal, a counselor, or a cadre of teachers and students might be in charge of collecting and making available data about the variety of resources available in the school. Early in the year, the strength exercise (described in Chapter 5) might be used to gather and publicize information about school resources. Later, regular memos might include information about the kinds of special instructional activities occurring within learning groups. Staff meetings can also be used for resource-sharing discussions. Communication about what participants can and want to contribute is necessary to make the school an effective resource-using system.

THE COUNSELOR'S PART

Like other important professionals in American schools, counselors have not been successful in humanizing relationships between teachers and students. Their lack of success derives in part from the many diverse challenges they face. Not only must they deal with students who cry out for help, but they are expected also to work effectively even in the midst of sharply conflicting expectations from colleagues, administrators, students, and parents. Counselors are expected to act as sympathetic listeners, confrontative disciplinarians, friendly confidantes, well organized schedulers, supportive advisors, and troubleshooters. Their function is often defined so ambiguously, in fact, that they themselves have a fragmented, inconsistent, and confused view of their role. The first task of any counselor today is often to define his role for his own peace of mind, and second to define for others how his resources will be used. In this section, we describe how we believe the school counselor can modify his role to help humanize relationships in the school.

Counselors are in a strategic position to help build more wholeperson relationships in the school. Like the principal they have legitimate access to all school participants, but unlike the principal they do not have to exercise authority nor must they become preoccupied with time-consuming administrative chores. Like teachers they can have direct contact with students on a regular basis, but they have more freedom than teachers to decide on the kinds of relationships they will develop with individual students. Also, counselors usually have received formal training in interpersonal competencies and have learned to use some of the skills of process consultation discussed in Chapter 7. And finally, as the research by Willower, Eidell, and Hoy (1967), discussed in Chapter 4, indicates, counselors as a group tend to hold more humanistic values than others in the school: values congruent with the goals of process consultation and organization development. All in all, counselors seem to be in a good position to help humanize relationships in schools.

1. Basic assumptions about the counselor's role

We think significant changes must be made in what the counselor does as he carries out his role. The changes we have in mind entail a much greater emphasis on the social dynamics of the school than on the personality dynamics of students who are in psychological trouble. In other words, we believe that a counselor should not look at a student's troubles in isolation from his social relationships within the school.

The counselor's role has been strongly influenced in the past by a therapeutic point of view: helping students to adjust to the school culture. We believe that the counselor's role should be influenced more by the human-systems application discussed in Chapter 3. The role we have in mind calls for a counselor to adopt more of a group or organizational application. He would diagnose student problems in relation to the context of the school's social environment. He would adopt the point of view that emotional tensions are influenced strongly by the interpersonal environment and that interpersonal norms and processes should be dealt with just as much as the student's inner thoughts and feelings. In this way, the counselor's role would be influenced more by the mental health and group applications. His work would involve attempts to create a school culture which is supportive of the positive mental health of individuals and which is characterized by healthy group interactions.

The counselor would continue to do some work with students who are experiencing difficulties but probably in small groups rather than on a one-to-one basis. Primarily, he would work with all school participants—the teachers, administrators, students, and even parents—to provide training in interpersonal skills or help to lead problem-solving discussions. Moreover, he would work to improve interpersonal relationships and to foster healthy climates for learning in key subsystems such as classroom groups, professional departmental units, teaching teams, and the student government. Instead of reacting to crises and disturbances as they arise, the counselor would initiate diagnoses and training sessions for the members of these subsystems. The energy that counselors have spent on only a handful of students would be redirected toward working with subgroups of students and staff, thereby producing some impact on the culture of the school as well as on individuals.

Of course, particular individuals would still need special help. Norm violators, disturbed students, and overloaded teachers would still require special assistance. Our hypothesis is that they would not take up so much of the counselor's time because other people could help them. And, even within the one-to-one conferences that counselors might continue to have, they would act more as collaborator and facilitator than as expert and prescriber. Indeed, counselors' effectiveness, in the role we have in mind, might well be measured by how successful they are in getting all school participants to help one another to cope with emotional stresses and strains.

2. Counselor as a process consultant

A counselor can help to humanize relationships in the school by consulting with three kinds of groups: faculty groups, learning groups, and school groups that involve most, if not all, of the school's participants. All three such groups could place the counselor in a third-party, outside role, and so would share some of the benefits of using an external, objective consultant.

a. Consulting with staff groups

Almost every staff we have worked with or observed has had difficulty making faculty meetings productive. To improve the flow of communication during such meetings, a counselor could assume the role of process consultant. The counselor could function as an observer, giving feedback to the group periodically on their interpersonal processes. He could also initiate the use of questionnaires and present feedback about the results. The kinds of leadership and interpersonal norms that develop in faculty meetings are integrally related to the effectiveness of the meetings. He might also comment during meetings on communication patterns and ambiguities that seem to be present, and the points at which decisions seem to be unclear or not fully shared. He might encourage the airing of interpersonal conflicts or tensions that would probably remain hidden without his help. Through process consultation, the counselor could help teachers and administrators to pay more attention to one another's feelings and ideas even during task-centered meetings.

The counselor could also assume the role of process consultant appropriately in many other settings in which faculty groups meet. For example, he could perform as a process consultant in the meetings of teaching teams, special ad hoc curriculum committees, departmental groups, and the administrative leadership group. The counselor might join such groups during their first few meetings to help them decide on the ways in which they want their leadership, discussions, and decision-making to function; then later he might occasionally return to give feedback on how well the group is living up to its own group agreements. The counselor also might be asked to attend a meeting if a special problem has arisen for the group. He could then serve as an objective third party to help clarify thoughts and feelings and to bring problem-solving techniques to the group's work.

b. Consulting with learning groups

Another way the counselor could help to improve interpersonal relationships in the school is to serve as a consultant to learning groups. This sort of consultation should be aimed at humanizing the climate of the group—the teachers and the students in interaction—and not just at helping a teacher cope with "problem students." The counselor might help the group to talk about itself by collecting diagnostic data and by feeding it back to the group. He might observe the group in action and present his observations on either a formal or informal basis. He might design a training program for a guidance group which involved practicing communication and group skills. He could help the members of an instructional group to give one another feedback about their interpersonal dynamics, or he could help the members of an application group to use role-playing as part of their learning design. Ideally, his services would be available to all sorts of learning groups with all sorts of special issues, and his time would be available to both students and teachers.

c. Consulting with the larger school organization

Considerable interest now exists in bringing educators and students into more effective communication to determine goals and procedures for an entire school. We believe that the counselor is an appropriate person to help prepare the groundwork for this sort of large-scale meeting. There are several ways this can be done. Some schools, for example, have formed a senate or governing board composed of administrators, teachers, and students. Counselors could act as process consultants to such a group, helping the members to keep communication clear and open, to agree upon decision-making procedures, and to discuss how their interpersonal processes are going during meetings. As in other settings, the counselor could design a training program to help educators and students to hold more effective meetings. In some instances counselors have initiated a weekend retreat so that the educators and students could get to know one another and make some agreements about operating procedures before being inundated with the work of the school year. It is important, however, for counselors to follow up their work by offering continued training to the group and helping to solve subsequent problems.

THE PRINCIPAL'S PART

The principal can have more influence on a school's climate than any other single person within the building. A principal's formal behavior, for example, can be especially important. Whether the principal makes decisions unilaterally or collaboratively, whether he evaluates teachers in a consultative fashion or as a supervisor, and whether his philosophy about students is primarily custodial or humanistic constitute some of the central motives for the type of influence exerted. At the same time, his informal behavior or even some of his unintended actions can also be very influential. For instance, is his office easily accessible and open to students? Does the principal's secretary warmly greet teachers and students who come into the office? In meetings with teachers, does the principal encourage diffused participation? Does he chat informally and openly with students? The answers to these questions are important ways he influences the culture of the school. The principal's formal and informal behavior can have profound effects on shaping the interpersonal relationships that occur regularly in the school.

1. The traditional role of the principal

Principals who attempt to enter into whole-person relationships with teachers and students face some very strong obstacles. Traditional expectations make it very difficult for principals to initiate close and open interpersonal relationships with others. A brief review of history may help to clarify the barriers which principals face in attempting to humanize schools.

In early America when schools were small and the curriculum was simple, principals were expected to teach for a major part of the day.

The teaching-principal devoted only a small portion of work time to administrative details and managerial matters and was often able to work closely and informally with colleagues and students. As schools increased in size and community importance, principals gradually reduced their teaching loads and moved into the top position in the school's hierarchy. During this period of transition, the principal obtained more and more prestige and power, eventually gaining the legitimate functions of hiring, supervising, evaluating, and firing teachers. Moreover, he decided upon many aspects of the school's curriculum and became ultimately responsible for the advancement or expulsion of students. Along with new legitimacy and these reward and coercive bases of influence, the principal was expected to have the highest level of expertise in the school in relation to new curriculum materials, instructional methods, and educational programs. The principal became the most powerful educational leader in the school.

As the population continued to grow and schools formed together into districts, the building principal changed from the primary instructional leader of an educational program to the primary manager of a bureaucracy. Functions such as checking on expenditures, record keeping, supervising the maintenance of the physical plant, attending district meetings, and speaking in the community became the predominant elements of the job. Other personnel took over many of the previous professional functions. Curriculum specialists and personnel directors took part in evaluating instructional programs and the performances of professional personnel. Department heads, assistant principals, and grade-level coordinators took over the day-to-day leadership of the instruction programs within learning groups. By the 1960s, principals had become further removed than ever before from personal and direct involvement with teachers and students.

As he has come to serve as instructional leader or bureaucratic manager, or as some combination of the two, principal's relationships with staff and students have grown shallow and impersonal. In addition, the sheer size and complexity of the social structure of the average district have increased formality and distance between the principal and other participants. While teachers may work closely with students in the school's learning groups and meet with one another in departmental or committee meetings, principals have very little opportunity to participate or even to observe in these settings. In the main, principals meet with teachers or with students either on a one-to-one basis or in large, formal meetings. Seldom does the principal participate in lengthy small-group discussions with teachers or students. Indeed, the principal probably is known best and understood most completely by his secretary. Even though principals are charged with giving critical and helpful feedback to teachers (and students) about their school performances, rarely, if ever, do teachers or students confide in the principal or ask him for help in solving a difficult school-related problem.

Unfortunately, most principals seem to have a typical bureaucratic role relationship with their teachers. The staff norms typically support hiding personal anxieties and job-related weaknesses, avoiding public expressions of affect, and adopting a universalistic perspective from which all colleagues are treated alike regardless of their particular interests or personal styles. Even in the face of these barriers, many principals still have attempted to act more informally or openly and to establish a more relaxed atmosphere in the school. Many of them have met resistance on the parts of others; social pressures for maintaining appropriate "professional distance" between the principal and teachers come from the central office, from the community, and from the teachers' organizations themselves. These various pressures help to maintain social distance between the principal and the teachers; the principal remains distant, surpassing in loneliness even the individual teachers.

2. The job of the principal

Most principals take the role that is expected of them. Principals are bombarded with pressures from all directions; they receive inputs from teachers, aides, service personnel, and students on the one hand, and from the central office, parents, community groups, and the school board on the other. Placed in the middle of a myriad of social pressures, principals are the object of continual and contradictory expectations and demands. Some students demand school experiences that are more relevant to their lives, others will go along with anything the teachers mete out, and still others will not go along with anything and do not care. Some teachers ask for more collective decisions and a greater opportunity to help run the school, while others want to be left alone. Some students and teachers want more freedom and flexibility in the schools, while others want more structure. The central office—in itself the object of multiple pressures—calls for new programs in math, sex education, the arts, PPBS, etc. And parents want their youngsters to feel better, more challenged, or even more fearful about school. Naturally, in the midst of this, the principal must find ways of insulating himself. Often the most sensible way to cope with the continual and conflicting demands seems to be to go along with the school norms of formality, low public affect, universalism, the reduction of differences, and the hiding of weaknesses and deficiencies.

Even though the inertia of tradition and the force of these multiple demands mitigate against changes in the principal's role, we have found many principals who desire a different and more personalized relationship with teachers and students. Indeed, the number is large enough that we are optimistic about the part that principals can play in helping to humanize public schools. The middle 1970s seem ripe for principals to start behaving differently in the school.

3. The principal's part in the humanized school

The most important behavioral changes for principals to make are in the interpersonal interactions with staff and students. The changes we have in mind involve more direct and open ways of communicating ideas, opinions, and feelings in face-to-face interactions. Principals especially should be more open and direct in describing their own feelings and values about education. The most important organizational changes principals must make involve broadening the customary unilateral and authoritarian decision-making patterns so as to use more teacher and student resources and to encourage deeper involvement and commitment from the school's participants. The principal should make fewer unilateral decisions, stimulate more active group interaction, and encourage more collaborative decision-making than has been the case in the traditional role.

We also wish to point out, however, that we do not see the principal as adopting a "soft" human relations role, whereby he merely relates with others in pleasant and friendly ways, letting their wishes prevail. While we see the principal as more pleasant and friendly in the new role, we also see him taking an active part in bringing conflict and differences of opinion out into the open, as well as being very direct and open about his own opinions, thoughts, and feelings.

Six leader functions will be particularly important to the principal as he attempts to humanize relationships within the school: (a) the way he exerts his leadership, (b) how he makes decisions, (c) his skill in confronting staff members, (d) how he uses evaluation, (e) how he organizes the group for problem-solving, and (f) how he relates to the district administration.

a. Flexible leadership

How the principal performs his leadership functions will have significant effect on the climate of the school. A principal should exert many different types of influence and be flexible enough to perform a variety of functions when needed. For example, sometimes the principal may need to present information to his staff, but other times he will need to gather information and ideas from them. Sometimes he may need to be supportive and helpful as a group of teachers carries out a job, while at other times he may initiate his own projects and organize support from others. Sometimes he will be the "sympathetic ear" or the "soft shoulder," while at others he may have to confront teachers or students for falling short of their own goals.

Although the principal is always the formal leader of the school, obviously he does not have to execute all of the functions of leadership. In fact, we think the principal's power should be dispersed so that many people have some influence over what transpires in the school. Not only is the dispersal of influence congruent with humanized values; it also helps to increase the effectiveness of a staff. Often the most effective leadership that principals can adopt is to refrain from taking a firm position, thereby allowing others to be influential. Schutz (1966) has referred to this concept in terms of the "leader as completer"; the leader performs those functions in a group that others are not doing. We do not mean here that the principal should abdicate his power position and assume a laissez-faire orientation. The effective principal gives others the chance to be the center of attention and to display their particular skills, while maintaining his position of legitimate authority.

b. Facilitating decision-making

Ultimately, principals are responsible for how the school is run. Today many school districts are implementing some form of Program Planning and Budgeting System (PPBS) and, with growing demands for accountability, many principals feel even greater pressures from the central office and the public than previously. Unfortunately, many administrators are reacting to these demands for the implementation of

Everybody's part in humanizing the school

PPBS by making decisions individually and unilaterally. We think that PPBS programs for schools will be successful only if administrators actively encourage collaborative goal-setting and decision-making on their staffs.

In facilitating collaborative decision-making, the principal guides and encourages his staff and students to open up and clarify their communication so that everyone is clear about who makes what decisions and how they will proceed in making such decisions. Decision-making thus becomes an open process rather than a secretive one. While decisions are being made the principal should not sit by passively, letting others discuss a topic in hopes that they will eventually come to his point of view; he should state his opinions and ideas as freely as other members. Nor should he try to avoid or hide conflicts and disagreements, but rather he should use disagreements to energize the group's efforts to reach decisions and to move on. Consensus decisions are the best method that principals can use to assure open and collaborative work.

Consensus does not mean a unanimous agreement. Consensus means that everyone can paraphrase the issue to indicate that he or she understands it, that everyone has had a chance to describe his feelings about the issue, and that those who continue to disagree or have doubts will nevertheless say publicly that they are willing to give the decision an experimental try for a prescribed period of time. It means that a sufficient number of people are in favor of the decision to carry it out, while others understand what is happening and will not obstruct it.

c. Confronting staff members

After the principal has dispersed the decision-making power in a school and has stimulated a consensual decision on a particular issue, it is quite appropriate that he direct his leadership efforts toward energizing others to pursue the chosen path. The principal should confront staff members or students who waver from their agreements.

The principal's confrontation skills involve more than just risking a show of strength. Confronting staff members means that the principal relinquishes the traditional formal role relationship and openly reveals his thoughts, opinions, hopes, and fears to staff members. By so doing, he does not abdicate his authority; he extends his power by keeping staff members on the courses they have determined for themselves. He confronts staff members with the discrepancies between where they want to go and where they are.

d. Providing for evaluation

The principal should insure that objective diagnosis of organizational processes is periodically carried out. Perhaps most importantly, the principal should find ways of assessing his own functioning and of encouraging the collection of data about his job as well as the roles of other school participants. In discussing the role of the counselor, we described how some diagnostic activities can be carried out in the school. Many of the same concepts apply here for the principal. Often, of course, the principal is too loaded with demands to take a major role as diagnostician. In such a case, he could provide support and encouragement for a counselor or cadre of teachers and students to collect data. Two useful, comprehensive collections of relevant diagnostic tools can be found in Fox, Jung, Schmuck, Ritvo, and Van Egmond (1973) and Schmuck, Runkel, Saturen, Martell, and Derr (1972). The collection and feedback of questionnaires, observations, and interviews should become a routine school function.

e. Convening group problem-solving

Although we recommend that some school participant, such as the counselor, should act routinely as a process consultant in the school, the principal's own leadership behaviors are crucial to the way in which work is carried out in groups. As we pointed out in Chapter 7, the skills of process consultation should not be the province of a single role-taker; they are important and functional interpersonal skills that all school participants can learn to use.

The principal as the formal leader and official convener of meetings is in a key position to employ the skills of process consultation. His behavior can be critical in determining the kinds of interpersonal relationships and problem-solving behaviors that will become prominent in the group. His uses of communication skills—his style of listening, probing, summarizing, and confronting—will encourage or discourage staff members to do the same. If he moves toward problems in systematic and deliberate ways, he will exhibit a model for handling problem-solving in the school.

The following five guidelines, paraphrased from Maier (1962), delineate some of the functions that principals should keep in mind as conveners of staff groups.

(1) Problem-solving groups often will move too rapidly toward the solution to a problem. Frequently solutions are decided upon before all participants have a clear idea of what the details of the problem are. One responsibility of the convener is to assure that everyone understands the nature and importance of the problem being discussed.

(2) Often group conveners attempt to discourage disagreement and open conflict in order to maintain an illusion of harmony and to avoid uncomfortable tensions. As we have already noted, we do not think that a principal should adopt soft human relations techniques in attempting to keep disagreement toned down. On the contrary, the convener should encourage respect for disagreement, helping to turn disagreements into stimulants for new ideas and practices.

(3) When new ideas are discussed within a group, people often reject them before they are fully explained. *Evaluation* of ideas also tends to slow down the *generation* of ideas. Thus, a job of a convener is to keep separate the functions of brainstorming (idea generation) and the later criticism and ultimate evaluation of the ideas.

(4) Ideas and suggestions from the formal leader of a group tend to be taken more seriously than the ideas of other members. The legitimate leader, the principal, should be aware of this norm and show by listening and acceptance of others that he welcomes ideas from everyone.

(5) Leadership involves a number of interpersonal activities that can be performed by many participants. The convener should encourage everyone to participate actively in trying to influence the group. He should encourage shared responsibility for the functions of leadership.

f. Relating to the district administration

A primary task of the principal is to bridge the communicative gap between the district administration and the participants of his own school. Indeed, our own experience, as well as some data-based research by Hornstein *et al.* (1967), indicates that teachers hold more respect for and are more willing to be influenced by principals whom they view as experts in their own right and whom they see as holding some influence at the district office.

A principal's role as a bridge to the central office is important for at least two reasons. First, along with the esteem he receives from teachers within the building, the principal's participation with the district administration can provide information about changing events in the district, the larger community, and even the nation. He can gain a different perspective, too, on the problem of his own building by learning about problems in other buildings. Furthermore, communication with fellow administrators can lead to the exchange of new ideas and programs that may be useful for his own school.

Second, the district office usually has additional resources that are not available within a single building. Resources such as specialized consultants, learning aides, experimental programs, or new materials may be housed in the district office without being used very much. A principal who is aware of particular services in the district office can use them in his building. In this way he helps maintain one aspect of the self-renewing school by using available outside resources.

THE STUDENT'S PART

Very few educational texts discuss the part that students might take in humanizing the schools. One reason may be that students are typically viewed as powerless in relation to the school's organizational functioning and management. Another is that text books are written for training programs in professional education. Unfortunately, a book of our sort does not reach many students or parents. We hope, of course, that students and parents will read this book, discuss it, and use it as a guide to help humanize schools, but we do not expect that many of them will study it unless educators take initiative in bringing it to them. With some initiation from educators, students can play just as important a part as teachers, counselors, and principals in humanizing the school climate.

The time when students—in particular, high school students—adopted *only* a quiet and passive stance in relation to adult professionals has passed. There are several indications that times are changing for students. The growing number of alternative schools strongly emphasizes that students want to make choices about the sort of education they experience. Virulent faculty-student conflict in many urban schools has led to the increased power of students in the organizational functioning of the school. The growing involvement of parents in schools usually is accompanied by giving students a greater voice as well.

Everybody's part in humanizing the school

Even within rather traditional schools students are being urged to initiate changes (as shown, for example, in the volume, *The Soft Revolution*, 1971, by Postman and Weingartner in which students are given ideas on how they might "revolutionize" schools through changes in their own behavior). However, this effort is still minuscule and has not broadly affected the majority of students.

For trend toward student involvement to continue, adult professionals will have to take initiative. Students should be more than informally influential; they should have formal and legitimate influence to determine some goals and procedures. It is still up to educators, essentially, to bring legitimate student influence to bear in our schools; it is still up to teachers, counselors, and administrators to take hold of these trends and to bring students into the management of the school.

This section is aimed primarily toward professional educators. We first demonstrate the ways in which the student culture does, in great part, determine what goes on between people in a school. We try to indicate how educators might energize those peer group dynamics toward constructive ends. We later give suggestions and ideas about how students can take on a legitimate decision-making function in the schools. We are hopeful that students can become more than just the consumers of education.

1. Students' influence on peers

The Coleman report (1966) argued strongly that improved instruction and better curriculum materials do not, in themselves, ameliorate the educational experiences of students. The Coleman findings have since been corroborated by Jencks *et al.* (1972). In both of these studies, emphasis is placed on particular sociological and social psychological variables associated with the peer group and the students' families and neighborhoods. In both, the influence of the school programs, as such, is played down. These reports clearly argue that other students constitute the most immediate and important environment for a student. Jencks writes, "Everything else—the school budget, its policies, the characteristics of the teachers—is either secondary or completely irrelevant."

Compared to the interactions with teachers and administrators, student interactions with other students are more varied and frequent, more intense, and have more influence on student self-identification.

Students have more influence over one another than any other single person or group within the school. Peers satisfy or frustrate one another's goals, help bridge emotional gaps during the period between the preschool years and adulthood, and interpret the cultural expectations and norms of the adult society to one another. Critical life issues such as relationships between the sexes, proper amounts of aggressiveness and hostility, and appropriate levels of competition, cooperation, and aspiration are heavily influenced by peers. They directly influence one another's information and feelings about success, power, prestige, respect, and ways of affiliating with others, as well as reinforcing norms about relating to superiors, colleagues, and subordinates. Through discussions and behavioral rehearsals with peers, youngsters learn to be disposed positively or negatively to sportsmanship, fairness, warmth, friendliness, informality, and spontaneity in social situations.

Peer relations influence more than generalized norms and skills in interpersonal relations; they also are instrumental in shaping a student's specific attitudes about school, success in school subjects, and academic achievement. For instance, students whose friends value academic success and who aspire to go to college will feel similar, and conversely those whose friends devalue education also tend to be negatively oriented to schooling. (See Wilson, 1959, and Alexander and Campbell, 1964.) The study by Hargreaves (1967) of the British schools, discussed in Chapter 5, fully delineated the kinds of influences the peer group has on a student's aspirations and success in school.

Educators should harness the power inherent in peer relations to humanize the climate in the school. Students as a group should become involved in understanding their own peer group dynamics and in deciding what their goals are, how they will reach them, and how their progress should be evaluated. The following suggestions can be used to involve students in decisions like these and to direct the energies of the peer group toward humanistic ends.

2. Students teaching other students

Involving students as formal teachers of one another is an effective way of directing the energies and resources of the peer group toward constructive ends. Ways in which students can act as teachers to one another are virtually endless. Of course, unplanned teaching in the form of informal influence already occurs naturally in school, and (as in the Hargreaves study) this influence can often be in opposition to

Everybody's part
in humanizing
the school

school learning. These informal interactions can be made formal, however, and with some training and guidance students can help one another to cope with school learning constructively. For example, students can teach same-age or different-age peers; they can help to teach the formal curriculum; or they can develop and teach subjects not now covered by the formal curriculum of the school.

a. One-to-one tutoring

A student who is doing poorly and has a negative attitude about his academic work will sometimes accept help more readily from another student whom he admires and respects than from an adult, no matter how skilled and well intentioned the adult may be. Putting students together in tutoring pairs can be a very effective way of insuring academic progress and raising both students' interest in school, and thus enhancing their performance expectations and confidence. A student may need remedial help or show interest in a subject on which the teachers do not have much information, or a student may simply have a difficult time with adults in authority. Any of these situations presents a good opportunity for one-to-one tutoring. For students in the teaching role, tutoring can increase their skill in emphasizing, listening, and helping others. For the recipients of the tutoring, such an experience can increase their attention-span, curiosity, and respect for others who are in teacher roles.

Several organizational arrangements can be used to encourage and allow students to work with one another on a formal teaching basis. Teachers might regularly assign a student to someone who needs additional help. A formal student tutoring service might be organized to serve as a clearing house for students who need help and those who have particular skills. Study hall periods or open times can be used to create informal rap sessions in which students talk about what is happening in their classes. The counselor's office might house a staff of students to offer immediate help to other students who are having academic problems and to seek longer-term help for students with more persistent problems.

b. Cross-age tutoring

One disadvantage of our age-graded schools is that youngsters have little opportunity to interact formally with younger or older students.

Cross-age tutoring can be a useful mechanism for formalizing cross-age relationships. The benefits of cross-age tutoring can be very similar to those listed above, with the added advantage of helping students to relate more effectively with their older and younger peers.

Two documented programs of cross-age tutoring have been successfully implemented. One by Fleming (1969) involved an entire fifth grade tutoring a class of second graders. Each fifth grader assisted a younger student in a variety of learning tasks for twenty to thirty minutes, two or three times per week. Fleming let the students choose their own partners and they were free to spend the time any way they wished. The tutor was to help his student with whatever he needed to work on. Very little training was given to the tutors, but teachers were available as resource persons while the tutoring was going on. The tutors held a few discussions about the problems they were encountering and tried to help one another become better tutors. The tutors also kept logs of their activities and prepared a final evaluation at the end of the year. Apparently the program worked out very well.

The second program of cross-age tutoring, by Lippitt and Lohman (1965), included a more extensive training program for the tutors and was started because many of the upper-grade elementary students felt very negatively about school. A deliberate attempt was made, in fact, to draft some of the most defiant students as tutors. The first group of tutors consisted of fourth and sixth graders who held high friendship and influence status in their classroom peer groups. Lippitt and Lohman believed that the tutoring program would have a better chance of achieving success if influential peers first had favorable experiences in the program.

The tutors met for a series of training sessions on how to help others; they also set their goals and instructional strategies during these sessions. Teachers chose the tutoring pairs and also scheduled their meeting times. All of the tutors would come together at regular times several times a week to discuss techniques and problems and to exchange ideas. These discussions typically were convened by the teachers, but the tutors did most of the talking. The teachers reported an increase in cooperation among the older students and an increased motivation to pursue academic work on the part of most of the students involved. The Northwest Regional Educational Laboratory, in Portland, Oregon, is currently producing a training package about cross-age tutoring, following this earlier work by Lippitt and Lohman.

c. Cross-school tutoring

Several programs of tutoring have been formed in which older students go to another school at specified times to tutor younger students. Junior high students go to elementary schools, senior high students go to junior highs and elementary schools, and college students go to all three. A program at the University of Oregon, for example, which is managed by college students, finds needful students in high schools, junior highs, and elementary schools, matches them up with college students, and then offers training to the college students in tutoring. The college students, in turn, receive college credit for tutoring younger students. In spring 1972, this program, known as ESCAPE, sent more than six hundred college students to thirty-two public schools for tutoring. The college students also attended weekly student-run seminars in which tutoring problems were discussed. This sort of program can work especially well for schools of education, which can use tutoring to give practice to future teachers before their formal practice teaching.

d. Mini-courses

Another arrangement for encouraging students to function as teachers is the use of mini-courses or interest classes. In addition, mini-courses can broaden the curriculum to include contemporary issues that have not yet entered the formal curriculum.

Mini-courses are developed primarily in response to interest and the availability of skills. They can be convened by students, teachers, the principal, parents, or other citizens. The arrangements can be simple or complex: one afternoon per week can be set aside for teaching a variety of mini-courses, or much of the regular curriculum can be made up of such courses, meeting for different lengths of time.

A committee of students and teachers (or perhaps a student committee with a teacher-advisor) can hold the responsibility for determining what courses will be taught, assigning educational leaders to the courses, and determining the logistics of scheduling. Groups might vary in interest from learning how to fix bicycles, to playing the autoharp, to studying the history of the Roman empire. Some of the mini-courses might require the resources of an expert, while others could merely have student conveners and hold discussions of mutual interest and concern. Mini-courses could well constitute the first step in helping students become more involved in and responsible for their own education. They might also help build new norms regarding the way in which the formal curriculum is taught.

Indeed, peer teaching embodies some of the key norms of a humanized school. It actualizes the themes of equalitarianism, of influence through resourcefulness, of responsibility for one's own learning, and of helping others. Through peer teaching, students can find out that teaching involves several different functions, and not just the transmission of information; that learning can take place between parties of equal status, and not just between high-status experts and low-status students; and that the school as an organization is much more than a cafeteria of resources. Many effective teachers already believe this and reinforce their values by using peer teaching in their classrooms. Staffs that set out to humanize their school should seriously consider some formal programs in which students teach one another.

3. Students sharing in decision-making power

We have pointed out that one important feature of the humanized school is the distribution of power among *all* of the participants. One way of sharing legitimate power is to grant students some formal opportunities for teaching one another and helping manage their own learning groups. But as the human systems application (Chapter 3) specifies, the discrete efforts of individual teachers and students generally do not produce viable and lasting changes in the organization itself. If school cultures are to become humanized, students must be encouraged to take a *central* part in managing the functioning of the entire school.

Currently in most public schools, students are granted only token involvement in the administrative processes of the school, if they are given any legitimate power at all. In some schools, however, parents and students have become organized and then negotiated for increased involvement in the functioning of the school. Most often, this process has been initiated by the community itself and not through the planned efforts of the professional educators. Indeed, teachers and administrators have been reticent to encourage student involvement in school decision-making.

There is sufficient evidence from a number of social psychological studies to justify the claim that students should take a more active part in school organizational matters. Studies done especially on industrial organizations have shown that participants who have no legit-

Everybody's part
in humanizing
the school

imate power in their places of work often feel alienated, disinterested, isolated, and uninvolved in the life of the organization. Similar feelings of alienation and isolation are common among students in many schools. It is really up to the educator to encourage students to become an integral and decisive voice in determining the goals, procedures, and policies of the school.

a. Models cf student governance

Three kinds of political structures might be tried to broaden the participation of students in school decision-making. The first is the representative bicameral system, in which two bodies constitute the whole. The students select a student senate and the faculty selects a faculty senate. Policy issues are decided upon separately in each body and then are brought to a linking group for action. The linking group (often called an executive committee or a steering committee) is convened by the principal and has as members students and teachers from their respective senates. This linking group implements policy and integrates it into the daily functioning of the school.

Another model is the representative unicameral system; a single body is formed to represent all of the various groups in the school. The Staples High Governing Board described in Chapter 6 is an example of a unicameral system. Such a governing body typically is kept small so that decision-making is not too cumbersome. Sometimes an executive committee is created out of the larger body to manage administrative details.

A third governance model is the town meeting, in which everyone in the school attends and decisions are made by the entire group. The town meeting is implemented best in small and intimate organizations; many alternative schools use it and it is often used within such subsystems of larger schools as learning groups, units, or houses.

Schools of various size naturally call for different sorts of governance structures. Large schools can easily incorporate several layers of structures; there would most likely be a small group to take care of administrative matters and other small groups throughout the school that could be charged with other sorts of special functions. Only once a month or so would a large group meeting of these senates take place. In smaller schools, the governance structure could consist of as simple a group as the principal and four or five participants elected at large from all relevant groups in the school. Occasional meetings would be held in which the entire school could communicate with such a governing body.

In any sort of school government, all members of the school should have formal opportunities to communicate with members of the governing board. Often a useful technique is to arrange the governing board in the center of a large room with the school participants seated around them, in the form of a theatre-in-the-round. An empty chair or two can be placed in the center circle so that anyone can sit with the governing board for interaction. Hearings can be held so that all participants have a chance to express their views and listen to the views of others. Also, some type of diagnostic instrument can be employed to survey opinions and feelings of the school's membership. The strength of any school governing body will be determined by how closely it remains in interaction with its constituency.

b. Implementing student governance

Ron Lippitt, an early advocate of participatory government in schools, used to surprise his young graduate students by telling of his experiences in preservice teacher training at Southern Illinois University. He would say that he trained the future teachers first to act as benevolent, authoritarian leaders. Then he led them through activities to show how such an authoritarian setting could be changed to a more democratic classroom organization. The reason for this was that the small rural schools of southern Illinois had a normative tradition in support of authoritarian rule by the teachers; newer teachers who were being trained to be more democratic were continually running into difficulties when they countered the prevailing norms and expectations of students and parents. Ron's mission became that of teaching the neophyte teachers to move gradually from authoritarian rule to more democratic arrangements.

One main point here is that students are often unprepared in their attitudes and skills to behave effectively in a democratic school. Teachers will often say that they once decided to democratize their classes but that the new procedures failed because students "wanted more structure," or "didn't know how to handle freedom," or "didn't do much of anything until I (the teacher) took the initiative." Unfortunately, students have learned all too well that the best way to get through school comfortably and successfully is to react in an accepting and passive manner to administrative and teacher demands.

For student government to function effectively, students should be trained initially in effective communication, group process techniques, problem-solving and decision-making. Since joint decision-making is costly in terms of time and energy, some assurance of its success should be built into the early phases of the program by training students in the skills described in Chapters 5, 6, and 7. In particular it is important to review the discussion of organization development in Chapter 6.

A quote from Bane and Jencks (1972) will serve as a link between discussion of the student's part and the parent's part which is the topic of the following section.

...the primary basis of evaluating school should be whether students and teachers find it a satisfactory place to be....

Since there is no evidence that professional educators know appreciably more than parents about what is good for children, it seems reasonable to let parents decide what kind of education their children should have while they are young and to let the children decide as they get older. (P. 41.)

THE PARENT'S PART

Middle-class parents typically have had some influence in relation to schools by virtue of the school's economic dependence on the community. In the early days of America, in fact, schools were formed only after community members supported buying a building as well as paying for a teacher who typically was granted payment in the form of free room and board at someone's home. As schools became larger and districts were created, economic control by some citizens still continued. Indeed, throughout our history richer communities typically have spent more money on schools and have been happier with their schools than poorer communities. (The unequal distribution of money between American school districts is now being seriously challenged in the courts.)

Nowadays, however, almost all school districts—regardless of the wealth or social class of the parents—are being confronted with community dissatisfaction, mostly in the form of defeated budgets and bond issues. Such economic control is, however, futile in attempting to produce humanistic change; a defeated budget or bond issue is not a direct way of improving the quality of interpersonal relationships in the school. Besides helping to build economic influence, concerned parents have been involved in the schools in superficial, social ways. They have served as room mothers (never room fathers), as cooks and bakers, as PTA officers, as helpers at open houses and fairs. They have attended conferences, plays, and musical performances, and it is clear that some of this involvement is important for their child's success in school. Indeed research evidence has shown that a student's perception of how his parents view the importance of school is closely associated with the student's own attitudes about school and his academic performance (Luszki and Schmuck, 1965).

Although baking cookies and attending fairs probably will always be important activities for parents, this last decade has seen changes occurring in the mode of parent participation in the schools. We see three major types of parent participation that hold a great deal of promise for further humanizing relationships in the school: (1) the increasing use of parents as paraprofessionals, (2) community control of schools through political action, and (3) the concept of a community school, which sees the school as a site for learning for all members of the community. In the final analysis the most effective participation is that in which parents are as involved as students and educators in determining what kinds of schools should be created or reformed.

1. Parents as paraprofessionals

Many school districts are already using the services of parents as paraprofessionals; typically these parents are mothers who have not gone to college but who have a strong interest in helping youngsters. The specific uses of paraprofessionals differ from one district to another. Generally, they assist in clerical functions (keeping attendance, typing, mimeographing) or they serve as instructional aides. Sometimes as instructional aides the parents assist the teacher in the classroom, while at other times parents take full responsibility for working with students. Paraprofessional parents may also assume such functions as managing the library or media center, or helping to set up instructional materials, audio-visual aids, and graphics.

Continued and even expanded use of parents as paraprofessionals can help in humanizing the schools. For one thing, the use of parents in lower-class neighborhoods serves as a means of employment for persons who may not have the required credentials. Using parents as paraprofessionals would create new patterns of social mobility for the poor; poor people could become effective employees of schools even without academic credentials. In some communities, career patterns of paraprofessionals already are being established. Some community colleges, for example, offer courses and some school districts have instituted mobility ladders for paraprofessionals so that they can move up into positions of more pay and responsibility.

For another thing, it is obvious that many chores and functions can be performed in the schools quite well by people who do not have the full credentials of teachers. And, at least theoretically, if some of these activities are performed by other personnel, skilled and experienced professionals should have more times to build close, whole-person relationships with their students. Furthermore, the use of people from the immediate neighborhood and from surrounding neighborhoods as paraprofessionals offers increased pluralism in the schools. Thus low-income, minority-group students, who have previously related primarily to the white-middle class teachers, might be tutored by a low-income paraprofessional; and middle-class students, who seldom interact with minority-group citizens, could be tutored by someone from a neighborhood and ethnic background quite different from theirs. As other examples, parents with special hobbies or particular skills could be enlisted to work for short periods of time in the school.

There are other quite different interesting programs for using parents in the schools. In Umpqua, Oregon, for example, parents are employed by the school district to carry out preschool training in their homes. The parents, who are mostly mothers, are given training in developing readiness skills in preschoolers. They visit the homes of the preschool children to meet with the mothers and children together. They suggest activities that the mothers can use routinely with their children (e.g., sorting out all the socks by color, counting the number of people for dinner, separating forks, knives, and spoons, etc.) and provide learning games that the parent and child can play together.

While using paraprofessionals from the community does increase the parent participation and involvement within the school (and we fully recommend it as a source of parent involvement), working in the role of paraprofessional does not necessarily increase the power or voice of the parents in educational decision-making. In most of these programs, the educators still retain most of the power to determine educational goals and programs for the students. Special training of the OD sort, discussed in Chapter 6, can be very helpful, however, in bringing parents and teachers into useful collaboration and shared power regarding goals and programs.

2. Community control through political activities

In many urban communities, school conditions have been assessed by the parents as being so detrimental to the students that they have decided that outsiders can do a better job than the professional educators. Attempts at control have been made by various parent and citizen groups, typically using strategies of confrontation, continual pressure, negotiation, and bargaining. They have initiated meetings, developed proposals, and demanded a part in the decision-making of the school.

One well-known example of community control took place in the Morgan school in Washington, D. C. The Morgan school, located in an ethnically and socio-economically mixed neighborhood, was still considered a legally segregated black school before the 1954 Supreme Court decision. Roots of discontent were apparent in both the white and black parents in the surrounding Adams-Morgan community.

The Washington school district, along with most other large American urban centers, wished to move toward greater decentralization, so that schools would have more local autonomy. The Adams-Morgan community council was organized and took an active part in altering the direction of the Morgan school. They established the school as an experimental community school and also created plans for raising the quality of education; they also developed a plan to increase the parents' legitimate power in the decision-making of the school. Despite many difficulties (high conflict, high teacher turnover, an aborted plan to involve college students in the teaching, and a reverberating teacher's strike in New York City), the Morgan school did gradually take on a new shape and form. It became a team-teaching school with nongraded classrooms. Favorable results included vast new uses of community resources, gains in standardized achievement tests, and a great deal of new and vigorous community participation.

We believe that some aspects of the community control of schools could be quite beneficial to schools in the long run. But community control has some problems of which educators and parents should be aware. First, the required time and energy, and attendant conflict and

Everybody's part
in humanizing
the school

emotional upheaval, may leave deep and long-lasting emotional scars among the participants. Second, parents themselves do not generally sustain the effort over the long haul, and reasonably so. Parents contribute their time, energy, and resources without payment and usually do not stay involved in confrontation activities on a full-time basis. And unfortunately our society has almost always held that educators should do the whole job of teaching. We believe that, along with wielding political power, other forms of parent participation should be found for humanizing relationships in the schools.

3. The community school

Another concept for parent participation resides in a total educational design called the community school. In this concept, the school is viewed as the center for the community where all members can come together as learners. The educational program is not just something for youngsters but is set up for people of all ages. Courses covering such diverse areas as the arts, recreation, cooking, child care, and first aid can be offered at any time of day or night.

The Mott program, in Flint, Michigan, has offered a model for the community school. In one form, the community school envisioned by the Mott program would open up its library doors, its cafeteria lines, and its classrooms to people of all backgrounds and ages. In another form, perhaps close to what Ivan Illich might imagine, all community participants would be seen as school participants. Everyone would be seen as possessing resources and needs, and the function of the school would be to get the needs and resources together. The staff of a community school would diagnose the learning needs in the community, discover the resources, manage the programming and the logistics, and help to organize the learning opportunities of all interested participants.

The community school, at its best, is the sort of humanized organization that we have been arguing for throughout this book. All members, regardless of age or occupation, are defined as learners, all have something to offer, and programs are based on interests, needs, and available resources. *The people themselves are the school.*

Unfortunately, most community schools have not become this sort of organization. School for students continues on in the same old ways; the building is merely used for more activities and the adults come in the evenings. Contact—real contact—between students and adults seldom occurs. Even though some relationships across generations do take place and more people make efficient use of the building, the basic culture of the school has not changed significantly.

4. Recommendations for parent participation

Parents should be involved more than they are now in helping to form the goals and policies of the education of their children. Parents today are better informed and more interested in schools than ever before. Many can talk as peers to the professional educators; others make up for a lack of sophistication with their strong interest. The current rush of popular books about schools elicits new hopes and gives parents some new ideas of what schools could be like. Parents more and more feel that they should be involved in their children's education and that they have a legitimate right to proclaim what they believe schooling should be like.

In our own neighborhood in Eugene, Oregon, we have seen all of these forces at work. An elementary school located in a rather affluent, stable neighborhood near the University of Oregon has accumulated a long record of academic excellence; most of the students surpass the average city scores in achievement; school budgets seldom, if ever, have been defeated in that neighborhood; most students go on to college; and the school lacks the sorts of problems that plague schools in low-income neighborhoods. And yet today this school is having "its problems."

In 1971, a small group of parents became actively dissatisfied with the school. The reasons behind their dissatisfaction of course were varied; some indeed had read Kohl, Silberman, or Dennison and had begun to have some ideas about what schools *could* be like; some were upset by the lack of innovativeness in the building compared with other buildings in the district; some felt troubled over the way their children were being treated by particular teachers; and some felt deflated by paternalistic responses of the principal and certain teachers who made it clear that the business of education was up to the professionals.

The parents commenced a series of coffees and cocktail parties to discuss their concerns informally. At one point at least sixty percent of the total number of parents were in informal communication with one another about the school. A subgroup of parents eventually prepared a list of demands for changes in the school and presented it to the principal. The principal initially was surprised and upset, and felt as if he had lost community confidence. He wanted to protect his teachers but he also thought that he should try to react constructively to the parental demands.

Just previous to this confrontation, a cadre of OD specialists had been formed within the Eugene district to deal with organizational problems. The principal decided to ask these OD specialists for help. The cadre agreed to help and conducted a series of meetings with the parents and the faculty. The cadre started by working with the parents and with the faculty separately to clarify the dissatisfactions, satisfactions, goals, and priorities of each group. Later the two groups met together (more than sixty parents and the entire professional staff attended) with the cadre as a third-party process consultant. The large meeting lasted five hours one evening; problem areas were agreed upon and several small problem-solving groups were formed. The small groups, made up of teachers and parents, met once every two weeks for about five sessions. Finally, the large group convened again to plan for actions to be taken.

At this writing, it is still unclear what will happen. The parents have been organized and energized; the school cannot stay as it was. Although some staff members and parents still feel upset and threatened, most teachers, and most parents have begun to seek new and constructive solutions. A new principal advocates parent participation. Many new projects have already been initiated, such as an artist-in-residence, parents as tutors, a woodworking room, and a new constitution for the PTA. The parents have, in other words, begun to help out within the school in new ways.

Although this project does not prove a great deal, it does indicate that parent involvement in educational decision-making can occur without undermining the professional status of the teachers. The project also showed us that our schools need to be more pluralistic organizationally to account for the variety of goals and needs of students and parents. Since people learn in different ways and under different circumstances, the way for a school district best to assure that all students have optimal conditions for learning is to provide a larger number of educational alternatives.

Parents can be an invaluable resource in helping schools to become functionally more pluralistic. With the involvement of parents, teachers, and students together to join problem-solving, new school structures and procedures can be conceived for increasing educational alternatives. Parents, with the help of administrative personnel, can provide ideas for educational alternatives ranging from traditional schools, community schools, schools with an art focus, and teams with a science focus, to schools within schools having an intercultural and interpersonal emphasis. While it will take time and energy to involve parents, it is appropriate and useful for educators to do so.

Everybody's part
in humanizing
the school

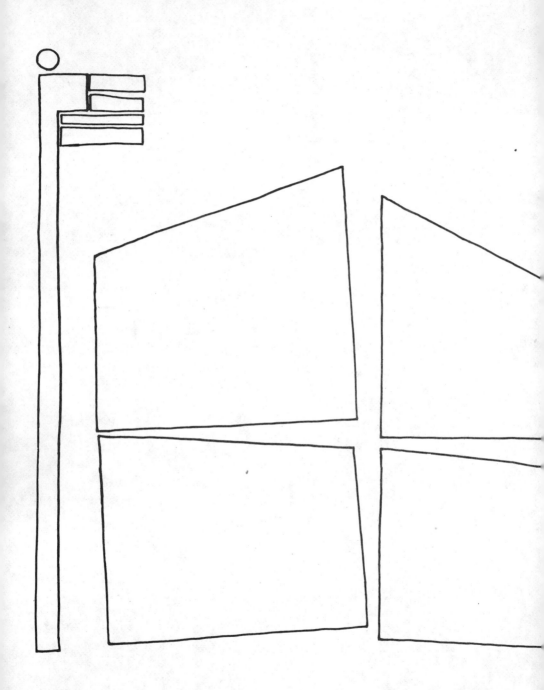

Epilogue

To bring into existence schools that belong to everybody is to redirect the focus of public education and to establish some new guidelines for schools to follow. In this book, we have tried to create such guidelines.

One of the unfortunate outcomes of America's rapid growth into a series of bureaucratized large-scale organizations has been to fragment the lives of participants who live and work within them. Classrooms are separated by age-grades; jobs are separated into professional and special occupation groups; neighborhoods into economic groups; coffee houses are for the freaks; and the Elks' Club is for the straights.

Current trends toward communes and new, more intimate living arrangements are attempts to stem the tide of this depersonalized and fragmented life style. The yearning is to bring more whole-person relationships back into existence. It is not only a yearning of young, long-haired people coming off drugs or into Jesus, but it also is a yearning of the middle-aged and middle-class among us who are trying to develop life styles which bring together their occupations, families, and social concerns into some fusion. There is a search for effective ways of rebuilding a diverse community of people who have become lost and alienated from themselves.

There are many people like us, who share the yearning but are not yet ready to give up their jobs, neighborhoods, social institutions, or schools to live with just a few friends in a secluded setting. We hope that humanistic changes can be brought about within the society as we generally know it today. As teachers, we want schools that are exciting and joyful to work in; as parents we wish to have wider choices for our own children's education; as students we want to have more chances to determine what and how we will learn; and as socially concerned citizens we hope for new political, religious, and educational structures to support increased human interdependence and collaboration. We hope for more ways to bring people together into real, authentic interaction with one another.

References

Alexander, C., and E. Campbell. 1964. "Peer Influences on Adolescent Aspirations and Attainments." *American Sociological Review*, 29, 4, 568-575.

American Association of Colleges for Teacher Education. 1967. *Teacher Productivity*. Washington, D.C.

Ames, A. A., Jr. 1955. *An Interpretative Manual for the Demonstration in the Psychology Research Center*. Princeton, N.J.: Princeton University Press.

Appleberry, James B., and Wayne K. Hoy. 1969, "The Pupil Control Ideology of Professional Personnel in 'Open' and 'Closed' Elementary Schools." *Educational Administration Quarterly*. 3, 74-85.

Argyris, Chris. 1970. *Intervention Theory and Method: A Behavioral Science View*. Menlo Park, Ca.: Addison-Wesley Publishing Co.

Asch, Solomon. 1956. "Studies of Independence and Conformity: I. A. Minority of the One Against a Unanimous Majority," *Psychology Monographs*. 70, No. 9. (Whole No. 416.)

Ashton-Warner, Sylvia. 1972. "Spearpoint." *Saturday Review*, June 24, 1972, 33-39.

Atkinson, John, and Norman Feather. 1966. *A Theory of Achievement Motivation*. New York: John Wiley and Sons.

Backman, Carl, and Paul Secord. 1968. *A Social Psychological View of Education*. New York: Harcourt, Brace, and World, Inc.

Baird, L. L. 1969. "Big School, Small School: A Critical Examination of the Hypotheses." *Journal of Educational Psychology*, 60. 253-260.

Bane, Mary Jo, and Christopher Jencks. 1972. "The Schools and Equal Opportunity." *Saturday Review*, Sept. 16, 1972, 37-42.

Barker, Roger, and Paul Gump. 1964. *Big School, Small School: High School Size and Student Behavior*. Stanford, Ca.: Stanford University Press.

Bassett, G. W. 1970. *Innovation in Primary Education*. New York: Wiley, Interscience.

Benjamins, James. 1950. "Changes in Relation to Influences Upon Self-Conceptualization." *Journal of Abnormal and Social Psychology*, 45, 473-480.

Berelson, Bernard, and Gary A. Steiner. 1964. *Human Behavior: An Inventory of Scientific Findings.* New York: Harcourt, Brace and World, Inc.

Berne, Eric. 1964. *Games People Play.* New York: Grove Press, Inc.

Bessell, Harold. 1972. "Human Development in the Elementary School Classroom," in L. Solomon and B. Berzon (eds.), *New Perspectives on Encounter Groups.* San Francisco: Jossey-Bass, Inc.

Bessell, H., and O. H. Palomares. 1967. *Methods in Human Development.* San Diego: Human Development Training Institute.

Bettelheim, Bruno. 1949. *Love Is Not Enough.* New York: The Free Press.

Bettelheim, Bruno. 1958. "Individual and Mass Behavior in Extreme Situations," in Eleanor Maccoby (ed.), *Readings in Social Psychology.* 3rd ed. New York: Holt, Rinehart, and Winston, 300-310.

Bigelow, Ronald. 1971. "Changing Classroom Climate Through Organization Development," in Richard Schmuck and Matthew Miles (eds.), *Organization Development in Schools.* Palo Alto, Ca.: National Press Books, 71-86.

Bion, W. R. 1948. "Experiences in Groups I." *Human Relations* I: 314-320.

Bloom, Benjamin, J. Thomas Hastings, and George F. Madaus. 1971. *Handbook on Formative and Summative Evaluation of Student Learning.* New York: McGraw-Hill Book Co.

Bradford, Leland, Jack Gibb, and Kenneth Benne. 1964. *T-Group Theory and Laboratory Method.* New York: John Wiley and Sons, Inc.

Bradford, Luther E. 1959. "Elementary School Teachers: Their Problems and Supervisory Assistance." *Educational Administration Supplement*, 45, 102-106.

Brophy, Jere, and Thomas Good. 1970. Teachers' Communication of Differential Expectations for Children's Classroom Performance." *Journal of Educational Psychology*, 61, 5, 365-374.

Brown, George. 1971. *Human Teaching for Human Learning: An Introduction to Confluent Education.* New York: Viking Press.

Bruner, Jerome. 1961. *The Process of Education.* Cambridge, Mass.: Harvard University Press.

Buber, Martin. 1958. *I and Thou.* New York: Charles Scribner's Sons.

Buckley, Walter. 1967. *Sociology and Modern Systems Theory.* Englewood Cliffs, N.J.: Prentice-Hall, Inc.

Carbaga, Diane. 1970. "The Story of the Monmouth Day School." *Outside the Net*, 1, 6-9.

Campbell, John P., and Marvin D. Dunnette. 1968. "Effectiveness of T-Group Experience in Managerial Training and Development." *Psychological Bulletin*, 70, 2, 73-104.

Charters, W. W. 1963. "The Social Background of Teachers," in N. Gage (ed.), *Handbook of Research on Teaching.* Chicago: Rand, McNally and Co., 715-813.

Chesler, Mark, and Robert Fox. 1966. *Role-Playing Methods in the Classroom.* Chicago: Science Research Associates.

Chesler, Mark, Richard Schmuck, and Ronald Lippitt. 1963. "The Principal's Role in Facilitating Innovation." *Theory into Practice*, 2, 5, 269-277.

Chesler, Mark, and John Lohman. 1971. "Changing Schools Through Student Advocacy," in R. Schmuck and M. Miles (eds.), *Organization Development in Schools.* Palo Alto, Ca.: National Press Books, 185-212.

Coffman, L. D. 1911. "The Social Composition of the Teaching Population." *Teachers College Contributions to Education.* No. 41.

Coleman, James. 1966. *Equality of Educational Opportunity.* Washington, D.C.: U.S. Government Printing Office.

Coleman, James. 1972. "The Children have Outgrown the Schools." *Psychology Today,* 5, 9 (February 1972), 72.

Collins, Barry, and Burt Raven. 1969. "Group Structure: Attraction, Coalitions, Communication, and Power," in *Handbook of Social Psychology.* Reading, Mass.: Addison-Wesley, Vol. 4, Chap. 30.

Conant, James B. 1959. *The American High School Today.* New York: McGraw-Hill.

Conant, James B. 1964. *The Education of American Teachers.* New York: Mc-Graw-Hill.

Cook, W. W., C. H. Leeds, and R. Callis. 1951. *The Minnesota Teacher Attitude Inventory.* New York: Psychological Corporation.

Cooperative Project for Educational Development (COPED). 1970. *Final Report.* COPED Data Analysis Project. Project No. 8-0069. Grant No. OEG-3-8-080069-0043 (010). Washington, D.C.: Office of Education. (Vol. I, *Research Outcomes.* Vol. II, *Case Studies.* Vol III, *Diagnosing the Professional Climate of Your School.*)

Criswell, Eleanor, and Severin Peterson. 1972. "The Whole Soul Catalog." *Psychology Today.* 5, 11, 57-64.

Cuban, Larry. 1964. "The Cardozo Peace Corps Project. Experiment in Urban Education." *The Sociology of Education.* 28, 446-449.

Cuban, Larry 1971 "An Open Letter to Bill Cosby." Reprinted from the D. C. Gazette in *Outside the Net,* 3, 6.

Cutler, Richard, and Elton McNeil. 1966. *Mental Health Consultation in the Schools: A Research Analysis.* Ann Arbor: Dept. of Psychology, University of Michigan.

Dennison, George. 1969. *The Lives of Children.* New York: Random House.

Dentler, Robert A. 1966. "Equality of Educational Opportunity—A Special Review." *Urban Review,* 1, 5, 27-29.

DeVita, Joseph. 1963. "A Stimulating Technique: Teachers Observe Other Teachers." *Clearing House.* 37, 549-550.

Dewey, John. 1904. "The Relation of Theory to Practice in Education." *Third Yearbook, Part I.* Bloomington, Ill.: Public School Publishing Co.

Dobson, Russell, Ron Goldenberg, and Bill Elsom. 1972. "Pupil Control Ideology and Teacher Influence in the Classroom." *Journal of Educational Research,* 66, 2 (October 1972), 76-80.

Dubin, Robert, G. Homans, F. Mann, and D. Miller. 1965. *Leadership and Productivity: Some Facts of Industrial Life.* San Francisco: Chandler Publishing Co.

Dutton, Wilbur H., and Reginald H. Hammond. 1966. "Two In-Service Mathematics Programs for Elementary School Teachers." *California Journal of Educational Research,* 17, 63-67.

ERIC clearing house on Educational Administration. 1970. *Alternative Organizational Forms.* Eugene, Oregon: University of Oregon. EA-003-056.

Erickson, Erik H. 1950. *Childhood and Society.* New York: W. W. Norton and Co.

Eysenck, Hans. 1952. "The Effects of Psychotherapy: An Evaluation." *Journal of Consulting Psychology*, 16, 319-334.

Fargo, George, Charlene Behrns, and Patricia Nolen. 1970. *Behavior Modification in the Classroom.* Belmont, Ca.: Wadsworth Publishing Co., Inc.

Farina, Amerigo, and Kenneth Ring. 1970. "The Influence of Perceived Mental Illness on Interpersonal Relations," in Henry Wechsler, Leonard Solomon, and Bernard Kramer (eds.), *Social Psychology and Mental Health*. New York: Holt, Rinehart, and Winston, Inc., 567-572.

Festinger, Leon A. 1954. "A Theory of Social Comparison Process." *Human Relations*, 8, 117-140.

Festinger, Leon A. 1957. *Theory of Cognitive Dissonance*. Evanston, Ill.: Row, Peterson and Co.

Flacks, Richard. 1967. "Student Activists: Result Not Revolt." *Psychology Today*, 6, 6 (Oct. 1967), 18-24.

Flanders, Ned, and S. Havumaki. 1960. "The Effect of Teacher-Pupil Contacts Involving Praise on the Sociometric Choices of Students." *Journal of Educational Psychology*. 51, 65-68.

Fleming, Carl. 1969. "Pupil Tutors and Tutees Learn Together." *Today's Education*. 58, 22-24.

Foster, Marcus. 1971. *Making Schools Work*. Philadelphia: Westminster Press.

Fox, Robert, Margaret Luszki, and Richard Schmuck. 1966. *Diagnosing Classroom Learning Environments*. Chicago: Science Research Associates.

Fox, Robert, Charles Jung, Richard Schmuck, Miriam Ritvo, and Elmer Van Egmond. 1973. *Diagnosing Professional Climate of Schools*. Fairfax, Va.: NTL Learning Resources Corp.

French, Elizabeth. 1958. "Effects of the Interaction of Motivation and Feedback on Task Performance," in J. Atkinson (ed.), *Motives in Fantasy Action and Society*. New York: Van Nostrand, 400-408.

French, John R. P., and Burt Raven. 1959. "The Bases of Social Power," in D. Cartwright (ed.), *Studies in Social Power*. Ann Arbor: Institute for Social Research, 150-168.

Friedlander, Fred. 1968. "A Comparative Study of Consulting Processes and Group Development." *Journal of Applied Behavioral Science*, 4, 4, 377-400.

Fromm, Eric. 1962. *The Art of Loving*. New York: Bantam Books.

Fuchs, Estelle. 1969. *Teachers Talk: Views from Inside City Schools*. Garden City, N.Y.: Anchor Books, Doubleday and Co., Inc.

Gardner, John. 1963. *Self-Renewal: The Individual and the Innovative Society*. New York: Harper and Row.

Geiger, Russell M. 1970. "Behavior Modification with a Total Class: A Case Report." *Journal of School Psychology*, 8, 2, 103-106.

Getzels, Jacob, and Herbert Thelen. 1960. "The Classroom Group as a Unique Social System," in N. Henry (ed.), *The Dynamics of Instructional Groups*, 59th Yearbook, Part 2. Chicago: National Society for the Study of Education.

Gibb, Jack. 1961. "Defense Level and Influence Potential in Small Groups," in Luigi Petrillo and Bernard Bass (eds.), *Leadership and Interpersonal Behavior*. New York: Holt, Rinehart and Winston, 66-81.

Gibb, Jack. 1964a. "Climate for Trust Formation," in L. Bradford, J. Gibb, and K. Benne (eds.), *T-Group Theory: A Laboratory Method*. New York: John Wiley and Sons, 279-309.

Gibb, Jack. 1964b. "Is Help Helpful?" *Forum* (February 1964) Association of Secretaries of the YMCA.

Gibb, Jack. 1971. "The Effects of Human Relations Training," in Bergin, Allen E. and Sol L. Garfield (eds.), *Handbook of Psychotherapy and Behavior Change: An Empirical Analysis*. New York: John Wiley and Sons. 839-862.

Glidewell, Jack, M. Kantor, L. Smith, and L. Stringer. 1966. "Classroom Socialization and Social Structure," in Martin Hoffman and Lois Hoffman (eds.), *Revew of Child Development Research*. New York: Russell Sage Foundation, 221-257.

Goldhammer, Robert, 1969. *Clinical Supervision*. New York: Holt, Rinehart, and Winston, Inc.

Goodacre, D. M. 1953. "Group Characteristics of Good and Poor Performing Combat Units." *Sociometry*, 16, 168-178.

Gorman, Alfred E. 1969. *Teachers and Learners: The Interactive Process of Education*. Boston: Allyn and Bacon.

Grier, William H., and Price M. Cobbs. 1968. *Black Rage*. New York: Bantam Books.

Gross, Neal, and Robert Herriott. 1965. *Staff Leadership in Public Schools*. New York: John Wiley and Sons.

Gross, Neal, Joseph B. Giacquinta, and Marilyn Bernstein. 1970. "Failure to Implement a Major Organizational Innovation," in Matthew Miles and W. W. Charters (eds.), *Learning in Social Settings*. Boston: Allyn and Bacon, Inc. 691-705.

Guskin, Alan, and Samuel Guskin. 1970. *A Social Psychology of Education*. Menlo Park, Ca.: Addison-Wesley Publishing Co.

Halpin, Andrew W. and Don B. Croft. 1963. *Organizational Climate of Schools*. Chicago: Midwest Administrative Center, University of Chicago.

Hargreaves, David H. 1967. *Social Relations in a Secondary School*. New York: Humanities Press.

Harris, Thomas A. 1969. *I'm OK, You're OK, A Practical Guide to Transactional Analysis*. New York: Harper and Row.

Heinicke, C., and Robert Bales. 1953. "Developmental Trends in the Structure of Small Groups." *Sociometry*. 16, 7-38.

Hentoff, Nat. 1966. *Our Children Are Dying*. New York: Viking Press, Inc.

Herndon, James, 1965. *The Way It Spozed To Be*. New York: Bantam Books.

Herndon, James, 1971. *How to Survive in Your Native Land*. New York: Simon and Schuster.

Herriott, Robert, and N. St. John. 1966. *Social Class and the Urban School*. New York: John Wiley and Sons.

Hoehn, A. J., and E. Saltz. 1956. "Effect of Teacher-Student Interviews on Classroom Achievement." *Journal of Educational Psychology*, 47, 424-435.

Hornstein, Harvey, D. Callahan, E. Fisch, and B. A. Benedict. 1967. "Influence and Satisfaction in Organizations: A Replication." Unpublished paper. New York: Teachers College.

Hughes, E., Heinz Becker, and Blanche Geer. 1962. "Student Culture and Academic Effort," in N. Sanford, *The American College.* New York: Wiley and Sons, Inc., 515-530.

Iannoccone, Laurence. No date. "Student Teaching: A Transitional Stage in the Making of a Teacher." Unpublished mimeographed paper, New York University.

Illich, Ivan. 1970. *Deschooling Society.* New York: Harpar and Row.

Institute for Development of Educational Activities, Inc. (IDEA). 1971. *Learning in the Small Group.* Suite 9950, 1100 Glendon Ave., Los Angeles, Ca.: 90024.

Iscoe, Ira, John Pierce-Jones, Thomas S. Friedman, and Joyce McGehearty. 1967. "Some Strategies in Mental Health Consultation; A Brief Description of a Project and Some Preliminary Results." In Cowne, Gardner, and Zax (eds.), *Emergent Approaches to Mental Health Problems.* New York: Appleton-Century-Crofts, 307-330.

Jacoby, Susan. 1972. *Saturday Review,* April 1, 1972, 49-53.

Jahoda, Marie. 1958. *Current Concepts of Positive Mental Health.* New York: Basic Books, Inc.

Jencks, Christopher, Marshall Smith, Henry Ackland, Mary Jo Bane, David Cohen, Herbert Gintis, Barbara Heyns, and Stephen Michelson. 1972. *Inequality: A Reassessment of the Effect of Family and Schooling in America.* New York: Basic Books, Inc.

Johnson, David. 1970. *The Social Psychology of Education.* New York: Holt, Rinehart, and Winston, Inc.

Katz, Daniel, and Robert Kahn. 1966. *The Social Psychology of Organizations.* New York: John Wiley and Sons.

Katz, Michael B. 1971. *Class Bureaucracy and Schools: The Illusion of Educational Change in America.* New York: Praeger.

Klausmeier, Herbert, and Roland Pellegrin. 1971. "The Multiunit School: A Differentiated Staffing Approach," in David Bushnell and Donald Rappaport (eds.), *Planned Change in Education.* New York: Harcourt, Brace, Jovanovich, Inc., 107-126.

Klausmeier, H., M. Quilling, and J. Sorenson. 1971. "The Development and Evaluation of the Multiunit Elementary School." Technical Report No. 158. Wisconsin Center for Cognitive Learning. University of Wisconsin.

Klein, Donald C. 1967. "Consultation Processes as a Method for Improving Teaching," in Eli Bower and William Hollister (eds.), *Behavioral Science Frontiers in Education.* New York: John Wiley and Sons.

Knoblock, Peter, and Arnold Goldstein. 1971. *The Lonely Teacher.* Boston: Allyn and Bacon.

Kohl, Herbert. 1969. *The Open Classroom: A Practical Guide to a New Way of Teaching.* New York: A New York Review Book.

Kohlberg, Lawrence, and Rochelle Mayer. 1972. "Development as the Aim of Education." *Harvard Educational Review.* 42, 4, 449-496.

Kolb, David, and Richard Boyatzis. 1970. "On the Dynamics of the Helping Relationship." *The Journal of Applied Behavioral Science,* 3, 6, 267-289.

Kolb, David, Irwin Rubin, and James McIntyre. 1971. *Organizational Psychology: An Experimental Approach.* Englewood Cliffs, N.J.: Prentice-Hall, Inc.

Kozol, Jonathan. 1967. *Death at an Early Age.* Boston: Houghton Mifflin Co.

Kozol, Jonathan. 1972. *Free Schools.* New York: Houghton Mifflin Co.

Krathwohl, David R., Benjamin S. Bloom, and Bertrand B. Masia. 1964. *Taxonomy of Educational Objectives: The Classification of Educational Goals. Handbook 2. Affective Domain.* New York: McKay.

Landry, Thomas. 1959 "Louisiana Supervisors Examine Their Practices." *Educational Administration Supplement*, 45, 305-311.

Lewin, Kurt, Ronald Lippitt, and Ralph White. 1939. "Patterns of Aggressive Behavior in Experimentally Created 'Social Climates.'" *Journal of Social Psychology*, 10, 271-299.

Lewis, Howard, and Harold Streitfeld. 1970. *Growth Games: How To Tune in Yourself, Your Family, Your Friends.* New York: Harcourt, Brace, Jovanovich, Inc.

Lieberman, M. 1956. *Education as a Profession.* Englewood Cliffs, N.J.: Prentice-Hall.

Lighthall, Frederick, F. 1969. "A Social Psychologist for School Systems." *Psychology in the Schools*, 6, 1, 3-12.

Likert, Rensis. 1961. *New Patterns of Management.* New York: McGraw-Hill Book Co., Inc.

Lippitt, Peggy, and John Lohman. 1965. "Cross-Age Relationships: An Educational Resource." *Children*, 12, 113-117.

Lippitt, Ronald. 1940. "An Experimental Study of the Effect of Democratic and Authoritarian Group Atmospheres." *University of Iowa Studies in Child Welfare*, 16, 43-195.

Lowen, Alexander. 1967. *The Betrayal of the Body.* New York: Macmillan Co.

Luft, Joseph. 1970. *Group Processes: An Introduction to Group Dynamics.* Palo Alto, Ca.: National Press Books.

Luszki, Margaret B., and Richard Schmuck. 1965. "Pupil Perception of Parental Attitudes Toward School." *Mental Hygiene*, 49, 2, 296-307.

Mackie, Romaine R. 1965a. "Converging Circles—Education of the Handicapped and Some General Federal Programs." *Exceptional Child*, 31, 250-255.

Mackie, Romaine, R. 1965b. "Spotlighting Advances in Special Education." *Exceptional Child*, 32, 77-81.

Maier, Norman. 1962. "Leadership Principles for Problem-Solving Conferences." *Michigan Business Review*, 14, 8-15.

March, James, and Herbert Simon. 1958. *Organizations.* New York: John Wiley and Sons.

Marin, Peter. 1969. "The Open Truth and Fiery Vehemence of Youth: A Sort of Soliloquy." *The Center Magazine*, 2, 1, 61-74.

Martell, George. 1971. "Class Bias in Toronto Schools: The Park School Community Council Brief." *This Magazine Is About Schools*, 5, 4 (Fall/Winter), 7-35.

Maslow, Abraham M. 1967. "Self-Actualization and Beyond," in Bugental, James (ed.), *Challenge of Humanistic Psychology.* New York: McGraw-Hill Book Co.

May, Rollo. 1969. *Love and Will.* New York: Norton.

Mayer, Martin. 1961. *The Schools.* New York: Harper and Bros.

McGregor, Douglas. 1967. *The Professional Manager.* New York: McGraw-Hill Book Co.

McKeachie, Wilbert, D. Pollie, and J. Spiesman. 1955. "Relieving Anxiety in Classroom Exams." *Journal of Abnormal and Social Psychology*, 50, 93-98.

McLuhan, Marshall, and Quentin Fiore. 1967. *The Medium is the Massage*. New York: Bantam Books.

Meacham, Merle, and Allen E. Wiesen. 1970. *Changing Classroom Behavior: A Manual for Precision Teaching*. Scranton, Pa.: International Textbook Co.

Meadow, Arnold S., Sidney Parnes, and Hayne Reese. 1959. "Influence of Brainstorming Instructions and Problem Sequence on Creative Problem-Solving Tests." *Journal of Applied Psychology*, 43, 413-416.

Meyers, Roger A. 1971. "Research on Education and Vocational Counseling," in Allen Bergin and Sol Garfield (eds.), *Handbook of Psychotherapy and Behavior Change: An Empirical Analysis*. New York: John Wiley.

Miles Matthew. 1959. *Learning to Work in Groups: A Program Guide for Educational Leaders*. New York: Bureau of Publications, Teachers College, Columbia University.

Miles, Matthew. 1964. *Innovation in Education*. New York: Bureau of Publications, Teachers College, Columbia University.

Miller, Daniel, and Guy Swanson. 1958. *The Changing American Parent*. New York: John Wiley and Sons, Inc.

Miller, James. 1955. "Toward a General Theory for the Behavioral Sciences." *American Psychologist*, 10, 513-531.

Miller, James. 1965. "Living Systems: Basic Concepts; Structure and Process; Cross Level Hypotheses." *Behavioral Science*, 10: 193-237, 337-379, 380-411.

Minuchin, Patricia, Barbara Biber, Edna Shapiro, and Herbert Zimiles. 1969. *The Psychological Impact of School Experience*. New York: Basic Books, Inc.

Myers, Karin. 1972. "The Self Concept of Students in Individually Prescribed Instruction." Paper presented at the Annual Meeting of th AERA, Chicago, Ill.

National Elementary Principals' Journal, Vol. 52, No. 3 (Nov. 1972).

Nelson, Jack. 1971. *Collegial Supervision in Multiunit Schools*. Unpublished doctoral dissertation, University of Oregon, Eugene, Ore.

Nelson, Margaret. 1972. *Attitudes of Intermediate School Children toward Substitute Teachers Who Receive Feedback on Pupil-Desired Behavior*. Unpublished doctoral dissertation, University of Oregon, Eugene, Ore.

Newman, Ruth. 1967. *Psychological Consultation in the Schools*. New York: Basic Books, Inc.

Northwest Regional Educational Laboratory. 1971-1972. *Research Utilizing Problem Solving*. Portland, Ore.: NWREL.

Northwest Regional Educational Laboratory. 1971-1972. *Preparing Educational Training Consultants*. Portland, Ore.: NWREL.

Noyes, Kathryn J., and Gordon L. McAndrew. 1968. "Is This What Schools Are For?" *Saturday Review*, Dec. 21, 1968.

Nyberg, David. 1971. *Tough and Tender Learning*. Palo Alto, Ca.: National Press Books.

Ohme, Herman. 1972. "Needed: Exportable Models of Significant Change in Education." *Phi Delta Kappan*, June 1972, 655-658.

Olton, Robert M., and Richard S. Crutchfield. 1969. "Developing Skills of Productive Thinking," in Mussen, Paul, Jonas Langer, and Martin Covington (eds.), *Trends and Issues in Developmental Psychology*. New York: Holt, Rinehart, and Winston.

Parker, John. 1971. "Teacher Training at Adams." *Phi Delta Kappan*, May 1971, 520-522.

Parsons, Talcott, and Edward Shils (eds.), 1952. *Toward a General Theory of Action.* Cambridge, Mass.: Harvard University Press.

Parsons, Talcott, and Robert Bales. 1955. *Family, Socialization and Interaction Process.* New York: Free Press.

Patterson, C. H. 1973. *Humanistic Education.* New York: Prentice-Hall, Inc.

Patterson, Gerald R. 1971. "Behavioral Intervention Procedures in the Classroom and in the Home," in Allen Bergin and Sol Garfield (eds.), *Handbook of Psychotherapy and Behavior Change: An Empirical Analysis.* New York: John Wiley and Sons. 751-775.

Pearson, Gerald. 1954. *Psychoanalysis and the Education of the Child.* New York: Norton Book Co.

Pendel, Mary Helen, and Erin Hennessey (eds.). 1971. *On The Move.* 2021 North Western Avenue, Los Angeles, Ca. 90027.

Perls, Fredericks. 1969. *Gestalt Therapy Verbatim.* Lafayette, Ca.: Real People Press.

Postman, Neil. 1970. "The Politics of Reading." *Harvard Educational Review,* 40, 2 (May 1970).

Postman, Neil, and Charles Weingarten. 1971. *The Soft Revolution.* New York: Delacorte Press.

Price, James L. 1972. *Handbook of Organizational Measurement.* Lexington, Mass.: D. C. Heath and Co.

Rasberry, Salli, and Robert Greenway. 1970. *Rasberry Exercises—How to Start Your Own School and Make a Book.* Freestone, Ca.: Freestone Publishing Co.

Redl, Fritz. 1959a, "Strategy and Techniques of the Life-Space Interview." *American Journal of Orthopsychiatry*, 29, 1-18.

Redl, Fritz. 1959b. "The Concept of Therapeutic Milieu." *American Journal of Orthopsychiatry*, 29, 721-727.

Redl, Fritz, and William Wattenberg. 1951. *Mental Hygiene in Teaching.* New York: Harcourt, Brace, and World.

Reich, Charles. 1971. *The Greening of America.* New York: Bantam Books.

Reisman, David, Nathan Glazer and Reuel Denney. 1950. *The Lonely Crowd.* New York: Doubleday Anchor Books.

Reissman, Frank. 1962. *The Culturally Deprived Child.* New York: Harper and Bros.

Resnick, Henry. 1971. "Promise of Change in North Dakota." *Saturday Review,* 54, 16 (April 17, 1971), 67.

Reynolds, Maynard. 1969. "Special Education," in R. Ebel (ed.), *Encyclopedia of Educational Research.* Toronto: Collier-Macmillan Canada, Ltd.

Rivlin, Harry N. 1965. "New Ways of Preparing Teachers for Urban Schools," in Michael D. Usdan and Frederick Bertolaet (eds.), *Development of School-University Programs for the Pre-Service Education of Teachers for the Disadvantaged Through Teacher Education Centers.* Cooperative Research Project No. f-068. Washington, D.C.: Office of Education, U.S. Dept. of Health, Education and Welfare, 77-99.

Rogers, Carl. 1969. *Freedom to Learn.* Columbus, O.: Charles E. Merrill, 303-373.

Rogers, Carl. 1970. *Carl Rogers on Encounter Groups.* New York: Harper and Row.

Rosenthal, Robert, and Loreen Jacobson. 1968. *Pygmalion in the Classroom.* New York: Holt, Rinehart, and Winston.

Rothney, John W. 1963. *Educational Vocational and Social Performance of Counseled and Uncounseled Youth Ten Years After High School.* Cooperative Research Project SAE 9231. Madison, Wisconsin: University of Wisconsin Press.

Runkel, Philip. 1962. "The Effectiveness of Guidance in Today's Schools: A Survey in Illinois." Unpublished report. ERIC No. Ed002998.

Runkel, Philip, Roger Harrison, and Margaret Runkel. 1969. *The Changing College Classroom.* San Francisco: Jossey-Bass, Inc.

Sanford, Nevitt (ed.). 1962. *The American College.* New York: John Wiley and Sons, Inc.

Sarason, S., K. Davidson, F. Lighthall, R. Waite, and Britton Ruebush. 1960. *Anxiety in Elementary School Children.* New York: John Wiley and Sons.

Sarbin, Theodore. 1970. "On the Futility of the Proposition That Some People Be Labeled Mentally Ill," in Henry Wechsler, Leonard Solomon, Bernard Kramer (eds.), *Social Psychology and Mental Health.* New York: Holt, Rinehart, and Winston, Inc. 52-60.

Savage, William W. 1952. *Educational Consultants and Their Work in Mid-Western State Departments of Education.* Chicago: Mid-West Administration Center, University of Chicago.

Savage, William W. 1959. *Consultative Services to Local School Systems.* Chicago: Mid-West Administration Center, University of Chicago.

Schein, Edgar H. 1969. *Process Consultation: Its Role in Organization Development.* Reading, Mass.: Addison-Wesley.

Schmuck, Richard. 1963. "Some Relationships of Peer Liking Patterns in the Classroom to Pupil Attitudes and Achievement." *School Review,* 71, 337-359.

Schmuck, Richard. 1966. "Some Aspects of Classroom Social Climate." *Psychology in the Schools.* 3, 1, 59-65.

Schmuck, Richard. 1968. "Helping Teachers Improve Classroom Group Processes." *Journal of Applied Behavioral Science,* 4, 4, 401-435.

Schmuck, Richard. 1971. "Developing Teams of Organizational Specialists," in Schmuck, R. and M. Miles (eds.), *Organization Development in Schools.* Palo Alto, Ca.: National Press Books.

Schmuck, Richard, Mark Chesler, and Ronald Lippitt. 1966. *Problem-Solving To Improve Classroom Learning.* Chicago: Science Research Associates.

Schmuck, Richard, and Philip Runkel. 1970. *Organizational Training for a School Faculty.* Eugene, Ore.: Center for the Advanced Study of Educational Administration, University of Oregon.

Schmuck, Richard, and Matthew Miles. 1971. *Organization Development in Schools.* Palo Alto, Ca.: National Press Books.

Schmuck, Richard, and Patricia Schmuck. 1971. *Group Processes in the Classroom.* Dubuque, Iowa: Wm. C. Brown.

Schmuck, Richard, Philip Runkel, Steven Saturen, Ronald Martell, and C. Brooklyn Derr. 1972. *Handbook of Organization Development in Schools.* Palo Alto, Ca.: National Press Books.

Schutz, William. 1958. *FIRO: A Three Dimensional Theory of Interpersonal Relations.* New York: Holt, Rinehart, and Winston.

Schutz, William. 1966. *The Interpersonal Underworld*. Palo Alto, Ca.: Science and Behavior Books.

Seidman, Jerome M. 1963. *Education for Mental Health: A Book of Readings*. New York: Thomas Y. Crowell Co.

Sexton, Patricia. 1961. *Education and Income: Inequality of Opportunity in Our Public Schools*. New York: Viking Press.

Shaevitz, Morton H., and Donald J. Barr. 1968. *The Assessment of Change: Interim Report to Western Behavioral Science Institute*. La Jolla, Ca.: Study of the Person. Unpublished mimeographed paper.

Sherif, M., O. Harvey, B. White, W. Hood, and C. Sherif. 1961. *Intergroup Conflict and Cooperation*. Norman, Okla.: University of Oklahoma Book Exchange.

Shils, Edward, and Morris Janowitz. 1948. "Cohesion and Disintegration in the Wehrmacht in World War II." *Public Opinion Quarterly*, 12, 1, 280-315.

Silberman, Charles E. 1970. *Crisis in the Classroom: The Remaking of American Education*. New York: Random House.

Simon, Sidney, Leland Howe, and Howard Kirschenbaum. 1972. *Values Clarification: A Handbook of Practical Strategies for Teachers and Students*. New York: Hart Publishing Co.

Skinner, B. F. No date. "Contingency Management in the Classroom." Unpublished mimeographed paper.

Skinner, B. F. 1968. *The Technology of Teaching*. New York: Appleton-Century-Crofts.

Skinner, B. F. 1971. *Beyond Freedom and Dignity*. New York: Alfred A. Knopf.

Smith, Mortimer, Richard Peck, and George Weber. 1972. *A Consumer's Guide to Educational Innovation*. Washington, D.C.: Council for Better Education.

Solomon, Lawrence, and Betty Berzon. 1972. *New Perspectives on Encounter Groups*. San Francisco: Jossey-Bass, Inc.

Spence, K., and J. Taylor. 1953. "The Relation of Conditioned Response Strength to Anxiety in Normal, Neurotic and Psychotic Subjects." *Journal of Experimental Psychology*, 45, 265-272.

Stanford, Gene, and Barbara D. Stanford. 1969. *Learning Discussion Skills Through Games*. New York: Citation Press.

Stolurow, Lawrence. 1969. "Programmed Instruction," in Robert Ebel, Victor Noll, and Roger Bauer (eds.), *Encyclopedia of Educational Research*. New York: Macmillan Co., 1017-1022.

Stufflebeam, Daniel L. 1971. *Educational Evaluation and Decision Making*. Itasca, Ill.: F. E. Peacock.

Terreberry, Shirley. 1968. "The Evolution of Organizational Environments." *Administrative Science Quarterly*, 12, 4 (March 1968), 590-613.

Thelen, Herbert. 1954. *Dynamics of Groups at Work*. Chicago: University of Chicago Press.

Thelen, Herbert. 1960. *Education and the Human Quest*. New York: Harper and Brothers.

Thompson, George, and C. W. Hunnicutt. 1944. "The Effect of Repeated Praise or Blame on the Work Achievement of 'Introverts' and 'Extroverts'." *Journal of Educational Psychology*, 35, 257-266.

Thorndike, Edward. 1903. *Educational Psychology*. Lemcke and Buechner.

Thorndike, Edward. 1912. *Educational Psychology*. Teachers College, Columbia University. Quoted in Lawrence M. Stolurow, "Programmed Instruction," in Robert Ebel (ed.), 1969, *Encyclopedia of Educational Research* (New York: Macmillan Company), 1017-1022.

Thorndike, Robert. 1968. "Review of Rosenthal, R. and Jacobson, L., *Pygmalion in the Classroom.*" *American Educational Research Journal*, 5, 708.

Trow, Clark, Alvin Zander, William Morse, and David Jenkins. 1950. "Psychology of Group Behavior: The Class as a Group." *Journal of Educational Psychology*, October 1950, 322-338.

Tuckman, Bruce, and W. Oliver. 1968. "Effectiveness of Feedback to Teachers as a Function of Source." *Journal of Educational Psychology*, 59, 4, 297-301.

Usdan, Michael D., and Frederick Bertolaet. 1966. *Teachers for the Disadvantaged*. New York: Follett.

Walberg, Herbert J. 1967. "Changes in the Self-Concept During Teacher Training." *Psychology in the Schools*, 4, 14-21.

Walberg, Herbert. 1968a. "Teacher Personality and Classroom Climate." *Psychology in the Schools*, 5, 163-169.

Walberg, Herbert. 1968b. "Structural and Affective Aspects of Classroom Climate." *Psychology in the Schools*, 5, 247-253.

Walberg, Herbert. 1969. "Predicting Class Learning: An Approach to the Class as a Social System." *American Educational Research Journal*, 6, 4, 529-542.

Walberg, Herbert, and Gary Anderson. 1968. "The Achievement—Creativity Dimension and Classroom Climate." *Journal of Creative Behavior*, 2, 4, 529-542.

Waller, W. 1932. *The Sociology of Teaching*. New York: John Wiley and Sons.

Watts, Alan. 1961. *The Book*. New York: Collier.

Willower, Donald J. The Teacher Sub-Culture. ERIC microfiche. ED-020-588.

Willower, Donald J., Terry L. Eidell, and Wayne K. Hoy. 1967. *The School and Pupil Control Ideology*. Pennsylvania State Studies Monograph, No. 24. University Park, Pa.: The Pennsylvania State University.

Willower, Donald J., Wayne K. Hoy, and Terry L. Eidell. 1967. "The Counselor and the School as a Social Organization." *Personnel and Guidance Journal*, 46, 228-234.

Willower, Donald J., and Ronald G. Jones. 1967. "Control in an Educational Organization," in J. D. Raths (ed.), *Studying Teaching*. Englewood Cliffs, N.J.: Prentice-Hall, Inc.

Wilson, A. 1959. "Residential Segregation of Social Classes and Aspirations of High School Boys." *American Sociological Review*, 836-845.

Wise, Arthur. 1969. *Rich Schools, Poor Schools; The Promise of Equal Educational Opportunity*. Chicago: University of Chicago Press.

Wocha, Peter. 1971. Letter in *Big Rock Candy Mountain*. 2, 2 (Fall 1971), 33.

Wolfe, D. 1954. *America's Resources of Specialized Talent*. New York: Harper Bros.

Yalom, Irvin, Morton Lieberman, and Matthew Miles. 1973. *Encounter Groups: First Facts*. New York: Basic Books, Inc.

Zand, Dale E. 1972. "Trust and Managerial Problem Solving." *Administrative Science Quarterly*, 17, 2, 229-239.

Zahorik, John, and Dale Brubaker. 1972. *Toward More Humanistic Instruction*. Dubuque, Iowa: Wm. C. Brown. Co.

Index

Michelson, Stephen, 370
Micro-teaching, 286
Middle school, 258
Miles, Matthew, 83, 165, 166, 229, 271, 272, 276, 316, 366, 369, 372, 374, 376
Milieu therapy, 62
Miller, Daniel, 9, 372
Miller, Delbert, 367
Miller, James, 372
Mini-courses, 23, 218, 349-50
Minnesota Teacher Attitude Inventory (MTAI), 143
Minuchin, Patricia, 276, 372
Models of student governance. *See* Governing boards
Morgan school, 356
Morse, William, 61, 64, 376
Motivation, 136, 152, 190, 194, 247, 255, 297; theory of, 107-8, 113-14, 241, 242, 294-95
Mott program, 357
Multi-unit schools, 136, 256-57, 258. *See also* Team teaching
Mussen, Paul, 372
Myers, Karin, 51, 372

National Defense and Education Act, 12
National Institute of Mental Health, 61
National Mental Health Act, 61
National Training Laboratories, Institute of Applied Behavioral Science, 73, 282
Nelson, Jack, 156, 372
Nelson, Margaret, 310, 372
Networks. *See* Communication
Newman, Ruth, 61, 64, 67, 88, 372
New Math, 103, 104, 151, 152, 153, 218
New School in Spokane (Washington), 17, 214-15
New Schools Exchange Newsletter, 16
Nixon, President, 33
Nolen, Patricia, 56, 87, 368
Noll, Victor, 375
Nonverbal communication, 117, 195, 199, 202, 210
Norms, 77, 94, 101, 108, 109, 116, 117, 121, 122, 123, 157, 163, 164, 238, 240, 263; clarification of,

213-14; in college, 142-45; about control, 158-62; of peer group, 170-74; of learning group, 177-83; in the humanized school, 240-48; in organization development, 266-74
North Dakota, 256. *See also* University of North Dakota
Northwest Regional Educational Laboratory, 282, 315, 348, 372
Noyes, Kathryn, 182, 372
Nyberg, David, 26, 27, 372

Objective evaluation, 284-93. *See also* Evaluation
Objectives, in self confrontation, 298-306
Observation, 156, 236, 293, 342
Observation sheets, 193, 197, 198, 220, 221
Observers, 193, 219-22
Office of Education, 30
Ohme, Herman, 259, 372
Oliver, W., 310, 376
Olton, Robert, 52, 372
On the Move, 79
One-room schoolhouse, 252, 253
One-to-one tutoring, 347
Open campus, 260-61
Open classroom, 26, 327, 328
Openness, 101, 124, 234, 235, 251, 262, 266
Organization Development, 115, 153, 234, 266-75, 276, 277, 330, 332, 356
Organization man, 105
Organization of humanized school, 240-48
Organizational efficiency, 327-29. *See also* Bureaucratic
Organizational specialists. *See* Cadre
Organizational structure, 136, 240-48, 251-66
Organizational variables, 238-40
Other-directed character, 10-12, 105
"Outside the Net," 16

Palomares, O. H., 255, 366
Paraphrasing, 193, 196, 198, 208, 211, 222, 262, 301, 308; in consensus, 341
Paraprofessionals, 121, 140, 354-56